Lecture Notes in Computer Science 4943

Commenced Publication in 1973
Founding and Former Series Editors:
Gerhard Goos, Juris Hartmanis, and Jan van Leeuwen

Editorial Board

David Hutchison
Lancaster University, UK

Takeo Kanade
Carnegie Mellon University, Pittsburgh, PA, USA

Josef Kittler
University of Surrey, Guildford, UK

Jon M. Kleinberg
Cornell University, Ithaca, NY, USA

Alfred Kobsa
University of California, Irvine, CA, USA

Friedemann Mattern
ETH Zurich, Switzerland

John C. Mitchell
Stanford University, CA, USA

Moni Naor
Weizmann Institute of Science, Rehovot, Israel

Oscar Nierstrasz
University of Bern, Switzerland

C. Pandu Rangan
Indian Institute of Technology, Madras, India

Bernhard Steffen
University of Dortmund, Germany

Madhu Sudan
Massachusetts Institute of Technology, MA, USA

Demetri Terzopoulos
University of California, Los Angeles, CA, USA

Doug Tygar
University of California, Berkeley, CA, USA

Gerhard Weikum
Max-Planck Institute of Computer Science, Saarbruecken, Germany

Roger Woods   Katherine Compton
Christos Bouganis   Pedro C. Diniz (Eds.)

Reconfigurable Computing: Architectures, Tools and Applications

4th International Workshop, ARC 2008
London, UK, March 26-28, 2008
Proceedings

 Springer

Volume Editors

Roger Woods
Queen's University Belfast
ECIT Institute, Queen's Road, Queen's Island, Belfast, BT 3 9DT, UK
E-mail: r.woods@qub.ac.uk

Katherine Compton
University of Wisconsin-Madison
1415 Engineering Drive, Madison, WI 53706, USA
E-mail: kati@engr.wisc.edu

Christos Bouganis
Imperial College London
Department of Electrical and Electronic Engineering
South Kensington Campus, London, SW7 2AZ, UK
E-mail: christos-savvas.bouganis@imperial.ac.uk

Pedro C. Diniz
Technical University of Lisbon
Instituto Superior Técnico, Av. Rovisco Pais, 1049-001 Lisboa, Portugal
E-mail: pedro.diniz@tagus.ist.utl.pt

Library of Congress Control Number: 2008923932

CR Subject Classification (1998): C, B, I.4

LNCS Sublibrary: SL 1 – Theoretical Computer Science and General Issues

ISSN   0302-9743
ISBN-10   3-540-78609-0 Springer Berlin Heidelberg New York
ISBN-13   978-3-540-78609-2 Springer Berlin Heidelberg New York

Springer is a part of Springer Science+Business Media

springer.com

© Springer-Verlag Berlin Heidelberg 2008
Printed in Germany

Typesetting: Camera-ready by author, data conversion by Scientific Publishing Services, Chennai, India
Printed on acid-free paper   SPIN: 12240425   06/3180   5 4 3 2 1 0

Preface

For many years, the idea of reconfigurable hardware systems has represented the *Holy Grail* for computer system designers. It has been recognized for a long time that the microprocessor provides high flexibility but at a very low performance merit in terms of MIPS/W or other such measures. *Reconfigurable systems* are thus attractive as they can be configured to provide the best match for the computational requirements at that specific time, giving much better area – speed – power performance.

However, the practicalities of achieving such a reconfigurable system are numerous and require the development of: suitable reconfigurable hardware to support the dynamic behavior; programming tools to allow the dynamic behavior of the reconfigurability to be modelled; programming languages to support reconfiguration; and verification techniques that can demonstrate that reconfiguration has happened correctly at each stage. While the problems are many, the existence and development of technologies such as the multi-core processor architecture, reconfigurable computing architectures, and application-specific processors suggest there is a strong desire for reconfigurable systems. Moreover, FPGAs also provide the ideal platforms for the development of such platforms.

The major motivation behind the International Workshop on Applied Reconfigurable Computing (ARC) series is to create a forum for presenting and discussing on-going research efforts in applied reconfigurable computing. The workshop also focuses on compiler and mapping techniques, and new reconfigurable computing architectures. The series of editions started in 2005 in Algarve, Portugal, followed by the 2006 workshop in Delft, The Netherlands, and last year's workshop in Mangaratiba, Rio de Janeiro, Brazil. As in previous years, selected papers have been published as a Springer LNCS *(Lecture Notes in Computer Science)* volume.

This LNCS volume includes the papers selected for the fourth edition of the Workshop (ARC 2008), held at Imperial College London, UK during March 26–28, 2008. The workshop attracted a large number of very good papers, describing interesting work on reconfigurable computing related subjects. A total of 56 papers were submitted to the workshop from 18 countries: UK (9), Republic of China (6), Germany (6), USA (5), The Netherlands (4), France (4), Greece (3), Portugal (3), Brazil (3), Republic of South Korea (2), Japan (2), Spain (2), Poland (2), India (1), Belgium (1), Turkey (1), Thailand (1) and Canada (1).

In most cases, submitted papers were evaluated by at least three members of the Program Committee. After careful selection, 21 papers were accepted as full papers (acceptance rate of 38.1%) and 14 as short papers (global acceptance rate of 63.6%). Those accepted papers led to a very interesting workshop program, which we consider to constitute a representative overview of on-going research efforts in reconfigurable computing, a rapidly evolving and maturing field.

Several people contributed to the success of the 2008 edition of the workshop. We would like to acknowledge the support of all the members of this year's workshop Steering and Program Committees in reviewing papers, in helping the paper selection, and in giving valuable suggestions. Special thanks also to the additional researchers who contributed to the reviewing process, to all the authors that submitted papers to the workshop, and to all the workshop attendees. Last but not least, we would like to thank Springer, and Alfred Hofmann in particular, for their continued support in publishing the proceedings as part of the LNCS series and to Jürgen Becker from the University of Karlsruhe for his continued support role.

January 2008

Roger Woods
Katherine Compton
Christos Bouganis
Pedro C. Diniz

Organization

Organizing Committee

General Chairs	Christos-Savvas Bouganis (Imperial College London, UK)
	Pedro C. Diniz (Instituto Superior Técnico, Portugal)
Program Chairs	Katherine Compton (University of Wisconsin-Madison, USA)
	Roger Woods (Queen's University Belfast, UK)
Proceedings Chair	Pete Sedcole (Imperial College London, UK)
Local Arrangements Chairs	Alastair Smith (Imperial College London, UK)
	Terrence Mak (Imperial College London, UK)
Web Design	Iosifina Pournara (Birkbeck College, UK)
Secretary	Wiesia Hsissen (Imperial College London, UK)

Steering Committee

George Constantinides	Imperial College London, UK
João M.P. Cardoso	IST/INESC-ID, Portugal
Koen Bertels	Delft University of Technology, The Netherlands
Mladen Berekovic	Braunschweig University of Technology, Germany
Pedro C. Diniz	Instituto Superior Técnico, Portugal
Walid Najjar	University of California Riverside, USA

In memory of Stamatis Vassiliadis [1951–2007], Steering Committee Member for ARC 2006 and 2007.

Program Committee

Jeff Arnold	Stretch Inc., USA
Nader Bagherzadeh	University of California, Irvine, USA
Jürgen Becker	University of Karlsruhe (TH), Germany
Mladen Berekovic	Braunschweig University of Technology, Germany
Neil Bergmann	University of Queensland, Australia
Koen Bertels	Delft University of Technology, The Netherlands
Christos-Savvas Bouganis	Imperial College London, UK
Gordon Brebner	Xilinx Corp., USA
Mihai Budiu	Microsoft Research, USA
Tim Callahan	Carnegie Mellon University, USA

João M.P. Cardoso   IST/INESC-ID, Portugal
Mark Chang   Olin College, USA
Peter Cheung   Imperial College London, UK
Paul Chow   University of Toronto, Canada
Katherine Compton   University of Wisconsin-Madison, USA
George Constantinides   Imperial College London, UK
Oliver Diessel   University of New South Wales, Australia
Pedro C. Diniz   Instituto Superior Técnico, Portugal
Tarek El-Ghazawi   George Washington University, USA
Robert Esser   Xilinx Corp., Ireland
Antonio Ferrari   University of Aveiro, Portugal
Reiner Hartenstein   University of Kaiserslautern, Germany
Román Hermida   Complutense University of Madrid, Spain
Ryan Kastner   University of California, Santa Barbara, USA
Andreas Koch   Darmstadt University of Technology, Germany
Philip Leong   Chinese University of Hong Kong, China
Wayne Luk   Imperial College London, UK
John McAllister   Queen's University Belfast, UK
Maria-Cristina Marinescu   IBM T.J. Watson Research Center, USA
Eduardo Marques   University of São Paulo, Brazil
Kostas Masselos   University of Peloponnese, Greece
Seda Ö. Memik   Northwestern University, USA
Oskar Mencer   Imperial College London, UK
Walid Najjar   University of California Riverside, USA
Horácio Neto   INESC-ID/IST, Portugal
Joon-seok Park   Inha University, Seoul, South Korea
Andy Pimentel   University of Amsterdam, The Netherlands
Joachim Pistorius   Altera Corp., USA
Marco Platzner   University of Paderborn, Germany
Bernard Pottier   University of Bretagne, France
Tsutomu Sasao   Kyushu Institute of Technology, Japan
Pete Sedcole   Imperial College London, UK
Lesley Shannon   Simon Fraser University, USA
Russell Tessier   University of Massachusetts, USA
Pedro Trancoso   University of Cyprus, Cyprus
Ranga Vemuri   University of Cincinnati, USA
Markus Weinhardt   PACT Informationstechnologie AG, Germany
Stephan Wong   Delft University of Technology, The Netherlands
Roger Woods   Queen's University Belfast, UK

Additional Reviewers

Esther Andres   Qiang Liu
Kubilay Atasu   Antonio Roldao Lopes
Alberto del Barrio   Enno Lübbers
David Boland   Yi Lu

Vanderlei Bonato
Lars Braun
Hagen Gädke
Carlo Galuzzi
Angamuthu Ganesan
Heiner Giefers
Jose I. Gomez
Laiq Hasan
José Arnaldo Mascagni de Holanda
Jae Young Hur
Matthias Kuehnle
Mahendra Kumar
Loic Lagadec
Y.M. Lam
Martin Langhammer

Terrence Mak
Thomas Marconi
Shahnam Mirzaei
Abhishek Mitra
Shinobu Nagayama
Juanjo Noguera
Christian Plessl
Fredy Rivera
Mojtaba Sabeghi
Thomas Schuster
K. Susanto
Timothy Todman
Kieron Turkington
Qiang Wu

Table of Contents

Reconfigurable Computing Hardware and Systems

Image Processing

Run-Time Behavior

Instruction Set Extension

Random Number Generation and Financial Computation

Posters

Synthesizing FPGA Circuits from Parallel Programs

Satnam Singh[1] and David Greaves[2]

[1] Microsoft Research Cambridge, UK
[2] Cambridge University, UK

Abstract. In this presentation we describe recent experiments to represent circuit descriptions as explicit parallel programs written in regular programming languages rather than hardware description languages. Although there has been much work on compiling sequential C-like programs to hardware by automatically "discovering" parallelism we work by exploiting the parallel architecture communicated by the designer through the choice of parallel and concurrent programming language constructs. Specially, we describe a system that takes .NET assembly language with suitable custom attributes as input and produces Verilog output which is mapped to FPGAs. We can then choose to apply analysis and verification techniques to either the high level representation in C# or other .NET languages or to the generated RTL netlists.

R. Woods et al. (Eds.): ARC 2008, LNCS 4943, p. 1, 2008.

From Silicon to Science: The Long Road to Production Reconfigurable Supercomputing

Keith Underwood

Intel Corporation, USA

Abstract. Over the last several years, multiple vendors have introduced systems that integrate FPGAs, as well as other types of accelerators, into machines intended for general purpose supercomputing. However, these machines have not broadly penetrated production scientific computing at any of the world's top supercomputing centers. With the excitement around accelerators and the numerous examples of their potential, why haven't they achieved widespread adoption in production supercomputing? This talk will discuss several barriers to adoption based on input from people who buy supercomputers and from people who use them. The short answer is that FPGA enhanced supercomputers look very little like traditional supercomputers and the performance advantage for scientific applications is often not as compelling as advertised. This talk will attempt to map barriers to adoption to specific research challenges that must be addressed to see widespread usage of FPGAs for scientific computing. These challenges include everything from the lowest level of circuit design to the programming of applications, and point to a lot of work between the current state of the art and widespread adoption of reconfigurable computing.

R. Woods et al. (Eds.): ARC 2008, LNCS 4943, p. 2, 2008.
© Springer-Verlag Berlin Heidelberg 2008

The von Neumann Syndrome and the CS Education Dilemma

Reiner Hartenstein

Technical University of Kaiserslautern, Germany
http://hartenstein.de/

Abstract. Computing the von Neumann style is tremendously inefficient because multiple layers of massive overhead phenomena often lead
to code sizes of astronomic dimensions, thus requiring large capacity slow
off-chip memory. The dominance of von-Neumann-based computing will
become unaffordable during next decade because of growing very high
energy consumption and increasing cost of energy. For most application
domains a von-Neumann-based parallelization does not scale well, resulting in the escalating many-core programming crisis by requiring complete
remapping and re-implementation—often promising only disappointing
results. A sufficiently large population of manycore-qualified programmers is far from being available. Efficient solutions for the many-core
crisis are hardly possible by fully instruction-stream-based approaches.
Several HPC celebrities call for a radical re-design of the entire computing discipline. The solution is a dual paradigm approach, which includes
fundamental concepts known already for a long time from Reconfigurable
Computing. Whistle blowing is overdue, since these essential qualifica-
tions for our many-core future and for low energy computing are obsti-
nately ignored by CE, CS and IT curriculum task forces. This talk also
sketches a road map.

R. Woods et al. (Eds.): ARC 2008, LNCS 4943, p. 3, 2008.
© Springer-Verlag Berlin Heidelberg 2008

Optimal Unroll Factor for Reconfigurable Architectures

Ozana Silvia Dragomir, Elena Moscu-Panainte, Koen Bertels,
and Stephan Wong

Computer Engineering, EEMCS, Delft University of Technology,
Mekelweg 4, 2628 CD Delft, The Netherlands
{O.S.Dragomir,E.Moscu-Panainte,K.L.M.Bertels,J.S.S.M.Wong}@tudelft.nl

Abstract. Loops are an important source of optimization. In this paper, we address such optimizations for those cases when loops contain kernels mapped on reconfigurable fabric. We assume the Molen machine organization and Molen programming paradigm as our framework. The proposed algorithm computes the optimal unroll factor u for a loop that contains a hardware kernel K such that u instances of K run in parallel on the reconfigurable hardware, and the targeted balance between performance and resource usage is achieved. The parameters of the algorithm consist of profiling information about the execution times for running K in both hardware and software, the memory transfers and the utilized area. In the experimental part, we illustrate this method by applying it to a loop nest from a real-life application (MPEG2), containing the DCT kernel.

1   Introduction

Reconfigurable Computing (RC) is becoming increasingly popular and the common solution for obtaining a significant performance increase is to identify the application kernels and accelerate them on hardware. As loops represent an important source of performance improvement, we investigate how existing loop optimizations can be applied when hardware kernels exist in the loop body. Assuming the Molen machine organization [1] as our framework, we focus our research in the direction of parallelizing applications by executing multiple instances of the kernel in parallel on the reconfigurable hardware.

Optimal is defined in this paper as the largest feasible unroll factor, given area constraints, performance requirements and memory access constraints, taking into account also that multiple kernels may be mapped on the area. The contributions of this paper are: a) an algorithm to automatically determine the optimal unroll factor, based on profile information about memory transfers, available area, and software/hardware execution times; b) experimental results for a well known–kernel – DCT (Discrete Cosine Transformation), showing that the optimal unroll factor is 6, with a speedup of 9.55x and utilized area of 72%.

The paper is organized as follows. Section 2 introduces the background and related work. In Section 3, we give a general definition of the problem and present

R. Woods et al. (Eds.): ARC 2008, LNCS 4943, pp. 4–14, 2008.

the target architecture and application. We propose a method for solving the problem in Section 4 and show the results for a specific application in Section 5. Finally, concluding remarks and future work are presented in Section 6.

2   Background and Related Work

The work presented in this paper is related to the Delft WorkBench (DWB) project. The DWB is a semi-automatic toolchain platform for integrated hardware-software co-design in the context of Custom Computing Machines (CCM) which targets the Molen polymorphic machine organization [1]. More specifically, the DWB supports the entire design process, as follows. The kernels are identified in the first stage of profiling and cost estimation. Next, the Molen compiler [2] generates the executable file, replacing function calls to the kernels implemented in hardware with specific instructions for hardware reconfiguration and execution, according to the Molen programming paradigm. An automatic tool for hardware generation (DWARV [3]) is used to transform the selected kernels into VHDL code targeting the Molen platform.

Several approaches – [4], [5], [6], [7], [8], [9] are focused on accelerating kernel loops in hardware. Our approach is different, as we do not aggressively optimize the kernel implementation, but we focus on the optimization of the application for any hardware implementation, by executing multiple kernel instances in parallel.

PARLGRAN [10] is an approach that tries to maximize performance on reconfigurable architectures by selecting the parallelism granularity for each individual data-parallel task. However, this approach is different than ours in several ways: (i) they target task chains and make a decision on the parallelism granularity of each task, while we target loops (loop nests) with kernels inside them and make a decision on the unroll factor; (ii) in their case, the task instances have identical area requirements but different workloads, which translates into different executions time (a task is split into several sub-tasks); in our algorithm, all instances have the same characteristics in both area consumption and execution time; (iii) their algorithm takes into consideration the physical (placement) constraints and reconfiguration overhead at run-time, but without taking into account the memory bottleneck problem; we present a compile-time algorithm, which considers that there is no latency due to configuration of the kernels (static configurations), but takes into account the memory transfers.

3   Problem Statement

Loops represent an important source of optimization, and there are a number of loop transformations (such as loop unrolling, software pipelining, loop shifting, loop distribution, loop merging, loop tiling, etc) that are used to maximize the parallelism inside the loop and improve the performance. The applications we target in our work have loops that contain kernels inside them. One challenge we address is to improve the performance for such loops, by applying standard loop transformations such as the ones mentioned above.

In this paper, we focus on loop unrolling and present the assumptions and parameters for our model. Loop unrolling is a transformation that replicates the loop body and reduces the iteration number. Traditionally it is used to eliminate the loop overhead, thus improving the cache hit rate and reducing branching, while in reconfigurable computing it is used to expose parallelism.

The problem definition is: find the optimal unroll factor u of the loop (loop nest) with a kernel K, such that u identical instances of K run in parallel on the reconfigurable hardware, leading to the best balance between the performance and area utilization. The method proposed in this paper addresses this problem, given a C implementation of the target application and a VHDL implementation of the kernel.

We target the Molen framework, which allows multiple applications to run simultaneously on the reconfigurable hardware. The algorithm computes (at compile time) the optimal unroll factor, taking into consideration the memory transfers, the execution times in software and hardware, the area requirements for the kernel, and the available area (without physical details, P&R, etc). Thus, because of the reconfigurable hardware's flexibility, the algorithm's output depends on the hardware configuration at a certain time.

The main benefits of this algorithm are that it can be integrated in an automatic toolchain and it can use any hardware implementation of the kernel. Thus, performance can be improved even when the kernel is already optimized. Our assumptions regarding the application and the framework are presented below.

Target architecture. The Molen machine organization has been implemented on Vitex-II Pro XC2VP30 device, utilizing less than 2% of the available resources of the FPGA. The memory design uses the available on-chip memory blocks of the FPGA.

The factors taken into consideration by the proposed method are:

- area utilized by one kernel running on FPGA;
- available area (other kernels may be configured in the same time);
- execution time of the kernel in software and in hardware (in GPP cycles);
- the number of cycles for memory transfer operations for one kernel instance running in hardware;
- available memory bandwidth.

General and Molen-specific assumptions for the model:

1. There are no data dependencies between different iterations of the analyzed loop. Practical applications that satisfy this assumption exist, for example MPEG2 multimedia benchmark.
2. The loop bounds are known at compile time.

3. Inside the kernel, all memory reads are performed in the beginning and memory writes in the end. This does not reduce the generality of the problem for most applications.
4. The placement of the specific reconfiguration instructions is decided by a scheduling algorithm which runs after our algorithm, such that the configuration latency is hidden.
5. Only on-chip memory is used for program data. This memory is shared by the GPP and the CCUs.
6. All data that are necessary for all kernel instances are available in the shared memory.
7. The PowerPC and the CCU run at the same clock.
8. All transfers to/from the shared memory are performed sequentially.
9. Kernel's local variables/arrays are stored in the FPGA's local memory, such that all computations not involving the shared memory transfers can be parallelized.
10. As far as running multiple applications on the reconfigurable hardware is concerned, for now we take into consideration only the area constraints.
11. The area constraints do not include the shape of the design.
12. Additional area needed for interconnecting Molen with the kernels grows linearly with the number of kernels.

Motivational example. Throughout the paper, we will use the motivational example in Fig. 1(a). It consists of a loop with two functions – one function is executed always in software ($CPar$), and the other is the application kernel (K) – implicitly, the execution time for $CPar$ is much smaller than for K. In each iteration i, data dependencies between $CPar$ and K exist, as $CPar$ computes the parameters for the kernel instance to be executed in the same iteration. The example has been extracted from the MPEG2 encoder multimedia benchmark, where the kernel K is DCT.

```
for (i = 0; i < N; i++ ) {
    /*Compute  parameters  for
    K()*/
    CPar (i, blocks);
    /*Kernel function*/
    K (blocks[i]);
}
```

```
for (i = 0; i < N; i += u) {
    CPar (i + 0, blocks);
    . . .
    CPar (i + u − 1, blocks);
    /*u instances of K() in parallel*/
    #pragma parallel
        K (blocks[i + 0]);
    . . .
        K (blocks[i + u − 1]);
    #end parallel
}
```

(a)Loop containing a kernel call   (b)Loop unrolled with a factor u

Fig. 1. Motivational example

4   Proposed Methodology

In this section we present a method to determine the optimal unroll factor having as input the profiling information (execution time and number of memory transfers) area usage for one instance of the kernel. We illustrate the method by unrolling with factor u the code from Fig. 1(a). Figure 1(b) presents a simplified case when $N \bmod u = 0$. Each iteration consists of u sequential executions of the function $CPar()$ followed by the parallel execution of u kernel instances (there is an implicit synchronization point at the end of the parallel region).

Area. Taking into account only the area constraints and not the shape of the design, an upper bound for the unroll factor is set by

$$u_a = \left\lfloor \frac{Area_{(available)}}{Area_{(K)} + Area_{(interconnect)}} \right\rfloor \text{, where:}$$

- $Area_{(available)}$ is the available area, taking into account the resources utilized by Molen and by other configurations;
- $Area_{(interconnect)}$ is the area necessary to connect one kernel with the rest of the hardware design (we made the assumption that the overall interconnect area grows linearly with the number of kernels);
- $Area_{(K)}$ is the area utilized by one instance of the kernel, including the storage space for the values read from the shared memory. All kernel instances have identical area requirements.

Memory accesses. In the ideal case, all data are available immediately and the degree of parallelism is bounded only by the area availability. However, for many applications, the memory bandwidth is an important bottleneck in achieving the ideal parallelism. We consider that T_r, T_w, respectively T_c are the times for memory read, write, and computation on hardware for kernel K. Then, the total time for running K in hardware is $T_r + T_w + T_c$. Without reducing the generality of the problem for most applications, we assume that the memory reads are performed at the beginning and memory writes in the end. Then, as illustrated in Fig. 2, where we consider $T_w \leq T_r < T_c$ and $T_r + T_w > T_c$, a new instance of K can start only after a time T_r (we denote kernel instances by $K^{(1)}$, $K^{(2)}$, etc)[1].

The condition that memory access requests from different kernel instances do not overlap sets another bound (u_m) for the degree of unrolling on the reconfigurable hardware[1]:

$$u \cdot \min(T_r, T_w) \leq \min(T_r, T_w) + T_c \quad \Rightarrow \quad u \leq u_m = \left\lfloor \frac{T_c}{\min(T_r, T_w)} \right\rfloor + 1 \quad (1)$$

The time for running u instances of K on the reconfigurable hardware is[1]:

$$T_{K(hw)}(u) = \begin{cases} T_c + T_r + T_w + (u - 1) \cdot \max(T_r, T_w) & \text{if } u < u_m \\ u \cdot (T_r + T_w) & \text{if } u \geq u_m \end{cases} \quad (2)$$

Since we are interested only in the case $u < u_m$, from (2) we derive the time for u instances of K in hardware as:

$$T_{K(\text{hw})}(u) = T_C + \min(T_r, T_W) + u \cdot \max(T_r, T_W) \qquad (3)$$

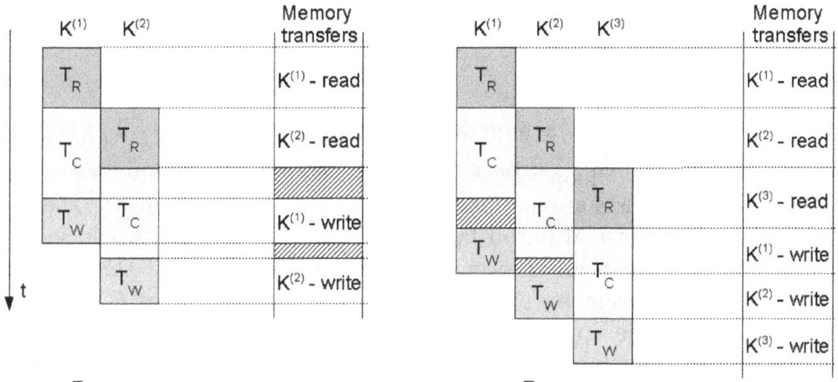

(a) $u < \dfrac{T_C}{T_W} + 1 \rightarrow T_{k(\text{hw})}(u) = T_C + T_W + u \cdot T_r$ (b) $u \geq \dfrac{T_C}{T_W} + 1 \rightarrow T_{k(\text{hw})}(u) = u \cdot (T_r + T_W)$

Fig. 2. Parallelism on reconfigurable hardware

Note that when applied to the example in Fig. 2, the case $u < u_m$ corresponds to Fig. 2(a) and the case $u \geq u_m$ corresponds to Fig. 2(b). In our example, $T_W \leq T_r$, thus $\max(T_r, T_W) = T_r$ and $\min(T_r, T_W) = T_W$. In Fig. 2(a), the time for running in parallel two kernel instances ($K^{(1)}$ and $K^{(2)}$) is given by the time for $K^{(1)}$ ($T_C + T_r + T_W$) plus the necessary delay for $K^{(2)}$ to start (T_r). In Fig. 2(b), $K^{(1)}$ writing to memory is delayed because of $K^{(3)}$ reading from memory; in this case, the actual kernel computation is hidden by the memory transfers and the hardware execution time depends only on the memory access times ($u \cdot (T_r + T_W)$).

Speedup. In order to compute the optimal unroll factor, we use the following notations:

- N- initial number of iterations (before unrolling);
- $N(u)$ - number of iterations after unrolling with factor u: $N(u) = \lceil N/u \rceil$;
- T_{sw} - number of cycles for that part of the loop body that is always executed by the GPP (in our example, the $CPar$ function);
- $T_{K(\text{sw})}$ / $T_{K(\text{hw})}$ - number of cycles for one instance of K() running in software/hardware;

---

[1] (1) and (2) are derived from an exhaustive analysis of all possible cases with different relations between T_C, T_r, and T_W. Fig. 2 represents only one of the 8 possible cases ($T_W \leq T_r < T_C$ and $T_W + T_r > T_C$).

- $T_{\text{loop(sw)}}$ / $T_{\text{loop(hw)}}$ - number of cycles for the loop nest with K() running in software/hardware (considering that the unroll factor satisfies the condition $u < u_{\text{m}}$):

$$T_{\text{loop(sw)}} = (T_{\text{sw}} + T_{K(\text{sw})}) \cdot N \tag{4}$$

$$T_{\text{loop(hw)}} = (T_{\text{sw}} + \max(T_{\text{r}}, T_{\text{w}})) \cdot N + (T_{\text{c}} + \min(T_{\text{r}}, T_{\text{w}})) \cdot N(u) \tag{5}$$

The speedup at loop nest level is: $$S_{\text{loop}}(u) = \frac{T_{\text{loop(sw)}}}{T_{\text{loop(hw)}}} \tag{6}$$

For $u < u_{\text{m}}$, $T_{\text{loop(hw)}}$ is a monotonic decreasing function; as $T_{\text{loop(sw)}}$ is constant, it means that $S_{\text{loop}}(u)$ is a monotonic increasing function for $u < u_{\text{m}}$.

When multiple kernels are mapped on the reconfigurable hardware, the goal is to determine the optimal unroll factor for each kernel, which would lead to the maximum performance improvement for the application. For this purpose, we introduce a new parameter to the model: the calibration factor F, a positive number decided by the application designer, which determines a limitation of the unroll factor according to the targeted trade-off. (For example, you would not want to increase the unrolling if the gain in speedup would be with a factor of 0.5%, but the area usage would increase with 15%.) The simplest relation to be satisfied between the speedup and necessary area is:

$$\Delta S(u + 1, u) > \Delta A(u + 1, u) \cdot F$$

where $\Delta S(u+1, u)$ is the relative speedup increase between unroll factors u and $u + 1$:

$$\Delta S(u + 1, u) = \frac{S(u + 1) - S(u)}{S(u)} \cdot 100 \ [\%] \tag{7}$$

and $\Delta A(u+1, u)$ is the area increase. Since all kernel instances are identical, the total area grows linearly with the number of kernels and $\Delta A(u + 1, u)$ is always equal to the area utilized by one kernel instance $(Area_{(K)})[\%]$.

Thus, F is a threshold value which sets the speedup bound for the unroll factor (u_{S}). The speedup bound is defined as:

$$u_{\text{S}} = \min(u) \quad \text{such that} \quad \Delta S(u + 1, u) < F \cdot Area_{(K)}.$$

Note that when the analyzed kernel is the only one running in hardware, it might make sense to unroll as much as possible, given the area and memory bounds (u_{a} and u_{m}), as long as there is no performance degradation. In this case, we set $F = 0$ and $u_{\text{S}} = u_{\text{m}}$.

Local optimal values for the unroll factor u may appear when u is not a divisor of N, but $u+1$ is. To avoid this situation, as S is a monotonic increasing function for $u < u_{\text{m}}$, we add another condition for u_{S}: $\Delta S(u_{\text{S}} + 2, u_{\text{S}} + 1) < F \cdot Area_{(K)}$.

By using (4) and (5) in (6) and the notations

$$x = \frac{T_{\text{c}} + \min(T_{\text{r}}, T_{\text{w}})}{(\max(T_{\text{r}}, T_{\text{w}}) + T_{\text{sw}}) \cdot N} \quad \text{and} \quad y = \frac{T_{\text{sw}} + T_{K(\text{sw})}}{\max(T_{\text{r}}, T_{\text{w}}) + T_{\text{sw}}},$$

the total speedup is computed by:
$$S_{\text{loop}}(u) = \frac{y}{1 + x \cdot N(u)} \qquad (8)$$

On the base of (8) and given the fact that the maximum unrolling factor is known – being the number of iterations N –, binary search can be used to compute in $O(\log N)$ time the value of u_S that satisfies the conditions $\Delta S(u_S + 1, u_S) < F \cdot Area_{(K)}$ and $\Delta S(u_S + 2, u_S + 1) < F \cdot Area_{(K)}$.

Integrated constraints. In the end, speedup, area consumption and memory accesses need to be combined in order to find the feasible unroll factor, given all constraints. If $u_S < \min(u_a, u_m)$, then the optimal unroll factor is $\min(u)$ such that $u_S < u \leq \min(u_a, u_m)$; else, we choose it as $\max(u)$ such that $u \leq \min(u_a, u_m)$.

5   Experimental Results

The purpose of this section is to illustrate the presented method which computes automatically the unroll factor taking into account the area constraints and profiling information. The result and also the performance depend on the kernel implementation. The order of magnitude of the achieved speedup in hardware compared to software is not relevant for the algorithm, although it influences its output. Instead, we analyze the relative speedup obtained by running multiple instances of the kernel in parallel, compared to running a single one.

The loop from Fig. 3, containing the DCT kernel (2-D integer implementation), was extracted from MPEG2 encoder multimedia benchmark and executed on the VirtexII Pro board. We used the following parameters: $width = 64$, $height = 64$, $block\_count = 6$ (the picture size is 64×64, leading to $N = 96$ iterations).

The DCT implementation operates on 8×8 memory blocks, therefore one kernel performs 64 memory reads and 64 memory writes. The memory blocks in different iterations do not overlap, thus there are no data dependencies and the first assumption in Section 3 holds.

```
for (j = 0, k = 0; j <height; j=j+16) {
    for (i = 0; i <width; i=i+16 ) {
        for (n = 0; n <block_count; n++ ) {
            /*Compute parameters for K()*/
            CPar (n, i, j, k, blocks);
            /*Kernel function*/
            DCT (blocks[k*block_count+n]);
        }
    }
}
```

Fig. 3. MPEG2 loop with DCT kernel

The VHDL code was **automatically** generated with DWARV [3] tool and synthesized with Xilinx XST tool of ISE 8.1; it is not optimized, each memory access and each loop are synchronization points. One instance of the DCT kernel uses 12% of the total available area on VirtexII Pro. The execution times measured using the PowerPC timer registers presented in Table 1 are for one DCT instance (including the parameter transfer using exchange registers).

Table 1. Initial execution time (cycles)

	Hardware	Software	Percent	Speedup
T_K	37 278	106 626	34.96%	2.86
T_{par}	5 292	5 292	100%	-
T_{loop}	4 093 308	10 751 868	38.07%	2.63

We used the following notations: (i) T_K - the number of cycles for one instance of the DCT kernel; (ii) T_{par} - the number of cycles for $CPar()$; (iii) T_{loop} - the number of cycles for the loop nest.

The experiment was performed with one instance of the kernel running on the FPGA. We extrapolated these results for all possible unroll factors, computing the number of cycles for software and hardware execution of the kernel, and also for the loop nest. We observe that the theoretical (computed) execution time (in cycles) for the loop nest (T_{loop}) with the kernel executed in software does not depend on the unroll factor. Comparing with the measured execution time, there is an error of approx 0.072%, due to not taking into account the loop overhead; this error is negligible. Next, we compute the unroll factor applying the method described in Section 4.

Area. The upper bound that satisfies the area constraints is:

$$u_a = \left\lfloor \frac{Area_{(total)} - Area_{(Molen)}}{Area_{(DCT)} + Area_{(interconnect)}} \right\rfloor = 8.$$

Memory accesses. For the considered implementation, the shared memory has an access time of 3 cycles for reading and storing the value into a register and 1 cycle for writing a value to memory; since there are 64 memory reads and 64 memory writes, $\min(T_r, T_w) = 64$ cycles. The computation time is $T_C = T_{K(\text{hw})} - (T_r + T_w) = 37\,022$ cycles. Using these values in (1), $\Rightarrow u_m = 579$.

Speedup. To compute the speedup limit u_s, we use the data from Table 1. Thus, $T_{\text{par}} = 5\,292$, $T_{K(\text{sw})} = 106\,626$, $T_C = 37\,022$, $\max(T_r, T_w) = 192$, $N = 96$, then $x \approx 0.07$ and $y \approx 20.9$. According to (6), $S_{\text{loop}}(u) \approx \dfrac{20.9}{1 + N(u) \cdot 0.07}$.

Figure 4 presents the speedup for different unroll factors. One is the speedup at kernel level, and the second at loop level.

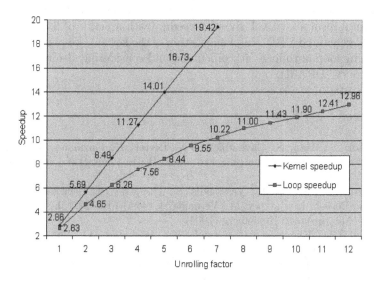

Fig. 4. Speedup obtained with loop unrolling

Assuming that we are interested in a relative speedup increase greater than the area increase ($\Delta S(u+1,u) > Area_{(K)}$ and $\Delta S(u+2,u+1) > Area_{(K)}$) for two consecutive unroll factors, $\Rightarrow u_S = 6$.

Integrated constraints. The condition $u_S < min(u_a, u_m)$ is satisfied, meaning that $u = 6$, leading to a loop speedup of 9.55 and 72% area utilization of the VirtexII Pro total area.

6   Conclusion and Future Work

In this paper, we presented a method to automatically compute the optimal number of instances of a kernel K that will run in parallel on reconfigurable hardware by applying loop unrolling. The algorithm uses only the profiling information about memory transfers, execution times in software and hardware, and information about area usage for one kernel instance and area availability. Its implementation in the compiler decreases the time for design-space exploration and makes efficiently use of the hardware resources.

One of the main benefits of this algorithm is that it can be used to improve performance even when given an already optimized VHDL implementation of the kernel, if there are enough resources available (for instance, when moved to a different platform). Different results will be obtained for different kernel implementations, depending on how much optimized they are.

The presented method takes into account the area constraints when running multiple applications on the reconfigurable hardware, but not the memory constraints for this case. This will be addressed in future work. However, as our approach demonstrates the potential for significant performance improvement (experimental results for DCT show a speedup with a factor of 9.55, for an automatically generated VHDL implementation of the kernel), we plan to extend it by combining loop unrolling with pipelining and considering also transfers from a slow memory (DRAM).

References

1. Vassiliadis, S., Wong, S., Gaydadjiev, G.N., Bertels, K., Kuzmanov, G., Panainte, E.M.: The MOLEN Polymorphic Processor. IEEE Transactions on Computers, 1363–1375, (October 2004)
2. Panainte, E.M., Bertels, K., Vassiliadis, S.: The PowerPC Backend Molen Compiler. In: Becker, J., Platzner, M., Vernalde, S. (eds.) FPL 2004. LNCS, vol. 3203, pp. 434–443. Springer, Heidelberg (2004)
3. Yankova, Y.D., Kuzmanov, G., Bertels, K., Gaydadjiev, G., Lu, J., Vassiliadis, S.: DWARV: DelftWorkbench Automated Reconfigurable VHDL Generator. In: The 17th International Conference on Field Programmable Logic and Applications (FPL 2007) (August 2007), pp. 697–701 (2007)
4. Guo, Z., Buyukkurt, B., Najjar, W., Vissers, K.: Optimized Generation of datapath from C codes for FPGAs. In: DATE 2005: Proceedings of the conference on Design, Automation and Test in Europe (March 2005), pp. 112–117 (2005)
5. Gupta, S., Dutt, N., Gupta, R., Nicolau, A.: Loop shifting and compaction for the high-level synthesis of designs with complex control flow. In: DATE 2004: Proceedings of the conference on Design, Automation and Test in Europe (February 2004), pp. 114–119 (2004)
6. Mei, B., Vernalde, S., Verkest, D., Man, H.D., Lauwereins, R.: Exploiting Loop-Level Parallelism on Coarse-Grained Reconfigurable Architectures Using Modulo Scheduling. In: DATE 2003: Proceedings of the conference on Design, Automation and Test in Europe (March 2003), pp. 296–301 (2003)
7. Cardoso, J.M.P., Diniz, P.C.: Modeling loop unrolling: approaches and open issues. In: Pimentel, A.D., Vassiliadis, S. (eds.) SAMOS 2004. LNCS, vol. 3133, pp. 224–233. Springer, Heidelberg (2004)
8. Weinhardt, M., Luk, W.: Pipeline vectorization. IEEE Transactions on Computer-Aided Design of Integrated Circuits and Systems, 234–248 (February 2001)
9. Liao, J., Wong, W.F., Mitra, T.: A model for hardware realization of kernel loops. In: Y. K. Cheung, P., Constantinides, G.A. (eds.) FPL 2003. LNCS, vol. 2778, pp. 334–344. Springer, Heidelberg (2003)
10. Banerjee, S., Bozorgzadeh, E., Dutt, N.: PARLGRAN: parallelism granularity selection for scheduling task chains on dynamically reconfigurable architectures. In: ASP-DAC 2006: Proceedings of the 2006 conference on Asia South Pacific design automation (January 2006), pp. 491–496 (2006)

Programming Reconfigurable Decoupled Application Control Accelerator for Mobile Systems

Samar Yazdani[1,2], Joël Cambonie[1], and Bernard Pottier[2]

[1] STMicroelectronics, Grenoble 38019, France
samar.yazdani@univ-brest.fr
[2] Université de Bretagne Occidentale
LESTER, CNRS,
Brest 29200, France

Abstract. This paper presents an innovative multimedia reconfigurable accelerator for mobile systems associated to a programming model and a compiler flow. The architecture implements a flexible memory subsystem based on software controlled scratchpad shared memory banks. The main concern of the paper is shared memory management as it is a dominant factor in current designs and influences the performance of embedded systems as well as their energy consumption. An embedded shared-memory programming model is presented that abstracts the details of the hardware architecture but yet exposing parallelism to the user. It is open and user friendly while the hardware can execute complex data feeding on heavily pipelined datapath for compute intensive kernels. The architecture has been designed, and synthesized for 65nm technology for an operating frequency of 200MHz.

Keywords: coarse-grain architecture, shared-memory programming model, multimedia applications, embedded systems.

1 Introduction

Many application circuits available in the market today adopt a heterogeneous multiprocessor "SoC"[1] architecture, based on a control processor (often an ARM controller), one or several DSP cores, a set of dedicated hardware IPs which perform the heavy computation burden, and an interconnect network to support the data transfers between compute blocks and memories. In addition, a low power silicon technology allows a low clock speed operation, in the order of a few hundreds of MHz, to meet the stringent power requirements of the mobile terminal.

The use of reconfigurable accelerators is attractive to avoid the presence of several processing IPs, and to keep high flexibility. This paper will present such an accelerator with aspects of its software support. The hardware implements

---

[1] System on Chip.

R. Woods et al. (Eds.): ARC 2008, LNCS 4943, pp. 15–26, 2008.

an array of compute resources and reconfigurable routing network, providing high acceleration ratio for iterative kernels execution as found in multimedia applications.

A very powerful addressing mechanism allows synchronized concurrent accesses on a multibanked memory thus sustaining high data throughput for the compute nodes. This level of performance is mandatory to support the needs of portable multimedia applications of the incoming years. The proposed architecture shows good adaptability and scalability characteristics, preserving the possibility to implement complex algorithms due to its shared memory orientation.

We know that it is not enough to offer hardware support for the evolution of the integrated portable platforms toward more applications and denser technologies. It is also mandatory to provide an easy access to the huge computing power of this platform to the programmer through an adequate programming model, and proper tools. To meet this strong requirement, the details of the hardware architecture are abstracted, but yet exposing parallelism to the user. The programming model based on shared memory is open and user friendly while the hardware can execute complex data feeding on heavily pipelined datapath for compute intensive kernels.

The paper outline is as follows. Section 2 describes the target architecture model implemented in 65nm technology. Section 3 describes the programming concepts, with a discussion on dynamic aspects of the execution model. Section 4 gives a brief account of compiler flow. Related work is presented in section 5 and application results are presented in section 6.

2   Architecture

2.1   Reconfigurable Decoupled Application Control Architecture

The target Reconfigurable Multimedia Accelerator (RMA) is in the category of access/execute decoupled architecture. We refer this architecture as an RMA[2] accelerator. Figure 1 shows the internal organization of our current target.

In an RMA architecture, an external control processor (CP) is in charge of setting up and monitoring the components for a given application execution. This CP is not shown here since it relies on specific reconfiguration and control support.

The blocks appearing in the RMA architecture are as follow:

Address Generators (AG): 3 of thems are displayed on the right part. Another one appears in the main memory DMA engine.

DMA engine: Connected to a network on chip (NoC) interface, in relation with 2 FIFOs for decoupling local execution from NoC and main memory availability.

Clusters: Grouped around a multiplexor allowing exchange between them and local memories or DMA engine. Clusters are data path enabling to set-up computation graphs. The DSP Fabric holds the clusters and their multiplexor.

---

[2] Reconfigurable Decoupled Application Control.

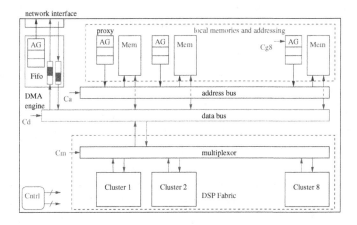

Fig. 1. Reconfigurable Multimedia Accelerator (RMA) block diagram

Address bus: Shared by all the local addressing mechanisms.
Data bus: Allows exchanges between the local memories, the FIFO internal to
  the DMA engine, and the DSP fabric.

The control of the RMA comes partly from the configuration and AG micro-
programs participating in the configuration. A Control Unit (CU) also receives
its program from the configuration, this program being the dynamic part of the
control. The CU is connected to all the control points shown on figure 2.

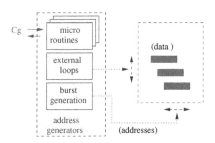

Fig. 2. Addressing mechanism block diagram producing data structure accesses

Address generators (AG) are an assembly of three components hierarchically
connected by control lines:

Burst Generators (BGen): That produces a serie of addresses based on a
  count and a starting point,
Address Generators (AGen): That produces the external loop over a linear
  data structure set-up in memory,

Micro-control sequencement: Defining possible repetition for address pattern generation in terms of micro-routines.

All the memory accesses are thus to be defined as AG microprogram configuration, including for main memory accesses. The CU program is critic since it must bind the feeding of the compute part to the address generation part. As there is a lot of potential concurrency in data use and communication, there is also a serious problem in coordinating the data transfers and conflicts.

The architecture can also be seen as a tighly coupled shared memory machine with conflicts resolved with a hardware support.

DSPFabric description. Figure 3 gives an overall picture of a 64 nodes/16 clusters DSPFabric co-processor. At level 0, it can be seen as an array of four 16-issues PEs, communicating through a collection of multiplexers, which realize a multi input/output switch.

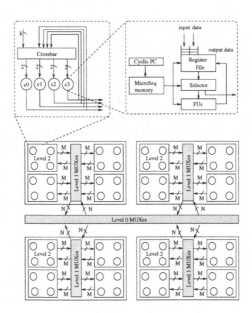

Fig. 3. Hierarchical clustered DSPFabric

Each cluster set has N input wires and N output wires, output wires being possibly broadcasted to all the others. At the contrary, input wires can be connected to only one source. Figure 3 shows a feasible data path at level 0, assuming N equal to 4. At level 1, the spatial structure replicates itself inside each set of clusters, presenting again an array of 4-issue processors, connected together by multiplexers with capacity M. The last level is composed of computation node (CNs) connected through a reconfigurable crossbar, which takes as input the internal connection and K of the wire incoming from level 1. Each computation node has two incoming wires and one outgoing wire. The computation nodes are single issue pipelined machines, accessing their own register file and functional units. Since DSPFabric has been specifically designed as loop accelerator coprocessor, each cluster is equipped with hardware features for better executing modulo scheduled code[1] like support for instruction predication and rotating registers. Precisely, the application is scheduled using the Kernel-only modulo Scheduling technique [1], which fully predicates loop prologue and epilogue. Thus, no branches are allowed and the execution is controlled by a cyclic counter. The inter-cluster copies are controlled by receive primitives executed by the destination cluster. Two regions of its register file are organized as input buffers, which push the incoming values on top, but can be read randomly by the receiver. To keep it as basic as possible, the compute node has no data memory and all temporary results and constants must be stored in the local register file, or in the memory banks of the RMA.

DSPFabric tools. Two different methods are used to map code on the DSP-Fabric. Kernel only modulo scheduling and code cloning. Kernel only modulo scheduling technique fully predicates prologue and epilogue of the loop, systematically speculates all branches of the if/then else expressions, and flattens all the internal loops in the procedure, so that a pure data flow graph expression of the algorithm is used as input to the schedule/place and route tool [2]. An other technique uses a code cloning technique, where group of nodes execute the same code shifted in time so that interconnect resources are time multiplexed between the nodes. This last method allows preservation of the control structure of the algorithm (loops are kept rolled and 'if' statement are mapped to jump instructions). In some cases, this last method can give better results that the former in terms of throughput, because inactive 'if/then/else' branches don't need to be speculatively executed.

This last method allows preservation of the control structure of the algorithm, and can give good code compaction caracteristics compared to the former.

Flexible streaming engine. The DSPFabric cyclically executes a sequence of instructions that consume and produce data through its I/Os primary ports. Those streams of data are produced by a DMA attached to that port, which reads and writes from a local buffer memory. In a steady state, a new data can be accessed on each primary port by the DSPFabric at each clock cycle, and so the maximum throughput can be sustained to feed the DSPFabric. The streaming engine has been designed to meet this high throughput requirements. It is composed of a local memory and a set of address generation units to drive the DMAs attached to the DSPFabric ports. A multibanked multiported memory block is used to store data prefetched from system memory, and to store temporary results of computation from the DSPFabric. This local buffer is useful to minimize traffic on the system interconnect, to mask bus latencies and keep a high compute efficiency for the RMA.

The DMAs of the DSPFabric ports are under control of the address generation units (AGU). This is their task to update the DMA burst descriptors. *Burst*

Descriptor is a structure that contains the start address, increment and last address of the memory bank under access according to the application requirements. These processors are single issue machines with an instruction memory and a data memory, and they communicate with each other through a set of shared registers that are read/write accessed by all the AGU, for instance to implement sync protocols.

3   Embedded Shared Memory Programming Model - Dynamic Aspects

An important aspect in streaming applications is the dataflow management between off-chip and on-chip memory hierarchies. Our data-memory architecture consists of a main memory and a scratch-pad memory. A scratch-pad memory is a fast software-managed SRAM as compared to cache-memory which is hardware-managed.

Smalltalk runtime environment (VM[3]) is used for the co-execution of different functional units of the heterogeneous reconfigurable accelerator (cf. section 2). The goal is to separate application from its resource management logic and to make resource management invisible from application's point of view. This abstract approach allows application validation and *rapid prototyping* in a unified framework. Application processes are defined as proxies. We define proxies as objects that implement a list of tasks (interfaces) specified at runtime on an instance. These tasks contribute to:

- **load**: pre-fetch data from virtual memory to SPM banks.
- **transmit**: feed data to the execution unit(s).
- **retrieve**: write back filtered data from execution unit(s) back to SPM banks.
- **store**: write data from SPM banks back to the virtual memory

The behavior of tasks is specified at method-level as:

- the natural encapsulation provided by methods can be used to drive hardware-software partitioning
- it facilitates capturing the method invocation by injecting specialized objects (discussed later)
- process and context management can be handled efficiently and dynamically

3.1   Method Wrappers

A transition of the execution state of a program module occurs when a designated program module is called or returns from another program module, and when the other program is called or returns from the designated program module. The first step is to detect method invocation calls. In the second step, using detection of calls

---

[3] Virtual Machine.

and returns among program modules as triggers, transitions in execution state are recorded, and the execution state of the designated program module is managed.

The transition between the objects is managed by injecting specialized objects *method wrappers* [3], referred MW hereafter. It allows to determine dynamically who calls a method, and which methods are called. In this manner, the communication between objects can be tracked and traced.

MW is a technique by virtue of which it replaces the method calling selector or symbol with a new one which in turn invokes the old method. Thus, changing the compiled method associated with a symbol or selector handles message-passing control. It also specializes the controlling method which is called each time the encapsulated method is invoked. For example, pseudocode below illustrates the encapsulation of a method by *beforeMethod* and *afterMethod*.

```
controlMethod(argument)
    //beforeMethod
        [//original method source]
    //afterMethod
```

At each invocation of the original method, the *controlMethod* is called. As a natural consequence, we can:

- track the method invocations of all the methods that have been installed with MW
- change at runtime what executes before and after the original method

The latter point is the key to handle proxies (described earlier) dynamically.

3.2   Dynamic Execution

At runtime, *beforeMethod* is efficiently used for context analysis. The decisions or conditions that require context switch could be determined before the execution of the method itself. The object which calls current active method is called *sender* while the object being is called *receiver*. Analyzing this sequence during execution helps in the application analysis. Encapsulation interfaces cause the control method to be called at each invocation and hence allows to deduce the active objects in the input application. We rely on this runtime analysis to schedule memory accesses and allocate optimally the data from virtual memory to scratch-pad memory banks.

3.3   Memory Access Scheduling

In a multi-threaded environment, synchronization between concurrent threads is a critical aspect. Our solution is based on lock-free synchronization of shared data structures. A shared object is lock-free (nonblocking) if it guarantees that whenever a thread executes some finite number of steps, at least one operation on the object by some thread must have made progress during the execution of these steps. We rely on runtime scheduling which guarantees the atomicity of operations dynamically. At each macro-pipeline step all the active tasks are analyzed. Clock step and memory access projection of each thread's memory access is determined by native code analysis. Bounding rectangles by loop indices analysis are determined for each thread's access. The overlap between bounding rectangles representing memory access durations helps in the conflict inference between concurrent threads. Runtime analysis also allows to record execution steps of each concurrent thread. Complete control of local states of active objects as stated earlier allows to record the active or inactive phases of parallel application execution.

The algorithms 1 and 2 illustrate the steps of the methodology described above.

Algorithm 1. Algorithm for lock-free dynamic memory allocation management in the shared SPM banks

---

Require: A linked list of processes: P_{List}
Require: Sorting Queue: S_{queue}
Ensure: initialize method wrappers
   while $time_{observed} < time_{simulation}$ **do**
      select process P_i from P_{List}
      evaluate beforeMethod
      if $P_i \mathrel{!=} P_{root}$ **then**
         memory access analysis (cf. Algorithm 2)
         schedule memory accesses
            sort the tasks in list, S_{queue}
            (by giving priority to write access over read)
         P_i suspend
      else
         set context to the process P_j of S_{queue}
         evaluate executeMethod
      end if
   end while

Algorithm 2. Runtime memory access analysis

Require: Processes sampled for a macro-pipeline step: $P_{sampled}$
   num $\Leftarrow$ size of $P_{sampled}$
   while num $\mathrel{!=} 0$ **do**
      calculate memory access projection (bounding rectangles)
      determine access duration (native code analysis, start clock step, stop clock step)
      num $\Leftarrow$ num - 1
   end while

---

4   Synthesis for Architecture

A comprehensive high-level synthesis system requires step-by-step transformations of system specification or description with an objective of overlapping

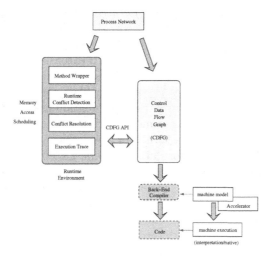

Fig. 4. Compiler Flow

computation and communication optimally. In addition to this, it requires an adequation of such transformations into a set of available system components which could be synthesized and validated. A complete flow of our framework is shown in figure 4.

Design of an appropriate intermediate representation (IR) is of crucial importance to the effectiveness of an HLS environment. Our intermediate representation, CDFG, captures simple operators, hierarchical constructs and control structures. Hierarchical constructs are used both for readability and to force parallel/sequential execution of branches/processes of the CDFG. The control structure of the algorithm is reflected from conditional statements, loops, function call, etc. Concurrency appears at two levels: application process nodes and a control structure inside the CDFG (parallel nodes). In addition to these elements, synchronization is achieved through send/receive operations over channels.

The representation, IR, is then scheduled vis-à-vis the architectural constraints to generate code for the target architecture. This code which represents the data and program memory mappings specific to an application execution drives the structural model of the architecture. This execution is traced/ visualized with a discrete-event simulator which represents the gantt-diagram of the overall execution. The framework is expected to integrate synthesis, co-simulation, performance estimation and design space exploration and graphic visualization tools.

5   Related Work

Bringing flexibility to the SoC has been a research challenge for years and has lead to many proposals. Among them, the coarse grained approach has received much attention with the concept of compute intensive kernel mapped on a cluster of very simple processing unit executing iteratively the same sequence of instructions. CoMAP[4] is an academic project proposing a weakly programmable array of processors. The cell processor [5] from IBM/Sony/Toshiba consortium proposes a cluster of processing elements with SIMD extension providing big MIPS, with a ring interconnect for nearest neighbors connections, and a centralized high throughput memory. It uses a streaming like programming model, with task level granularity. ADRES[6] is a research program from IMEC, proposing a coarse grained fabric of processing elements with a small register file and a mesh interconnect. It supports compute kernels of a few tens of operations. It is tightly coupled to a VLIW[4] processor for data transfers. Except some very particular cases, heavy control structures are embedded in the application code, and many are even data dependent (like in adaptive filters) and those control structures somehow decreases the benefit of using coarse grained fabric, and restrain their deployment in a low cost product. The smart memory project [7] from Stanford is an array of microcontrollers with reconfigurable distributed memory banks. It supports either a streaming like or a shared memory with cache coherence programming model. UCDavis reports an other array of processing elements with fine granularity [8], and with a streaming programming model. The fact is that all solutions showing fine granularity report high MIPS/mm^2, but are difficult to program by non architecture savvy developers. They all use a rigid memory hierarchy based on data streaming transfers that also restrict their use by a wider community.

This paper presents an innovative architecture with a flexible sub-memory system based on software controlled scratch-pad memories. The programming model is then responsible to manage data-transfers from main memory to the local memory banks. Cited methodologies related to memory allocation under the control of software can be categorized as *static* [9,10] and *dynamic* [11,12] methods.

To the best of our knowledge, none of the cited methods considers the dynamic allocation of heap data to scratchpad memory banks in a multi-threaded runtime environment which favors communication and computation overlap. In addition to the conventional memory allocation steps, the runtime environment also has to schedule explicit data transfers between the offchip memory and the SPM so as to maximize the communication and computation overlap or hide processor-memory latency gap. To accomplish this, the runtime environment needs to take into account the data layout in the off-chip memory, the application access pattern, and the available memory space in the SPM.

6   Results - Mapping of the Deblocking Kernel on the DSPFabric

The DFG of the kernel has 376 basic nodes once loop unrolling and if/then/else to multiplexer transformation has been done. The graph is mapped on DSPFabric

---

[4] Very Large Instruction Word.

Table 1. Mapping of the deblocking kernel on DSPFabric

Kernel	Number of ops	Number of compute nodes	Data rate (pix/sec)	Cycle budget	Schedule density
	376	32	2 XVGA 30 fps (luma+chroma)	14	84%
MPEG-4 deblock		16	VGA 30 fps (luma+chroma)	29	81%

using the joint scheduling/place and route method described in [2]. The mapping routine tries to make the best use of the available resources to reach a specified initiation interval for the input kernel.

Several trials have been performed targeting different initiation interval constraints, and the results are given in the table 1.

A solution with 16 nodes gives a pixel rate good enough for a VGA stream format (640×480 pixels), while with 32 nodes we sustain 2 VGA streams. This shows that performance grows linearly with the number of resources available, and this comes with a good schedule density (ration of useful operations performed during iteration execution).

7   Conclusion

The results shown in this paper are still of a preliminary development , but appear very promising and worth deeper exploration of this methodology. This research is paving the way for programming toolsets and methods for massively parallel architectures with distributed memory, as envisioned in future compute platforms for portable applications.

Acknowledgements

This work has been achieved partly at the University of Bretagne Occidentale, LESTER, FRE CNRS, France and at STMicroelectronics, Grenoble, France. It has been funded by STMicroelectronics and ANRT CIFRE grant.

References

1. Rau, B.R.: Iterative modulo scheduling: An algorithm for software pipelining loops. In: MICRO 27: Proceedings of the 27th annual international symposium on Microarchitecture, pp. 63–74. ACM, New York (1994)
2. Sykora, M., Pavoni, D., Cambonie, J., Costa, R., Reghizzi, S.C.: Hierarchical cluster assignment for coarse grained reconfigurable coprocessor. In: Proceedings of RAW 2007, (August (2007)
3. Johnson, R.E., Brant, J., Foote, B., Roberts, D.: Wrappers to the rescue. In: Jul, E. (ed.) ECOOP 1998. LNCS, vol. 1445, Springer, Heidelberg (1998)

4. Dutta, H., Hannig, F., Kupriyanov, A., Kissler, D., Teich, J., Schaffer, R., Siegel, S., Merker, R., Pottier, B.: Massively Parallel Processor Architectures: A Co-design Approach. In: Proceedings of the 3rd International Workshop on Reconfigurable Communication Centric System-on-Chips (ReCoSoC), Montpellier, France (June 2007)
5. J.K., et al.: Introduction to the cell multiprocessor. IBM J. Research and Development, 589–604 (September 2005)
6. Mei, B., Vernalde, S., Verkest, D., Lauwereins, R.: Design methodology for a tightly coupled vliw/reconfigurable matrix architecture: A case study. In: Proceedings of the Conference on Design, Automation and Test in Europe, February 16 - 20, 2004, vol. 2, p. 21224. IEEE Computer Society, Washington (2004)
7. Labonte, F., Mattson, P., Buck, I., Kozyrakis, C., Horowitz, M.: The stream virtual machine. In: PACT (September 2004)
8. Meeuwsen, M., Yu, Z., Baas, B.: A shared memory module for asynchronous arrays of processors. EURASIP Journal on Embedded Systems, 2007, Article ID 86273, 13 pages (2007)
9. Avissar, O., Barua, R., Stewart, D.: Heterogeneous memory management for embedded systems. In: Proceedings of the ACM 2nd International Conference on Compilers, Architectures, and Synthesis for Embedded Systems (CASES) (November 2001)
10. Banakar, R., Steinke, S., Lee, B.S., Balakrishnan, M., Marwedel, P.: Scratchpad memory: A design alternative for cache on-chip memory in embedded systems. In: Tenth International Symposium on Hardware/Software Codesign (CODES), Estes Park, May 6-8, 2002, ACM Press, New York (2002)
11. Udayakumaran, S., Dominguez, A., Barua, R.: Dynamic allocation for scratchpad memory using compile-time decisions. The ACM Transactions on Embedded Computing Systems (TECS) 5(2) (to appear, 2006)
12. Kandemir, M., Ramanujam, J., Irwin, M.J., Vijaykrishnan, N.I., Parikh, A.: Dynamic management of scratch-pad memory space. In: Design Automation Conference, pp. 690–695 (2001)

DNA Physical Mapping
on a Reconfigurable Platform

Adriano Idalgo and Nahri Moreano

Department of Computing,
Federal University of Mato Grosso do Sul, Brazil
adriano.idalgo@gmail.com, nahri@dct.ufms.br

Abstract. Reconfigurable architectures enable the hardware function to be implemented by the user and, due to its characteristics, have been used in many areas, including Bioinformatics. One application of Bioinformatics is the consecutive ones problem, which consists in finding a permutation of columns in a binary matrix, in such a way that all the ones in each row are consecutive. This matrix represents information about DNA fragments and probes, which allow the determination of the order of the nitrogenated bases that form the original DNA.

This work proposes a hybrid software/hardware system for solving the consecutive ones problem. Since this problem processes large volumes of data, the goal is to reduce its execution time, compared to a SW algorithm. We present and analyze several implementations, in the reconfigurable hardware, of sections of this algorithm, using a Virtex-II FPGA. Experiments performed using real chromosomes produced speedups of up to 29.62 and show potential for further optimizations exploiting dynamic reconfiguration.

Keywords: Consecutive ones problem, Reconfigurable architectures, Software/hardware partitioning.

1 Introduction

Reconfigurable computing characterizes the hardware in which the logic implemented is created and modified by the user and not by the manufacturer. It introduces many application possibilities that could not be developed using a hardware with fixed and predefined functionality. There is also a performance improvement potential of the application implemented on a reconfigurable hardware with respect to their implementation in software [1].

In another research area, the Bioinformatics, achievements have been reached recently on DNA mapping, using computational techniques to assist the sequencing task, which consists of identifying the order of base pairs in a chromosome. Due to technical limitations, the DNA is not directly sequenced and must be broken into fragments. One approach is to represent the information of fragments and probes as a binary matrix and to arrange the columns of the matrix so that all ones in each row are consecutive, in order to determine the order among the fragments. This problem is called the *Consecutive Ones Problem* [2].

R. Woods et al. (Eds.): ARC 2008, LNCS 4943, pp. 27–38, 2008.

Besides its vast practical application, DNA mapping requires manipulating huge volumes of data. In particular, the consecutive ones problem handles binary data. Such characteristics motivate the study and implementation, on reconfigurable devices, of solutions to this problem, in order to obtain a better performance in its execution.

In this work we present a hybrid Software/Hardware (SW/HW) solution for the consecutive ones problem. We developed several implementations, on a reconfigurable hardware, of operations with high execution frequency in a well-known algorithm [3] to the consecutive ones problem. These implementations exploit different trade-offs between computation and communication costs, on the processor/FPGA platform used. We performed an experimental evaluation, in order to analyze our solutions and compare them to the pure SW solution, using chromosomes of two living beings. The results show large performance gains and possibilities for improvements using reconfiguration.

This paper is organized as follows: Section 2 describes previous works with solutions for Bioinformatics problems using reconfigurable architectures. The consecutive ones problem and an algorithm for it are introduced in Section 3. Section 4 presents our hybrid implementations for this problem, while the results obtained through experiments are analyzed in Section 5. Finally, in Section 6 the conclusions and future extensions of this work are discussed.

2 Related Work

Most of works which solve Bioinformatics problems using reconfigurable architectures focus on the sequence alignment problem using the Smith-Waterman algorithm, which is based on the dynamic programming technique. The works in [4,5] implemented this algorithm on a FPGA, using processing elements which form a linear structure and operate in parallel. This processing elements compute the similarity between two sequences and compute in parallel all the values in each diagonal of the dynamic programming matrix.

The authors in [6] implemented the Smith-Waterman algorithm on a multi-FPGA network. In [7], a prefetching scheme for search in a sequence database is implemented, in order to accelerate the sequence alignment task on a FPGA, overlapping computation with communication.

The work in [8] presents a hybrid SW/HW system for the reconstruction of the phylogenetic tree of DNA sequences. This tree represents the evolution history of different organisms. A genetic algorithm is implemented in SW and a maximum likelihood function is implemented on a FPGA.

In [9] the authors designed a variant of BLAST, a well-known similarity search tool to compare DNA sequences. The goal was to build a specialized BLAST accelerator using a system with a general-purpose processor and a reconfigurable hardware (FPGA) associated with the disk controller.

There is not, to our knowledge, any previous solution to the consecutive ones problem in hardware, with either fixed or reconfigurable logic.

3   DNA Physical Mapping

Many DNA molecules are over millions of base pairs long, therefore too large to be sequenced as a whole. A physical map of a DNA contains the location of certain markers along the molecule. Given a sequenced fragment of the DNA, the physical map is used to locate the fragment in the DNA by matching markers in the fragment and the physical map.

In order to create a physical map, it is necessary to obtain several copies of the DNA, to use restriction enzymes to break each copy into fragments, and to clone each fragment, producing a collection of clones. Then we need to examine the clones for overlaps among them. The hybridization technique can be applied to obtain overlap information from the clones, using probes (short sequences) and verifying if each probe binds to each clone. If a probe hybridizes to two clones, then the clones overlap each other. Using the overlap information from the clones, it is possible to determine their relative order in the DNA.

3.1   Consecutive Ones Problem and Algorithm

The information produced by hybridization experiments with n clones and m probes can be modeled by a binary matrix M, $n \times m$, where the M_{ij} position says if probe j hybridized ($M_{ij} = 1$) or not ($M_{ij} = 0$) to clone i. M is said to own the *consecutive ones property* for rows (C1P), if all ones in each row are consecutive. In order to get the DNA physical map it is necessary to solve the consecutive ones problem, i.e., to find a permutation of columns (probes) such that all ones in each row (clone) are consecutive.

We describe briefly the polynomial time complexity algorithm proposed in [3] to this problem. Other solutions can be found in [10,11]. The algorithm uses certain criteria to separate the rows of M into components. If each component has the C1P, then M will also have this property. The algorithm performs the following steps: separate rows into components, permute the columns of each component, and join the components [2]. The following relations between rows and the number of intersections between their column sets are used to form the components and to guide the permutation of their columns.

Definition 1. *For each row i of M, let S_i be the set of columns k where $M_{ik} = 1$. Given two rows i and j three situations can arise:*

1. $S_i \cap S_j = \emptyset$;
2. $S_i \subseteq S_j$ or $S_j \subseteq S_i$;
3. $S_i \cap S_j \neq \emptyset$, and none of them is a subset of the other.

An undirected graph G_C is built, where each vertex in G_C corresponds to a row of M. There is an edge between vertices i and j if $S_i \cap S_j \neq \emptyset$, and none of them is a subset of the other. The components of M are the connected components of G_C. Thus, each component is a sub-matrix of M with the same number of columns and possibly fewer rows than M.

In order to permute the columns of a component, the rows are processed one by one. We permute the first two rows placing the exclusive 1s of one row in a direction (right or left), the exclusive 1s of the other in the opposite direction, and the intersection 1s in the middle. To insert a new row k it is necessary to find two previously placed rows, i and j, such that there are edges (k, i) and (i, j) in G_C. If $|S_j \cap S_k| < min(|S_j \cap S_i|, |S_i \cap S_k|)$, k is placed in the same direction of i (with respect to j); otherwise, k will have the opposite direction.

We represent the permutation solutions by associating a set of possible columns to each component column. These sets indicate which original matrix columns correspond to the component column. In the end, the column sets codify the order in which the columns must be arrange so that matrix M has all 1s consecutive in each row.

To join the components, a directed graph G_M is built, where vertices correspond to components of G_C. There is a directed edge from vertex α to β if, for every row i of component β, the set S_i is contained at least in one set S_j of component α. Since the relationship between components is given by edge direction, the topological order of G_M vertices indicates the order the components must be joined. The first component, α, is fixed, and to join another component β, the row l of β that has the leftmost 1 is chosen. Let c_β be this column. We must find all rows in α that contain S_l, and find the leftmost column c_α where all these rows have 1. Then, c_α and c_β are made the same column and the rows of β are joined to α. The final matrix with C1P is obtained after joining all components.

Fig. 1 illustrates the algorithm steps [2]. Matrix M in Fig. 1(a) represents hybridization results of 8 clones with 9 probes, and the corresponding graphs G_C, with four connected components, and G_M are shown in Figs. 1(b) and 1(c). Fig. 1(d) shows the result from the permutation of M.

4 Hardware/Software Solution

We use, in our solutions to the consecutive ones problem, an hybrid architecture composed of general purpose processor with a reconfigurable component attached to it. The reconfigurable hardware (a FPGA) is used to implement a hardware accelerator for this application. Due to the characteristics of this architecture, the coupling between host processor and FPGA is weak, and the fastest available communication between them is through the network interface present in both devices. Therefore, the communication overhead can cause a major impact on the application total execution time, and consequently, the implementation strategy chosen for the communication is very important.

Initially, we implemented a SW solution to the problem, which uses only the host processor. Then, we profiled this implementation, determining the sections of the algorithm that consume most of the execution time. Based on these profile information, we performed the SW/HW partitioning. The application operations are divided, such that operations that can not be easily mapped on reconfigurable logic are executed on the host processor, and operations that can benefit from hardware implementation and consume substantial execution time are executed

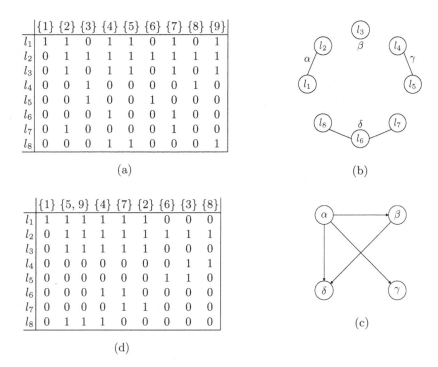

	{1}	{2}	{3}	{4}	{5}	{6}	{7}	{8}	{9}
l_1	1	1	0	1	1	0	1	0	1
l_2	0	1	1	1	1	1	1	1	1
l_3	0	1	0	1	1	0	1	0	1
l_4	0	0	1	0	0	0	0	1	0
l_5	0	0	1	0	0	1	0	0	0
l_6	0	0	0	1	0	0	1	0	0
l_7	0	1	0	0	0	0	1	0	0
l_8	0	0	0	1	1	0	0	0	1

(a)

(b)

	{1}	{5, 9}		{4}	{7}	{2}	{6}	{3}	{8}
l_1	1	1	1	1	1	1	0	0	0
l_2	0	1	1	1	1	1	1	1	1
l_3	0	1	1	1	1	1	0	0	0
l_4	0	0	0	0	0	0	0	1	1
l_5	0	0	0	0	0	0	1	1	0
l_6	0	0	0	1	1	0	0	0	0
l_7	0	0	0	0	1	1	0	0	0
l_8	0	1	1	1	0	0	0	0	0

(c)

(d)

Fig. 1. (a) Matrix M and corresponding (b) graph G_C (with components α, β, γ, and δ), (c) graph G_M, and (d) final matrix

on the FPGA. Thus, some sections of the application code executed originally in software have been replaced by function calls for communication to the FPGA.

We selected for hardware implementation two critical operations: clones comparison and construction of the column sets for each component. For each operation, we developed different hardware implementations, producing several hybrid SW/HW solutions. The main goal is to reduce the execution time of the consecutive ones problem solution, when compared to its SW implementation.

The HW component of the hybrid solutions is composed of the main modules described below. In addition to these modules, it can use memory banks available on the board that contains the FPGA to increase the processing capacity.

- **Control:** Manages the data flow necessary for the other modules in the FPGA, so it is the most complex module. The control consists of a state machine which coordinates all steps of the HW operations.
- **Compare clones:** Compares two rows and counts their intersections.
- **Construct sets:** Constructs the column sets for each component.
- **Receive data:** Receives input data from the SW part of the application.
- **Send data:** Sends the operation results to the SW part of the application.

4.1   Comparing Clones

The comparison of rows (clones) of M determines whether two rows belong to same component and also the number of intersections between their column sets. The rows, represented as sequences of bits, are sent from the SW program to the FPGA. Given that the rows can be very long, the HW implementation of this operation performs comparisons and intersection counting in blocks of bits. In order to process two rows i and j, we operate the first block of i with the first block of j, then the second block of i with the second one of j, and so on. At each clock cycle, the circuit processes a pair of blocks, until the two rows are entirely operated. We use 32 bit-blocks.

The circuit of Fig. 2 shows how the row comparison operation is implemented in HW. At each cycle, the row comparator performs the following operations:

- Perform an AND operation with the two blocks, obtaining the auxiliary result R.
- In parallel:
  - If R is different from 0, the blocks have intersection. The relation result is set appropriately.
  - Perform a XOR operation with the first block and R. If the result is different from 0, the first block is not contained by the second one. The relation result is set accordingly.
  - Perform a XOR operation with the second block and R. If the result is different from 0, the second block is not contained by the first one. The relation result is set accordingly.
  - Count the number of 1s in R and accumulate the partial result.

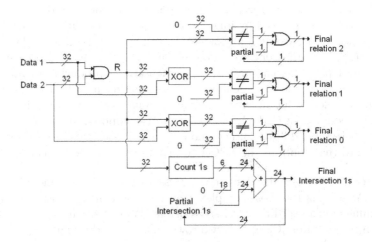

Fig. 2. Circuit for clone comparison

4.2   Constructing Column Sets

After permuting the component columns, the construction of the column sets of each component is performed processing the components by columns. When scanning column c, if the position corresponding to row i contains 1, it indicates that at least one element from the set S_i of columns of row i belongs also to the column set of c. If this is the first 1 found, the set S_i is copied to this column set. Otherwise, only the columns belonging to both sets will be part of the column set of c. If the position corresponding to row i contains 0, the columns belonging to S_i do not belong to this column set. So any element in S_i should be removed from the column set of c.

The column set construction operation implemented in HW uses memory banks of the FPGA board to store the matrix M, the permuted component stored by columns, and the indexes of the rows of M that belong to the component. The set constructor uses the same strategy of the clone comparator and process the input data in blocks. The input data to the set constructor are a block from the component column and a block from the column set of a row. The output is the block from the column set of the component.

The circuit of Fig. 3 shows how this operation is implemented in HW. The constructor receives a column block every 32 clock cycles and a row block each cycle. It maintains the partial result P and an index indicating the position to be accessed in the column. After receiving a row block, the constructor verify the column current position and performs the following operations:

- If this position has 0, the block of the row set is inverted (operation NOT) and perform an AND operation with this result and P.
- If this position has 1, perform an AND with the block of the row set and P.
- The result is stored in P, and the column index is decremented.

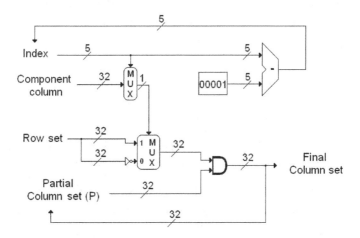

Fig. 3. Circuit for column set construction

4.3   Hybrid Implementations

We developed five different hybrid solutions using several implemented versions of the two operations (clone comparison and set construction), with increasingly functionality and control complexity, and exploring different trade-offs between computation and communication costs.

SW/HW 1: Demand Sending and Clone Comparison
    This solution implements in HW only the row comparison operation. There is no use of memory banks and the communication is stream-based. The SW determines which pairs of rows must be compared and for each pair, sends a package containing the two rows to be compared. The rows are processed in HW in a pipelined way: while some blocks are unpacked, others are compared.

SW/HW 2: Complete Sending and Demand Clone Comparison
    The second solution also implements in HW only the row comparison operation, but it uses a memory bank to store the entire matrix M. The SW initially sends the entire M to the HW. Then the SW determines which pairs of rows must be compared and for each pair, sends a package containing only the two row indexes (rather than the two entire rows). The packages are smaller and the replicated sending of the same row is eliminated (when it is compared to several distinct rows). Therefore the communication overhead can decrease.

SW/HW 3: Complete Sending, Demand Clone Comparison, and Set Construction
    This solution is similar to the previous one, but it includes the column set construction operation in HW. Since more memory banks are used, the control becomes more complex accordingly.

SW/HW 4: Complete Clone Comparison, and Set Construction
    The fourth solution implements in HW both the row comparison and the column set construction operations. The SW initially sends the entire M to the HW, which performs all row comparisons (each row is compared to every row). The SW does not need to send a comparison request for each pair of rows. The goal is to reduce the communication overhead when there are many row comparisons. The set construction control is not changed with respect to the previous implementation.

SW/HW 5: Parallel Clone Comparison and Parallel Set Construction
    The last solution also implements in HW both operations and introduces the exploitation of parallelism in their execution. There are in the HW two modules for row comparison and another two for set construction. Additional memory banks are used and matrix M is stored in an interleaved way in two banks. This way, both row comparison modules (as well as the set constructors) can work in parallel and provide twice the performance for each operation.

5   Experimental Results

The platform used to implement our solutions consists of a computer with a general purpose processor Athlon 64 with 2.2 GHz clock frequency, 2 GB of RAM, and a 100 Mb/s network connection, and a multimedia board from Xilinx [12] containing a Virtex-II XCV2000 FPGA operating at 50 MHz clock frequency and five memory banks of 2 MB each one. The pure SW implementation, as well as the SW parts of the hybrid solutions were developed in the C programming language. The HW parts of the hybrid solutions were developed using the VHDL hardware description language and synthesized with the Xilinx/ISE tool.

We used chromosomes from two living beings to generate the clones and probes, which in turn produced the binary matrices used in the experiments. The first was the chromosome 5 of *Arabidopsis thaliana* (a plant of the mustard family), and the second was a chromosome 2 contig of *Homo sapiens*, both obtained from NCBI [13]. For the first chromosome, 3,285 clones and 4,096 probes were generated, and for the second chromosome, 2,881 clones and 4,096 probes.

For each input matrix, the pure SW algorithm and the five hybrid solutions described in Subsection 4.3 were executed. Table 1 shows the results for the various solutions, applied to the matrix formed with the *Arabidopsis thaliana* data. For each operation implemented in HW (row comparison and set construction), we show the time spent only on FPGA processing and the total time spent performing the operation. The latter includes communication, FPGA processing, and SW processing times. The number of row comparisons performed is also shown. Finally, the table shows the total execution time of the solution and the speedup of each hybrid implementation with respect to the SW algorithm.

The results show that, for the *Arabidopsis thaliana* data, a few comparisons between rows are necessary, indicating that the matrix has few components. Therefore, the comparison of all row pairs (performed by implementations SW/HW 4 and 5) offers no benefits because it makes a far greater number of comparisons than are actually necessary. For this operation, the best solutions are implementations SW/HW 2 and 3.

Considering the set construction operation, the first two hybrid implementations perform the set construction in SW, while implementations SW/HW 3 and 4 use one single constructor module in HW, and reduce in more than 16 times

Table 1. Results for *Arabidopsis thaliana* chromosome (execution times in seconds)

Implementation	Row Comparison			Set Construction		Total time	Speedup wrt. SW
	Number of comparisons	Time in FPGA	Total time	Time in FPGA	Total time		
SW	7,879	–	0.70	–	571.45	573.11	–
SW/HW 1	7,879	0.04	1.30	–	589.34	591.45	0.97
SW/HW 2	7,879	0.04	0.67	–	572.59	574.11	1.00
SW/HW 3	7,879	0.04	0.63	34.45	35.17	36.67	15.63
SW/HW 4	5,393,970	27.72	29.95	34.45	35.16	65.89	8.70
SW/HW 5	5,393,970	13.92	16.14	17.22	17.94	34.86	16.44

Table 2. Results for *Homo sapiens* chromosome (execution times in seconds)

Implementation	Row Comparison			Set Construction		Total time	Speedup wrt. SW
	Number of comparisons	Time in FPGA	Total time	Time in FPGA	Total time		
SW	2,080,334	–	214.83	–	272.42	487.73	–
SW/HW 1	2,080,334	10.65	351.53	–	280.55	633.56	0.77
SW/HW 2	2,080,334	11.07	137.08	–	248.28	386.47	1.26
SW/HW 3	2,080,334	11.15	124.12	15.11	15.61	145.53	3.35
SW/HW 4	4,148,640	21.32	23.06	15.11	15.59	39.02	12.50
SW/HW 5	4,148,640	10.70	12.44	7.55	8.03	20.84	23.40

the total time spent on this operation. In the last implementation, the introduction of a new set constructor module provided a performance gain around 100% when compared to the previous solution.

We can see from the SW solution results that, for this matrix, most of the total execution time is spent on the set construction operation. We can develop a SW/HW implementation 6, combining *Complete Sending and Demand Clone Comparison* (as SW/HW 3) *and Parallel Set Construction* (as SW/HW 5). This solution produces the best results for the *Arabidopsis thaliana* matrix, with 19.35 seconds of total execution time and yielding a speedup of 29.62 with respect to the SW algorithm.

Table 2 presents the results obtained with the second matrix, containing the *Homo sapiens* data. We can see that, for this matrix, it is necessary to compare many more row pairs, and consequently the time spent on the row comparison operation represents a considerable portion of the SW algorithm total execution time. Thus, the implementation of this operation in HW has enabled all hybrid implementations (except the first one) a substantial performance gain when compared to the SW solution. The approach used in solution SW/HW 1 sends to the FPGA a message with the pair of rows, for each row comparison, and produces a negative impact on the communication time. Solutions SW/HW 2 and 3 send all M rows once and, for each comparison, send only the row indexes, reducing the communication time and yielding an average performance gain of 65%, for this operation, with respect to the SW algorithm. Implementation SW/HW 4, which makes all comparisons and does not send row indexes, reduces even further the communication time and produces a performance gain of 832% in the time spent on this operation, compared to the SW algorithm. The last hybrid solution nearly doubles this gain, using two row comparison modules. Therefore, we can conclude that if the number of comparisons is significant, it is better to perform all comparisons than to send messages with comparison requests.

The results from Table 2 also show significant performance gains for implementations that perform in FPGA the set construction operation. The use of parallel row comparison and set construction (solution SW/HW 5) produced the hybrid implementation with the best results, for this matrix, yielding a speedup of 23.4 when compared to the SW algorithm. Both operations benefit from parallelism, because their data can be partitioned and processed independently.

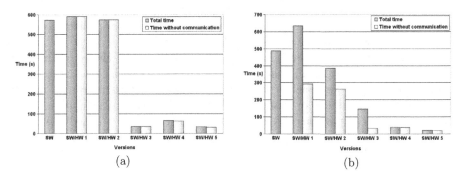

Fig. 4. Execution time for (a) *Arabidopsis thaliana* and (b) *Homo sapiens* chromosomes

Fig. 4 shows the total execution time for all implementations and for both chromosomes. In order to analyze the impact of communication overhead in each hybrid solution, the figure also shows the execution time without the communication overhead, but including both FPGA and SW processing. We can see that, for the *Homo sapiens* chromosome, some hybrid solutions can benefit from a platform with a stronger coupling between processor and FPGA, and consequently lower communication overhead.

6   Conclusions and Future Research

This paper presented several SW/HW solutions to the consecutive ones problem, used in DNA physical mapping. We developed these solutions on a platform with a processor and a reconfigurable component attached to it, and also implemented the pure SW algorithm. The hybrid solutions perform in hardware operations that most contribute to the SW algorithm total execution time. We performed experiments with real chromosomes in order to compare the performance of these solutions to the SW implementation, and analyze different trade-offs between communication overhead and computation.

The results showed the reconfigurable device capability in efficiently execute the operations, clone comparison and set construction, and both provided performance gains. These operations perform repetitive tasks that require a continuous data flow and present a considerable amount of data parallelism, features that are benefited from the implementation in hardware.

We achieved drastic performance improvements using approaches with reduced communication and with pipeline and parallelism. The hybrid implementations yielded speedups up to 29.62, with respect to the SW algorithm, for the *Arabidopsis thaliana* chromosome. For the *Homo sapiens* chromosome, we produced speedups up to 23.4.

We can further improve these results using an architecture with stronger coupling and a reconfigurable component without the strict limitations of low clock frequency and small memory capacity. This way, communication time can be reduced and more parallelism can be exploited. The solutions developed employ at most two hardware modules, for each operation, working in parallel, due to memory limitations. However, the application offers more parallelism potential and there was still plenty of area available in the FPGA.

From the experimental evaluation we conclude that the choice of the best SW/HW solution may be different for each input matrix with clones and probes data. A challenging approach is to identify which characteristics of this matrix influence it to have a few or many components and affect the demand of a few or many clone comparisons. Based on this investigation, we can dynamically reconfigure the FPGA to implement the best solution to that matrix.

References

1. Bondalapati, K., Prasanna, V.K.: Reconfigurable Computing Systems. Proceedings of the IEEE 90(7), 1201–1217 (2002)
2. Setubal, J.C., Meidanis, J.: Introduction to Computational Molecular Biology. PWS Publishing Company (1997)
3. Fulkerson, D., Gross, O.: Incidence Matrices and Interval Graphs. Pacific Journal of Mathematics 15(3), 835–855 (1965)
4. Jacobi, R.P., Rincón, M.A., Carvalho, L.G., Llanos, C.H., Hartenstein, R.W.: Reconfigurable Systems for Sequence Alignment and for General Dynamic Programming. In: Proceedings of the Brazilian Workshop on Bioinformatics, pp. 25–32 (2004)
5. Oliver, T., Schmidt, B., Maskell, D.: Hyper Customized Processors for Bio-Sequence Database Scanning on FPGAs. In: Proceedings of the International Symposium on Field-Programmable Gate Arrays, pp. 229–237 (2005)
6. Regester, K., Byun, J.H., Mukherjee, A., Ravindran, A.: Implementing Bioinformatics Algorithms on Nallatech-Configurable Multi-FPGA Systems. Xcell Journal Online (53), 100–103 (2005)
7. Meng, X., Chaudhary, V.: An Adaptive Data Prefetching Scheme for Biosequence Database Search on Reconfigurable Platforms. In: Proceedings of the ACM Symposium on Applied Computing, pp. 140–141 (2007)
8. Mak, T.S.T., Lam, K.P.: Embedded Computation of Maximum-Likelihood Phylogeny Inference Using Platform FPGA. In: Proceedings of the IEEE Computational Systems Bioinformatics Conference, pp. 512–514 (2004)
9. Krishnamurthy, P., Buhler, J., Chamberlain, R.D., Franklin, M.A., Gyang, K., Jacob, A., Lancaster, J.: Biosequence Similarity Search on the Mercury System. In: Proceedings of the International Conference on Application-Specific Systems, Architectures and Processors, pp. 365–375 (2004)
10. Hsu, W.L.: A Simple Test for the Consecutive Ones Property. In: Ibaraki, T., Iwama, K., Yamashita, M., Inagaki, Y., Nishizeki, T. (eds.) ISAAC 1992. LNCS, vol. 650, pp. 459–468. Springer, Heidelberg (1992)
11. Booth, K.S., Lueker, G.S.: Testing for the Consecutive Ones Property, Interval Graphs, and Graph Planarity Using PQ-tree Algorithms. Journal of Computer and System Sciences 13(3), 335–379 (1976)
12. Xilinx: Xilinx Multimedia Board (2005), http://www.xilinx.com
13. NCBI - National Center for Biotechnology Information: NCBI (2007), http://www.ncbi.nlm.nih.gov/

Hardware BLAST Algorithms with Multi-seeds Detection and Parallel Extension

Fei Xia, Yong Dou, and Jinbo Xu

Department of Computer Science, National University of Defence Technology,
Changsha, P.R. China, 410073
{xcyphoenix,yong_dou,JinboXu}@hotmail.com

Abstract. As one of the most widely used bio-sequence searching tools, BLAST adopts index-based approach to detect the matches between two substrings by looking up a large table and processing one match per query. In this paper, we propose a systolic array approach to detect string matches without using looking up tables. The pipelining systolic array is implemented as a multi-seeds detection and parallel extension pipeline engine to accelerate the first two stages of NCBI BLAST algorithm. Different from the index-based approach, our implementation consumes little memory resources and eliminates redundant string extensions by merging multiple adjoin seeds into a valid seed. Our FPGA implementation achieves superior performance results in both of processing element number and clock frequency over related works in the area of FPGA BLAST accelerators. The experimental results also show the speedup can reach about 17 and 48 compared to the NCBI BLASTp and TBLASTn programs for 3072-residue queries on Intel P4 CPU, respectively. Furthermore, the idea of multi-seeds detection also can be adopted in other seed-based heuristic searching applications.

1   Introduction

The comparison of DNA or protein sequences has become a fundamental task of modern molecular biology. BLAST (Basic Local Alignment Search Tool) [1] as one of the most important tools has been designed to run on commodity PC clusters at present to search for sequence similarity in genomic databases. With the exponential growth of the bio-sequence databases, such as the NCBI (National Center for Biotechnology Information) GenBank [2], which has doubled in size every 12~16 months for the last decade and now stands at over 56 billion characters, the computational requirements for sequence comparisons have far exceeded the computing capability.

General-purposed microprocessors typically provide very limited bit-level parallelism. However, sequence comparison algorithms exhibit a much higher degree of bit-level data parallelism, typically hundreds of bit-level operations can be performed in parallel. Therefore, many researchers keen on implementing BLAST algorithms in hardware to avoid the low efficiency in general-purposed microprocessors. Recently, FPGA chips have emerged as one promising application accelerator, using a combination of FPGAs and general-purposed CPUs to

R. Woods et al. (Eds.): ARC 2008, LNCS 4943, pp. 39–50, 2008.

accelerate BLAST algorithm attracts much more attention. A number of parallel architectures have been proposed, such as Mercury BLASTn [3], [4], [5], Tree-BLAST [6], Mercury BLASTp [7], RC-BLAST [8], FPGA/FLASH Accelerator [9],Multi-engine BLASTn Accelerator [10], [11] and many commercialized system, BEE2 [12], CLC Cube [13], Mitrion [14] and DeCypher [15] et.al. have been built.

Most of the current implementations adopt the index-based searching approach, which builds all kinds of tables to record the position of each *word* in query sequence, then drives the *words* (or named *w-mers*) in database flowing through the accelerator one by one and looks up the table to find the *seeds*. However, this method typically suffers two drawbacks. Firstly, only one word can be searched per cycle (meaning at most one seed can be detected per cycle), with the limitation on memory port number, no matter what the table is stored in internal or external memory. Second, the storage and access overhead of lookup table become the resource bottleneck.

Specifically, Mercury BLASTn [4] and Mitrion [14] implement a pre-filter using hashing, then check *words* in database against a hash table constructed from the query one by one. Hash table is stored in an external SRAM attached to FPGA, since the internal block RAMs are too limited in size to hold the tables for large query sequence. The accessing delay to external SRAM incurs long pipeline cycle time. RC-BLAST [8] and BEE2 [12] implement the word-finding stage by using query index. Each word from subject sequence is then used as an index to lookup the table in order. Because of the limitation of on-chip memory size, the design in RC-BLAST assumes that no word in query sequence is repeated more than three times. Obviously, the assumption is unreasonable. Compared with other designs, FPGA/FLASH adopted a novel approach, the database is also formatted as an index structure. Each word is associated with its position in the sequence and its neighboring environment. This information allows short un-gapped alignments to be immediately computed, avoiding millions of random accesses to the database. Unfortunately, the size of the database index has to be very large. As an example, storing a 40 amino acid substring environment leads to a 150 GB index for the Human genome. This is 50 times more than the raw data [9]. The storage cost will be intolerable with the steeply growth of database. To improve searching efficiency, Multi-engines BLASTn [11] fitted 64 identical computing machines in single chip to compare the query with 64 subject sequences in database concurrently and Mercury BLASTp [7] implemented a two-seed generator for accelerating the first stage of BLASTp. Unfortunately, these approaches are still based on the query index essentially.

Besides the index-based searching approach, there exists another searching strategy, which uses systolic array without lookup tables. D.Hoang et. al. [16], [17] implemented the Needleman-Wunsch and dynamic programming algorithms using systolic array implementation on SPLASH 2. Using JBits S.Guccione et. al. [18]implements the Smith-Waterman algorithm. The most recent implementations were the Hyper Customized Processors in Nanyang Tech University [19] and FPGA-Based Accelerators by Tom Van Court et. al [20]. It is a natural approach to use systolic array to mapping dynamic programming algorithms on FPGAs. But it is rare to use systolic array for mapping the BLAST algorithm, only Tree-BLAST [6] can be found.

At present, most of the seed-based solutions test the words from database stream in a serial mode, one match per cycle. The searching efficiency can be improved if hardware can detect multiple "*seeds*" concurrently and extend them in parallel. In this paper we present a *Multi-seeds Detection and Parallel Extension Engine* to accelerate BLAST algorithm. Our design is based on systolic array rather than the static lookup table. It lessens the storage requirement to on-chip memory because all positions of match points can be calculated dynamically at seeds detection pipelines. The multi-seeds detection has three advantages: Firstly, it improves the searching capability in word-matching stage, which can execute up to 3072 matches/cycle and report all the match points contemporarily with the help of 3072 PEs. Secondly, all the reported seeds at a time are located in identical diagonal, which is convenient for filtering some invalid seeds. Finally, the mechanism of multiple seeds detection supplies enough seeds to reduce the empty time in the extension stage.

2   BLAST Algorithm Overview

BLAST family is composed of five subprograms: BLASTn, BLASTp, BLASTx, TBLASTn and TBLASTx. They provide functionalities for comparing all possible combinations of query and database sequence types by translating the sequences. Nevertheless, the algorithms for each type of search operate are almost identically. The kernel of the algorithm can be summarized as 3 steps: **Seeds Hitting**, **Ungapped Extension** and **Gapped Extension**. Previous study [4] showed most of the execution time is spent in the step 1 and 2, over 99%, especially in the first one, over 80%. Therefore, how to detect and locate word matching quickly is critical to accelerate BLAST algorithm.

3   The Structure of Multi-seeds Detection and Parallel Extension Engine

Our BLAST searching system consists of an algorithm accelerator engine and a host processor. The accelerator scans database for an input query sequence and produces a HSP list. Then the host analyses the HSP list in order to assign statistical significance to those matches. The accelerator engine comprises one FPGA chip (Altera StratixII EP2S130C5), two 1GB SDRAM modules (Micron MT16LSDT12864A) and an USB2.0 interface which is connected to the host. The structure is shown in Fig.1(A). The design fitted in the FPGA includes SDRAM&PE Array Interface Module, Sequence Memory Group, Multi-seeds Detection Array, Seeds Merging Module and Multi-seeds Ungapped Extension Module. SDRAM&PE Array Interface is responsible for system initialization and providing the subject data stream. Sequence Memory holds the query and

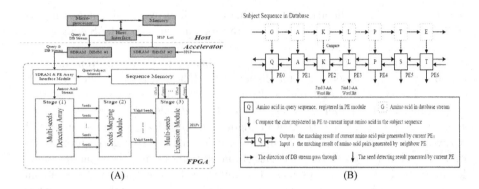

Fig. 1. (A) The Structure of Multi-seeds Detection and Parallel Extension Engine, (B) The Structure of Multi-seeds Detection Array

current subject sequence, and produces the subsequence including seeds for ungapped extension. The last three modules compose the algorithm core. In the following subsections, we take BLASTp algorithm as example to illustrate our implementation in detail.

3.1 Multi-seeds Detecting

The function of this stage is similar to word matching in NCBI BLASTp. It finds out the common appearance of subsequence with 3 amino acids (*3-AA word*) in both query sequence and subject sequence in database. The main difference is that with the help of systolic array, multiple seeds can be detected at each clock cycle, instead of one match per cycle in usual index-based method. Suppose $q_{i-1}q_iq_{i+1}$ and $s_{j-1}s_js_{j+1}$, $(i, j \geq 1)$ are substrings in query and subject sequence respectively. If $(q_{i-1} = s_{j-1}) \wedge (q_i = s_j) \wedge (q_{i+1} = s_{j+1})$ that means a 3-AA word matching occurred and a seed had been detected. The structure of systolic seed detecting array as shown in Fig.1(B).

The array consists of a series of *Processing Elements* (PEs), which holds the query(a char per PE) while the database stream flows through the array. *PE[i]*(the *ith* PE) compares q_i with s_j, then send the match flag to previous and next PEs, per cycle. At the same time, *PE[i]* receives the match flags, compares results of amino acid pairs (q_{i-1}, s_{j-1}) and (q_{i+1}, s_{j+1}) , generated by neighbour PEs and judges if a seed has been detected. Therefore, the array is capable of processing word matching at up to L Matches/cycle (L is the PE array size) and can report multi-seeds per cycle if they are detected. The array reports two seeds (word *AKL* on PE2 and *KLP* on PE3) at the same time, as shown in Fig.1(B). The multi-seeds detect algorithm is illustrated in Fig.2(A).

Seed detecting and locating are two key functions of PE module implemented. Statement S3 in algorithm1 implements the seed-detecting. The location of word hit consists of the offsets in query and in subject, the subject sequence ID in database, which calculated dynamically by S2(Initial phase), S1 and S2 in processing phase respectively.

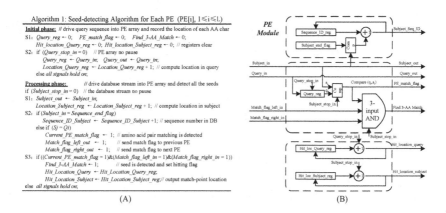

Fig. 2. (A) The Seeds Detecting Algorithm for Each PE, (B) PE Module Structure

3.2 Successive Seeds Merging

The systolic array implements the multi-seeds detect procedure very quickly. The array may report a lot of seeds contemporarily when there is enough similarity between the query and subject. It is hard for ungapped extension stage to catch up with the speed of multi-seeds detect with the growth of the array size. Finally, it will cause the unbalance in processing capability between the two stages. To address the problem, we add a seeds merging stage to merge the adjacent successive word-hits (because those seeds belong to identical HSP) into a valid seed and pass it to extension stage as shown in Fig.3(A). The benefit of merging seeds is that the number of valid seed can be reduced significantly. As result, the efficiency of ungapped extension stage is improved since the duplication extension of single HSP had been eliminated.

3.3 Multi-seeds Extension

This stage extends the seeds to either side to identify a longer pair of protein sequence with the score exceeds the threshold. To improve the extension efficiency, we adopt the Multi-channel Parallel Extension Strategy, which will be introduced particularly in section 4.4.

4 FPGA Implementation and Optimization

4.1 Multi-seeds Detection Array

As for the basic cell in multi-seeds detection array, *PE Module* performs the character comparison in pipeline mode and calculates the hit position. The kernel in PE module is a 3-input AND Gate(the middle rectangle area in Fig.2(B)), which implements seed detection. The two input signals named *Match_flag_left_in* and *Match_flag_right_in* generated by adjacent PEs and the current pair match-flag are sent to input ports of the 3-input AND to generate a hit signal when all inputs are TRUE. Three accumulators calculate the offsets of the seed by counting the amino acid characters passed through. Since the *Find 3-AA Match* flag depends on the comparing result of amino acid pairs calculated by adjacent PEs, the calculating the hit flag is the critical path. Timing analysis shows the path delay is less than 3ns, thus it is not the bottleneck in FPGA implementation.

The PE array size is limited by logic (LUT) resource in FPGA. Generally, the larger array size is, the higher searching efficiency can be reached since more words are scanned and more seeds may be detected at the same time. However with the increase in seed-detection capability, multi-seeds recording becomes a critical issue because the number and location of seeds generated by PE array at each time is random. When there is enough similarity between the query and subject, a lot of seeds are reported contemporarily. The overhead recording the seeds orderly will lead to a long pause and low efficiency since the array must be held up until all the seeds have been recorded. To address this problem, we adopt two schemes: decomposing the PE array and merging successive seeds.

4.2   Decomposing the Detection Array

The idea of this strategy is decomposing the Multi-seeds Detection Array into *PE Groups* to record the seeds in parallel. To record the seeds detected by the array, the *Seeds Merging Module* should also be partitioned into some *SM subModules* (corresponding to *PE Groups*), each of which records and merges the seeds detected by local *PE Group* then sends it to a local *Hit FIFO*. The seed in *Hit FIFOs* is delivered to *Hit information FIFO* by multilevel *Fifo Merger Modules*. The partition and hierarchical merging process is illustrated in Fig.3(A). The other advantage of decomposing the detection array is eliminating the bottleneck in implementing the huge multiplexer (MUX) between the *Multi-seeds Detection Array* and *Seeds Merging Module* as shown in Fig.3(B). We transform the huge multiplexer into several smaller ones (subMUX) by partitioning the large array

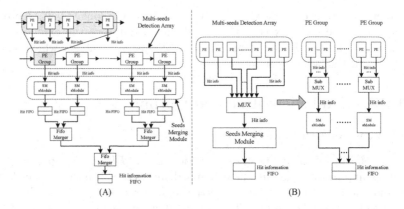

Fig. 3. (A) The Array Partition and Hierarchical Multi-seeds Merging Process, (B) The Port Connection between PE Array and Seeds Merging Module

and *Seeds Merging Module* into small groups. Thus the multiplexer units no longer become the bottleneck in FPGA implementation. The synthesis results show that the 64 PEs compose a group is an optimal choice. The clock frequency of the detection array with 512 PEs increases from 55MHz to 156MHz since the large *MUX* (512-line to one) is divided into eight small *subMUX* (64-line to one) and it does not change visibly with the array size growth.

4.3   The Algorithm of Merging Successive Seeds

As far as each *PE Group* is concerned, recording multi-seeds still have to be processed in order. If the two subsequences in query and current subject are highly similar, many seeds will be reported by adjacent PEs contemporarily. It will take a long time to record them one by one. Additionally, it will cause redundant extension if every seed in successive position is sent to the *Hit FIFO* because the seeds belong to the identical HSP.

To filter the redundant seeds and reduce unnecessary extension overhead, we adopt a merging seeds strategy in *SM sModule*. The successive seeds merging algorithm is illustrated in Fig.4. Each *SM sModule* registers the seed flags as statement S1 in processing phase and checks whether word matches are detected. The *function* in S4 finds the first position "1" ("1" means a word hit), which corresponds to the location of first seed detected. The loop in S6 merges the successive word hits into a valid seed then reports it (S8). Suppose the current

Algorithm 2: Successive Seeds Merging

Initial phase:
S1: $Hit\_location \leftarrow 0$; $Subject\_stop \leftarrow 0$; $Word\_hit\_reg[1..m] \leftarrow 0$; $i \leftarrow 0$;
Processing phase:
S1: $Word\_hit\_reg[1..m] \leftarrow Word\_hit[1..m]$; $Hsp\_flag \leftarrow 0$; $i \leftarrow 0$;
S2: While $(Word\_hit\_reg[1..m] != 0)$
  Do S3 ~ S8;
    S3: $Subject\_stop \leftarrow 1$;   // Stop current subject sequence passing through
    S4: FUNCTION $Find\ the\ first\ location\ of\ '1'\ (n)$;   // The value returned is n ($1 \leq n \leq m$).
    S5: $Word\_hit\_reg[n] \leftarrow 0$; $n \leftarrow n+1$; $i \leftarrow 1$;
    S6: While $(Word\_hit\_reg[n] = 1)$
      Do { $Word\_hit\_reg[n] \leftarrow 0$;   // record the match point and clear the hit flag
        $n \leftarrow n+1$; $i \leftarrow i+1$; }
    S7: If $(i > T)$ // judge if finds a segment matched exactly with enough length
      $Hsp\_flag \leftarrow 1$;
    S8: $Hit\_location \leftarrow \{ Hsp\_flag, Hit\_info[n] \}$;
S9: $Subject\_stop \leftarrow 0$; Returns S1;

Fig. 4. Successive Seeds Merging Algorithm for Each SM subModule

status of *PE Group* as shown in Fig.1(B). Both PE2 and 3 find a seed at the same time. The *SM sModule* will deliver the two seeds to *Hit FIFO* and the extension operation will be executed twice without the phase of merging seeds. In fact only one extension is needed since the seed *AKL* and *KLP* can be merged into a bigger seed *AKLP*.

Statement S7 judges whether it finds a segment matched exactly with enough length from the count of successive hit flags (variable i). If i is greater than the value set by user (suppose $T = 8$, that means the substring with more than 10 amino acid pairs matched exactly is detected), then *Hsp_flag* is set active.

The extension module will no longer extend the seed but output it directly because the extension have finished. Our method reduces unnecessary extension and endows the PE array with a measure of "*macroscopic*" searching ability.

4.4   Multi-channel Parallel Extension Strategy

In this stage seeds are read out from *Hit information FIFO* and extended (adopting Blosum62 Matrix) to either side to identify a HSP. So the *seed's context characters* are needed for extension. However, because of the powerful capability of multi-seeds detecting and the serial extension procedure (only one amino acid pair can be read out per cycle from *Sequence Memory*), the seed-extension capability can't catch up with the throughput of multi-seeds detection units.

To solve the problem, we adopt the *Multi-channel Parallel Extension* method by setting several *Ungapped Extension Modules* as shown in Fig.5. Because each *Extension Module* accesses query and subject sequence memory contemporarily to get the seed's context characters, several *Qry/Sub Memory* copies are fitted to supply enough access ports for multi-channel extension. Thus, multiple seeds from different *Hit info FIFO* can be extended in parallel.

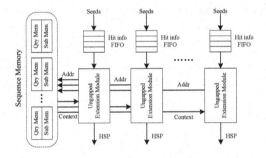

Fig. 5. The Structure of Multi-channel Parallel Extension

5   Experiments and Performance Comparison

The NCBI BLAST software with default parameters (Ver:2.2.16) runs on a desktop computer with a 2.60GHz P4 CPU and 1.5GB Memory. Theoretically, the *Multi-seeds Detection Array* can detect all seeds. We searched a sequence selected in Swiss-Prot with 2048 residues against a small part of Swiss-Prot with 65536 total letters. As a result, 12629 seeds have been detected and 793 seeds have been extended successfully. Using the merging seeds strategy, the number of seeds reported in our design is greatly less than that of the software, but the HSP list accords with the software version. We did a series of tests to evaluate our implementation in the aspects of synthesis performance, storage requirement, actual searching capability and speedup over related works.

Test 1: Comparing Synthesis Performance to Systolic Array Approaches. We fit our design on FPGA EP2S130C5 with 3072 PEs as shown in Table 1. Without seed-detecting, Tree-BLAST [6] finds HSP directly by adding up the scores of individual alignments between two amino acids. It allocates a BRAM for every four PEs to index the scoring matrix, therefore the BRAM count limits the query size up to 600 on XC2VP70 and 1024 on XC4VLX160. Different from Tree-BLAST, the array size is not limited by BRAM but LUTs in our implementation. It only consumes 38% on-chip memory resource of FPGA XC4VLX160, compared with nearly 88% of related work. We also implement 1024 PEs on XC2VP70-5, the same platform with Tree-BLAST. The result shows our design is superior to Tree-BLAST in both PE number and clock frequency.

Table 1. Performance results and comparison

	Ours			Tree-BLAST [6]	
FPGA	EP2S130C5	XC2VP70-5	XC4VLX160	XC2VP70-5	XC4VLX160
PEs Fitted	3072	1024	3072	600	1024
ALUT/Slice (%)	92098/(87%)	20007/(60%)	48272 /(71%)	− −	78%
Memory (%)	741376 bits/(11%)	36 BRAM/(11%)	110 BRAM/(38%)	− −	88%
Clock (MHz)	113	140	189	110	178
Single PE	42 ALUTs or 31 Slices			− −	− −

Test 2: Comparing Storage Requirement to Index-based Approaches. As stated before, the systolic array storage requirements less than index-based approaches. The main storage expense in our design is *Sequence Memory* and multistage *Hit FIFO* (When the array size is 3072, the memory overhead is $692K$bits, which is only 11% of the memory capacity in EP2S130C5). On the contrary, the index-based approach is limited to the capacity of on-chip block RAMs. RC-BLAST [8] fitted a query index with the size of $64K \times 64$bits in Xilinx 4085XLA, which can only record three offsets for each word. Due to the same reason, Mercury [4] and Mitrion [14] have to store the hash table to external SRAM. The delay of memory access becomes the performance bottleneck. Compared to index-based RC-BLAST and systolic-based Tree-BLAST, our approach reduced the storage requirement by about 90% and 50% respectively. Furthermore, in our implementation, little memory requirement reduces the complexity of memory access and lessens the difficulty in FPGA layout and routing.

Test 3: Comparing to Index-based Hardware Accelerators
(1) Word-scanning Capability. Most of the current implementations can execute only one word-match per cycle, such as [3], [4], [5], [8], [12], [14]. The word-scanning capability in Mercury BLASTn [3] is 96M matches/s. Mercury BLASTp [7] designed a two-seed generator, the processing capability reaches up to 219M matches/s for 2048-residue queries. The capability in Multi-engine BLASTn Accelerator [11] achieves 6400M matches/s by using 64 identical parallel engines. Comparatively, our searching engine can execute 294912M word matches per second, over 40 times, by using the multi-seeds parallel detecting approach.

(2) Actual Searching Capability. We use the measurement unit, the number of *Kilo Amino Acids (Kaa)* compared to the number of *Mega nucleotides (Mnt)* performed every second, *KaaMnt/s*, to measure the actual computing power, because of the variation in the hardware structure, the amount of FPGA resource and clock frequency among all kinds of accelerators. The computational power of FPGA/FLASH and Timelogic Decypher Engine reported in [9] is 451 and $182KaaMnt/s$ respectively. In our implementation, it took 424ms to search a 3072-residue query against drosoph.nt downloaded from NCBI BLAST Database [21] on our engine. We calculate our computational capability:

$$\frac{3Kaa \times 122Mnt}{424ms} = 863KaaMnt/\sec$$

Hence, as for the actual searching capability, our design is 1.91 and 4.74 times as fast as the FPGA/FLASH and Timelogic Decypher Engine respectively.

Test 4: Comparing Execution-time to Software Version. We fit the design on our testbed to accelerate the first two stages of BLASTp and TBLASTn. The experimental results are listed in Table 2.

Table 2. Execution time (ms) and speed-up for different queries

Array Size	BLASTp			TBLASTn		
(Query length)	Software	Hardware	Speedup	Software	Hardware	Speedup
128	1901	1047	1.82	3203	150	21.3
256	3087	1057	2.92	3641	163	22.3
512	5603	1090	5.14	5156	199	25.9
1K	9327	1157	8.06	9891	254	38.9
2K	17814	1227	14.5	15438	358	43.0
3K	25132	1487	16.9	20328	424	47.9
4K	32469	1620 (simulated)	20.0	25656	480 (simulated)	53.4
8K	61162	2207 (simulated)	27.7	47797	570 (simulated)	83.8

(1) Comparing to BLASTp. We did a series of experiments to search queries selected in Swiss-Prot with different length(128~8K, which equals array size) among the database Swiss-Prot, including 274,295 sequences, 100,686,439 total letters, downloaded from EBI [22]. The software execution time, with the growth of query size, is increasing very fast. It only took 1901 ms to search the database with 128-residue queries, while the time added up to 61162 ms to finish the mission with 8K-residue queries. The reason is the cost in both index constructing and searching object increasing greatly with the query size growth. However, the time on our accelerator increases very slowly. This is due mainly to searching cycles of our accelerator equals to the time of database stream flow through the array (that is $L + S$, where L is the array size and S is the database size) plus the pausing time. In the above factors, S is a const and the variation in L can be ignored compared with S. In addition, the pausing cost is related to the number of seeds detected directly. When searching domain (DB) is certain, the valid seeds number and the extension overhead will not increase sharply with the query size growth since the optimized strategies introduced in section 4 are used in our implementation. Thus, the larger the array size is, the better the speedup achieves. It is about 17 times faster than the desktop computer for 3072-residue queries. Simulation result shows it can reach 27.7 with the array size of 8K.

(2) Comparing to TBLASTn. Queries were selected in Swiss-Prot with the length from 128 to 8K residues. The run time of TBLASTn is tested for searching the database drosoph.nt downloaded from NCBI BLAST Database [21], which includes 1170 sequences, 122,655,632 letters and the accelerator searches against the *Coding Sequence* (CDS) picked out from drosoph.nt. TBLASTn is used for searching protein sequence against DNA database. It translates all the DNA sequences into the 6 possible potential proteins before searching. Therefore, for the same query, it is slower than BLASTp. However, the execution time of our accelerator does not increase steeply with the query size growth for the same reason as the Test4(1), so the higher speedup can be achieved. Our implementation has a speedup of approximately 48 for 3072-residue queries using the array with 3072 PEs and the value can reach about 84 for 8K-PE array.

6   Conclusion

In this paper we present a systolic array, which supports Multi-seeds Detection and Multi-channel Ungapped Extension in parallel, to accelerate the first two stages of NCBI BLASTp and TBLASTn. Our implementation reduces unnecessary extension by using merging seeds strategy and decreases the memory requirement on-chip as a result of eliminating the lookup tables. The experimental results show about 17 and 48 times faster than BLASTp and TBLASTn program running on a desktop computer with 2.60GHz P4 CPU and 1.5GB Memory for 3072-residue queries, respectively. Furthermore, our design is suitable to BLASTn and the Multi-seeds Detecting Array also can be used to accelerate the seed detection stage in other seed-based heuristic searching applications.

Acknowledgments. This work is supported by the National High Technology Research and Development Program of China (2007AA01Z106) and National Natural Science Foundation of China (60633050).

References

1. Altschul, S.F., Gish, W., et al.: Basic local alignment search tool. Molecular Biology, 403–410 (1990)
2. NCBI, GenBank Growth Statistics (2006),
   http://www.ncbi.nlm.nih.gov/Genbank/genbankstats.html
3. Buhler, J.D., Lancaster, J.M., et al.: Mercury BLASTN: Faster DNA Sequence Comparison Using a Streaming Hardware Architecture. In: Proc. 3rd Annual Reconfigurable Systems Summer Institute (2007)

4. Krishnanurthy, P., Buhler, J., et al.: Biosequence Similarity search on the Mercury system. In: Proc. 15th IEEE International Conference on Application-Specific Systems, Architectures and Processors, pp. 365–375 (2004)
5. Lancaster, J., Buhler, J., et al.: Acceleration of Ungapped Extension in Mercury BLAST. In: Proc. 7th Workshop on Media and Streaming Processors, pp. 50–57 (2005)
6. Herbordt, M.C., Model, J., et al.: Single Pass, BLAST-Like, Approximate String Matching on FPGAs. In: Proc. 14th Annual IEEE Symposium on Field-Programmable Custom Computing Machines, pp. 217–226 (2006)
7. Jacob, A., Lancaster, J., et al.: FPGA-accelerated seed generation in Mercury BLASTp. In: Proc. 15th Annual IEEE Symposium on Field-Programmable Custom Computing Machines, pp. 95–106 (2007)
8. Muriki, K., Underwood, K.D., et al.: RC-BLAST: Towards a Portable, Cost-Effective Open Source Hardware Implementation. In: Proc. 19th IEEE International Parallel and Distributed Processing Symposium (2005)
9. Lavenier, D., Xinchun, L., Georges, G.: Seed-based Genomic Sequence Comparison using a FPGA/FLASH Accelerator. In: IEEE International Conference on Field Programmable Technology, pp. 41–48 (2006)
10. Sotiriades, E., Dollas, A.: Design Space Exploration for the BAST Algorithm Implementation. In: Proc. 15th Annual IEEE Symposium on Field-Programmable Custom Computing Machines (2007)
11. Sotiriades, E., Kozanitis, C., Dollas, A.: FPGA based Architecture for DNA Sequence Comparison and Database Search. In: Proc. 20th IEEE International Parallel and Distributed Processing Symposium (2006)
12. Chang, C.: BLAST Implementation on BEE2. Electrical Engineering and Computer Science University of California at Berkeley (2005), http://bee2.eecs.berkeley.edu
13. CLC Desktop Hardware-Acceleration. White paper on CLC Bioinformatics Cube (2006), http://www.clccube.com
14. Mitrion.Inc.: NCBI BLAST Accelerator (2007), http://www.mitrionics.com
15. Timelogic.Inc.: Timelogic DeCypher BLAST Engine (2006), http://www.timelogic.com/decypher_blast.html
16. Hoang, D., et al.: FPGA Implementation of Systolic Sequence Alignment. In: Proc. 2nd International Workshop on Field-Programmable Logic and Applications, Lecture Notes in Computer Science, pp. 183–191 (1992)
17. Hoang, D., et al.: Searching Genetic Databases on Splash2. In: Proc. IEEE Workshop on FPGAs for Custom Computing Machines, pp. 185–191 (1993)
18. Guccione, S.A., Keller, E.: Gene Matching Using JBits. In: Glesner, M., Zipf, P., Renovell, M. (eds.) FPL 2002. LNCS, vol. 2438, Springer, Heidelberg (2002)
19. Oliver, T., et al.: Hyper Customized Processors for Bio-Sequence Database Scanning on FPGAs. In: Proc. ACM/SIGDA 13th international symposium on Field programmable gate arrays, pp. 229–237 (2005)
20. Court, T.V., Herbordt, M.C.: Families of FPGA-Based Accelerators for Approximate String Matching. Microprocessors and Microsystems 31, 135–145 (2007)
21. NCBI BLAST Database, National Center for Biotechnology Information (2006), http://www.ncbi.nih.gov/BLAST
22. EBI, European Bioinformatics Institute (2007), http://www.ebi.ac.uk/uniprot/database/download.html

Highly Space Efficient Counters for Perl Compatible Regular Expressions in FPGAs*

Chia-Tien Dan Lo and Yi-Gang Tai

Department of Computer Science
University of Texas at San Antonio
{danlo,ytai}@cs.utsa.edu

Abstract. Signature based network intrusion detection systems (NIDS) rely on an underlying string matching engine that inspects each network packet against a known malicious pattern database. Traditional static pattern descriptions may not efficiently represent sophisticated attack signatures. Recently, most NIDSs have adopted regular expressions such as Perl compatible regular expressions (PCREs) to describe an attack signature, especially for polymorphic worms. PCRE is a superset of traditional regular expression, in which no counters are involved. However, this overloads the performance of software-based NIDSs, causing a big portion of their execution time to be dedicated to pattern matching. Over the past decade, hardware acceleration for the pattern matching has been studied extensively and a marginal performance has been achieved. Among hardware approaches, FPGA-based acceleration engines provide great flexibility because new signatures can be compiled and programmed into their reconfigurable architecture. As more and more malicious signatures are discovered, it becomes harder to map a complete set of malicious signatures specified in PCREs to an FPGA chip. Even worse is that the counters used in PCREs typically take a great deal of hardware resources. Therefore, we propose a space efficient SelectRAM counter for PCREs that involve counting. The design takes advantage of components that consist of a configurable logic block, and thus optimizes space usage. A set of PCRE blocks has been built in hardware to implement PCREs used in Snort/Bro. Experimental results show that the proposed sheme outperforms existing designs by at least 5-fold. Performance results are reported in this paper.

1   Introduction

Signature based network intrusion detection systems (NIDS) such as Snort [1] and Bro [2], inspect packets on a network segment and seek for known malicious attacks against a rule database. The advance of attack techniques create a need to describe sophisticated attack signatures using Perl compatible regular expressions (PCRE)[3], which have been adopted and implemented in the

---

* This project is partially supported by the Center for Infrastructure Assurance and Security at UTSA and US Air Force under grant #26-0202-10.

R. Woods et al. (Eds.): ARC 2008, LNCS 4943, pp. 51–62, 2008.

aforementioned NIDSs. Based on our previous study [4,5], more than 70% of the Snort execution time is found to be on string comparisons and their related manipulations. Such computations need to move network packets from the media access control (MAC) layer across the system bus to the CPU. This data path can be shortened and efficiently implemented in FPGAs with their flexibility and parallelism to achieve high performance.

PCREs are not traditional regular expressions (which typically are composed of a set of alphabet with operations such as concatenation, alternation, and Kleene star). However, the PCREs allow counting operations such as Exactly, AtLeast, and Between a range of matches. For example, $a\{n\}$ is looking for n continuous matches of the character a; $a\{n,\}$ specifies at least n continuous matches of the character a, and $a\{n,m\}$ indicates a match when the number of matches is between n and m, inclusively. Obviously, PCREs require counters in addition to a typical implementation via either non-deterministic final automata (NFA) or deterministic final automata (DFA). Furthermore, each PCRE of the above forms will be associated with one or two counters. When implemented in hardware, these counters may take a large portion of hardware resources.

PCRE is a superset of regular expression which can be constructed as an equivalent NFA using the Thompson's construction method [6]. Each NFA can be derived to an equivalent DFA using the subset construction process [6]. However, the exponential space complexity ($O(2^n)$, where n is the length of a regular expression) may not be suitable for a hardware implementation. NFA, on the other hand, are suited for hardware implementations for their parallel nature and expressiveness. Over the past decade, NFA based hardware implementations of string matching have been widely studied. However, the efficiency of hardware implementations for PCREs with constrained repetitions remains to be studied.

The rest of this paper is organized as follows. Section 2 discusses previous related work in hardware implementations for PCREs. Section 3 describes PCREs used in NIDSs. Our proposed 20-bit SelectRAM counter will be depicted in Section 4, followed by the performance evaluation and comparisons with other approaches in Section 5. Section 6 concludes the paper.

2   Related Work

Regular expression string matching implemented in hardware has been extensively studied over the past decade. Back in 1982, Floyd and Ullman proposed a technique to compile regular expressions into integrated circuits [7] using the McNaughton-Yamada algorithm [8]. In 2001, Sidhu and Prasanna presented an efficient method for fast regular expression matching using FPGAs. Regular expressions such as a single character, alternation, concatenation, and Kleene star are converted to NFA which are placed and routed on a self-reconfigurable gate array (SRGA) device. Afterwards, a number of authors have proposed to enhance the performance of pattern matching using hardware. In 2002, Hutchings, Franklin, and Carver [9] studied a JHDL-based module generator using the basic regular expression blocks proposed by Sidhu and Prasanna. This generator additionally supports regular expressions such as meta-characters "?", ".", and "[]", and optimizes space usage via common prefix sharing.

Clark and Schimmel (2004) proposed a pre-decoding technique to share hardware matchers with an attempt to reduce resource usage [10]. Sutton proposed a partial character decoder for NFA-based regular expression matching to reduce the number of signals needed to be routed around the FPGA [11]. Lin, Huang, Jiang, and Chang minimized hardware space by sharing sub-regular expressions [12]. Brodie, Taylor, and Cytron proposed an approach to translate static patterns and regular expressions to DFA based on a pipelined state-machine representation that uses encoding and compression techniques to improve density [13]. Baker, Jung, and Prasanna proposed a microcontroller architecture to emulate DFA-based regular expressions stored in run-time programmable memory tables [14]. This flexible design allows regular expressions to be swapped in and out hardware on-the-fly.

Yusuf, Luk, Szeto, and Osborne proposed a uniform hardware-based network intrusion detection engine based on content addressable memory (CAM) and binary decision diagrams (BDDs) [15]. Bispo, Sourdis, Cardoso, and Vassiliadis proposed a space efficient NFA-based regular expression matcher with constraint repetitions used in PCREs [16]. Their approach employs built-in shift registers (SRL16) for counting to reduce resource usage. These authors also pointed out open issues in synthesizing regular expressions in FPGAs [17], in which one of the emerging issues is area reduction. DFA-based approaches [18,13,14] may result in a significant space demand. The related works in NFA-based approaches may not implement constraint repetitions except the work conducted by Bispo, Sourdis, Cardoso, and Vassiliadis [16].

3   Perl Compatible Regular Expressions Used in Network Intrusion Detection Systems

Due to their expressiveness, PCREs have been adopted by NIDSs such as Snort, and Bro to describe sophisticated attack signatures. The official Snort ruleset is certified by the Sourcefire Vulnerability Research Team (VRT) and is available to the public [1]. The Snort ruleset released on October 15, 2007 is used in this paper. Bro analyzes network traffic against rules that describe activity restrictions, policies, and signatures of known attacks. Signatures defined in Snort can be converted to Bro using a utility called "snort2bro." Currently, there are about 47,355 static patterns and 18,350 PCREs defined in Snort. However, the repeated rates are over 85% as shown in Table 1.

A typical implementation will share identical patterns among rules, and common prefix sharing can also further reduce space requirement [16,14]. For example, there is a signature that describes "IMAP create buffer overflow," defined in Snort and Bro, which is listed in Table 2 and Table 3.

PCRE is defined using "pcre" keyword in Snort; Bro uses "payload" keyword to specify a PCRE. This PCRE describes any string that starts with a space, followed by "CREATE", followed by another space, and followed 1024 non-new

Table 1. Statistics of Signatures Used in Snort

Pattern Type	# of instances	repeated rate	total characters	repeated rate
Static	47,355	85%	560,401	64%
Non-Repeated Static	7,127		203,133	
PCRE	18,350	87%	775,797	51%
Non-Repeated PCRE	2,427		378,066	

Table 2. The Signature That Describes IMAP Create Buffer Overflow Attemp Used in Snort

```
alert tcp $EXTERNAL_NET any -> $HOME_NET 143 (msg:"IMAP create buffer
overflow attempt"; flow:to_server,established; content:"CREATE";
isdataat:1024,relative; pcre:"/\sCREATE\s[^\n]{1024}/smi";
metadata:service imap; reference:bugtraq,7446; classtype:misc-attack;
sid:2107; rev:5;)
```

line characters (ASCII value 10). The ".*" prefixed in the Bro payload attribute is to filter out non-matched characters, and it is semantically identical to the PCRE defined in Snort. Other portions of the signature define the condition of a header in a packet to be inspected, such as source/destination IP addresses, ports, protocols, etc.

Table 3. The Signature That Describes IMAP Create Buffer Overflow Attemp Used in Bro

```
signature sid-2107 {
  ip-proto == tcp
  src-ip != local_nets
  dst-ip == local_nets
  dst-port == 143
  event "IMAP create buffer overflow attempt"
  tcp-state established,originator
  payload /.* CREATE [^\x0a]{1024}/
  }
```

4   Our Proposed 20-Bit SelectRAM Counter

In a Xilinx Virtex-II Pro configurable logic block (CLB), there are four slices, each of which includes two 4-input function generators, two flip-flops (FFs), carry logic, arithmetic logic gates, and multiplexers. The 4-input function generator can be configured as a 4-input lookup table (LUT), 16 bits of distributed memory (RAM16), or a 16-bit shift register (SRL16). In order to save space, a function generator is confgiured as a RAM16 which keeps a count value, and another is programmed as another RAM16 which acts as a counter. Figure 1 shows the schematic design of our proposed 20-bit counter. Since the RAM16 is 16 bits long and one bit wide, it requires 16 clock cycles to reset and a 4-bit address bus. Therefore, we will need a 4-Bit counter to provide an address and a 16 cycles reset (Ready signal) for the RAM16 counter. Once reset, the RAM16 counter will be reset in the first 16 cycles and will count up by one in every 16 cycles achieved by the half adder (HA). A 1-Bit comparator is used to compare the RAM16 counter and the RAM16 value. The RAM16 value is set to be 32 far from the final count for the sentinel register to set timely. The relation of the final count and the RAM16 value is $RAM16\_value = \lceil (final\_count - 32)/2 \rceil$. After the sentinel register is set, the output is high if the 4-Bit decoder detects the leftover counts, i.e., $final\_count$ mod 16.

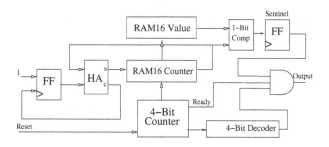

Fig. 1. Our Proposed 20-Bit SelectRAM Counter

For example, a count to 33 will require 16 cycles to reset RAM16, 16 cycles to increase the RAM16 counter to 1 (the 17th cycle), and 16 cycles to increase its value to 2 (the 34th cycle). It will be too late if we check the counter at the 34th. Therefore, the RAM16 value is set to 1. In our design, the sentinel register is set at the 32nd cycle. Thus, if a decoder is used for "0001", then in the 33rd cycle, the circuit will signal that the count has been reached.

Characteristics of the 20-Bit SelectRAM Counter. Based on the design of the proposed 20-bit counter, it will count to any number as large as 2^{20} using the same hardware resource, i.e., the resource usage is constant and is not dependent on the count value. A count value is decomposed into two portions: multiple of 16 (stored in a RAM16) and residue of 16 (detected by the 4-Bit decoder). Each RAM16 can be mapped to a LUT nicely with a design goal to miminize hardware resource usage (the two RAM16 can be mapped to a single slice). For small counts less than 16, a simple LUT configured as SRL16 will be a good option instead. A 16-cycle reset is required to initialize the 20-bit counter because the RAM16 is 16 bits deep and 1 bit wide. Another 16 cycles are required to read its value. Therefore, by its nature, the counter will count any number larger than 32. Once started, the counter can not be stopped unless there is a reset. However, it will output high for one cycle when the final count is reached. A detailed description of using the counter in designing PCRE hardware will be delineated in a later section. The characteristics of the proposed 20-bit SelectRAM counter are summarized as follows:

- needs 16 clocks to reset.
- 4-bit counter counts for the RAM16's addresses and the residue counts.
- is either reset or +1 in any 16 clock cycles.
- can only count by 16.
- can count any value between 32 and 2^{20}.
- two LUTs (one slice) are used for the counter and the final count.

4.1 A PCRE Exactly Block Based on the 20-Bit SelectRAM Counter

Assume that the PCRE Exactly block will count any number larger than 32. A match signal driven from a previous PCRE block will be used to reset the 20-bit SelectRAM counter and enable the output. The reasons why the 20-bit SelectRAM is reset whenever a pre-match is asserted are as follows. First, if a counter is not mature and the following pre-match is found to be within 16 cycles, there would not be enough time for the counter to reset its RAM16 to zero. Second, similarly, if the couter is reset once a mismatch is found, it would miss the following prematch during the 16 cycles of reset. On the other hand, if two or more pre-matches are found within 16 cycles, the counter would not be reset completely until the last pre-match. It should not be a problem in our design because any count less than 32 is taken care of by other simple LUT counters. Figure 2 shows the design of a PCRE Exactly block, such as $a\{n\}$, based on the proposed 20-bit SelectRAM counter.

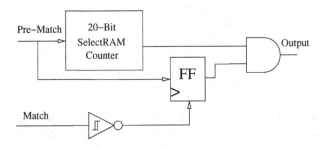

Fig. 2. A PCRE Exactly Block Based on the 20-Bit SelectRAM Counter

Whenever there is a mismatch, the FF is reset to disable the output. Note that the counter will not stop regardless if a mismatch character is found. However, the 20-bit SelectRAM counter will output high for one cycle when a final count is reached. Therefore, the Exactly block will output high for that cycle even though there are more matches.

4.2 A PCRE AtLeast Block Using the Proposed SelectRAM Counter

Our PCRE AtLeast block is composed of a PCRE Exactly block and a register that keeps the state of when the minimal number of matches are reached. When a

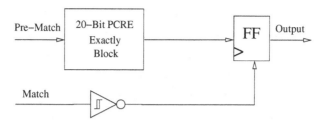

Fig. 3. A PCRE AtLeast Block Based on the 20-Bit SelectRAM Counter

pre-match occurs, the Exactly block will be reset and start counting. Once a designated count is reached, the output from the Exactly block will be kept in the register and the the output will remain high until a mismatch occurs. Figure 3 illustrates our design for a PCRE AtLeast block using the 20-bit SelectRAM counter $(a\{n,\})$.

4.3   A PCRE Between Block Using the 20-Bit SelectRAM Counter

Our 20-bit SelectRAM counter can be modified with maximum resource sharing to implement a PCRE Between block such as $a\{n,m\}$ where n is the lower bound and m is the upper bound. The circuit should output high after a pre-match and n continuous matches of a pattern. The output remains high until the upper bound is reached. Whenever there is a mismatch, the output goes to low. Instead of two full counters, we add a RAM16 (one LUT) to keep the upper bound and some mux logic blocks to switch the 1-bit comparator to the upper bound when the lower bound is reached. It is worth mentioning that there are mux'es in a logic cell and this modificatin should be space efficient. Figure 4 depicts our design for a space efficient PCRE Between block using the 20-bit SelectRAM counter. Because the sentinel register is set every 16 cycles, one more sentinel register is needed in order to check if the upper bound is reached. Otherwise, the Match_lb register will be reset immediately after it is set by the lower bound match logic. Moreover, there should be two sets of residue decoders: one for the lower bound and the other for the upper bound. Since the sentinel register is set 32 cycles ahead of the final count, and reset in the first clock of a 16-cycle update period, then there is an intrinsic limit that the minimal difference between an upper bound and a lower bound is 16. For small counts, they can be implemented using one LUT instead.

4.4   Kleene Star and Plus Blocks

The Kleene star $(a*)$ operator used in PCRE can be easily implemented in hardware based on a PCRE Plus block $(a+)$. For example, $a * b$ is equivalent to $b|a + b$. In practice, it is hard to have a dedicated hardware block to the Kleene star because it depends on the next character. The PCRE Plus block, however, does not need to have a counter to keep its states. Therefore, it can be simply implemented using a register as shown in Figure 5.

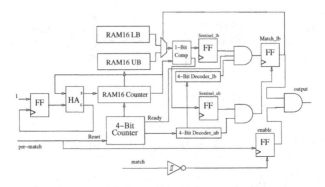

Fig. 4. A PCRE Between Block based on the 20-Bit SelectRAM Counter

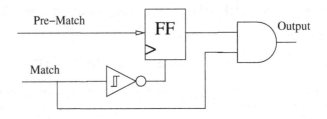

Fig. 5. A PCRE Plus Block

5   Performance Evaluation and Comparison

We have implemented the proposed 20-bit SelectRAM counter on a Xilinx Vertex II pro device and a similar result also applies to other devices. Table 4 shows a performance comparison of our proposed 20-bit SelectRAM counter with other approaches. The results are optimized either in area or in speed set in the Xilinx Synthesis Tool (XST), i.e., the numbers are the same either optimized by area or by speed. Data are collected after place and route operations are complete. The 8 ~ 20-bit LUT counters are purely based on a 4-bit LUT counter which is composed of 4 LUTs. Each bit is latched using a register as shown in the Table 4, in which the number of FFs is increasing accordingly. The SRL16-based 11-bit counter proposed by Bispo *et al.* [16] is based on the shifter register (16 bits deep and 1 bit wide) in a typical Xilinx logic cell. However, the number of SRL16 needed for a counter depends on the count value, i.e., the larger the count value, the more space is required. Nevertheless, the SRL16-based approach is the fastest (397 MHz Vertex V5-3) among all the approaches. Also, its performance would not be degraded when the count value increases. The Xilinx 32-bit counter is synthesized by XST whenever a counter is inferred in a VHDL process. The Xilinx ISE 8.2i will always generate a 32-bit counter, and even a smaller width is set for the counter. It is worth mentioning that a basic Xilinx 20-bit counter will cost 20 FFs in 10 slices. However, when compared to a designated count, it

Table 4. A Performance Comparison on the Proposed 20-Bit SelectRAM Counter with Other Approaches

	FF	LUT	Slice	V2P-7(MHz)	V4-12(MHz)	V5-3(MHz)
Our Proposed 20-bit	11	19	15	185	224	234
20-bit LUT	20	25	17	199	187	183
16-bit LUT	16	21	13	181	169	201
12-bit LUT	12	16	10	181	169	201
8-bit LUT)	8	11	7	204	185	261
SRL16-based 12-bit [16]	246	247	486	304	255	397
SRL16-based 8-bit [16]	21	22	36	304	255	397
Xilinx XST 32-bit	32	73	37	239	282	322

adds up as shown in Table 4. Among the listed approaches, our proposed 20-bit SelectRAM counter outperforms others in terms of space usage and performance.

Based on the 20-bit SelectRAM counter, the PCRE blocks such as Exactly, AtLeast, Between, and Plus, are implemented and their performances are listed in Table 5 and Table 6. Resource usages for the PCRE basic blocks are tabularized in Table 5, in which the targeted device is Virtex-II Pro with speed and area optimization. Implementation on Virtex-II Pro, Virtex-4 and Virtex-E shows exactly the same resource usage. It is worth noting that the Exactly block and the AtLeast block use exactly the same amount of resource whereas the SRL16-based design [16] may vary. Our approach takes advantage of the space efficient design of the 20-bit SelectRAM counter in those two PCRE blocks. As a result, there is only an AND gate difference as shown in Figure 2 and Figure 3. Moreover, the PCRE Between block shares most of the hardware resource used in the Exactly Block in our design. It only uses 19 LUTs as it may require more than 26 LUTs if two Exactly blocks are to be built, in which one is in charge of lower bound counting and the other is in charge of upper bound counting.

Table 5. Resource Usage for the Proposed PCRE Basic Blocks

	FF	LUT	Slice
Character	1	1	1
Plus	1	2	2
Exactly	9	13	12
AtLeast	9	13	12
Between	11	19	15

The maximal frequencies (MHz) of the PCRE basic blocks over different FPGA devices measured from Xilinx ISE tools are reported in Table 6. The results for the Exactly block and the AtLeast block are almost identical and Virtex-5 shows higher performance among the others. The Between block performs slower but is very close to the other two PCRE blocks.

Table 6. Maximum Frequency (MHz) for the Proposed PCRE Basic Blocks

	Character	Plus	Exactly	AtLeast	Between
Virtex-II Pro -7	1,011	480	185	185	183
Virtex-4 -12	1,122	441	224	224	191
Virtex-5 -3	1,039	468	234	234	229

Table 7. Performance Indices of All Approaches

	V2P-7	V4-12	V5-3
Our Proposed 20-bit	195	236	246
20-bit LUT	159	150	146
16-bit LUT	138	129	153
12-bit LUT	136	127	151
8-bit LUT	148	135	190
SRL16-based 12-bit	15	12	19
SRL16-based 8-bit	111	93	144
Xilinx XST 32-bit	105	124	141

Table 8. Comparison between Our Proposed PCRE Pattern Matching Engine and Other PCRE Approaches

Approaches	Bits /Clk	Device	Throu-ghput (Gbps)	Logic Cells	Logic Cells /char	MEM Kbits	# of Char-acters	PEM
Our Approach	8	Virtex-4-200	1.5	5947	0.15	0	40,209	10.26
Bispo et al.[16]	8	Virtex-4	2.9	25,074	1.28	0	19,580	2.27
Lin et al.[12]	8	Virtex-E 2000	-	13,734	0.66	0	20,914	-
Brodie et al.[13]	64	ASIC	16.0	~247K	22.2	2,296	11,126	0.66
Baker et al.[14]	8	Virtex-4-100	1.4	-	2.56	6,000	16,175	0.22
Sidhu et al.[19]	8	Virtex-100	0.46	1,920	66	0	29	0.01

In order to fairly compare overall performance among different designs, we use a performance index that takes into considerations the maximum frequencies and hardware resources used. The performance index is defined as follows:

$$performance\_index = maximum\_frequency/total\_logic\_cell * number\_bits$$

Table 7 shows performance index of the designs over different devices (Virtex II, Virtex-4, and Virtex-5). The results show that our proposed 20-bit SelectRAM approach outperforms other approaches in terms of the performance index. The performance can be 1.2 to 19 times better (in the instance of SRL16-based on Virtex-4).

To measure space efficiency of our proposed PCRE building blocks, a tool written in PERL is developed to automatically extract and compile PCREs defined in Snort to VHDL modules. As an experiment instance, 700 PCRE rules are converted into VHDL, in which 733 Plus blocks, 2,877 Kleene Star blocks, 96 Exactly blocks, 217 AtLeast blocks, 4 Between blocks, and 36,282 static characters are implemented and synthesized. Table 8 lists detailed performance efficiency metric (PEM) [16] numbers among related schemes. Since our proposed PCRE building blocks are highly space efficient, the overall performance implemented on Virtex-4-LX200 is at least 5-fold compared to other related works.

6   Conclusions

As powerful PCREs are being used to describe sophisticated network attack signatures for NIDSs, the performance of PCRE-based pattern matching engines may be a bottleneck to the overall system throughput. To cope with a high speed network, NIDSs have to process incoming network traffic in a timely pace; otherwise, malicious packets would not be detected. Software implementations typically suffer from I/O intensive operations and complicated PCREs pattern matching. With the advanced VLSI techniques, it is inevitable to map software routines (such as PCREs) to hardware, which improves system throughput. However, these PCREs involve counters which may consume a tremendous amount of hardware resources. In this research, a highly space efficient PCRE implementation on FPGAs is proposed. Our scheme takes advantage of CLB structures in FPGAs to optimize resource usage, and thus its performance is at least 5-fold compared to existing designs when implemented for NIDSs. This design can also be applied to other fields such as Bioinformatics that requires extensive string comparisons.

References

1. Snort: Snort intrusion detection system (2007), http://snort.org
2. Bro: Intrusion detection system (2007), http://www.bro-ids.org
3. PCRE: Perl compatible regular expressions (2007), http://www.pcre.org
4. Lo, C.T.D., Tai, Y.G., Psarris, K., Hwang, W.J.: Super fast hardware string matching. In: Proc. of the 2006 IEEE International Conference on Field Programmable Technology, Bangkok, Thailand (December 2006)
5. Roan, H.C., Hwang, W.J., Lo, C.T.D.: Shift-or circuit for efficient network intrusion detection pattern matching. In: Proc. of the 16th International Conference on Field Programmable Logic and Applications (FPL 2006), Madrid, SPAIN (August 2006), pp. 785–790 (2006)
6. Aho, A., Sethi, R., Ullman, J.: Compilers - Principles, Techniques, and Tools, pp. 117–123 (1988)
7. Floyd, R., Ullman, J.: The compilation of regular expressions into integrated circuits. Journal of the ACM (JACM) 29, 603–622 (1982)
8. McNaughton, R., Yamada, H.: Regular expressions and state graphs for automata. IEEE Transactions on Electronic Computers 9, 39–47 (1960)
9. Hutchings, B.L., Franklin, R., Carver, D.: Assisting network intrusion detection with reconfigurable hardware. In: Porc. of the 10th Annual IEEE Symposium on Field-Programmable Custom Computing Machines (FCCM 2002), Napa, CA (April 2002), pp. 111–120 (2002)

10. Clark, C., Schimmel, D.: Scalable parallel pattern-matching on high-speed networks. In: Proc. of IEEE Symposium on Field-Programmable Custom Computing Machines (2004)
11. Sutton, P.: Partial character decoding for improved regular expression matching in fpgas. In: Proceedings of IEEE International Conference on Field-Programmable Technology (FPT), pp. 25–32 (2004)
12. Lin, C.H., Huang, C.T., Jiang, C.P., Chang, S.C.: Optimization of regular expression pattern matching circuits on fpga. In: DATE 2006: Proceedings of the Conference on Design, Automation and Test in Europe, pp. 12–17 (2006)
13. Brodie, B., Taylor, D., Cytron, R.: A scalable architecture for high-throughput regular-expression pattern matching. In: the 33rd International Symposium on Computer Architecture (ISCA 2006), pp. 191–202 (2006)
14. Baker, Z., Prasanna, V., Jung, H.J.: Regular expression software deceleration for intrusion detection systems. In: The 16th International Conference on Field Programmable Logic and Applications (August 2006), pp. 1–8 (2006)
15. Yusuf, S., Luk, W., Szeto, M.K.N., Osborne, W.: Unite: Uniform hardware-based network intrusion detection engine. In: Reconfigurable Computing: Architectures and Applications, pp. 389–400 (2006)
16. Bispo, J., Sourdis, I., Cardoso, J., Vassiliadis, S.: Regular expression matching for reconfigurable packet inspection. In: Proc. of the 16th International Conference on Field Programmable Logic and Applications (FPL 2006), Madrid, SPAIN (August 2006), pp. 119–126 (2006)
17. Bispo, J., Sourdis, I., Cardoso, J., Vassiliadis, S.: Synthesis of regular expressions targeting fpgas: Current status and open issues. In: Reconfigurable Computing: Architectures, Tools and Applicatins (June 2007), pp. 179–190 (2007)
18. Moscola, J., Lockwood, J., Loui, R., Pachos, M.: Implementation of a content-scanning module for an internet firewall. In: Proc. of IEEE Workshop on FPGAs for Custom Computing Machines, Napa, CA (April 2003), pp. 31–38 (2003)
19. Sidhu, R., Prasanna, V.K.: Fast regular expression matching using fpgas. In: Proceedings of the IEEE Symposium on Field-Programmable Custom Computing Machines (April 2001), pp. 227–238 (2001)

A Custom Processor for a TDMA Solver in a CFD Application*

Filipe Oliveira[1], C. Silva Santos[3], F. A. Castro[3], and José C. Alves[1,2]

[1] Instituto de Engenharia de Sistemas e Computadores do Porto (INESC-Porto)
[2] Faculdade de Engenharia da Universidade do Porto (FEUP)
[3] Centro de Estudos de Energia Eólica e Escoamentos Atmosféricos (CEsA)

Abstract. This paper presents a custom processor designed to execute a time consuming function in a CFD application. The selected function implements the method TDMA (Tri-Diagonal Matrix Algorithm) for solving a tri-diagonal system of equations. The custom processor was implemented in a commercial PCI prototyping board based on Virtex4LX FPGAs and uses a dedicated memory cache system, address generators and a deep pipelined floating-point datapath. Running at 100MHz and assuming the input data already in the cache memories, the system reaches a throughput greater than 1.4GFLOPS.

1 Introduction

Computational Fluid Dynamics (CFD) are numeric intensive computer applications to simulate the behavior of a fluid flow over a given physical domain, under certain initial and boundary conditions. The CFD application addressed in this work is the simulation of wind flow over complex terrain. In this class of applications, a CFD simulation is carried out over a 3D rectangular volume corresponding to the location under study, that is divided into a 3D mesh with a variable grid size. Final results of a simulation are the physical properties of the air flow at each point in that mesh like the 3 orthogonal components of wind speed, pressure and kinetic energy of the air. These values allow to construct a 3D map of the wind flow in the domain under study at a given point in time (stationary simulations) or to evaluate the steady state behavior of these variables over time, at a selected point in the simulation domain (transient simulations).

These simulations are performed by numeric iterative processes well known by the scientific community, for which stable resolution methods exist. These techniques rely on solving numerically a set of partial differential equations that describe the physical relationship among the variables at each grid node and its neighbors (the Navier-Stokes equations) as an approximation by finite-difference equations. In the work addressed in this paper, a function was selected from a FORTRAN software code [1], [2], [3] that uses the method SIMPLE, (Semi-Implicit Method for Pressure-Linked Equation) [4] to model the Navier-Stokes equations and the TDMA algorithm to solve the system of equations.

Duration of simulations, performed by desktop computers, may range from hours to days, depending on the number of points of the 3D grid that represent the domain

---

* This work is funded by FCT (*Fundação para a Ciência e Tecnologia*), project POSC/EEAESE/58513/2004.

R. Woods et al. (Eds.): ARC 2008, LNCS 4943, pp. 63–74, 2008.

under simulation and the speed of convergence of the iterative process (this if affected, for example, by the complexity of the terrain that may slow the convergence process). This way, even a modest speedup in the computation process may represent a significant amount of absolute time saved to run a simulation. Preliminary profiling of the original software code has shown that approximately 60% of the overall execution time is spent in a very regular sequence of computations that implement the method TDMA (from now we will refer to this function as 'solver'). This routine is formed by a set of 6 similar FOR loops, where the inner computations share the same structure and use only elementar arithmetic operations performed on single precision floating-point data. This regularity and the high cost of the execution of this small code in the overall program has selected this as the first candidate for migration to a custom processor. Measuring the real CPU time taken by this section of code and counting the number of elmentar floating point operations executed has shown an average performance around 100MFlops, for a typical sized problem (121x36x62 nodes). With appropriate pipelined datapaths, control and memory strutctures this value can be easily overtaken by current FPGA technology, thus the motivation for this development.

Little previous work has been found on FPGA-based acceleration applied to this class of problems. A first proposal for a custom computer for CFD applications was the DREAM-1 and DREAM-1A machines [5]. The authors propose a parallel processing system made of vector processing nodes and local memory partially implemented by hard disks. By this time, FPGA technology had no capacity for such applications and the hardware system was built with discrete chips. In [6] a custom processing architecture is proposed for CFD computations, targeted to the BenNUEY card and BenDATA modules [7]. The authors propose a computing architecture tailored for that hardware platform, using massive parallel memory access and mapping each arithmetic operation in the software code to a floating-point hardware operator in the computation pipelines. Actual datapath architecture and implementation data is presented for only a specific function and performance results presented are based on projections for some of the most computing intensive functions. However, some critical aspects are not addressed, like the operation scheduling and techniques to overcame the data dependencies that otherwise will stall the pipelines.

This paper presents the implementation of a FPGA-based custom processor for acceleration of the most time consuming function in a CFD application. The rest of the paper is organized as follow. Section 2 presents the function targeted in this work. Section 3 addresses the high-level transformations that were exploited to resolve data dependencies and maximize the pipeline efficiency. Section 4 presents the reconfigurable hardware platform that is being used in this work. In section 5, the organization of the custom processor is presented, including the cache memory subsystem and computation datapath. Closing the paper, section 6 shows preliminary results and draw the final conclusions.

2   CFD - The Problem

The CFD application addressed in the work was derived from a FORTRAN software code to simulate the wind flow over complex terrain. The TDMA solver selected to be implemented in the custom computing platform has a very regular structure with various nested FOR loops and performs a set of arithmetic operations on single-precision floating-point matrices. Current FPGA technology can easily surpass the 100MFLOPS performance measured for a typical sized simulation running on a 3.2GHz PC, through custom design of the datapath, controlpath and, in particular, the memory subsystem.

Figure 1 shows the structure of the function 'solver'. The input variables are 8 three-dimensional matrices representing the coefficients of the system of equations being solved, plus another three-dimensional matrix (phi()) containing the data that represents the current solution. The output results of this computation are placed in the matrix phi(). In each iteration, this function is called with a set of different coefficients computed by other sections of the program that were not addressed in this work.

```
for n=1 to nsweep
  for k=kmin to nk
    a(jminml)=0
    for i=imin to ni
      c(jminml)=phi(i,jminml,k)
      for j=jmin to nj
        a(j) = an(i,j,k)                              forward
        b(j) = as(i,j,k)                              loop
        c(j) = ae(i,j,k) * phi(i+1,j,k) +
               aw(i,j,k) * phi(i-1,j,k) +
               at(i,j,k) * phi(i,j,k+1) +
               ab(i,j,k) * phi(i,j,k-1) + su(i,j,k)
        d(j) = ap(i,j,k)
        term = 1 / ( d(j) - b(j) * a(j-1) )
        a(j) = a(j) * term
        c(j) = ( c(j) + b(j) * c(j-1) ) * term

      for j=nj to jmin step -1                        backward
        phi(i,j,k) = a(j) * phi(i,j+1,k) + c(j)  loop
```

Fig. 1. The pseudo-code illustrating the structure of one of the six blocks in function 'solver'. The other 5 blocks are similar to this by permuting the i, j and k control variables of the three nested FOR loops.

The sequence of operations shown in figure 1 can be divided into 2 sections: forward loop and backward loop. The forward loop produces as output the vectors c(j) and a(j), executing 8 multiplications, one division and 6 additions/subtractions in each loop iteration (for each j). The backward loop uses these two vectors to compute the final elements of the output matrix phi(i,j,k), along the dimension j; this section performs one more multiplication and one addition. A straightforward mapping of the dataflow graph of each section into an arithmetic datapath can be obtained easily, as shown in figure 2.

In spite of the simple structure of these circuits, there are two problems that must be solved in order to exploit efficiently the low level parallelism afforded by these datapaths, considering their implementations as a network of pipelined floating-point operators. One is the (relatively) large number of operands required for the forward datapath. To maximize the efficiency of the pipeline, the 15 operands must be issued at the pipeline clock rate, what requires a convenient organization of the memory system and dedicated address generators. The other problem is the data dependencies that exist in the forward loop: to start the computation of one instance of c(j) and a(j) the previously computed values for c(j-1) and a(j-1) must be ready at the pipeline inputs.

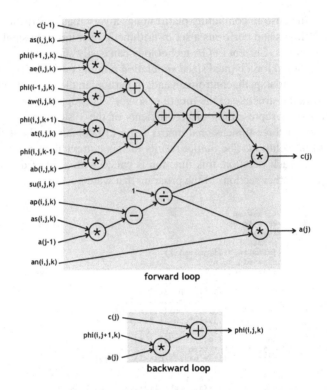

Fig. 2. The datapath that implements the core operations of the forward loop and the backward loop

This means it will not be worth to schedule the computations through the pipeline in the same sequence represented by the original code, because that would require an issue rate for the input data equal to the pipeline latency. On the other hand, if the scheduling of the computations do not follow the same order as in the original code, the final numerical results may alter in some way the overall output of the iterative process.

3   High-Level Transformations

Analyzing the figures 1 and 2, the inner computation in both loops is performed along index j, for a fixed k and i (note the outer loop is just a repetition nsweep times of the whole process). Assuming a pipeline with N stages and considering the original scheduling, the input dataset for index j+1 could only be issued to the pipeline inputs N clock cycles after the input dataset for index j, thus leaving $N-1$ empty slots in the pipeline. Besides, in the original code, the calculation of each c(j) uses the most recent values of phi(i±1,j,k±1). According to the iteration order, the loops along j (inner loop) for a given i and k will always use the results of phi(i-1,j,k-1) already computed for the previous values of i and k ($i-1$ and $k-1$, respectively).

To fully utilize the pipeline slots, the solution adopted was to dispatch into the computation pipeline (forward loop) a sequence of input data for the same j (inner loop) but for k and i (the two outer loops) addressing the elements of the (i,k) plane in a checkerboard fashion: first, compute all the elements along j on the "black" cells and then on the "white" cells. Considering a pipeline with N pipestages, the computations corresponding to the loop instance $(i,j+1,k)$ may be started N clock cycles after the instance (i,j,k). This is when the c(j) and a(j) values required to start iteration $(i,j+1,k)$ are ready at the pipeline outputs and may be feed back to the datapath inputs. This is functionally equivalent to the pseudo-code shown in figure 3.

```
for n = 1 to nsweep*2
  for k = kmin to nk
    a(jminm1) = 0
    k1 = k - kmin + (n-1)%2
    for i = imin + k1%2  to ni step 2
      c(jminm1) = phi(i,jminm1,k)
      for j = jmin to nj
        a(j) = an(i,j,k)                          forward
        ...                                       loop
        c(j) = ( c(j) + b(j) * c(j-1) ) * term

      for j = nj to jmin step -1                  backward
        phi(i,j,k) = a(j) * phi(i,j+1,k) + c(j)   loop
```

Fig. 3. The modified pseudo-code of the main loop in function 'solver', modified to reflect the scheduling implemented by the hardware system

To verify the feasibility of the application of this process, in terms of the numeric results obtained for a real CFD simulation, the original FORTRAN code of function 'solver' was modified to execute in the same fashion depicted in figure 3. The execution of a few typical CFD simulations using this new arrangement of the function 'solver' has shown surprisingly good results. All the runs experimented have reached the convergence criteria of the iterative process not slower than the original code. In one case, the solution has even converged after running only 50% of the number of iterations required by the original program. Besides, the final simulation results that represent the physical parameters of the simulated wind flow differ from the "golden" results by differences that, in terms of their physical meaning, can be considered negligible. Although these results cannot formally prove the validity of the method for all the cases, we can affirm with an high degree of confidence that the same behavior will certainly be observed in simulations with similar characteristics.

3.1   Example of Scheduling

This strategy is exemplified in figure 4, assuming a datapath with 8 pipeline stages and issue rate equal to 1 clock cycle. For a matter of clarity, we will call *j-column(i,k)* to the vector formed by all the elements of a matrix along the dimension j, for a given (i,k); a *black* j-column starts in a black cell of the checkerboard and a *white* j-column starts in a white cell. First iteration (stage 1) starts with $(i,j,k)=(0,0,0)$; next dataset sent to the pipeline inputs is the position $(i,j,k)=(2,0,0)$, then $(4,0,0)$ and so on, until the results of the first input data are present at the output of the pipeline, 8 clocks later (the schedule

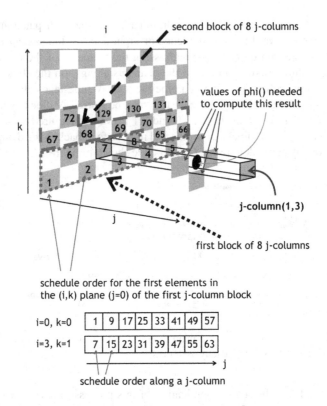

Fig. 4. Scheduling the operations through the forward loop pipeline

order of the first elements in each j-column is represented by the numbers 1 to 8 in the black cells of the checkerboard in figure 4).

At this point (stage 9), these results are re-injected in the pipeline inputs c(j-1) and a(j-1) to execute the iteration $j + 1$: (i,j,k)=(0,1,0), then (2,1,0), (4,1,0) and so on. Sixty-four clock cycles after the first dataset was sent to the pipeline inputs, the computation of the first block of 8 j-columns (dot-dot contour) is complete and the results stored in 8 vectors c(j) and a(j). This happens at stage (clock cycle) 65, when the computation of a new block composed by the next 8 black j-columns can start (dash-dash contour). At the same time, the backward loop is executed along the freshly computed j-columns, using a similar scheduling mechanism to compute the final phi() values for the matrix positions corresponding to the black j-columns.

Note the value of the results computed during the forward loop (the vectors c(j) and a(j)) only use the phi() values of the neighbor nodes corresponding to the original input data. Thus, there are no data dependencies among the calculation of the results for each j-column.

When the first outer loop iteration is concluded (corresponding to $n = 1$ in the code of figure 3, the matrix phi() has newly computed values in the positions corresponding to the black j-columns, and the original input values in the positions of white j-columns. The second iteration along i repeats the process described above for the white j-columns. During this phase, the computation of each element of the vectors c(j) and a(j) performed during the forward loop will use the four neighbor values phi(i±1,j,k±1) computed during the previous phase.

3.2 Memory Requirements

In order to fully utilize the computation pipeline shown in figure 2, a set of 14 single precision floating-point data values (32 bit) must be issued to the datapath inputs at the pipeline clock rate. This suggests the necessity of having local RAMs (on-chip) dedicated to hold each vector, because a single RAM would not be capable of sustaining such throughput. For example, assuming a 100MHz clock rate (this is the clock frequency our processor runs), this represents a throughput equal to 5.6GByte/s (14 floats ×4 bytes per float × 100MHz). However, the limited amount of on-chip SRAM in current FPGAs cannot hold the complete input, temporary and output data set needed to run the function 'solver' for realistic CFD simulations (tens of nodes in each dimension). One solution to overcame this consists in dividing the simulation domain (the 3D rectangular volume) in smaller volumes partially overlapped and execute separately the processing of each volume. This is the same solution adopted in [6] and was also experimented with success to run parallel versions of CFD applications on clusters of workstations.

4   The FPGA-Based Platform

The hardware platform chosen for this project was the Virtex-4 based DN8000K10PSX from the DiniGroup, USA [8] populated with one V4LX40 and two V4LX80 FPGAs and one module with 512MB of DDR2 SDRAM. By the time this was bought (end of 2006), this board was found to be the most adequate to host the implementation of our

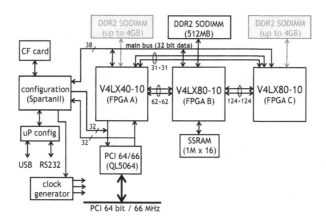

Fig. 5. Simplified block diagram of the DN8000K10PSX board. Presently, only one module of 512MB of DDR2 SDRAM, 200MHz is installed in the slot of FPGA B.

CFD processor, for the budget available (around USD $8000). Figure 5 shows a simplified block diagram of the DN8000K10PSX board, with the actual devices installed in the system used in this project.

Although the board supports the 64bit/66MHz PCI, only the 32bit/33MHz interface is being used due to the unavailability of a 64 bit PCI slot in the host PC. At power up the FPGAs are configured from a set of bit files stored in the compact flash memory card. Later reconfiguration can be done via USB or PCI using functions and software applications provided by the vendor. The transfer of data between the host PC and the FPGAs is done through a 32 bit data/address bus driven by the configuration FPGA (Main bus), that is supported by library functions for easy interface with software applications.

5   Hardware Implementation

Presently we have implemented a first prototype processor capable of executing the function 'solver', according to the schedule presented in section 3.1. Current implementation uses only FPGA B and the DDR2 SDRAM module directly attached to this FPGA. All the communication with the host PC is done through the PCI interface and, locally in the board, using the main bus. Due to on-chip memory limitations (BRAMs), the processor is limited to three-dimensional matrices of a maximum 16x16x16 nodes. The execution of larger problems will require the partitioning of the simulation domain into smaller volumes that can fit the local memories.

Figure 6 presents the general organization of the custom processor. Interfacing with the host is made through a bank of registers accessed by the host computer via the PCI interface and the board main bus. This block accesses the local cache memory to upload the data matrices and download the result matrix. This module was not yet subject of special attention and there is some room to improve the transfer rate with the host computer (using, for example, automatic address generators).

5.1   Address Generation

The address generation unit produces the addresses for the local memories, corresponding to the sequence of loop indexes, according to the scheduling presented above. As explained above, the complete code of the 'solver' routine is composed of 6 instances of the loop with the same structure of the pseudo-code shown in figure 1, for the 6 permutations of the loop indexes i, j and k. A finite-state machine generates the same sequence of i, j and k indexes for the 6 loops, using the iteration limits selected for each loop instance by a set of multiplexers. After that, another set of multiplexers perform the permutation of the three indexes, according to the loop being computed (figure 7).

5.2   Cache Memory

The local cache memory feeds the forward and the backward loop with 13 single-precision floats and stores the final result computed by the backward loop pipeline (figure 8). This unit is built with 13 dual-port RAMs, each with a total of $16 \times 16 \times 16 \times 4$

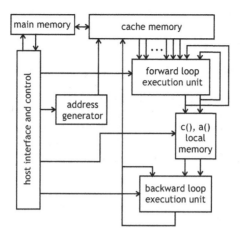

Fig. 6. Organization of the custom processor

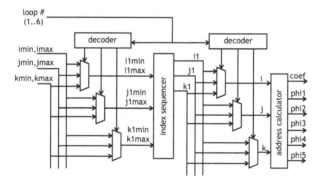

Fig. 7. The address generation unit

bytes/float each (16 KBytes). Eight of these RAMs store the 8 matrices of coefficients (vectors `as()`, `ae()`,...,`su()`) and share a common address bus because their elements are always accessed for the same indexes (i,j,k). Five other memories store 5 replicas of the input matrix `phi()`: four of them feed the inputs of the forward loop pipeline with the 4 elements `phi(i±1,j,k±1)`; a fifth memory is required to feed the backward loop execution unit with a different element of the `phi()` matrix, during the execution of the backward loop. All these memories were implemented with BRAMs by the Xilinx tool Coregen.

5.3   Execution Units

The forward loop execution unit implements the pipelined datapath by mapping directly the dataflow graph shown in figure 2. The single-precision floating-point operators were built by the Coregen Xilinx tool. Dummy pipestages were introduced where necessary

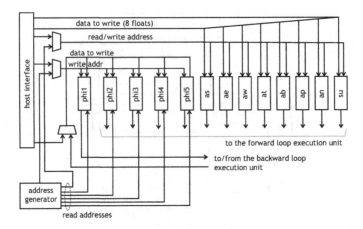

Fig. 8. The cache memory system

to balance the latency to the inputs of each arithmetic operator. The forward pipeline has 8 multipliers, 5 adders, one subtracter and one divider. The pipeline latency is 44 clock cycles with an issue rate equal to 1 clock.

The backward loop execution unit includes a pipeline with only one multiplier and one adder. Although the minimum latency of this datapath is 12 clock cycles, an additional delay of 32 clock cycles was introduced to facilitate the synchronization of the two pipelines during the parallel execution of the forward loop and the backward loop. This unit includes four additional dual-port RAMS to store the vectors c() and a() computed by the forward loop execution unit for a j-column block (total of 44×16 floats), and to feed them to the backward loop execution unit. These four memories (two for vector c() and the other two for vector a()) switch their role for each j-column block being computed: while one pair is being read by the backward loop execution unit during the computation of one j-column block, the other pair is being written by the forward loop execution unit with the results computed for the next j-column block.

6   Results and Conclusions

The first prototype processor implemented uses only the FPGA B and executes on data matrices already stored in the cache memories. The host processor loads the memories through the PCI interface, starts the processor and pools a status register to wait for the end of execution. Final results (the contents of phi() matrix) are then read from the cache memory. The functional correctness of the computation process was verified by comparing the contents of the output matrix with the results calculated on the PC by a C program implementing exactly the same sequence of calculations.

The processor runs at 100MHz, although the two arithmetic datapaths alone may be clocked at 200MHz. In the current version the global clock frequency is being limited by the path from the cache address generator through the cache memories. This is related with the dispersion of the various cache memories within the FPGA array and may be improved by replicating the cache address generators and forcing their placement near each memory.

Table 1 summarizes the FPGA occupation. Although only 14% of the LUTs are used, the BRAM occupation is 57% (the aditional 5% is used by the DDR2 interface) invalidates the implementation of a second processor within the FPGA.

Table 1. Summary of the FPGA occupation (Virtex4 LX80-10)

4-input LUTs	10,137 (14%)
Flip-flops	16,116 (22%)
Occupied slices	12,187 (34%)
LUTs used as route-thru	162 (<1%)
LUTs used as SRAM	32 (<1%)
LUTs used as shift-registers	448 (<1%)
FIFO16/BRAM16	124 (62%)
DSP48	36 (45%)
Equivalent gate count	8,369,419

Running at 100MHz, the total time needed to process the data matrices stored into the $16 \times 16 \times 16$ cache memories is 43μ seconds. A total of 61200 floating point operations are executed, which corresponds to an average throughput of 1.4GFLOPS. This figure shows, apparently, a good result, but it cannot be fairly compared to the performance obtained by the original software code running in a PC (around 100MFlops measured for a real simulation problem). Although the incorporation of the scheduling optimizations done in the hardware processor into the original software code has shown no significant modification of the overall running times of the function 'solver', the custom processor runs with the data already placed into its local cache, which is not the case for software version. Besides, smaller problems will certainly reach higher throughput for the software version due to the increase of data locality in the memory accesses to the data matrices.

Further developments will implement a mechanism to load the data matrices from the DDR2 main memory in blocks (partially overlapped) that can fit the dimensions of the cache memories. Although a similar domain decomposition strategy is valid for dividing a simulation domain into smaller parts dispatched to different processors, it is still needed to validate the approach of applying such partitioning only at the level of the function 'solver' addressed in this work.

References

1. Castro, F.A.: Métodos Numéricos para Simulação de Escoamentos Atmosféricos sobre Topografia Complexa, PhD thesis, Faculdade de Engenharia da Universidade do Porto (1997)
2. Castro, F.A., Palma, J.L., Lopes, S.: Simulation of the Askervein flow. Part 1: Reynolds Averaged Navier-Stokes equations (k-epsilon turbulence model), Boundary Layer Meteorology 107, 501–530 (2003)
3. Ventos simulation program, http://www.fe.up.pt/ventos

4. Patankar, S.V., Spalding, D.B.: A Calculation Procedure for Heat, Mass and Momentum Transfer in Three-dimensional Parabolic Flows. International Journal for Heat and Mass Transfer 15, 1787–1806 (1972)
5. Ohno, Y., Makino, J., Hachisu, I., Ebisuzaki, T., Sugimoto, D.: DREAM-1A: Special Purpose Computer for Computational Fluid Dynamics. In: Proceedings of the Twenty-Seventh Annual Hawaii International Conference on System Sciences (1994)
6. Smith, W.D., Schnore, A.R.: Towards an RCC-Based Accelerator for Computational Fluid Dynamic Applications. The journal of Supercomputing 30, 239–261 (2004)
7. Nallatech, http://www.nallatech.com
8. The DiniGoup, http://www.dinigroup.com

A High Throughput FPGA-Based Floating Point Conjugate Gradient Implementation[*]

Antonio Roldao Lopes and George A. Constantinides

Electrical & Electronic Engineering,
Imperial College London,
London SW7 2BT, England
{aroldao,g.constantinides}@ic.ac.uk

Abstract. As Field Programmable Gate Arrays (FPGAs) have reached capacities beyond millions of equivalent gates, it becomes possible to accelerate floating-point scientific computing applications. One type of calculation that is commonplace in scientific computation is the solution of systems of linear equations. A method that has proven in software to be very efficient and robust for finding such solutions is the Conjugate Gradient algorithm. In this paper we present a parallel hardware Conjugate Gradient implementation. The implementation is particularly suited for accelerating multiple small to medium sized dense systems of linear equations. Through parallelization it is possible to convert the computation time per iteration for an order n matrix from $\Theta(n^2)$ cycles for a software implementation to $\Theta(n)$. I/O requirements are scalable and converge to a constant value with the increase of matrix order. Results on a VirtexII-6000 demonstrate sustained performance of 5 GFLOPS and projected results on a Virtex5-330 indicate sustained performance of 35 GFLOPS. The former result is comparable to high-end CPUs, whereas the latter represents a significant speedup.

1 Introduction

One area where Field Programmable Gate Arrays (FPGAs) are increasingly important is in the acceleration of scientific computations. Some important examples of these applications include genetics, robotics, computer graphics and optimization problems. This paper introduces some typical solutions for solving systems of linear equations, a basic and recurring sub-task in scientific computation, and goes on to detail the Conjugate Gradient (CG) method [1]. A parameterizable hardware implementation of this algorithm is outlined, a comparison with software is made and results reported.

Due to deep pipelining, our proposed implementation is particularly suitable for accelerating computations of multiple small to medium sized dense systems in parallel. An example of such application arises when solving large banded

---

[*] The authors would like to acknowledge the support of the EPSRC (Grant EP/C549481/1 and EP/E00024X/1) and the support of Dr. Eric Kerrigan.

R. Woods et al. (Eds.): ARC 2008, LNCS 4943, pp. 75–86, 2008.

linear systems using the parallel algorithm described in [2] or in Multiple-Input-Multiple-Output adaptive equalization [3]. These computations are widespread and include the numerical solution of partial differential equations used in optimal control problems [4].

The main contributions of this paper are thus:

- a parameterizable deeply pipelined hardware design for solving systems of linear equations,
- a detailed analysis of the Conjugate Gradient algorithm and its affinity for FPGA based implementation,
- a design capable of 5 GFLOPS on VirtexII, and projected results predicting that a sustained performance of 35 GFLOPS is possible for a Virtex5-330; a speedup of 5× compared to the *peak* theoretical performance of a Pentium IV running at 3 GHz, and an order of magnitude compared to the measured performance of this processor.

After discussing the relevant background in Section 2, we present an overview of the CG method in Section 3. Section 4 presents the proposed hardware design. Section 5 details resulting resource utilization, achievable throughput, I/O requirements, and comparison to a high performance CPU is made. Section 6 concludes the paper.

2 Background

Most scientific computation involves the solution of systems of linear equations. To address this problem there are some well studied and proven methods. These are divided into two main categories: direct, where the solution is given by evaluating a derived formula, and iterative where the solution is approximated based on previous results until a certain acceptable value is reached. Examples of direct methods include Cholesky factorization and Gaussian Elimination, while iterative methods include Generalized Minimal Residual Methods (GMRES) and the Conjugate Gradient Method that is described in this paper.

For large problems, matrix and vector operations can be computationally intensive and may require significant processing time. Nonetheless they can be accelerated by performing, whenever possible, parallel operations. As a result of advancements in FPGA density, massively parallel floating point computation has become feasible. Although there has been an increasing interest into the use of Field Programmable Gate Arrays to accelerate scientific computation, with recent supercomputers incorporating these devices [5,6], only very recently there has been research focused on developing hardware optimized linear algebra [7]. This has led to the study and comparison of the performance and precision against conventional microprocessors. The results forecast a very promising future for FPGAs by predicting that by the year 2009 they will be an order of magnitude faster in peak performance [8].

Some typical methods for solution of linear equations finding have already been implemented on FPGAs. A Cholesky implementation has demonstrated a performance increase by 50% over software on a APEX EP20K1500E FPGA [9]. A Jacobi solver has been implemented on a Xilinx VirtexII Pro XC2VP50 and demonstrated a speedup of 1.3 to 36.8 relative to uniprocessor implementations, depending on the matrix structure [10]. There are also two papers that discuss an implementation of the Conjugate Gradient method: one uses a Logarithmic Number System (LNS) and achieves up to 0.94 GFLOPS on a VirtexII-6000 [11], the other uses a rational number representation and achieves 0.27 GFLOPS using a VirtexII Pro XC2VP4 [12] and projects that it will be able to sustain 1.5 GFLOPS with Virtex4-55. In contrast, we present a parallelised and deeply pipelined Conjugate Gradient method using the IEEE 754 [13] single precision floating point number representation. We are able to achieve approximately 5 GFLOPS on a readily available VirtexII-6000 and 35 GFLOPS on a high-spec Virtex5-330, for matrices of order 16 and 58 respectively.

Table 1 summarizes FPGA implementations of Conjugate Gradient method in terms of year of publication, number system, device and GFLOPS achieved.

Table 1. Previous FPGA-based Conjugate Gradient implementations

Year	Reference	Number System	Device	GFLOPS
2005	[11]	LNS	VirtexII-6000	0.94
2006	[12]	Rational	Virtex4-25	1.5
2007	this paper	FP single	VirtexII-6000	5
2007	this paper	FP single	Virtex5-330	35

3   Conjugate Gradient Method

The Conjugate Gradient Method is an iterative method for solving systems of linear equations of the form given in (1), where the n by n matrix A is symmetric (*i.e.*, $A^T = A$) and positive definite (*i.e.*, $x^T A x > 0$ for all non-zero vectors x in $\mathbb{R}^n$) [1]. When matrix A is positive definite, the associated quadratic form given by $J(x)$, defined in (2), is convex. $J'(x)$, the differential of $J(x)$, is given in (3). Notice that setting $J'(x) = 0$ is identical to (1), hence the the solution to the linear system is equivalent to minimizing the quadratic function given in (2). This is the basic intuition of CG and other iterative algorithms.

$$Ax = b$$

$$\begin{bmatrix} a_{11} & a_{12} & \cdots & a_{1n} \\ a_{21} & a_{22} & \cdots & a_{2n} \\ \vdots & \vdots & \ddots & \vdots \\ a_{n1} & a_{n2} & \cdots & a_{nn} \end{bmatrix} \begin{bmatrix} x_1 \\ x_2 \\ \vdots \\ x_n \end{bmatrix} = \begin{bmatrix} b_1 \\ b_2 \\ \vdots \\ b_n \end{bmatrix} \tag{1}$$

$$J(x) = \frac{1}{2}x^T A x - b^T x \qquad (2)$$

$$J'(x) = \begin{bmatrix} \frac{\partial}{\partial x_1} J(x) \\ \frac{\partial}{\partial x_2} J(x) \\ \vdots \\ \frac{\partial}{\partial x_n} J(x) \end{bmatrix} = Ax - b \qquad (3)$$

3.1   Algorithm Description

The algorithm, described in Fig. 1, consists of two parts. The first is an initialization that produces a 'residual' or search direction. The second part iterates until the residual error is sufficiently small. The algorithm is intuitive and comprises of the following steps:

1. Determine a search direction, d, of steepest descent in $J(x)$. ($cg1$) and ($cg12$).
2. Perform a line search to determine the best step length, α, in the steepest descent direction. ($cg5$) and ($cg6$).
3. Generate the new solution by adding the vector d times the determined step length α to the current solution x and update the residual r. ($cg7$) and ($cg8$).
4. Iterate until the residual error is negligible. ($cg13$).

4   Implementation

4.1   Overview

The dataflow of this iterative algorithm is depicted in Fig. 2. The most computationally intensive operation is the matrix-by-vector multiplication in ($cg5$). To obtain scalable performance, the proposed design implements this computation by sequentially operating on each matrix row in turn; each constituent vector-by-vector multiplication, however, is fully unrolled and parallelised (see Fig. 3). We also use the same vector-by-vector unit for operations ($cg2$), ($cg6$) and ($cg10$). These operations are represented in the double lined boxes on dataflow diagram of Fig. 2. This vector-by-vector unit is fully pipelined, with a new vector introduced each cycle. As a result, this implementation is able to complete a conjugate gradient iteration every $n + 3$ cycles. This throughput is given by the vector-by-vector computational unit that has to compute for n cycles to perform the block matrix-by-vector operation and another 3 cycles to compute the remaining vector-by-vector operations ($cg2$), ($cg6$) and ($cg10$).

The latency of one CG iteration is given by (4) where the linear growth comes from the row-by-row processing, the logarithmic growth comes from the addition tree in the inner-product computation, and the constants are due to the pipeline depths of the components. The discrepancy between a throughput of one iteration every $n + 3$ cycles and the latency given in (4)is used to our

$$
\begin{array}{ll}
Input: & \text{Matrix } A, \text{ Vector } b, \\
& \text{Error tolerance } \varepsilon \\
Output: & x \text{ Such that } \|Ax - b\|_2 \le \varepsilon \|b\|_2 \\
\end{array}
$$

$$
\begin{array}{ll}
d \leftarrow b & (cg1) \\
r \leftarrow b & (cg2) \\
\delta_0 \leftarrow r^T r & (cg3) \\
\delta_{new} \leftarrow \delta_0 & (cg4) \\
\text{do} & \\
\quad q \leftarrow Ad & (cg5) \\
\quad \alpha \leftarrow \frac{\delta_{new}}{d^T q} & (cg6) \\
\quad x \leftarrow x + \alpha d & (cg7) \\
\quad r \leftarrow r - \alpha q & (cg8) \\
\quad \delta_{old} \leftarrow \delta_{new} & (cg9) \\
\quad \delta_{new} \leftarrow r^T r & (cg10) \\
\quad \beta \leftarrow \frac{\delta_{new}}{\delta_{old}} & (cg11) \\
\quad d \leftarrow r + \beta d & (cg12) \\
\text{while } \delta_{new} > \varepsilon^2 \delta_0 & (cg13) \\
\end{array}
$$

Fig. 1. Conjugate Gradient Algorithm [14]

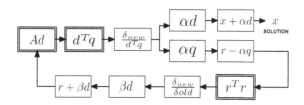

Fig. 2. Circuit data flow diagram. Single boxed operations are implemented using a single floating point unit each. Double boxed operations are implemented on the single matrix/vector by vector module that requires $2n - 1$ FP units.

advantage, by using the slack to operate on multiple different matrix/vector pairs in a pipelined fashion. The total number of linear systems that can be processed simultaneously by the pipeline is therefore given by (5), a $\Theta(1)$ function that converges to 7 for large n as shown in Fig. 4. Note that in order to continuously process problems every $n + 3$ cycles, a constant κ is introduced into (4) so that the number of clocks per iteration is a multiple of $n + 3$. This is implemented through the addition of a FIFO at the output of last operation ($cg12$). This guarantees the new value of d is output at the start of a new iteration in ($cg5$) ensuring full pipeline utilization.

One of the major advantages of the proposed row-based scheme is its scalable FPGA I/O requirements, eliminating I/O bottlenecks. The conjugate gradient algorithm completes in n iterations under infinite precision, and $\Omega(n)$ iterations under finite precision [1] [15]. Since one iteration is completed by our design every $\Theta(n)$ cycles and to find the solution for this system under its finite precision we

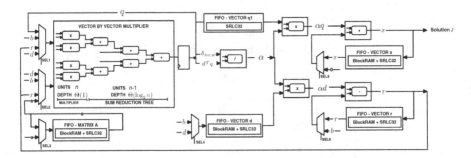

Fig. 3. Partial circuit schematic displaying the vector-by-vector module, two of constant by vector multiplications, a vector by vector summation, vector by vector subtraction and FIFOs. Some of these FIFOs use a combination of Xilinx SRLC32 primitives and BlockRAMs and store various vectors including A matrices in the row-by-row form.

require at least n iterations, the the data transfer bandwidth required is a $\Theta(1)$ function, *i.e.* approaches a constant for large n. Section 5 quantifies this I/O requirement for synthesized designs, and shows it to be well within PCI-express bandwidth limitations.

$$\text{Clocks per Iteration}(n) = 7n + 36\lceil \log_2 n \rceil + 127 + \kappa \tag{4}$$

$$\text{Pipeline Depth}(n) = \frac{7n + 36\lceil \log_2 n \rceil + 127 + \kappa}{n+3} \tag{5}$$

4.2 Performance

In order to optimize for throughput, floating point modules with the highest latency were selected from the Xilinx Coregen Library. From results gathered, the maximum frequency achievable on the Virtex5-330 is 364MHz limited by the divider. In practice, when included with the other logic, this falls to 287MHz on the Virtex5-330 (and 126MHz for the VirtexII-6000).

Since this implementation does not have every floating point computational module in operation for the entire iteration of the CG method, as described in Section 4.3, two performance formulas were deduced. One describes the peak performance (6) when all the modules are in operation simultaneously (*e.g.* at the start of a $n+3$ period when the pipeline is full) and the other counts the number of operations per iteration divided by clocks per iteration (7). This second formula accounts for the idle time of floating point units involving vector operations that only function for n cycles, every $n+3$ cycles.

$$\text{FLOPS Peak}(n) = (2n + 7) \times \text{MaxFreq} \tag{6}$$

$$\text{FLOPS Sustained}(n) = \frac{2n(n+5)}{n+3} \times \text{MaxFreq} \tag{7}$$

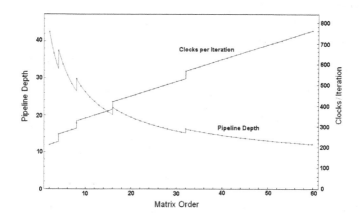

Fig. 4. Pipeline depth and required cycles per iteration with matrix order

4.3   Floating Point Unit Operations

Due to the iterative nature of the algorithm it is possible to reutilize all allocated floating point units. A single module is instantiated to perform all vector-by-vector multiplications, n times in ($cg5$), and once in ($cg2$), ($cg6$) and ($cg10$). This module implements the double boxed computations in Fig. 2, and operates continually processing and outputting new values every $n+3$ cycles. The remaining vector operations, in order to output a solution every $n + 3$ cycles, require a single floating point unit each. These units operate for n (+ latency) clock cycles before a vector solution is output. After this solution is output, each unit is idle for 3 cycles to compensate for the matrix and vector by vector operation module delay. In brief, every constant by vector multiplication and vector by vector addition/subtraction operates for n cycles every $n + 3$ cycles. The divisions in ($cg6$) and ($cg12$) only operate for 1 (+ latency) clock cycle every $n + 3$ cycles. The total number of floating point units is detailed in Table 2.

Table 2. Floating Point units used in this implementation

Operation	FP units
Matrix/Vector by Vector Multiplier	$2n - 1$
Constant by Vector Multiplier	3
Vector by Vector Summation	2
Vector by Vector Subtraction	1
Floating Point Divider	2
Total (FP_{units})	$2n + 7$

5   Results

5.1   Resource Utilization

Theoretical floating point resource utilization grows as $\Theta(n)$. However for this method to be efficient the coefficients of each problem to be solved need to be stored or generated within the FPGA. This requires a storage that grows with $\Theta(n^2)$ ($\Theta(n^2)$ for one problem, with $\Theta(1)$ problems in the pipeline). To store these values a mixture of embedded BlockRAMs [16] and SRLC32 primitives are used. This mixture depends on the length of the FIFO. When this length is equal to or below 64, they are implemented solely using SRLC32 primitives. When above 64, they are implemented by combining BlockRAMs and SRLC32 primitives for efficiency. This is due to the fact that Xilinx Coregen BlockRAM FIFOs are only available in sizes of 2^n with $n > 3$; thus SRLC32 primitives are used to take up any slack. Fig. 5 depicts resource usage as a function of the matrix order. Growth of each resource is approximated linearly as predicted, with the exception of BlockRAMs that are also used for matrix storage. The usage of these BlockRAMs is asymptotically quadractic, however for the depths in the range of our implementation, this growth is at most $O(n \log n)$, since the BlockRAMs are deep enough to implement the required FIFOs and a further $O(\log n)$ units can be used to help fill the slack mentioned earlier.

For the Virtex5-330, resources are saturated for matrices orders above 58 having depleted all BlockRAMs. Best fit resource usage for REGisters, LUTs, BlockRAMs and DSP48Es usage as a function of matrix order is described in (9), (10), (11) and (8) respectively. BlockRAMs usage varies significantly, from the best fit, because they are used in conjunction with SRLC32s, as explained previously.

$$DSP48Es(n) = 2n + 2 \tag{8}$$

$$REG\ Slices(n) = 3007n + 6446 \tag{9}$$

$$LUT\ Slices(n) = 2361n + 3426 \tag{10}$$

$$BlockRAMs(n) = 25n \log_2 n - 2n - 3 \log_2 n - 39 \tag{11}$$

5.2   Software Comparison and Discussion

Acceleration relative to software is provided by pipelining and parallelization of vector operations. In this implementation considerable speedup is due to the block module that performs a fully parallelized vector by vector multiplication. Each of these operations requires $2n - 1$ sequential operations in software while in hardware they can be reduced to $Lm + Ls\lceil \log_2 n \rceil$ cycles for a single problem, where Lm is the latency of the multiplication core, Ls the latency of the addition

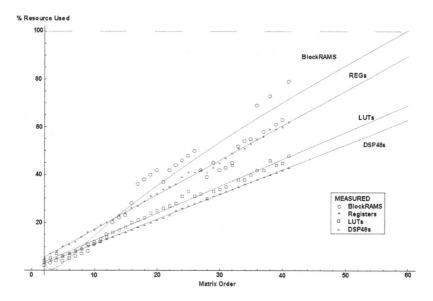

Fig. 5. BlockRAMs, REGisters and LUTs resource utilization with matrix order for the Virtex5-330. Lines represent the best fit based on the synthesis reports of Look-Up-Tables, REGisters, BlockRAMs and DSP48Es usage.

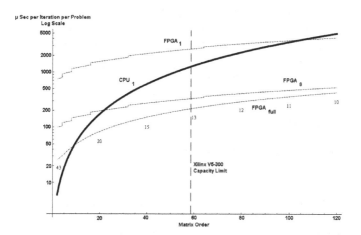

Fig. 6. Iteration time required for solving a number of CG problems as a function of matrix order on a CPU and FPGA. The bold line represents a high end CPU operating at 6 GFLOPS [17]. The remaining lines show the FPGA Virtex5-330 implementation with a single problem in the pipeline, with 8 problems and a fully loaded pipeline. This last line also depicts the number of problems in the pipeline for that matrix order in accordance with (5).

core and n, the matrix order. In the case where several vectors need to be multiplied, they can be pipelined and a result provided for every clock cycle at the initial cost of filling the pipeline.

The overall speedup given by the combination of parallelization and pipelining is illustrated in Fig. 6, which compares the processing time, for each CG iteration, on an FPGA and on a Pentium IV running at 3.0 GHz. Three lines are shown for the FPGA implementation: one representing the pipeline containing only a single problem, another intermediate line showing the pipeline with 8 problems, and a third line representing a full pipeline. Below this last line, the number of problems pipelined and being concurrently solved, given by (5), is shown for every 20 matrix orders. The dark bold line represents the CPU at its best case scenario of peak theoretical performance at 6 GFLOPs [17]. Comparing the FPGA with a full pipeline and a CPU, it is possible to observe that the FPGA is faster than the CPU for orders greater than 10. For a single problem in the FPGA pipeline, the CPU becomes slower than the FPGA for matrix orders above 105. With the intermediate FPGA line showing the time required to process 8 pipelined problems it is possible to observe its convergence to the FPGA full line as demonstrated in (5). Thus with only eight parallel problems, FPGA superiority is clearly established, even for low matrix orders.

5.3   Input/Ouput Considerations

As input, this method requires a matrix A and a vector b to be introduced. As a output, it requires the solution vector x, which, under finite precision, is generated after at least n iterations [15]. This translates to the need to transfer $32(n^2 + 2n)$ bits per problem for a total number of problems given by (5). This transfer can occur over a period given by at least n times the clocks per iteration (4) because this is the time it takes to generate a solution and start a new problem. Combining these data we can deduce the a minimum bit rate as given in (12). For the Virtex5-330 limit matrix order of 58, running at 287MHz this, translates to a data rate requirement of 1.1GB/s, a value well within the operation range of PCI-Express [18].

$$\text{I/O Bits per Clock Cycle} = 32 - \frac{32}{n+3} \tag{12}$$

6   Conclusions

This paper describes a Conjugate Gradient implementation. It analyzes its resource utilization growth with matrix order, peak performance achievable, compares this performance with a high end processor and demonstrates that this method exhibits high performance with scalable I/O requirements.

It is demonstrated that multiple dense problems of matrix order 16 can be solved in parallel with a sustained floating point performance of 5 GFLOPS, for the VirtexII-6000 and multiple dense matrices of order 58, with a sustained floating point performance of 35 GFLOPS, for the Virtex5-330. Multiple parallel solutions of these orders are required, for example, in Multiple-Input-Multiple-Output communication systems using adaptive quantization [3] and in solving large banded matrices using the algorithm described in [2]. These banded systems arise in a number of problems including optimal control systems [4].

For the lower density VirtexII-6000 FPGA, the GFLOPS are between peak theoretical performance and the measured performance of a Intel Pentium IV 3.0 GHz CPU, based on a Linpack benchmark [17]. Taking advantage of hardware parallelization, the required latency for a single iteration is reduced from $\Theta(n^2)$ to $\Theta(n)$, at the cost of increasing hardware computational utilization from $\Theta(1)$ to $\Theta(n)$.Since generating each solution requires at least n iterations under finite precision [1] and each iteration requires $n + 3$ clock cycles, this design exhibits scalable I/O transfer rates that converge to a constant number, as matrix order n increases. Hence, its inherent properties make it exceptionally suited for FPGA implementation.

Future work will be focused on the direct solution of structured systems originating in [4] and matrix sparsity will also be exploited to accelerate the solutions of especial cases.

References

1. Hestenes, M., Stiefel, E.: Methods of conjugate gradients for solving linear systems. Journal of Research of the National Bureau of Standards 49(6), 409–436 (1952)
2. Wright, S.: Parallel Algorithms for Banded Linear Systems. SIAM Journal on Scientific and Statistical Computing 12(4), 824–842 (1991)
3. Biglieri, E., Calderbank, R., Constantinides, A., Goldsmith, A., Paulraj, A.: MIMO Wireless Communications. Cambridge University Press, Cambridge (2007)
4. Wright, S.: Interior Point Methods for Optimal Control of Discrete Time Systems. Journal of Optimization Theory and Applications 77(1), 161–187 (1993)
5. Cray, XD1 Datasheet (2005) (Accessed on 2/03/2007)
   http://www.cray.com/downloads/Cray-_XD1_Datasheet.pdf
6. SGI, RASC RC100 Blade (2006) (Accessed on 2/03/2007)
   http://www.sgi.com/-pdfs/3920.pdf
7. Zhuo, L., Prasanna, V.K.: High Performance Linear Algebra Operations on Reconfigurable Systems. In: Proc. of SuperComputing, pp. 12–18 (2005)
8. Underwood, K.: FPGAs vs. CPUs: Trends in Peak Floating-Point Performance. In: Proc. ACM. Int. Symp. on Field-Programmable Gate Arrays, pp. 171–180 (2004)
9. Haridas, S., Ziavras, S.: FPGA Implementation of a Cholesky Algorithm for a Shared-Memory Multiprocessor Architecture. Journal of Parallel Algorithms and Applications 19(6), 411–226 (2004)
10. Morris, G., Prasanna, V.: An FPGA-Based Floating-Point Jacobi Iterative Solver. In: Proc. of the 8th International Symposium on Parallel Architectures, Algorithms and Networks, pp. 420–427 (2005)
11. Maslennikow, V.L.O., Sergyienko, A.: FPGA Implementation of the Conjugate Gradient Method. In: Proc. Parallel Processing and Applied Mathematics, pp. 526–533 (2005)
12. Callanan, A.N.O., Gregg, D., Peardon, M.: High Performance Scientific Computing Using FPGAs with IEEE Floating Point and Logarithmic Arithmetic For Lattice QCD. In: Proc. of Field Programmable Logic and Applications, pp. 29–35 (2006)

13. IEEE, 754 Standard for Binary Floating-Point Arithmetic (1985) (Accessed on 18/03/2007), `http://grouper.ieee.org/groups/754/`
14. Shewchuk, J.: An Introduction to the Conjugate Gradient Method Without the Agonizing Pain, Edition $1\frac{1}{4}$ (2003) (Accessed on 28/02/2007), `http://www.cs.cmu.edu/~jrs/+jrspapers.html#cg`
15. Meurant, G.: The Lanczos and Conjugate Gradient Algorithms from theory to Finite Precision Computation, SIAM, 323–324 (2006)
16. Xilinx, DS100 (v3.0) Virtex5 Family Overview - LX , LXT, and SXT Platforms (2007) (Accessed on 1/03/2007), `http://direct.xilinx.com/bvdocs/publications/ds100.pdf`
17. Dongarra, J.: Performance of Various Computers Using Standard Linear Equations Software (2007) (Accessed on 15/03/2007), `http://www.netlib.org/benchmark/performance.ps`
18. Bhatt, A.: PCI-Express - Creating a Third Generation I/O Interconnect (2007) (Accessed on 19/06/2007), http://www.intel.com/technology/pciexpress/devnet/docs/WhatisPCIExpress.pdf

Physical Design of FPGA Interconnect to Prevent Information Leakage

Sumanta Chaudhuri[1], Sylvain Guilley[1], Philippe Hoogvorst[1], Jean-Luc Danger[1], Taha Beyrouthy[2], Alin Razafindraibe[2], Laurent Fesquet[2], and Marc Renaudin[2,*]

[1] GET / Télécom Paris, CNRS – LTCI (UMR 5141)
46 rue Barrault, 75 634 PARIS Cedex 13, France
[2] TIMA Laboratory (INPG), CIS group
46 avenue Félix Viallet, 38 031 GRENOBLE, France

Abstract. In this article we discuss dual/multi-rail routing techniques in an island style FPGA for robustness against side-channel attacks. We present a technique to achieve dual-rail routing balanced in both timing and power consumption with the traditional subset switchbox. Secondly, we propose two switchboxes (namely: Twist-on-Turn & Twist-Always) to route every dual/multi-rail signal in twisted pairs, which can deter electromagnetic attacks. These novel switchboxes can also be balanced in power consumption albeit with some added cost. We present a layout with pre-placed switches and pre-routed balanced wires and extraction statistics about the expected balance. As conclusion, we discuss various overheads associated with these techniques and possible improvements.

1   Introduction

Due to their increasing integration capability, current FPGAs can be programmed with entire system-on-chips (SoCs.) This makes them an attractive alternative to ASICs for low to medium production volumes.

In the mean time the applications have become communication-centric, which explains why virtually every SoC embeds a cryptographic engine.

Standard cryptographic algorithms are chosen to be resistant against exhaustive key search and various mathematical attacks, such as linear or differential cryptanalyses. However their implementations in CMOS face a severe challenge from *Side-Channel Attacks* (SCA) [5,13]. The attacker can use either known or chosen plaintexts/ciphertexts and concomitantly gather information leaked through various side-channels, such as timing, power consumption, electromagnetic (EM) radiations [1], *etc.*

To the authors' knowledge, this paper is the first published initiative towards a *secured by design* FPGA. Our goal is to propose a secure reconfigurable hardware which enables implementation of proved counter-measures at the logical level.

The rest of this article is organized as follows. Section 2 motivates the need for new FPGA interconnect styles that allows FPGAs to resist SCA. We introduce sound

---

* Part of this work was funded by the French National Research Agency (ANR) project "SAFE": http://projects.comelec.enst.fr/safe/

R. Woods et al. (Eds.): ARC 2008, LNCS 4943, pp. 87–98, 2008.

specifications suitable for trusted computing in FPGAs. Section 3 states the basic assumptions, security objectives, and notations used throughout the article. Section 4 discusses a routing technique balanced in power consumption using the conventional subset switchbox. Section 5 presents two variants of a novel switchbox, called "twisted-bus switchbox", that aims at reducing EM emissions. A possible implementation of this switchbox is proposed. Section 6 details the secured connection between switchboxes and logic blocks. The CMOS layout of the switchbox, and its security evaluation are presented in section 7. As conclusion, we compare in section 8 the costs associated with these routing techniques and additional measures that can be taken to improve immunity against SCAs.

2   Why Do We Need Secure FPGAs?

The security of FPGAs in general is a wide problem, that encompasses, amongst others, bitstream format confidentiality (FPGA vendor IP), bitstream protection (user IP) and the application itself (user data). A comprehensive survey of the issues raised by FPGA security is given in [20].

In this article, we do not address the question of bitstream reverse-engineering feasibility. Instead, we focus on protecting the data handled by the FPGA. Our goal is to show that unprotected applications programmed in FPGAs leak information in a similar way as ASICs. Nevertheless, in the rest of the paper, we argue that the structure of the FPGA can be devised in such a way that the implementations of counter-measures be efficient. Our methodology consists in adapting the counter-measures used to protect ASICs to the FPGA; in the sequel, we thus consider FPGAs as special ASICs.

An efficient attack to retrieve secrets from a cryptographic device the differential power attack (DPA, [5]). The DPA is a special case of SCA. Its principle is to correlate a physical leakage (power as for DPA, electromagnetic emanations as for EMA [3], *etc.*) with results expected from a power consumption model. Although the first SCA has been realized on a commercial smart card, this attack can target an FPGA as well. To the authors' knowledge, the first successful DPA on an FPGA was performed on a stand-alone DES [7] block cipher, programmed in a Xilinx Virtex XCV800 by Standaert *et al.* [10].

We have been able to reproduce this attack independently on a DES co-processor embedded in a SoC (10,157 logic elements and 286,720 memory bits), programmed in an Altera Stratix EP1S25. As illustrated in Fig. 1, we found that less than 2 000 traces were enough to retrieve the full key. The rapidity of the attack demands that adequate and sound counter-measures be researched.

Some counter-measures against SCAs have been proposed in the literature. Notably, the wave dynamic differential logic (WDDL [15]) consists in the usage of dual-rail logic to obtain a power-constant design. The WDDL technique has been adapted by its inventor, Tiri, to Xilinx FPGAs in [17]. Nonetheless, this protection strategy is implemented at the register transfer level (RTL), on top of an off-the-shelf FPGA fabric. Quoting Tiri [13]: *"for the RTL counter-measures (e.g. dual-rail logic) to be effective [...], matching the interconnect capacitances of the signal wires is essential."*. Other counter-measures at the logical level include asynchronous styles [6,9] which demands

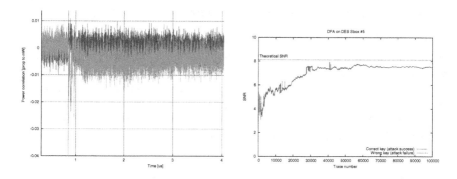

Fig. 1. DPA on DES (in an Altera EP1S25B672C7) first round: Bad and correct subkey (*left*) and signal-to-noise ratio of the attack (*right*)

the balancing of interconnect capacitances as well. This motivates researches towards granting a natively balanced interconnect. In the paper, we investigate generic geometrical routing techniques that allow to meet the balancedness constraint.

3 Principles of Balanced Bus Routing in FPGA

3.1 Delay Model

Delays in integrated circuits can be modeled at three different levels, presented below in increasing accuracy order:

D1: Sum of routing segments R × C making up a point-to-point connection (Elmore's formula.)
D2: The impedance of each terminal is taken into account, leading to standing waves according to S-matrix transmission lines theory.
D3: The coupling with the EM environment is part of the model. This introduces the notion of cross-talk.

For our purpose we assume the simplified Elmore delay model, while being aware of the impedance and crosstalks effects. We define *equitemporal lines* based on this delay model. An equitemporal line (‒·‒·‒·) is the set of points attainable simultaneously by signals originating from synchronized sources (*i.e.* wave fronts.) Furthermore, we make the following assumption: the same length of wire of same width, charging the same capacitances, causes the same delay irrespective of any bends.

3.2 Power Consumption Model

We use a simplified power consumption model in which only *active* gates consume power depending on their output capacitive load. Tri-state buffers and multiplexors are *active*, whereas pass-transistors or transmission gates are *passive* (*i.e.* do not leak any observable syndrome.) We also assume that equal lengths of wire of equal width present the same amount of load to its driving active gate.

3.3   Embedding Security Against SCAs into FPGAs

Intensive efforts have been deployed to secure custom circuits (ASICs.) Many types of primitive gates suitable for secure computation have been proposed [14,15,6,4,9]. Two papers address this issue of balancing interconnects: the "*fat wires*" routing [16] and the "*backend duplication*" method [12]. These methods are presented on dual-rail circuits, but can easily be generalized to any bus width. As illustrated in Fig. 2, the fat wires equitemporals make a $\pi/4$ angle with the cell rows, whereas the backend duplication equitemporals are collinear with the (x, y) vector, where x is the routing *pitch* and y is the placement *cell height*.

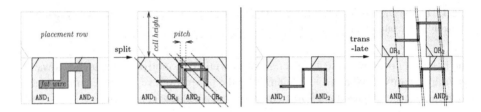

Fig. 2. Fat wire (*left*) and backend duplication (*right*) paths balancing illustration in semi-custom ASICs using WDDL (logic in which AND & OR gates are mutually dual)

In [18], Kris Tiri shows how to implement WDDL in Xilinx. However, only the security at the gate level is tackled with. The routing is done automatically, and thus opens up potential vulnerabilities. Some techniques, such as dynamic masking [8], can be used to alleviate the routing security issue. However, such tricks add extra activity and require more logic than strictly necessary. *Static* and *secure* routing in FPGAs is thus an issue, for which we provide two solutions in this paper. Off-the-shelf FPGAs are not suitable, because balanced interconnect is not part of their specification. A custom layout meticulously drawn by hand is thus needed; our methodology consists in transposing ASIC secured routing techniques to FPGAs. The problematic is however different, in the sense that:

– ASIC secured bus routing is a matter of properly constraining CAD tools, whereas
– FPGA secured bus routing consists in proposing one tile secured by design.

The security of custom FPGAs has thus two complementary aspects:

– A *balanced* layout,
– *Security-centric* FPGA CAD tools which allow the designer to implement the desired dependability level.

3.4   Secured Routing Objectives

In an ideally secured scheme, each wire in a n-wire signal should be indiscernible from each other w.r.t. power consumption and EM emission.

Indiscernability in power consumption. This constraint implies not only the same average power consumption for all the signals in a bus, but also the same delay between each active gate commutation. For example, if the same number of buffers are placed along two parallel wires but not at the same position, the average power consumption is the same for two wires but their power consumption pattern distinguishes them.

Indiscernability in EM emission. The radiation pattern measured at any point in space should be the same for each wire of a n-wire bus. For example, given a set of parallel wires (not twisted), we can choose a point closer to one of the wire and further from others. At that very point in space, radiation patterns emitted from different wires will be distinguishable.

Although we disassociate these two aspects for convenience, in reality they are related one to each other. In a programmable device the n-wires buses can be of varying size depending on applications. Thus we loose generality by fixing a particular bus width. We aim to plan a routing fabric where a n-wire signal can be routed as a bus from point-to-point for different values of $n \geq 2$.

In addition, only the functional parts of the routing resources will be balanced. The functional switchbox and connection boxes constructions can all be laid out with only two metal layers, and do not add extra vias w.r.t. to other interconnect styles. Metal levels 2 and 3 will typically be used to perform the secured interconnect: by this way, it will be buried below higher metallization levels, and so protected against malevolent probing attacks. The remaining silicon area and routing tracks (metal 2, 3, and above) are devoted to the static programmation logic, placed-and-routed automatically without any security constraints. This approach is similar to the security partitioning in cryptographic ASICs; only the datapath, that handles secret data, is designed with the care. By contrast, the control block is allowed to leak, because it only manipulates public information about the algorithm.

3.5 Notations

We will use the following notation [19] to describe switchboxes: each terminal is represented as $t(j, i)$, where j denotes each subset corresponding to each side ($0 =$ left, $1 =$ top, $2 =$ right, $3 =$ bottom) and $i \in [0, W[$ denotes the position of the terminal in that subset. For example, a $W \times W$ "subset" switchbox **S** can be represented as a set of arcs between these terminals:

$$\mathbf{s} = \bigcup_{i=0}^{W-1} \left\{ \begin{array}{l} [t(0, i), t(2, i)], \\ [t(1, i), t(3, i)], \\ [t(0, i), t(1, i)], \\ [t(1, i), t(2, i)], \\ [t(2, i), t(3, i)], \\ [t(3, i), t(0, i)]. \end{array} \right\}$$

4 Balanced Bus Routing with Subset SwitchBox

A subset switchbox [2] can be built by repeating a basic six-way switchpoints along a diagonal, as shown in figure 3(a). We consider that the diagonal formed by the six-way switchpoints makes up equitemporal signals if these signals are outputs of the same FPGA logic element CLB. Figure 3(b) shows the routing matrix using a subset

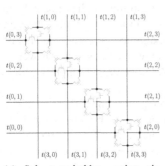

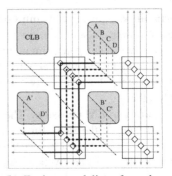

(a) *Subset* switchbox using six-way switchpoints.

(b) Equitemporal lines for *subset* switchbox routing.

Fig. 3. *subset* switchbox

switchbox. Connection boxes from the equitemporal lines to the CLB inputs/outputs are considered as equitemporals. They are discussed in section 6. In figure 3(b), the dual pair signals corresponding to connections {A, A'} and {D, D'} have exactly the same length and the same electrical characteristics. The same goes for buses {B, B'} and {C, C'}. Notice that the dual-rail signals are not necessarily routed in an adjacent way (case of A and D) and that it is possible to route in the same fashion multi-wires signals.

5   Balanced Routing with Twisted-Bus SwitchBox

As a countermeasure against information leakage through EM radiations, we propose to route every n-rail signal as a twisted bus. Figure 4(a) shows the advantages of using a twisted pair compared to parallel routed wires. If we consider the twisted pair as made up of several elementary radiating loops, we see that the radiation from a loop is canceled by that of adjacent loops.

In addition to reducing EM compromising radiations (outputs), the twisted bus gains immunity from its EM vicinity (inputs). Consequently, twisting signals bundles reduces cross-talk, which enhances the routing security by meeting the equitemporal requirements under D1, D2 and also now D3 delay models refinements (*cf.* definitions of section 3.1.)

In order to route any n-rail signal as a twisted bus throughout the FPGA, two novel switchboxes are introduced.

5.1   Twist-on-Turn Switch Matrix

The basic idea behind this switchbox is that every pair or n-uplets of signals deflected by the switchbox must come out twisted. As shown in figure 4(b), every $\pm\pi/2$ bend through this switchbox is a twisted pair. We can express this switchbox using the notation described in section 3 as:

$$\mathbf{s} = \bigcup_{i=0}^{W-1} \left\{ \begin{array}{l} [t(0, i), t(2, i)], \\ [t(1, i), t(3, i)], \\ [t(0, i), t(1, i)], \\ [t(1, i), t(2, W-i-1)], \\ [t(2, i), t(3, i)], \\ [t(3, i), t(0, W-i-1)]. \end{array} \right\}$$

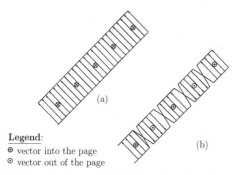

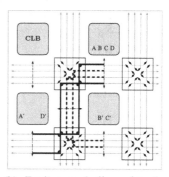

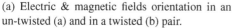

Legend:
⊕ vector into the page
⊙ vector out of the page

(a) Electric & magnetic fields orientation in an un-twisted (a) and in a twisted (b) pair.

(b) Equitemporal lines for the *twisted-pair* switchbox.

Fig. 4. *twisted-pair* switchbox

Connection boxes from the equitemporal lines to the CLB inputs/outputs are considered as being equitemporal perpendicular to the routing channel. They are discussed in section 6. In figure 4(b), the dual pair signals corresponding to connections {A, A'} and {D, D'} have exactly the same length even if they cross at the switching box. It is exactly the same for buses {B, B'} and {C, C'}.

When turning, this switch matrix introduces a small imbalance for the arrival time on the deflecting switch point. If the switch point is implemented thanks to a *passive* gate, this balance violation is not observable by an attacker. The counterpart is that the channels must be buffered, which can safely be done with *active* gates, because every wire in a channel is equitemporal.

5.2 Twist-Always Switch Matrix

The twist-on-turn matrix does not twist buses when they are routed straight. This matrix can be transformed in a twist-always matrix by twisting the wire i wire with wire $W - 1 - i$ for straight connections, as shown in figure 5, W being the number of channels.

This matrix allows the use any 1-of-n (asynchronous) style, as it is possible to twist a number of lines greater than two.

This switchbox cannot be implemented with traditional six-way switchpoints, even if the number of transistors remains the same. A possible implementation of the twist-always switch box is shown in figure 5(b). It can be laid out in silicon with two interconnect layers and by repeating two basic patterns over space. Note that for straight (*e.g.* from left to right) connections, the outer rails are drawn wider than the inner rails to compensate for the difference in lengths. Alternatively, every wire can keep the same nominal width, but inner rails are forced to zigzag so as to make up for their shorter length. For bends, every rail traverses an equal distance, hence this compensation is not required.

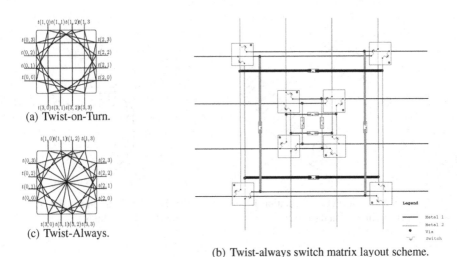

(a) Twist-on-Turn.

(c) Twist-Always.

(b) Twist-always switch matrix layout scheme.

Fig. 5. The twisted-pair switchboxes

These new switchboxes are close to conventional universal/subset switchbox in terms of connectivity. Hence we can expect similar performance in routability of netlists in the FPGA.

6   Balanced Bus Routing at Connection Box Level

6.1   Cross-Bar Connection Box

As depicted in figures 3(b) and 4(b), a signal routed from one equitemporal line to another have the same delay. Therefore the connection box (C-Box) between the W channel wires and the CLB $I \in [0, W[$ inputs/outputs should also keep this equitemporality. We propose to use a crossbar connection box based on balanced binary trees, built according to the following three rules: *(i)* from the channel, W trees have I equal-length branches, *(ii)* from the CLB, I trees have W equal-length branches, *(iii)* the two trees are superimposed orthogonally and the $W \times I$ branches from each tree type meet via a switch point.

Figure 6(a) illustrates the layout of the balanced crossbar with $W = 4$ and $I = 4$, using only two metal layers (represented with two different thicknesses.) The crossbar area is $W \cdot \lceil \log_2 (I) \rceil \times I \cdot \lceil \log_2 (W) \rceil$ square routing pitches, and can be freely depopulated without altering its security level.

6.2   C-Box for Subset and Twisted-Pair Switch Matrix

The equitemporal lines are either diagonal (for the subset switch matrix, *cf* Fig. 3(b)) or horizontal/vertical (for the twisted switch matrix, *cf* Fig. 5(b).) The connections between the channel and the crossbar should compensate the wire length delays. A solution for both cases is illustrated in figure 6.

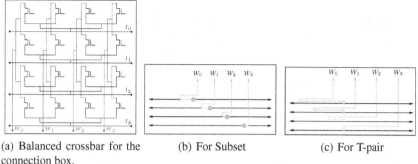

(a) Balanced crossbar for the connection box.

(b) For Subset

(c) For T-pair

Fig. 6. Balanced Crossbar and Connections between channel wires and crossbar

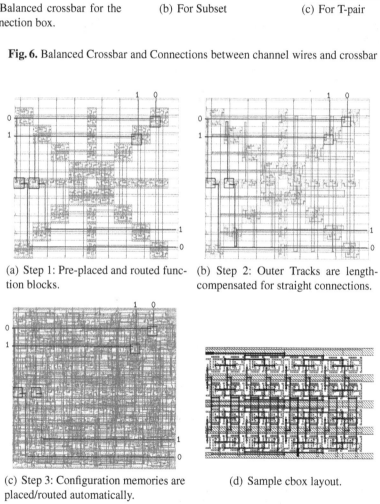

(a) Step 1: Pre-placed and routed function blocks.

(b) Step 2: Outer Tracks are length-compensated for straight connections.

(c) Step 3: Configuration memories are placed/routed automatically.

(d) Sample cbox layout.

Fig. 7. Semi-custom layout for The T-Pair SwitchBox and Connection Box

7   Physical Layout

Figure 7 shows the layout of the T-pair switchbox with 8 channels in STMicroelectronics 65 nm 7 metal layer process. The functional part (see fig. 7(a)) of the switchbox is laid out according to the scheme presented in fig 5(b). Note that we used tri-state buffers from the standard library as basic switches. The slight asymmetry in the pin positions of the tri-state buffer switches could be improved with a full-custom layout. The rest (i.e. the configuration memory points and programmation logic) is placed and routed automatically as shown in figure 7(c). We used SOC ENCOUNTER 5.1.41 from Cadence. The final layout makes use of 5 levels of metal; the switchbox is thus constraint by the logic, and by the routing. The layout area is as 2216 μm^2 (47.0 × 47.16) compared to an automatically generated layout [11] 2199 μm^2. The overhead of the manual placement is acceptable.

Table 1. Average and worst-case unbalancedness (E_{01})

E_{01}	No Compensation	After Compensation
Average	0.073	0.018
Worst Case	0.178	0.045

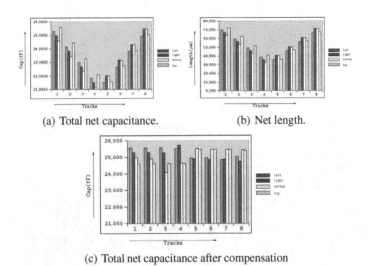

(a) Total net capacitance.   (b) Net length.

(c) Total net capacitance after compensation

Fig. 8. Security evaluation of T-pair switchbox

Figure 8 shows a comparative chart for total capacitances and net lengths for each track. The capacitance profile is as expected: the capacitance of track i is roughly equal to that of track $8 - i$. Indeed the outer tracks traverse more length than the inner tracks for straight connections. Figure 7(d) shows a sample layout of 4x8 connection box. One tree (horizontal) with equal length branches from CLB i/o (see fig 6(a)) and one tree from the channel side (vertical) is highlighted.

7.1 Security Evaluation

The proposed *twisted-pair* switchbox is designed to prevent leakage of information through the EM side-channel. We can see from figure 8(a) that it introduces an unbalancedness in power consumption of dual rails. In figure 7(b) we show the layout where the inner tracks are routed with more length of wire for straight connections. Due to this compensation this switchbox can minimize information leakage through the power-consumption side-channel as well. In fig. 8(c) we show the capacitances after compensation. Note that in fig. 5(b) we have shown the outer tracks compensated in width, however in the actual layout (see fig. 7(b)) we length-compensated the inner tracks so that all the dual rail connections charge the same capacitance.

To quantitatively evaluate the security (unbalancedness in dual rails) w.r.t. power *side-channel* we use the following metric (since in CMOS the power consumption is proportional to the capacitance of an equipotential):

$$E_{01} = \left| \log(\frac{C_0}{C_1}) \right| ,$$

where C_0 and C_1 denotes the total capacitance of the rail 0 and rail 1. To evaluate the security of the *twisted-pair* switchbox we take all possible dual rail routes possible through this switchbox and calculate the average unbalancedness. Table 1 shows the results before and after compensation.

8 Conclusion

This paper presents solutions to secure island-style FPGAs at the interconnect level for multi-rail signals. The proposals aim mainly at balancing interconnections for both the switch matrix and the connection box. An effort has been made to satisfy stringent timing, power consumption and EM radiation constraints: all the wires of a bus travel through the same length of wire and an identical number of switch points. Additionally, equi-temporal multi-rail signals are easily obtained with classical subset switch matrix; this ensures that switch points are reached simultaneously for all wires in a bus. Improvements to impede electromagnetic attacks while reducing crosstalk can be obtained with two proposed twisted-pairs switch matrices. Connection boxes take advantage of a fully balanced crossbar which allows to connect wire channels to CLBs with few place/route effort. Based on a case-study in 65 nm technology, the switchbox is shown to remain balanced (hence secured) even after layout extraction. The proposed solutions are very generic and can thus be used for mixed single/multi-rail signals in synchronous/asynchronous FPGAs. Future works will focus on the security evaluation of an actual silicon implementation of a prototype FPGA natively robust against side-channel attacks.

References

1. Agrawal, D., Archambeault, B., Rao, J.R., Rohatgi, P.: The EM Side-Channel(s). In: Kaliski Jr., B.S., Koç, Ç.K., Paar, C. (eds.) CHES 2002. LNCS, vol. 2523, pp. 29–45. Springer, Heidelberg (2003)
2. Betz, V., Rose, J., Marquardt, A.: Architecture and CAD for Deep-Submicron FPGAs. Kluwer Academic Publishers, Dordrecht (1999)

3. Gandolfi, K., Mourtel, C., Olivier, F.: Electromagnetic analysis: Concrete results. In: Koç, Ç.K., Naccache, D., Paar, C. (eds.) CHES 2001. LNCS, vol. 2162, Springer, Heidelberg (2001)
4. Guilley, S., Hoogvorst, P., Mathieu, Y., Pacalet, R., Provost, J.: CMOS Structures Suitable for Secured Hardware. In: Proceedings of DATE 2004, Paris, France, (February 2004), pp. 1414–1415 (2004)
5. Kocher, P.C., Jaffe, J., Jun, B.: Differential Power Analysis. In: Wiener, M.J. (ed.) CRYPTO 1999. LNCS, vol. 1666, Springer, Heidelberg (1999)
6. Moore, S., Anderson, R., Cunningham, P., Mullins, R., Taylor, G.: Improving Smart Card Security using Self-timed Circuits. In: Proceedings of ASYNC 2002, Manchester, United Kingdom (April 2002), pp. 211–218 (2002)
7. NIST/ITL/CSD. Data Encryption Standard. FIPS PUB 46-3 (October 1999)
   http://csrc.nist.gov/publications/fips/fips46-3/fips46-3.pdf
8. Popp, T., Mangard, S.: Masked Dual-Rail Pre-charge Logic: DPA Resistance without the Routing Constraints. In: Rao, J.R., Sunar, B. (eds.) CHES 2005. LNCS, vol. 3659, pp. 172–186. Springer, Heidelberg (2005)
9. Razafindraibe, A., Robert, M., Maurine, P.: Asynchronous Dual Rail Cells to Secure Cryptosystems against Side Channel Attacks. In: Proc. of SAME 2005 forum, 8th edn., Sophia Antipolis, France, (October 6, 2005),
   http://www.same-conference.org/same_2005
10. Standaert, F.-X., Örs, S.B., Quisquater, J.-J., Preneel, B.: Power analysis attacks against FPGA implementations of the DES. In: Field Programmable Logic and Applications, London, UK, (August 2004), pp. 84–94. Springer-Verlag, Heidelberg (2004)
11. Chaudhuri, S., Danger, J.-L., Guilley, S.: Efficient Modeling and Floorplanning of Embedded-FPGA Fabric, FPL, Netherlands (August 2007), pp. 665–669 (2007)
12. Guilley, S., Hoogvorst, P., Mathieu, Y., Pacalet, R.: The Backend Duplication Method. In: Rao, J.R., Sunar, B. (eds.) CHES 2005. LNCS, vol. 3659, pp. 383–397. Springer, Heidelberg (2005)
13. Tiri, K.: Side-Channel Attack Pitfalls. In: 44th Design Automation Conference (DAC), San Diego, California, USA, (June 4 & 8, 2007), pp. 15–20 (2007)
14. Tiri, K., Akmal, M., Verbauwhede, I.: A Dynamic and Differential CMOS Logic with Signal Independent Power Consumption to Withstand Differential Power Analysis on Smart Cards. In: Proceedings of ESSCIRC 2002, pp. 403–406 (September 2002)
15. Tiri, K., Verbauwhede, I.: A Logic Level Design Methodology for a Secure DPA Resistant ASIC or FPGA Implementation. In: Proceedings of DATE 2004, pp. 246–251 (February 2004)
16. Tiri, K., Verbauwhede, I.: Place and Route for Secure Standard Cell Design. In: Proceedings of CARDIS 2004, pp. 143–158 (August 2004)
17. Tiri, K., Verbauwhede, I.: Secure Logic Synthesis. In: Becker, J., Platzner, M., Vernalde, S. (eds.) FPL 2004. LNCS, vol. 3203, pp. 1052–1056. Springer, Heidelberg (2004)
18. Tiri, K., Verbauwhede, I.: Synthesis of Secure FPGA Implementations. In: Proceedings of IWLS 2004, (June 2004) pp. 224–231. Springer, Heidelberg (2004)
19. Wilton, S.J.: Architectures and Algorithms for Field-Programmble Gate Arrays with Embedded Memories. PhD thesis, University of Toronto (1997)
20. Wollinger, T., Guajardo, J., Paar, C.: Security on FPGAs: State-of-the-art implementations and attacks. Transactions on Embedded Computing Systems 3(3), 534–574 (2004)

Symmetric Multiprocessor Design for Hybrid CPU/FPGA SoCs

Shane Santner[1], Wesley Peck[2], Jason Agron[3], and David Andrews[4]

[1] University of Kansas, Lawrence KS 66045, USA
[2] The NNSA's Kansas City Plant managed and operated by Honeywell FM&T,
Kansas City MO 64141, USA

Abstract. This paper presents the design of a Symmetric Multiprocessor (SMP) hybridthreads (hthreads) system that allows multiple threads to execute in parallel across multiple processors controlled by a single hardware scheduler. This approach increases the performance of software at a minimal cost to hardware. The issues that must be addressed for extending a uniprocessor kernel include system initialization, processor identification, context switching and concurrency control. As a proof of concept this paper shows how hthreads, an existing hardware/software co-designed kernel can be extended to control multiple processors from a single, centralized hardware scheduler. Analysis results from executing on hardware reveal that for computationally intensive programs the typical speedup is in the range of 1.65x. This shows improvement in system performance while also illustrating issues associated with bus arbitration and memory access times.

1 Introduction

The hybridthreads project is a real-time embedded operating system that allows programmers to run threads simultaneously on the embedded processor and the FPGA fabric [6]. The previous hthreads design targeted a single processor and focused on achieving software acceleration through hardware co-processors attached to one of the peripheral buses. The new version of hthreads builds upon the foundation from the previous design while making use of the previously idle second PowerPC that is embedded in the FPGA. Utilizing this resource would allow two software threads to execute in parallel with the potential to increase the overall system performance in direct proportion to the number of processors in the system. This would be useful for a wide range of applications where performance and real-time execution are critical factors.

As previously mentioned, the work in this paper builds upon the original hthreads design and therefore a basic understanding of this design is required to understand the principles and design decisions used when extending the hthreads kernel to multiple processors. The details of the original hthreads design is outside the scope of this paper, however it is available through previous publications from the hthreads project [3] [4] [5] [6] [7].

R. Woods et al. (Eds.): ARC 2008, LNCS 4943, pp. 99–110, 2008.
© Springer-Verlag Berlin Heidelberg 2008

The remainder of the paper is partitioned as follows: System Initialization, Hardware and Software design (due to the nature of hardware/software co-design, there will be some overlap on certain topics), Implementation Results (from executing the hthreads kernel on a Virtex-4 FX FPGA) and the Conclusion.

2   System Initialization

The hardware configuration for the SMP hthreads system is a combination of processors, bus architectures, memory and hardware cores. The performance of the processors embedded in the FPGA will be severely crippled if they cannot access shared resources such as memory and the custom hardware cores. This responsibility lies with the Processor Local Bus (PLB) and the On-Chip Peripheral Bus (OPB), which can both be used to connect these vital components together. Figure 1 shows a block diagram view of the SMP version of hthreads.

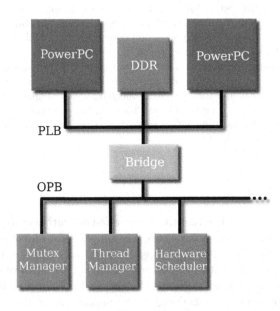

Fig. 1. Block Diagram of the SMP hthreads system

From figure 1 it is evident that both PowerPC's share the same PLB which allows the DDR SDRAM to be placed directly on the PLB. As a result of this placement, the access times to global memory are faster compared to accessing memory that is placed on the OPB because of the additional overhead that is associated with transmitting information across the bridges between the PLB and OPB. One final note of interest is that the custom hardware cores are placed on the OPB. This placement reduces the traffic on the PLB, reducing the amount of arbitration necessary to communicate with global memory on the PLB.

3   Design

3.1   Hardware

The first modification required was to the hardware scheduler core. To implement a multi-processor hardware scheduler required adding additional current thread registers to the scheduler and thread manager cores. The purpose of the current thread register is to identify which threads are currently executing on each processor. Since the design now includes more than one processor the number of current thread registers were increased to equal the number of processors in the system.

Similar in concept to the current thread register is the next thread register which contains the thread id of the highest priority thread on the ready-to-run queue. For this design the decision was made to continue to use only one next thread register. This allows the deterministic scheduling that was achieved in the previous design to continue through this version of the hthreads kernel.

An integral part of the new scheduler design was to develop a method for determining the next thread to execute from the pool of available threads on the ready-to-run queue. Several factors must be considered when making a scheduling decision. First, the scheduler needs to know the priorities of all currently running threads. This required creating a new register solely responsible for tracking this information (current_priority_reg). Secondly, the scheduler needs to ensure that if multiple processors could be preempted, that only one processor is interrupted and furthermore that the processor that is interrupted is the processor currently executing the lowest priority thread. For example, if the first processor is executing a thread of priority equal to ten and the second processor is currently running a thread of priority equal to seven, and the highest priority thread on the ready-to-run queue has a priority equal to five, then for proper operation the scheduler must ensure that the first processor is interrupted and not the second one (zero is the highest priority in the hthreads system).

To ensure that this occurs the check_preempt function was created to handle these scenarios. This function takes the highest priority thread on the ready-to-run queue and the priority register as parameters, and determines which processor if any should be preempted. The method used to make this determination is to compare priorities, and if the highest priority thread on the ready-to-run queue is better than the currently executing thread then the function tracks the difference between these priorities. In the end the highest difference corresponds to the processor that should be preempted. Figure 3.1 helps to illustrate this point.

If there does not exist a higher priority thread in the ready-to-run queue to execute then C_NUM_CPUS is returned which is an indication to the caller that preemption should not occur. This is because C_NUM_CPUS will always be one value higher than the highest Processor Identification Number (PIN) assignment in the system.

State Machine Modifications to the Hardware Scheduler. Once the check_preempt function was added to the hardware scheduler, preexisting

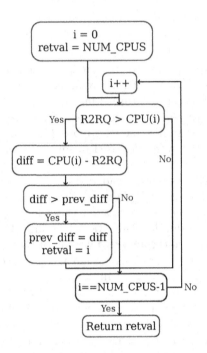

Fig. 2. Illustration of the check_preempt function implemented in the hardware scheduler

internal states within the scheduler now required modifications, the first state being the ENQUEUE operation. To account for multiple processors, the first change is to read the processor id from the bus, encoded into the request itself. Due to bit mapping definitions from the previous design the mapping of the processor id bits into the request was limited to bits 14 and 15 of all memory mapped reads, regardless if the operation is requested from the hardware scheduler or thread manager. Extracting this information from the bus has become a common procedure in the SMP version of the design. The second modification to the ENQUEUE operation is to determine if the thread being added to the ready-to-run queue is an idle thread. This check is done because idle threads cannot exist on the ready-to-run queue because then it would be possible for an idle thread to be put into the next thread register which means that it could be dequeued by the wrong processor (idle threads are processor specific in hthreads). If this check returns true, then the hardware simply returns without adding the thread to the queue. The final modification required to the ENQUEUE request was to determine which processor needs to be preempted when a thread with a higher priority becomes available to execute. This is handled by the check_preempt function as previously described.

The second modification to the internal states of the hardware scheduler involved the DEQUEUE operation. Like the ENQUEUE operation, the first modification is to again read the processor id from the bus. This information is necessary because the scheduler needs to track the priorities of the threads that are currently executing on all the processors in the system. This is one of two places where this information gets updated, the other being inside the IDLE_ID_DEQ operation where an idle thread is chosen to execute on a particular processor because there are no threads in the ready-to-run state. The other change to the DEQUEUE operation occurs when the ready-to-run queue is empty. When this happens, the next_thread is invalidated. Previously the idle thread was set up as the next_thread to run, however due to the nature of SMP systems and how idle threads are handled, this was changed because again if an idle thread is placed into the next_thread register it is possible that the wrong processor could attempt to dequeue and execute the idle thread which was initialized for the other processor.

SET_SCHED_PARAM begins as the previous two operations, by acquiring the processor id from the bus. The second change to this set of states within the finite state machine of the scheduler is to skip the preemption check if the thread is not on the ready-to-run queue. This is important because a thread could have its priority elevated above a currently executing thread, however the thread that is being updated might not be in the ready-to-run state. Therefore this would cause a processor to respond to an interrupt and attempt to execute a thread that is not on the ready-to-run queue. Conversely, if the thread being modified is on the ready-to-run queue then the check_preempt function is called to determine if a processor should be preempted in light of the updated scheduling parameters for this particular thread. This operation and the ENQUEUE operation are the only places in the hardware scheduler where preemption can occur.

Because idle threads are handled differently in the SMP hthreads system, there must now be a way to 'dequeue' idle threads when a better thread is not available to execute. To accomplish this the IDLE_REQUEST_ID state was added to the state machine. This is a request from the thread manager when either a YIELD or DEQUEUE system call has been requested. The thread manager checks to see if the ready-to-run queue is empty, and if so it instead requests the idle thread for the requesting PIN. This functionality allows each processor to have its own unique idle thread to execute.

System calls were one area that was identified as a critical region of code in the design which needed the protection of a lock. These regions of code modify critical shared data which are used to store information about threads in the system. If both processors have access to this region of code at the same time then race conditions can occur with the outcome of the data being inconsistent. To protect this region of code a shared lock between both processors has been implemented through the SYSCALL_LOCK state in the hardware scheduler.

Adding this functionality into the system required modifying the hardware scheduler core to include this critical lock around system calls. This is a memory-mapped read operation from the kernel with the type of request being encoded into the address. Two types of requests exist around the call to lock system calls, a request to lock the critical region of code and a request to release the lock around the critical region of the code. The scheduler implements this functionality by creating two new registers, syscall_mutex and syscall_mutex_holder.

The register syscall_mutex is used to track whether or not the mutex is locked and the syscall_mutex_holder keeps track of which processor currently holds the lock. When a request is made to acquire the lock the scheduler checks the status of the mutex. If the mutex is in use then a zero is returned on the bus and the scheduler returns to the idle state. However, if the mutex is not in use then syscall_mutex is updated to a value of one and the value of the requesting processor is stored in the syscall_mutex_holder. This is important because it allows the scheduler to only release a lock if it is owned by the processor requesting the release. This safeguard is used to ensure that only the processor which owns the lock is allowed to release the lock. In this scenario, the scheduler will update both registers and return the value of one on the bus to show that the release operation was successful. Conversely, the scheduler will return a zero on the bus when a request to release the lock has been denied. Figure 3 illustrates the SYSCALL_LOCK scheduler implementation.

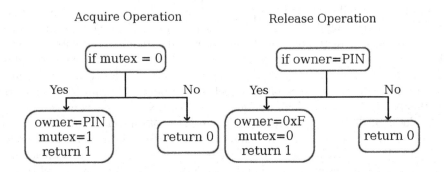

Fig. 3. Illustration of the SYSCALL_LOCK implemented in the hardware scheduler

MALLOC_LOCK is also critical for system stability in SMP systems. This is because malloc is not thread-safe by default [8]. The libc implementation of malloc calls two functions to lock around critical regions of software - malloc_lock and malloc_unlock. However, by default these calls do nothing unless the system designer implements these calls. This means that without modification it would be possible for malloc to allocate the same region of memory for multiple threads. It would also be possible for the libc function free to attempt to deallocate memory that is still in use. This scenario only worsens when caching is enabled (because of the lack of a snoopy cache implementation). Malloc also requires the locks to be recursive, therefore a completely new type of lock had to be added to the hardware scheduler, however most of the basic concepts from the SYSCALL_LOCK could be carried into the MALLOC_LOCK operation. Bit 13 is still used to encode the type of operation into the request. However this time instead of locking on the PIN, the lock is based on the thread id. This allows the malloc call to complete before another thread can call malloc. Also, a new signal was added to the state machine called lock_count which tracks the depth of the recursion. Only when this signal returns to zero can the lock be released, and of course only when the correct thread id is requesting the release. This ensures the correct functional operation of the recursive lock required by malloc.

State Machine Modifications to the Thread Manager. Similar to the hardware scheduler, the thread manager also required changes to internal states within the state machine. The first addition to the thread manager was to add the ASSIGN_CPU state which returns the PIN to the requesting processor. This is a memory mapped read from the thread manager and returns the PIN on the two least significant bits of the bus. The logic is simple for this state - a counter tracks which PIN should be returned on the bus. Each time this operation is requested the counter increments. The counter is a two-bit register which allows for a maximum of four processors in the system. When the counter returns PIN three it overflows to zero.

The only other state requiring modification was the NEXT_THREAD state which is used to dequeue the thread stored in the next_thread register by the scheduler. The modification to this state involves dequeueing the idle thread from the scheduler. This state initially checks to see if the next_thread is valid, and if it is not then the hardware will check to see if the idle_thread is setup for the requesting processor and if so will request a 'pseudo dequeue' of the idle_thread for that processor. This ensures correct operation of the idle_threads with multiple processors.

3.2   Software

Transforming non-physically concurrent system-level software into SMP compatible code is challenging. Several problems exist either from hardware limitations or from troubleshooting concurrency issues. The following sections will describe the natural progression of the software as the project matured, along with the difficulties and successes that accompanied this progress.

Cache Coherency. Due to limitations of the hardware design provided by Xilinx, cache coherency is extremely difficult to achieve. Xilinx does not implement a snoopy cache protocol which severely limits the use of cache in SMP systems. Even worse, the implementation of a custom snoopy cache protocol is even more difficult because Xilinx does not extend the necessary hardware cache lines to perform this type of an operation. Initially, the SMP hthreads design attempted to incorporate data caching into the system. To work around this issue of incoherency the cached section of data was limited to the first 128 MB of main memory. Conversely, the non-cached section occupied the remaining memory. Through modifications to the linkerscript and special gcc directives, critical system variables that are shared between processors were specified to be stored in the non-cached region of memory. This does not prevent race conditions, however it does keep the data that is shared cache coherent. The data that is being stored in this region of memory is an array of hthread_thread_t struct's. This data is analogous to the Task Control Block (TCB) in linux. It is critical that this information is stored in the non-cached region of memory to eliminate erroneous errors that occur from reading the incorrect context of the thread or using the incorrect stack to access data.

After many attempts to enable data caching for limited portions of the software, it became obvious that the system would not stabilize and that it was hindering the overall goal of porting hthreads to an SMP architecture. Due to this limitation, data caching was completely removed from the system.

To further ensure stability in the developmental stages of this project certain portions of concurrency have been removed from the system. To accomplish this spin locks have been inserted around system calls in the system-level software as shown in figure 4.

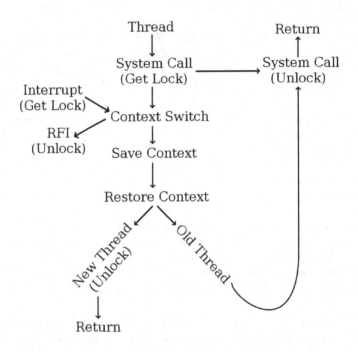

Fig. 4. Entry and Exit paths for acquiring system call locks

This will ensure that only one processor has access to shared system data at a time. The initial call to acquire the lock is immediately before the system call and inside the non-critical exception handling code. Entry into kernel-space occurs at these two entry points exclusively. Unlock calls are placed at the end of the system call, immediately before running a newly created thread and when returning from a non-critical interrupt. Exiting from kernel-space occurs at these three exit points exclusively.

After examining the possible scenarios for acquiring and releasing the system call lock in more detail it can be shown that in the hthreads system where a thread 'comes out' of a context switch depends on if the thread is a new thread or has already been executed and blocked. If the thread is new then it is 'boot-strapped' into execution and it is critical that the system call lock is released by this processor before the new thread begins execution. The other option for 'coming out' of a context switch is when the context of a previously executed thread has been restored which will then release the system call lock when returning from the system call handler. Also, interrupts acquire and eventually will release the system call lock inside the non-critical exception handling code. It is also important to remember that this lock is PIN specific, therefore different threads can acquire and release the lock as long as they both execute on the same processor.

Handling SMP Malloc. Finally, as previously stated the libc implementation of malloc is not thread-safe by default [8], and this became evident through numerous hours of debugging. The problem was encountered when the free routine was attempting to deallocate memory that was still valid - the pointer to the region of memory to be freed was actually pointing to a valid region of memory for another thread.

In order to have a thread-safe implementation of malloc, it is imperative that the system design implements the stub function calls to __malloc_lock() and __malloc_unlock(). These are required by the libc implementation of malloc to ensure that race conditions do not occur when attempting to allocate and deallocate memory. Furthermore, the locks which are used inside __malloc_lock() and __malloc_unlock() must be recursive locks [8] to ensure proper operation. The implementation of this lock is in the hardware scheduler state machine and is an atomic operation because the bus is locked until the scheduler returns the result of the request on the bus.

4   Implementation Results

The SMP version of hthreads has been successfully tested on the Xilinx XUP development board [1] and the Avnet Virtex-4 FX PCI Express Board [2]. The results in this section were obtained from executing on the Avnet Virtex-4 FX PCI Express Board.

Two software test cases were developed to stress the system and measure the capabilities of the SMP hthreads system. These tests were designed to illustrate the expected speedup when executing computationally intensive applications.

The first test is the producer/consumer (simple_buffer.c) problem which demonstrates nearly a 2x speedup for small buffer sizes - this is illustrated in figure 5. The almost linear speedup when the buffer size is one is caused by nearly constant context switching for the uniprocessor system. This buffer size however has no effect on the SMP version because each thread can execute exclusively on one of the PowerPC's, therefore eliminating the majority of context switching. It is also interesting to note the performance results as the buffer size increases, which relieves the amount of context switching required for the uniprocessor system. The data illustrates that as the buffer size increases, the performance

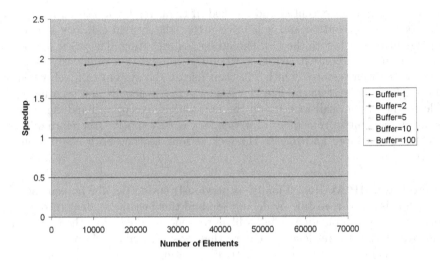

Fig. 5. simple_buffer.c results

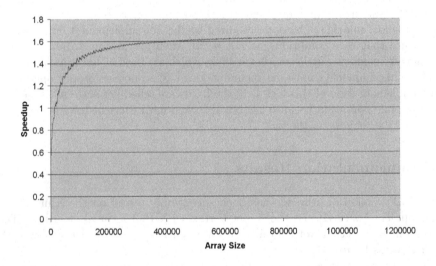

Fig. 6. dual_test.c results

improvement of the SMP system plateaus at around 1.2x. This is because parallelism is being removed from the application and the effect of context switching is being masked out by the increasing size of the buffer.

Similar to simple_buffer.c, dual_test.c is also computationally intensive. This application divides an array of N elements in half, allocating each half to a separate thread. Each thread will then perform a summation operation on the data, and the final value is the difference of the two summation results once both of the threads have completed. One important note about this application is that the data is not shared until the final difference operation. This eliminates the overhead of communicating between processors and should provide a greater amount of speedup compared to the producer/consumer test with large buffer sizes. Figure 6 illustrates this accurately, showing a speedup of approximately 1.65x compared to the single processor implementation for large amounts of data.

It is also interesting to note that the speedup does not plateau at 2x for this application. This is because of bus contention on the PLB between the two PowerPC's. Both processors are reading large amounts of data from main memory which results in collisions on the PLB. This leads to bus arbitration which restricts main memory access to only one processor due to limitations of the PLB arbitration scheme [12] provided by Xilinx. Other than providing fair arbitration between the PowerPC's, this issue could also be greatly improved by turning on the data cache for both processors which would relieve the amount of stress on the PLB.

5 Conclusion

The SMP version of the hthreads kernel now utilizes the second PowerPC processor which can significantly improve the performance of computationally intensive applications. This required making modifications to the hardware scheduler, the thread manager and the hthreads kernel software. Due to the lack of cache-coherency support data caching must be disabled to ensure proper operation. Furthermore, hardware locks were implemented to prevent race conditions and to ensure that memory allocation and deallocation calls were handled properly.

Two software tests were developed to show the performance of the new SMP hthreads system. Using a producer/consumer model with a buffer size of one, simple_buffer.c showed a performance improvement of 1.95x. This is explained by the almost constant context switching of the uniprocessor system between producer and consumer threads, contrasted with the SMP design where each thread occupies a PowerPC for exclusive execution. The second example, dual_test.c revealed more of a typical performance improvement for computationally intensive applications with a speedup of 1.65x when operating on large amounts of data.

For further information on the SMP port of hthreads please visit the hthreads wiki [6] or the main hthreads web-site [7].

References

1. Xilinx University Program, http://www.xilinx.com/univ/
2. Avnet Electronics Marketing, http://www.em.avnet.com/
3. Peck, W., Anderson, E., Agron, J., Stevens, J., Baijot, F., Andrews, D.: Hthreads: A Computational Model for Reconfigurable Devices (August 2006)
4. Agron, J., Peck, W., Anderson, E., Andrews, D., Komp, E., Sass, R., Baijot, F., Stevens, J.: Run-Time Services for Hybrid CPU/FPGA Systems on Chip (December 2006)

5. Andrews, D., Peck, W., Agron, J., Preston, K., Komp, E., Finley, M., Sass, R.: hThreads: A Hardware/Software Co-Designed Multithreaded RTOS Kernel (September 2005)
6. Hybridthreads - Wiki Page, http://wiki.ittc.ku.edu/hybridthread/Main_Page
7. Hybridthreads - Main Page, http://www.ittc.ku.edu/hybridthreads/
8. Sourceware: libc __malloc_lock/__malloc_unlock implementation, http://sourceware.org/newlib/libc.html
9. Xilinx - Programmable Logic Devices, http://www.xilinx.com
10. Silberschatz, A., Baer, P., Gagne, G., Gagne, G.: Operating System Concepts, 6th edn. (2001)
11. Xilinx: Designing Multiprocessor Systems in Platform Studio, http://direct.xilinx.com/bvdocs/whitepapers/wp262.pdf
12. Xilinx: Processor Local Bus (PLB) v3.4, http://www.xilinx.com/ipcenter/catalog/logicore/docs/plb_v34.pdf

Run-Time Adaptable Architectures for Heterogeneous Behavior Embedded Systems

Antonio Carlos S. Beck[1], Mateus B. Rutzig[1], Georgi Gaydadjiev[2], and Luigi Carro[1]

[1] Universidade Federal do Rio Grande do Sul – Porto Alegre/Brazil
2 Delft University of Technology, Computer Engineering – Delft/The Netherlands
{caco,mbrutzig}@inf.ufrgs.br, g.n.gaydadjiev@ewi.tudelft.nl,
carro@inf.ufrgs.br

Abstract. As embedded applications are getting more complex, they are also demanding highly diverse computational capabilities. The majority of all previously proposed reconfigurable architectures targets static data stream oriented applications, optimizing very specific computational kernels, corresponding to the typical embedded systems characteristics in the past. Modern embedded devices, however, impose totally new requirements. They are expected to support a wide variety of programs on a single platform. Besides getting more heterogeneous, these applications have very distinct behaviors. In this paper we explore this trend in more detail. First, we present a study about the behavioral difference of embedded applications based on the Mibench benchmark suite. Thereafter, we analyze the potential optimizations and constraints for two different run-time dynamic reconfigurable architectures with distinct programmability strategies: a fine-grain FPGA based accelerator and a coarse-grain array composed by ordinary functional units. Finally, we demonstrate that reconfigurable systems that are focused to single data stream behavior may not suffice anymore.

1 Introduction

While the number of embedded systems continues to grow, new and different devices, like cellular phones, mp3 players and digital cameras keep appearing on the market. Moreover, a new trend can be observed: the multi-functional embedded system, which performs a wide range of different applications with diverse behaviors, e.g. present day portable phones or PDAs. As a consequence, simple general purpose or DSP processors cannot handle the additional computational power required by these devices anymore. Although a large number of techniques that can solve the performance problem are available, they mainly exploit the instruction level parallelism (ILP) intrinsic to the application, e.g. the superscalar architectures. However, these architectures spend a considerable amount of power while finding the ILP [1]. For that reason, alternative approaches, such as reconfigurable fabrics, have been gaining importance in the embedded domain, speeding up critical parts of data stream oriented programs. By translating a sequence of operations into a hardware circuit performing the same computation, one could speed up the system and reduce energy consumption significantly [2]. This is done at the price of additional silicon area, exactly the resource mostly available in new technology generations.

R. Woods et al. (Eds.): ARC 2008, LNCS 4943, pp. 111–124, 2008.

Recent FPGA based reconfigurable devices targeting embedded systems are designed to handle very data intensive or streaming workloads. This means that the main design strategy is to consider the target applications as having very distinct kernels for optimization. This way, speeding up small parts of the software allows one to obtain huge gains. However, as commented before, the number of applications a single embedded device must handle is increasing. Nowadays, it is very common to find embedded systems with ten or more functions with radically different behaviors. Hence, for each of these applications, different optimizations are required. This, in consequence, increases the design cycle, since mapping code to reconfigurable logic usually involves some transformation, which is done manually or by the use of special languages or tool chains. To make this situation even more complicated, some of these applications are not as datastream oriented as they used to be in the past. Applications with mixed (control and data flow) or pure control flow behaviors, where sometimes no distinct kernel for optimization can be found, are gaining popularity. As it will be demonstrated, the JPEG decoder is one such example.

In accordance to the facts commented above, the main contributions of this paper are:

- To evaluate the potential performance of two representative run-time dynamically reconfigurable architectures with different programmability strategies for the same set of embedded systems benchmarks;
- To provide indication for the need of mixed behavior architectures supporting different reconfiguration mechanisms based on the above results.

This work is organized as follows: Section 2 discusses classic reconfigurable architectures and shows how they are applied in embedded systems. In Section 3 we discuss two representative architectures with different configuration strategies used in our study. Section 4 summarizes the analysis done on the benchmark set with these two systems. Finally, Section 5 draws conclusions and indicates some directions.

2 Related Work

Reconfigurable systems have already shown to be very effective in mapping certain pieces of the software to reconfigurable logic. Huge software speedups as well as significant system energy reductions have been previously reported [2]. Careful classification study in respect to coupling, granularity and instructions type is presented in [3]. In accordance with this study, in this section we discuss only the most relevant work. For instance, processors like Chimaera [4] have a tightly coupled reconfigurable array in the processor core, limited to combinational logic only. The array is, in fact, an additional functional unit (FU) in the processor pipeline, sharing the resources with all normal FUs. This simplifies the control logic and diminishes the communication overhead between the reconfigurable array and the rest of the system. The GARP machine [5] is a MIPS compatible processor with a loosely coupled reconfigurable array. The communication is done using dedicated move instructions.

More recently, new reconfigurable architectures, very similar to the dataflow approaches, were proposed. For example, TRIPS is based on a hybrid von-Neumann/ dataflow architecture that combines an instance of coarse-grained, polymorphous grid processor core with an adaptive on-chip memory system [6]. TRIPS uses three different execution modes, focusing on instruction-, data- or thread- level   parallelism. Wavescalar [7], on the other hand, totally abandons the program counter and the linear von-Neumann execution model that is limiting the amount of exploited parallelism. As these two examples, Piperench is also a reconfigurable machine highly relying on compiler driven resource allocation [8].

Specifically concerning embedded systems, Stitt et al. [9] presented the first studies about the benefits and feasibility of dynamic partitioning using reconfigurable logic, showing good results for a number of popular embedded system benchmarks. This approach, called *warp processing*, is based on a complex SoC. It is composed by a microprocessor to execute the application software, another microprocessor where a simplified CAD algorithm runs, local memory and a dedicated FPGA array. Firstly, the microprocessor executes the code, and a profiler monitors the instructions in order to detect critical regions. Next, the CAD software decompiles the application to a control flow graph, synthesizes it and maps the circuit onto the FPGA structure. At last the original binary code is modified to use the generated hardware blocks. In [10] another reconfigurable architecture is presented, called Computer Configurable Accelerator (CCA), working in granularity of the instruction level. The CCA is composed by very simple functional units, tightly coupled to an ARM processor.

We can observe two main trends concerning reconfigurable logic organization for embedded systems. The first one is aimed at optimizing the most executed kernels, with a fine grain array usually being relatively loosely coupled to the processor, or avoiding a central processor at all [6][7][8][9]. The second class are tightly coupled coarse grain units, embedded as ordinary FUs in the processor pipeline [4][5][10], attacking lowest levels of parallelism, such as ILP. That is why in this work we are considering two representative examples from these two distinctive groups for our evaluation.

3   Evaluated Architectures

In this study we are employing two different run-time dynamically reconfigurable systems to perform our analysis. Although they represent different programming paradigms, both are implemented using the same general-purpose processor (GPP): a MIPS R3000. The first one is Molen, an FPGA reconfigurable architecture [11]. Because of the high penalties incurred by reconfiguration, it is usually used to speed up the applications at loop and subroutine levels. Since it is based on fine grain devices and variable size of instruction blocks, code can be transformed into reconfigurable logic with huge potential for optimizations. However, one must take into account that there is a design effort to create the optimized hardware blocks for each kernel. Implementing huge parts of the code in a reconfigurable logic can sometimes become very complex, putting pressure on the development time, which, in turn, cannot be always tolerated. The design process can be seen as designing a VHDL engine for a specific subroutine inside the targeted program.

The second reconfigurable system is tightly coupled to the processor and has a coarse-grain nature [12], acting at the instruction level. This way, the allocation of reconfigurable resources becomes easier, since the implementation of execution blocks is usually based on a simple allocation of instructions to an array of ordinary functional units. However, as it does not work at bit level and optimizes smaller parts of the code, the degree of potential performance gains of such system is not the same as for fine grain approaches. The designer effort, however, can be significantly decreased (or avoided), and a vast number of different reconfigurations could be available, which makes this approach more suitable for systems with a large number of hot spots. In the two sub-sections to follow both systems are explained in more details.

3.1 Fine-Grain Based Reconfigurable System

The two main components in the Molen organization are depicted in Figure 1a. More precisely, they are the *Core Processor*, which is a GPP (in this case study MIPS R3000), and the *Reconfigurable Unit* (RU). The Arbiter issues instructions to both processors; and data transfers are controlled by the *Memory MUX*. The reconfigurable unit (RU), in turn, is subdivided into the *pµ-code unit* and the *Custom Computing Unit* (CCU). The CCU is implemented in reconfigurable hardware, e.g., a field-programmable gate array (FPGA), and memory. The application code runs on the GPP except of the accelerated parts implemented on the CCU used to speed up the overall program execution. Exchange of data between the main and the reconfigurable processors is performed via the *exchange registers* (XREGs).

The reconfigurable processor operation is divided into two distinct phases: *set* and *execute*. In the set phase, the CCU is configured to perform the targeted operations. Subsequently, in the execute phase, the actual execution of the operations takes place.

3.2 Coarse-Grain Based Reconfigurable System

This reconfigurable array operates as an additional functional unit in the execution stage, using an approach similar to Chimaera's in this aspect. This way, no external accesses (from the processor perspective) to the array are necessary. The array is two-dimensional, organized in rows and columns, and composed by ordinary functional units, e.g ALUs, shifters, multipliers, etc.

An overview of the general organization of the DIM system is shown in Figure 1b. Each instruction is allocated in an intersection between one row and one column. If two instructions do not have data dependences, they can be executed in parallel, in the same row. Each column is homogeneous, containing a determined number of a particular type of functional units. Depending on the delay of each functional unit, more than one operation can be executed within one processor equivalent cycle. It is the case of the simple arithmetic ones. On the other hand, more complex operations, such as multiplications, usually take longer to be finished. The delay can vary depending on the technology and the way the functional unit was implemented. Moreover, regular multiplexers are responsible for the routing (Figure 1c and Figure 1d). Presently, the reconfigurable array does not support floating point operations.

The array works together with a special hardware designed to detect and transform instruction groups for reconfigurable hardware execution. This is done concurrently while the main processor fetches other instructions. When this unit detects a minimum number of instructions worth being executed in the array, a binary translation is

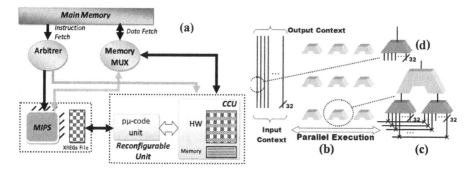

Fig. 1. The (a) FPGA-based and the (b) coarse-grain array reconfigurable architectures

applied to this code sequence. After that, this configuration is saved in a special cache, and indexed by the program counter (PC). The next time this sequence is found, the dependence analysis is no longer required: the processor just loads the configuration from the special cache and the operands from the register bank, then activating the reconfigurable hardware as functional unit. Thereafter, the array executes the configuration with that context and writes back the results, instead of executing the normal instruction flow of the processor. Finally, the PC is updated in order to continue with the execution of the normal (not translated) instructions.

4 Experimental Results

4.1 Benchmarks Evaluation

In our study we use the Mibench Benchmark Suite [13]. This suite has been chosen because it has a large range of different application behaviors. We are using all benchmarks with no representative floating point computations and that could be compiled successfully to the target architecture.

First, we characterize the algorithms regarding the number of instructions executed per branch (classifying them as control or dataflow oriented based on these numbers). As it can be observed in Figure 2b, the *RawAudio Decoder* algorithm is the most control flow oriented one (a high percentage of branches executed per program) while the *Rijndael Encoder* is quite the opposite. It is important to point out that, for reconfigurable architectures, the more instructions a basic block (BB) has, the better, since there is more room for exploiting parallelism (a basic block is code that has one entry point, one exit point and no jump instructions contained within it). Furthermore, more branches mean additional paths that can be taken, increasing the execution time and the area consumed by a given configuration, when implemented in reconfigurable logic. Our experiments presented in Figure 2b show similar trends as the ones reported in [13], where the same benchmark set was compiled on a different processor (ARM).

Figure 2a shows our analysis of distinct kernels based on the basic blocks present in the programs and their execution rates. The methodology involves investigating the number of basic blocks responsible for a certain percentage of the total number of basic block execution figures. For instance, in the *CRC32* algorithm, just 3 basic blocks are responsible for almost 100% of the total program execution time. Again, for typical reconfigurable systems, this algorithm can be easily optimized: one just needs to concentrate all the design effort on that specific group of basic blocks and implement them to reconfigurable logic.

However, other algorithms, such as the widely used *JPEG decoder*, have no distinct execution kernels at all. In this algorithm, 50% of the total instructions executed are due to 20 different BBs. Hence, if one wished to have a speedup of 2x (according to Amdahl's law), considering ideal assumptions, all 20 different basic blocks should be mapped into reconfigurable logic. This analysis will be presented in more details in the next section.

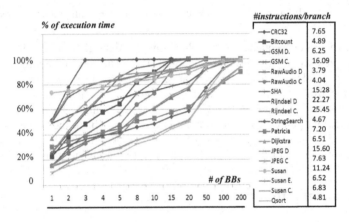

Fig. 2. (a) Instruction per Branch rate. (b) How many BBs are necessary to cover a certain amount of execution time.

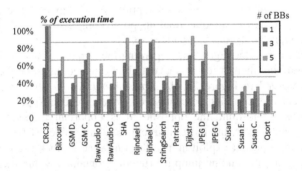

Fig. 3. Amount of execution time covered by 1, 3 or 5 BBS in each application

The problem of not having a clear group of most executed kernels becomes even more evident if one considers the wide range of applications that embedded systems are implementing nowadays. In a scenario when an embedded system runs *RawAudio decoder*, *JPEG encoder/decoder*, and *StringSearch*, the designer would have to transform approximately 45 different basic blocks into the reconfigurable fabric to achieve a 2x performance improvement.

Furthermore, it is interesting to point out that the algorithms with a high number of instructions per branch tend to be the ones that need fewer kernels to achieve higher speedups. Figure 3 illustrates this trend by using the cases with 1, 3 and 5 basic blocks. Note that, mainly when we consider the most executed basic block only (first bar of each benchmark), the shape of the graph is directly proportional to the instructions per branch ratios shown in Figure 2b (with some exceptions, such as the *CRC32* or *JPEG decoder* algorithms). A deeper study about this issue is envisioned to indicate some directions regarding the reconfigurable arrays optimization just based on very simple profile statistics.

4.2 Potential of Optimization

In this section, we first study the potentiality of fine grain reconfigurable arrays. Considering the optimization of loops and subroutines, we analyze the level of performance gains if a determined number of such hot spots is mapped to the Molen based reconfigurable logic.

Fine Grain reconfigurable architecture. In this first experiment, we are assuming that just one piece of reconfigurable hardware is available per loop or subroutine. This means that the only part of the code that will be optimized by the reconfigurable logic is the one which is common in all itterations. For example, let us assume a loop that should be executed 50 times. 100% of the code is executed 49 times, but just 20% is executed 50 times (all the iterations). This way, just this 20% is available for optimization, since it comprises the common instructions executed in all loop iterations. Figure 4a illustrates this case. The dark part is always executed, so just this part can be transformed to reconfigurable logic. Moreover, subroutines that are called inside loops are not suited for optimization.

Figures 5a and 5b show, in the y-axis, the performance improvements (speedup factor) when implementing a different number of subroutines or loops (x-axis) on reconfigurable logic, respectively. It is assumed that each one of these hot spots would take just one cycle for being executed on reconfigurable hardware. As it can be

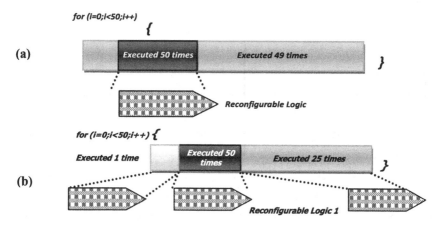

Fig. 4. (a) Just a small part of the loop can be optimized (b) Different pieces of reconfigurable logic are used to speed up the entire loop

observed, the performance gains demonstrated are very heterogeneous. For a group of algorithms, just a small number of subroutines or loops implemented on FPGA reconfigurable logic are necessary to show good speedups. For others, the level of optimization is very low. One reason for the lack of optimization is the methodology used for code allocation on the reconfigurable logic, explained above. This way, even if there is a huge number of hot spots subject to optimization, but presenting different dynamic behaviors, just a small number of instructions inside these hot spots could be optimized. This shows that automatic tools, aimed at searching the best parts of the software to be transformed to reconfigurable logic, might not be enough to achieve the necessary gains. As a consequence, human interaction for changing and adapting parts of the code would be required.

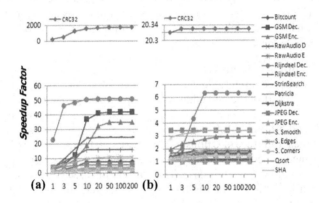

Fig. 5. Speedup factor considering different numbers of subroutines and loops being executed in 1 cycle

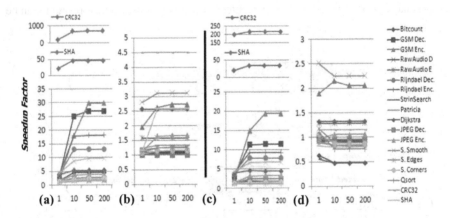

Fig. 6. Speedup factor considering different numbers of subroutines and loops being executed in (c) (d) 5 cycles and (e) (f) 20 cycles in reconfigurable logic

In the first experiment, besides considering infinite hardware resources and no communication overhead between the processor and reconfigurable logic, we were also assuming an infinite number of memory ports with zero delay, which is practically infeasible for any relatively complex configuration. Now, in Figures 6a and 6b, we consider a more realistic assumption: each hot spot would take 5 cycles to be executed on the reconfigurable logic. When comparing this experiment with the previous one, although the algorithms that present performance speedups are the same, the speedup levels vary. This obviously demonstrates that the performance impact of the optimized hot spots is directly proportional to how much they represent considering total algorithm execution time.

In Figure 6c and 6d we present the same analysis that was done before, but considering more pessimistic assumptions. Now, each hot spot would take 20 cycles to be executed on the reconfigurable hardware. Although usually a reconfigurable unit would not take that long to perform one configuration, there are some exceptions, such as really large code blocks or those that have massive memory accesses. Also, one can observe that some algorithms present losses in performance. This means that, depending on the way the reconfigurable logic is implemented and how the communication between the GPP and RU is done, some hot spots may not be worth to be executed on reconfigurable hardware.

In Figure 7 a different methodology is considered: a subroutine or loop that can have as much reconfigurable logic as needed to be optimized, assuming that enough reconfigurable hardware is available to support infinite configurations. This way, entire loops or subroutines could be optimized, regardless if all instructions inside them are executed in all iterations, in opposite to the previous methodology. Figure 4b illustrates this assumption. A reconfigurable unit would be available for each part of the code.

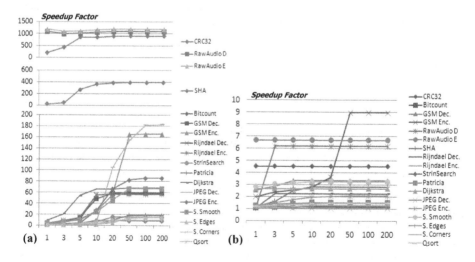

Fig. 7. Infinite configurations available for (a) subroutine or (b) loop optimizations: each one would take 5 cycles to be executed

In this experiment it is considered that the execution of each configuration would take 5 cycles. Comparing against Figures 6a and 6b (same experiment using a different methodology), huge improvements are shown, mainly when considering subroutine optimizations. This, in fact, reinforces the use of totally or partially dynamic reconfigurable architectures, which can adapt to the program behavior during execution. For instance, considering a partially reconfigurable architecture executing a loop: the part of the code that is always executed could remain in the reconfigurable unit during all the iterations, while sequences of code that are executed in certain time intervals could be configured when necessary.

Coarse Grain reconfigurable architecture. Now, we analyze the performance improvements when considering such architecture. Since it works at the instruction level, and in this version no speculative execution is supported, the optimization is limited to basic block boundaries. The level of optimization is directly proportional to the usage of BBs (Figure 2a): for a determined basic block, the more it is executed, more performance boost it represents. Even this coarse grain reconfigurable array does not demonstrate the same level of performance gains as fine grain reconfigurable systems show, more different configurations are available to be executed on this kind of system. This way, even applications which do not have very distinct kernels could be optimized.

Considering the ideal assumption of one configuration taking just one cycle to be executed, let us compare the instruction level optimization against the subroutine level, which had shown more performance improvements than the loop level, as expected. When comparing the results of Figure 8a against the ones of Figure 5a, one can observe that for some algorithms the number of basic blocks optimized does not matter: just executing one subroutine in reconfigurable logic would achieve a high performance speedup. However, mainly for the complex algorithms at the bottom of the figure, the level of optimization is almost the same for basic blocks or subroutines. This way, using the instruction level reconfigurable unit would be the best choice: it is easier and cheaper to implement 10 different configurations for that than 10 for the FPGA based one.

When assuming that 5 cycles are necessary for the execution of each configuration in coarse grain reconfigurable hardware, there is a tradeoff between execution time and how complex are the basic blocks (in number of instructions, kind of operations, memory accesses etc). This assumption is demonstrated in Figure 8b: in the *Rinjdael* algorithms, the optimization is worth until a certain number of basic blocks being implemented on reconfigurable logic. After that, there is a performance loss. In Figure 8c, considering 20 cycles per basic block execution on the reconfigurable array, this situation is even more evident.

Mixed Systems. Hybrid systems are envisioned as a mix of the two different reconfiguration approaches investigated above. In Figure 9a it is assumed that the most executed subroutine would be implemented into the FPGA reconfigurable logic. Then, considering that the first 3 most executed basic blocks would be contained in this subroutine, the next 17 would be executed on the coarse grain unit. In Figure 9b the same approach is used, but now considering 2 subroutines implemented on FPGA and 45 basic blocks on the coarse grain (assuming that the first 5 basic blocks are part of the two subroutines already implemented on FPGA).

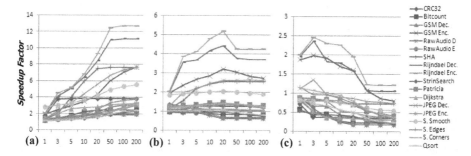

Fig. 8. Optimization at instruction-level with the basic block as limit. (a) 1 cycle, (b) 5 cycles and (c) 20 cycles per BB execution

As it can be observed, even though some algorithms do not present a significant performance gain while having this mixed architecture, the majority of the benchmark applications can take advantage of this system. This group would achieve almost the same performance boost when just using one or two pieces of FPGA-based reconfigurable logic together with the coarse grain unit, when comparing against a large number of huge blocks just implemented in FPGA.

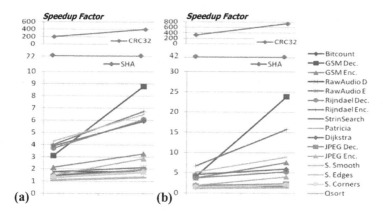

Fig. 9. Simulating a mixed system. (a) One subroutine optimized by FPGA and 17 basic blocks by coarse grain unit. (b) two subroutines - FPGA / 45 BBs – coarse grain

ILP, context loading and saving. Still assuming mixed systems, we repeat the previous examples but now considering the ILP available in each hot spot when computing their execution time. For instance, subroutines with more exposed ILP will execute faster than those with almost no parallelism. The algorithms chosen for this experiment are: *Rawaudio Decoder, Rijndael Encoder, CRC32* and *Quicksort*, since they are the most control and dataflow ones, and have a small or great number of distinct kernels, respectively.

The following assumptions have been done:

- Three simple arithmetic/logic execution per cycle, one multiplication, infinite memory ports, when executing on the coarse grain reconfigurable architecture;
- Nine simple arithmetic/logic execution per cycle, three multiplications, infinite memory ports when executing on the fine grain logic.

We also vary the reconfiguration (which comprises the configuration of the unit itself and the context loading, as register and memory reads) and write back times, considering them as being responsible for more 10%, 30% and 50% of the total execution time spent by each hot spot when using the coarse grain unit; and 3 times more when executing on fine grain logic. This way, if we are considering that FPGA is 3 times faster when executing its instructions, we are also assuming that it is 3 times slower for the reconfiguration process.

As it can be observed in Figures 10a and 10b, the importance of each architecture varies in each algorithm. In *CRC32*, there is no need of having a mixed architecture to speed up the system, since there is a small number of distinct kernels to be optimized. *Quicksort*, on the other hand, is quite different. Its gains are all presented by the coarse grain array, exactly because of its behavior is exactly the opposite of *CRC32*. Both *Rawaudio* and *Rijndael* benefits from the mixed system, but at different levels.

It is important to point out that the reconfiguration time starts to play an important role depending on the time it takes. For instance, in the *CRC32* algorithm, more time can be spent in the reconfiguration/write back than the in the execution itself. This way, for a given hot spot, one needs to pay attention on the size of the context and the resources available for its loading.

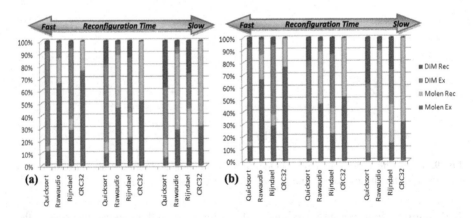

Fig. 10. Mixed system – Two subroutines executed on FPGA and 45 basic blocks on the coarse grain unit, considering different reconfiguration/write back times

5   Conclusions and Directions

Reconfigurable systems have already proven to be an efficient strategy to serve as platform for modern embedded systems. However, the number of different applications being executed on these systems has been increasing. In addition, the characteristics of the embedded system workloads have been changing as well. In this work we demonstrated that reconfigurable systems focusing just on the most executed kernels still can be used for some algorithms. This strategy, however, may require long development times that may not be acceptable. On the other hand, an alternative option is the employment of simpler reconfigurable architectures. The latter do not bring as much improvement as the fine grained approaches show, but could be easier to implemented due to its simplicity.

Considering fixed embedded applications, or yet those with long lifetime periods such as an MP3 player, FPGA based reconfigurable systems with high granularity grains can be a good choice. According to the results section, one can observe algorithms that present huge performance improvements, such as *CRC32*, *SHA* or *Dijkstra*. They need a small number of hot spots to achieve such gains, which would lead to a short development time.

On the other hand, there are other embedded devices, such as PDAs, with almost no pre installed applications. As they give to the user the freedom for installing applications, PDAs become a very heterogeneous environment. They will probably demand more flexible reconfigurable devices. Considering the benchmark set, some examples can be cited, as *Rijndael* and *Susan Corners*, which can just show good improvements when a large number of hot spots are optimized. As it was commented before, one also needs to take into consideration the assumption of having a great number of these applications being executed on the same device at the same time.

Finally, one could consider the example of next generation of mobile phones. Besides having fixed applications such as audio, image and video decompression, various Java applets can be installed. This way, mixed systems behavior appears as being a good choice. Moreover, we could envision some general directions when developing reconfigurable systems targeting to embedded applications, based on the discussion in section 3:

- Automated tools aimed at searching hot spots to be executed on reconfigurable logic may need human interaction;
- Algorithms with a great number of instructions/branch tend to present a small number of distinct kernels for optimization;
- For both level of granularities, some hot spots, even if they are highly used through program execution, may not be worth to be implemented in reconfigurable logic, due to low amount of ILP, great number of memory accesses for a given configuration, high overhead for context loading/saving;
- Partially reconfigurable systems may be a good choice in the sense that they can adapt themselves to parts of loops or methods that change while keeping other kernels always in the reconfigurable logic;
- The use of mixed systems, composed by both kinds of architectures, can be a good alternative. However, the reconfiguration/write back times must be taken into account when choosing the kernels to be optimized.

As future work, we will analyze both architectures in more details, as their area overhead and power consumption.

References

1. Wilcox, K., Manne, S.: Alpha processors: A history of power issues and a look to the future. In: CoolChips Tutorial An Industrial Perspective on Low Power Processor Design in conjunction with Micro, vol. 33 (1999)
2. Stitt, G., Vahid, F.: The Energy Advantages of Microprocessor Platforms with On-Chip Configurable Logic. IEEE Design and Test of Computers (2002)
3. Compton, K., Hauck, S.: Reconfigurable computing: A survey of systems and software. ACM Computing Surveys 34(2), 171–210 (2002)
4. Hauck, S., Fry, T., Hosler, M., Kao, J.: The Chimaera reconfigurable functional unit. In: Proc. IEEE Symp. FPGAs for Custom Computing Machines, Napa Valley, CA, pp. 87–96 (1997)
5. Hauser, J.R., Wawrzynek, J.: Garp: a MIPS processor with a reconfigurable coprocessor. In: Proc. 1997 IEEE Symp. Field Programmable Custom Computing Machines, pp. 12–21 (1997)
6. Sankaralingam, k., Nagarajan, R., Liu, H., Kim, C., Huh, J., Burger, D., Keckler, S.W., Moore, C.R.: Exploiting ILP, TLP and DLP with the Polymorphous TRIPS Architecture. In: Proc. of the 30th Int. Symp. on Computer Architecture, pp. 422–433 (2003)
7. Swanson, S., Michelson, K., Schwerin, A., Oskin, M.: WaveScalar. MICRO, vol. 36 (December 2003)
8. Goldstein, S.C., Schmit, H., Budiu, M., Cadambi, S., Moe, M., Taylor, R.R.: PipeRench: A Reconfigurable Architecture and Compiler. IEEE Computer, 70–77 (April 2000)
9. Lysecky, R., Stitt, G., Vahid, F.: Warp Processors. ACM Transactions on Design Automation of Electronic Systems (TODAES), 659–681 (July 2006)
10. Clark, N., Kudlur, M., Park, H., Mahlke, S., Flautner, K.: Application-Specific Processing on a General-Purpose Core via Transparent Instruction Set Customization. In: International Symposium on Microarchitecture (MICRO-37), pp. 30–40 (December 2004)
11. Beck, A.C.S., Rutzig, M.B., Gaydadjiev, G.N., Carro, L.: Transparent Reconfigurable Acceleration for Heterogeneous Embedded Applications. In: Design, Automation and Test in Europe (DATE), Munique (March 2008)
12. Vassiliadis, S., Cotofana, S.D., Wong, S.: The MOLEN $\rho\mu$-Coded Processor. In: Brebner, G., Woods, R. (eds.) FPL 2001. LNCS, vol. 2147, pp. 275–285. Springer, Heidelberg (2001)
13. Guthaus, M.R., Ringenberg, J.S., Ernst, D., Austin, T.M., Mudge, T., Brown, R.B.: MiBench: A Free, Commercially Representative Embedded Benchmark Suite. In: 4th Workshop on Workload Characterization, Austin, TX (December 2001)

FPGA-Based Real-Time Super-Resolution on an Adaptive Image Sensor

Maria E. Angelopoulou, Christos-Savvas Bouganis, Peter Y. K. Cheung,
and George A. Constantinides

Department of Electrical and Electronic Engineering, Imperial College London,
Exhibition Road, London SW7 2BT, UK
{m.angelopoulou,christos-savvas.bouganis,p.cheung,
g.constantinides}@imperial.ac.uk

Abstract. Recent technological advances in imaging industry have lead to the
production of imaging systems with high density pixel sensors. However, their
long exposure times limit their applications to static images due to the motion
blur effect. This work presents a system that reduces the motion blurring using
a time-variant image sensor. This sensor can combine several pixels together to
form a larger pixel when it is necessary. Larger pixels require shorter exposure
times and produce high frame-rate samples with reduced motion blur. An FPGA
is employed to enhance the spatial resolution of these samples employing Super
Resolution (SR) techniques in real-time. This work focuses on the spatial resolution enhancement block and presents an FPGA implementation of the Iterative
Back Projection (IBP) SR algorithm. The proposed architecture achieves 25 fps
for VGA input and can serve as a general purpose real-time resolution enhancement system.

1 Introduction

Every imaging system is based on an image sensor, a 2-D array of pixels that convert
incident light to an array of electrical signals (Fig. 1(a)) [1]. Two types of resolution
determine the quality of information collected by the sensor: the spatial and the temporal resolution. The *spatial* resolution depends on the spatial density of the photodiodes
and their induced blur. The most intuitive solution to increase the spatial resolution
corresponding to the same field of view would be reducing the pixel size, hence increasing the pixel density. However, the smaller the photodiodes become, the smaller
is the amount of incident light and, therefore, a longer integration time is required for
each photodiode to achieve an adequate signal to noise ratio [1, 2].

In the case of no relative motion between the camera and the scene, the reduction in
the amount of light can be compensated by increasing the exposure time of the pixels,
i.e. increasing the integration time of the photodiodes. However, in real-life systems either the camera is shaking or/and objects are moving in the scene during the integration
time. In this case, the integration time spans a large number of real-world 'frames', and
the output suffers from motion blur, thus reducing the temporal resolution. In Fig. 1(b),
the effect of motion blur is clearly visible: the exposure time was too long for the fast
moving bus to be captured. Thus, there is a fundamental trade-off in imaging systems:

R. Woods et al. (Eds.): ARC 2008, LNCS 4943, pp. 125–136, 2008.
© Springer-Verlag Berlin Heidelberg 2008

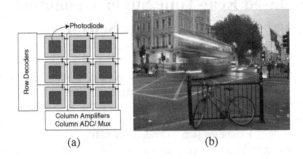

Fig. 1. (a) A hypothetical 3×3 CMOS image sensor. (b) A moving bus as opposed to a still bike. The first creates motion blur, whereas the second is fully captured.

an increase in the spatial resolution by reducing the pixel size reduces the temporal resolution and vice-versa. For the rest of the paper, 'LR' denotes the low spatial resolution and, thus, high temporal resolution image samples, while 'HR' refers to high spatial and low temporal resolution.

Recently researchers have focused on the problem of enhancing both spatial and temporal resolution. Resolution in both time and space can be enhanced by using multiple cameras to capture a fast moving scene with different subpixel spatial shifts and different subframe temporal shifts [3]. The main strength of the algorithm in [3] is that it treats motion blur independently of the cause of temporal change. Its main weakness lies in the large number of required cameras (such as 18). In real-life systems, this also introduces additional difficulties in the alignment of all the captured images from different cameras, a step known as registration. Apart from having to perform registration on many images, the large number of cameras increases the distances between the camera axes, making accurate registration difficult. This limits the applicability of the system.

In [4] the proposed system consists of a HR and a LR imaging device. The LR device deblurs the image captured by the HR device, by obtaining motion information for the estimation of the motion Point Spread Function (PSF). Then, the HR image is deblurred using deconvolution-based techniques. This approach mainly considers capturing a single image focusing in solving the blur caused by the undesired global motion due to camera shaking. The proposed system uses either two separate image sensors or a sensor with a LR periphery. If two separate image sensors are used, motion trajectories can be detected anywhere in the frame and, thus, the approach can be extended to dealing with the motion of objects. However, the use of two image sensors results in registration-related problems and an increased size of the device. In addition, the pixel size of the LR detector remains fixed over time regardless of the motion magnitude.

In summary, the contributions of the paper are: (1) The introduction of a motion-deblurring system which employs an FPGA to dynamically configure a time-variant image sensor. The size of the pixels is adapted according to local motions within the frame. The FPGA is used for the spatial enhancement of the high frame-rate areas, which are locally formed on the sensor, to provide super-resolution (SR) effects. (2) An efficient FPGA architecture is proposed for the implementation of the resolution enhancement module of the SR algorithm based on the Iterative Back Projection approach, and its performance is investigated. To the best of our knowledge, no FPGA implementation of an SR algorithm has been previously reported in literature.

The structure of the paper is as follows. Section 2 presents the architecture of the proposed FPGA-based motion-deblurring system and focuses on the spatial enhancement block, introducing SR and the Iterative Back Projection algorithm in particular. Section 3 describes the FPGA implementation of the SR block. In Section 4 hardware and quality results of the implementation are presented. Section 5 concludes the paper.

2 Surpassing the Fundamental Trade-off: Our Proposal

2.1 Description of the Motion-Deblurring System

The state of the art in imaging technology has produced sensors that are no longer subject to the constraint of time-invariant fixed pixel size [6, 5]. Elementary pixels can be grouped together over time, to form neighborhoods of different resolution. Taking advantage of what imaging technology has to offer, this work proposes an FPGA-based system that uses an adaptive image sensor to locally form areas of larger pixels and execute on-line, real-time motion deblurring. Fig. 2 presents an overview of this system.

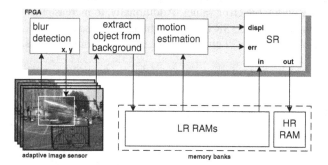

Fig. 2. The proposed motion-deblurring FPGA-based system that uses an adaptive image sensor. Areas of large pixels are formed where motion exists and the LR samples are spatially enhanced.

Let S_h denote the size of the elementary pixel of the sensor, corresponding to resolution HR (*i.e.* the highest spatial and lowest temporal resolution). Let m and n be the height and width of an area of the sensor measured in S_h units. That area may include pixels larger than S_h and, thus, produce multiple time samples during the HR integration. If all pixels, *regardless of their size*, are considered as points in the 3-D space, then during the HR integration $m \times n$ such points will be produced for an $m \times n$ area. The distribution of these points between time and space is determined by the pixel size. Increasing the pixel size of a particular region, decreases the density of these points on the 2-D plane and increases their density along the time axis, as the total number of points should remain $m \times n$ for the given area. Therefore, in one end, there is the still regions - covered with HR pixels - with distribution $m \times n \times 1$ (m in x, n in y and 1 in t), and at the other end lies the configuration $1 \times 1 \times (m \times n)$, if all the available pixels are grouped together to form one large pixel. Thus, if the pixel size of area Q equals $2 \times 2\ S_h$, the LR spatial resolution is 4 times lower than the HR resolution, while the temporal resolution is 4 times higher, *i.e.* 4 LR time samples are produced for Q during the HR integration. If the spatial relation is 3×3, 9 LR samples are produced, *etc.*

The *Blur Detection* block of Fig. 2 reads the sensor's output and indicates the blurred regions. These regions of the sensor will be configured to larger pixel sizes. If the motion blur derives from camera shaking a single motion region spans the entire sensor. During the HR integration time, a sequence of LR frames will be produced at every motion region, where the blur effect is reduced. Before executing SR on this group of LR frames, the static background should be removed by applying a background extraction algorithm.

The *Motion Estimation* block of Fig. 2 reads the sequence of LR frames and returns the motion vectors, *i.e.* the displacements of selected features between each LR frame and the reference LR frame. Any frame of the LR sequence can be chosen as the reference frame. These displacements will then be used by the *SR* unit to enhance the spatial resolution. The spatial resolution and the frame-rate of the final deblurred output will be those corresponding to the HR sequence.

The robustness of the system is increased by applying the following two techniques. The error information at the output of the *Motion Estimation* block [7] is used by the SR block to weight the information of the different LR samples and decrease the contribution of those with large error values. Additionally, to increase the available spatial information at the input of the SR block, neighboring LR samples before and after the integration interval of interest contribute in SR with adjustable weights.

2.2 Super Resolution

The forward model of generating LR pixels is shown in Fig. 3. Many HR pixels are mapped on a single LR pixel, thus imitating the integration of a group of HR pixels on a single photodiode. The weights with which these HR pixels contribute in the formation of the particular LR pixel form a gaussian kernel–the 2-D PSF shown in Fig. 3. Every LR pixel can be thus expressed as a weighted sum of HR pixels, and the following linear system of equations is formed:

$$Ah = l \tag{1}$$

where h and l denote the vectors of unknown HR pixels and known LR pixels, and matrix A contains the relative contribution of each HR pixel to each LR pixel.

The aim of spatial SR is to solve the inverse problem of finding h. The HR grid on which reconstruction will occur is the HR grid underlying the LR reference grid (Fig. 3). Thus, h consists of the HR pixels of this grid. Each LR frame adds an extra set of equations in the system, one for every LR pixel.

Spatial SR is based on subpixel shifts on the LR reference grid. If a group of LR frames were shifted on the reference LR grid (Fig. 3) by integer LR pixel units, they would all give the same set of equations since the same groups of HR pixels would form in the same manner their LR pixels. Therefore, for a LR frame to contribute uniquely in the system of Eq. 1, it should be shifted by subpixel units on the LR reference grid compared to the other LR frames. However, although in theory the above statements

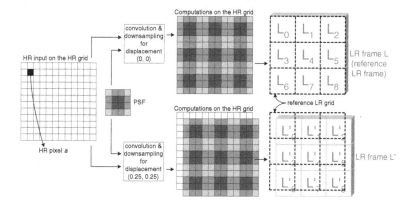

Fig. 3. The formation of the LR output presented mathematically. A 4×4 PSF is employed. Two simulated LR frames with displacements $(0, 0)$ and $(0.25, 0.25)$ are produced.

are true, in practice LR frames with the same integer displacements may give different sets of equations. This is partly due to errors in the motion estimation procedure [7] and partly due to the quantization of the LR grid on the HR grid on which reconstruction is executed. Therefore in practice it is preferable if more LR frames are considered, even if their displacements overlap.

The SR methods found in the literature solve the SR problem either in the spatial or in the frequency domain. In this work, a spatial domain method is implemented. This avoids the transformations between the two domains, and also removes the need to handle outputs with large dynamic range as produced by frequency domain analysis. Therefore, the need for long word-lengths in hardware implementations is not required. Among the spatial domain methods the Iterative Back Projection (IBP) [8] approach was selected because of its hardware-friendly characteristics. Instead of solving Eq. 1 for h, the IBP produces a simulated LR sequence and iteratively minimizes its difference from the observed LR sequence. This iterative scheme is suitable for hardware due to its potential for maximum parallelism and data re-use, as it will be demonstrated in Section 3.

Iterative Back Projection (IBP). The IBP employs an iterative refinement scheme on the HR grid, starting with an initial HR approximation such as the interpolation of the reference LR frame. Then, at every iteration of the algorithm the forward model of Fig. 3 is applied on the current HR approximation using the displacements of the corresponding observed LR frames to produce a simulated LR sequence. The aim of IBP is to minimize the difference between the observed and the simulated LR sequence, by refining the HR estimation.

All of the observed LR pixels and the corresponding simulated LR pixels which are influenced by a particular HR pixel contribute in the refinement of that HR pixel. This contribution is weighted according to the relative position of that HR pixel and the LR pair. For instance, in the refinement of HR pixel a (Fig. 3), pixel $L0$ of frame L participates with a weight proportional to $PSF(1, 1)$, whereas for $L'0$ of L' this weight will be proportional to $PSF(0, 0)$.

At iteration i, every pixel of the current HR approximation H_i is refined as follows:

$$H_{i+1}(x_h, y_h) = H_i(x_h, y_h) + \sum_{k=0}^{K-1} \sum_{(x_l, y_l) \in Y} (Lo_k(x_l, y_l) - Ls_k^{(i)}(x_l, y_l)) \times W(k, x_l, y_l),$$

(2)

where Lo_k and $Ls_k^{(i)}$ denote the kth observed and simulated LR frame, (x_h, y_h) and (x_l, y_l) denote the HR and LR coordinates, Y is the set of LR coordinates of the pixels of Lo_k and $Ls_k^{(i)}$ which are influenced by point (x_h, y_h), W is the weight with which $Lo_k(x_l, y_l)$ and $Ls_k^{(i)}(x_l, y_l)$ contribute in the refinement of $H_i(x_h, y_h)$, and K is the number of LR frames.

3   Architecture of the SR System

Figure 4 shows an overview of the proposed system. For every new group of LR frames, produced during a particular HR integration interval (Sect. 2.1), an SR stage occurs. At the beginning of each SR stage an initial HR approximation is produced by applying interpolation on the reference LR frame. Once this initial phase is completed, the iterations of the algorithm begin. When the iterations are over, the next LR group (associated with the next HR integration interval) is processed, and so on. The rest of the section focuses on the description of the individual blocks. It should be mentioned that the target system has 4 memory banks, each with a word-length of 4 bytes.

3.1   Off-Chip Memory Banks

LR RAMs. The LR memory banks store the incoming LR frames. As has been mentioned, the processing of the LR frames is performed in groups that correspond to one HR frame. However, in order to increase the spatial information available to the proposed system, a number of neighboring LR frames are used in addition to those produced during the HR integration (Fig. 5(a)). In hardware, this means that two memory

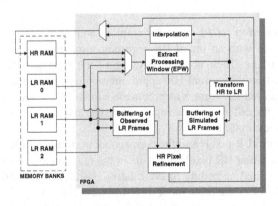

Fig. 4. Architecture overview

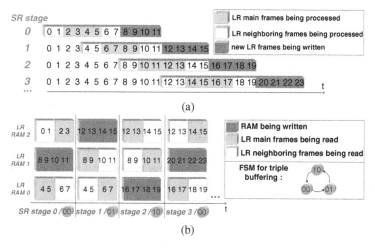

(a)

(b)

Fig. 5. The numbers correspond to the LR frame number. Four LR frames are produced during the HR integration and two pairs of neighboring frames (one pair at each side of the integration interval) are considered. (a) A sliding window indicates the group of LR frames processed during the current SR stage. While the processing occurs on these frames, a new group of four frames is written in the memory banks. (b) Triple buffering scheme applied on the LR RAMs. As the SR stages succeed one another the LR frames are written and read from the LR RAMs according to the current state of an FSM. There are three possible configurations.

banks need to be read in parallel, as Fig. 5(b) illustrates for the case of a 2×2 PSF and four neighboring frames. For instance, in SR stage 1 (Fig. 5(b)) frames 8-11 need to be read together with frames 4-7 which are in a different RAM bank due to the state of SR stage 0. In order to handle this we employ a triple buffering scheme. The access pattern of LR RAMs is shown in Fig. 5(b).

HR RAM. This external memory stores the computed HR pixels. During the initial phase of the current SR stage, data come into the HR RAM from the *Interpolation* unit. Once the initial estimation is computed, data come from the *HR Pixel Refinement* unit, which iteratively updates the content of the RAM until the end of the current SR stage. Before a pixel is written in HR RAM it is *rounded* to 8 bits. This allows storing HR pixels in groups of four in the 32-bit RAM, thus increasing the available memory bandwidth.

3.2   Individual Processing Units

The *Extract Processing Window* (EPW) unit of Fig. 4 produces the processing window for both the *Interpolation* and the *Transform HR to LR* units, at different phases of the SR stage. Thus, it operates in two modes. In *Mode 1* it returns a 2×2 window to the *Interpolation* unit, while in *Mode 2* it returns an $S \times S$ window to the *Transform HR to LR* unit, with S being the size of the PSF relating the LR to the HR grid. The EPW unit consists of $S - 1$ FIFOs which are connected to $S \times S$ registers to form the processing window.

To compute the initial HR guess, the *Interpolation* unit executes bilinear interpolation. Each interpolated HR pixel is a weighted sum of the surrounding 2×2 LR pixels.

The *Transform HR to LR* unit multiplies each HR pixel of an $S \times S$ processing window with the PSF weight corresponding to its location in the window. The Ls pixels of the simulated LR sequence (Sect. 2.2) will be produced by subsampling the output of the convolution of the last HR approximation. All possible subpixel displacements should be covered, therefore the HR pixels should 'move' in the FIFOs of the EPW unit one location at every cycle. This poses a minimum in the number of cycles of every iteration. This minimum will be equal to the number of HR pixels.

The *HR Pixel Refinement Unit* includes parallel processing branches each one of them associated with a LR frame. These parallel branches meet at a final adder, which corresponds to the external summation in Eq. 2, to produce the refined version of the HR pixel which is currently under process.

3.3   Data Re-use and Maximum Performance

To maximize data re-use every HR and Lo pixel are read from the corresponding RAM only once and remain on-chip until all the processing associated with them is over. Also, for maximum performance, one iteration requires the minimum number of cycles imposed by the HR convolution (Sect. 3.2). To achieve this, the EPW unit, which produces the processing window for convolution, is designed to produce the synchronization control signals for the entire system. When a HR pixel is first brought on-chip it is 'pushed' into the FIFOs of the EPW. When it is no longer needed by the EPW it will be the input of the next level of processing, that is the *HR Pixel Refinement Unit* unit. When this happens, all the LR pixels influenced by the particular HR pixel, both actual (Lo) and simulated (Ls), should be available on-chip.

3.4   On-Chip Memory

The units *Buffering of Simulated LR Frames* and *Buffering of Observed LR Frames* of Fig. 4 include the Ls and Lo groups of line-buffers, respectively. In order to achieve a throughput of one HR pixel per cycle, at every cycle all Ls and Lo buffers of all LR frames are accessed in parallel, while new data is brought in. Therefore, every group contains a separate buffer for every LR frame. These buffers only get updated when their content will not be used anymore at the current iteration. The width of the Ls buffers is equal to that of the LR frames. The Lo buffers are made wider, to surpass the limited memory bandwidth of the LR RAM. Specifically, the used Lo buffers are twice as wide as the LR frames and are written using a poling scheme.

4   Results

4.1   Implementation Requirements

The design was implemented on a Celoxica RC300 board using the DK5 Handel-C compiler, and was placed and routed using Xilinx ISE v.9.1. The RC300 board hosts

Table 1. Iterations for real-time performance for different HR sizes

$M_h \times N_h$	64×64	128×128	256×256	240×320	512×512	480×640	1024×1024
Iterations	585	146	36	31	8	7	2

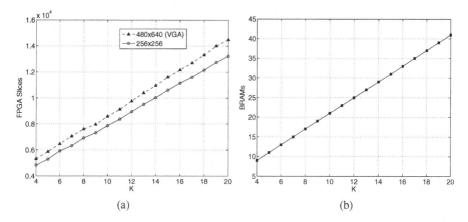

(a)   (b)

Fig. 6. The number of FPGA resources increases linearly with the number of LR frames (K). (a) Number of FPGA slices. (b) Number of BRAMs. The number of BRAMs is independent of the image sizes reported in Table 1.

a Xilinx Virtex-2 FPGA and on-board ZBT SRAMs. The operating frequency of the design on RC300 is 60 MHz. To meet real-time requirements the system should achieve 25 fps. The required number of cycles is: $C = reset\_cycles + M_l \times N_l + M_h \times N_h \times Iterations + [N_h \times (S - 1) + S] + Latency$, where M_h (M_l) and N_h (N_l) denote the number of rows and columns of the HR (LR) frame. Thus, C depends on the image size and on the number of LR frames (K) which contributes in $Latency$ by $\lceil log_2(K + 1) \rceil$, i.e. the latency of the final adder of the *HR Pixel Refinement* unit. For $K \in [8, 15]$ the number of maximum iterations of the IBP leading to 25 fps is given in Table 1.

The number of FPGA slices is mainly affected by K and does not significantly vary for different image sizes, as Fig. 6(a) demonstrates for 256×256 and 480×640 HR size. The number of BRAMs equals $(S - 1) + K \times 2$, as $(S - 1)$ BRAMs are used by the EPW unit, and K are occupied by each group of LR line-buffers (Fig. 6(b)).

4.2 Performance Evaluation

The performance of the system has been evaluated under two different scenarios. The first one is concerned with the classic SR problem where a sequence of shifted LR frames is used as the input to produce a HR output. The second deals with the motion deblurring of a moving object, presenting the SR results based on time samples read from a LR motion area. To incorporate motion estimation errors in the simulation process, the OpenCV Lucas & Kanade optical flow [7] and Shi & Tomasi good feature extraction [9] algorithms were used in both scenarios to calculate the motion vectors. The calculated motion vectors were inserted in the SR system.

(a)   (b)   (c)

Fig. 7. (a) Ground-truth reference frame (*i.e.* the real-world reference frame without any degradation). (b) Floating point bicubic interpolation of the reference LR frame. (c) Reconstructed frame:
Hardware output after 8 iterations (*i.e.* the number of iterations leading to real-time performance
for $M_h \times N_h = 512 \times 512$).

In the first experiment, a 512×512 natural image was used (Fig. 7(a)) and a sequence
of 8 shifted 256×256 LR images was generated. The LR sequence was synthetically
produced by first using randomly generated displacements to move the original image
on the HR grid and then applying a 2×2 spatial blur kernel on that HR sequence.

The produced LR sequence was used as input to the proposed system. Fig. 8(a) shows
the decrease in the Root Mean Square Error (RMSE) as the iterations of the algorithm
proceed. The vertical line indicates the number of iterations which complies with real-
time requirements for the given image size (Table 1). The results corresponding to the
8 bit rounding *of the output of every iteration* derive from the FPGA implementation of
the algorithm. Apart from those, Matlab results are reported for the following scenarios:
floating point version, floating point bicubic interpolation of the reference frame, 8 bits
truncated, 9 bits truncated and 9 bits rounded (the last three are bit-accurate models).
Fig. 8(a) illustrates that for large image sizes that impose a small number of iterations
for real-time performance, the 8 bit rounding scenario gives outputs of similar quality
as both larger word-lengths and the floating point SR, clearly prevailing against '8 bits
truncated'. The detail images of Fig. 7 show the higher quality obtained by the FPGA
implementation, after the number of iterations allowed for real-time performance, compared to floating point bicubic interpolation.

In the second experiment, a motion area employing pixels of 2×2 HR is considered,
which produces 4 time samples during the HR integration. The size of the HR frame is
240×320. To increase the robustness of the system a neighborhood of 2 LR frames at
each side of the integration interval is considered, so 8 LR frames are used in total.

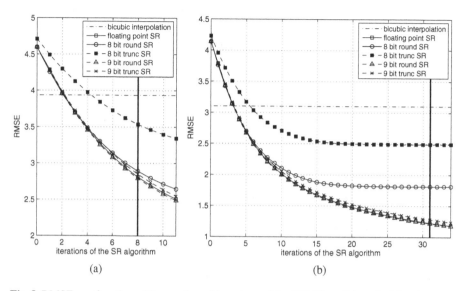

Fig. 8. RMSE as a function of the number of iterations of the IBP. The solid vertical line indicates the number of iterations allowed to obtain 25 fps for the given HR frame size ($M_h \times N_h$). (a) Experiment 1: $M_h \times N_h = 512 \times 512$ (b) Experiment 2: $M_h \times N_h = 240 \times 320$.

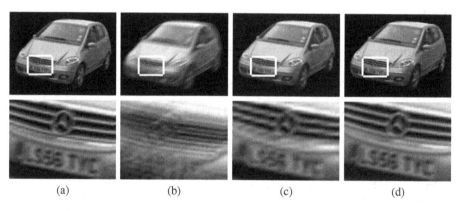

Fig. 9. (a) Ideal frame with HR spatial resolution and LR temporal resolution. This is the output of an ideal sensor that combines HR spatial resolution with LR integration time. (b) Motion-blurred output produced if the motion area had HR pixels. (c) Floating point bicubic interpolation of the reference LR frame. (d) Reconstructed frame for a motion area with LR pixels: Hardware output after the number of iterations leading to 25 fps. Using FPGA-based SR, the ideal combination of HR spatial resolution and LR temporal resolution is achieved.

If very fast motion is involved (as in Fig. 1(b)), the LR frames are blurred themselves. To incorporate this intra-LR-frame motion, we first generated a dense HR sequence of 32 frames, using random HR displacements, and then created the LR motion blurred sequence in two steps. First we averaged groups of 4 successive frames and produced sequence A, with LR pixel temporal resolution and HR pixel spatial resolution. This would be the output of an ideal but unrealistic sensor that combines LR temporal resolution with HR spatial resolution. A 2×2 PSF was then applied on sequence A to produce the actual LR sequence.

The desired output belongs to sequence A and is shown in Fig. 9(a). Note how close the detail of the reconstructed output presented in Fig. 9(d) is to Fig. 9(a), as opposed to Figures 9(b) and 9(c). The system can be easily modified to accommodate high precision in the pixels, which is required for further improvement in the quality. This is useful when a smaller frame size is considered and, therefore, more iterations can be performed (Fig. 8(b)).

5   Conclusions and Future Work

In this paper an FPGA-based system that forms areas of large pixels to cure motion blur was proposed. To compensate for the low spatial resolution of such areas FPGA-based SR is used. The reconstructed frame is of similar quality as the output of an ideal sensor with HR spatial resolution but LR temporal resolution, thus surpassing the fundamental trade-off between space and time. Future work includes the quantification of the scaling of the pixel size of the motion areas with the magnitude of motion, the use of bicubic interpolation as the initial estimation for faster convergence, and the implementation of the motion estimation, blur detection and background extraction blocks as well on FPGA.

References

1. Gamal, A.E., Eltoukhy, H.: CMOS image sensors. IEEE Circuits & Devices Magazine 21(3), 6–20 (2005)
2. Farrell, J., Xiao, F., Kavusi, S.: Resolution and Light Sensitivity Tradeoff with Pixel Size. In: SPIE Electronic Imaging 2006 Conference, vol. 6069, pp. 211–218 (February 2006)
3. Shechtman, E., Caspi, Y., Irani, M.: Space-Time Super-Resolution. IEEE Transactions on Pattern Analysis and Machine Intelligence 27(4), 531–545 (2005)
4. Ben-Ezra, M., Nayar, S.K.: Motion-based motion deblurring. IEEE Transactions on Pattern Analysis and Machine Intelligence 26(6), 689–698 (2004)
5. Constandinou, T.G., Degenaar, P., Toumazou, C.: An Adaptable Foveating Vision Chip. In: IEEE International Symposium on Circuits and Systems (ISCAS), May 2006, pp. 3566–3569 (2006)
6. http://www.foveon.com
7. Bouguet, J.-Y.: Pyramidal Implementation of the Lucas Kanade Feature Tracker - Description of the algorithm. Intel Corporation, Microprocessor Research Labs, Part of OpenCV Documentation, http://sourceforge.net/projects/opencvlibrary/
8. Irani, M., Peleg, S.: Improving Resolution by Image Registration. In: CVGIP: Graphical Models and Image Proc, May 1991 vol. 53(3), pp. 231–239 (May 1991)
9. Shi, J., Tomasi, C.: Good Features to Track. In: IEEE Conference on Computer Vision and Pattern Recognition (CVPR 1994) (June 1994), pp. 593–600 (1994)

A Parallel Hardware Architecture for Image Feature Detection

Vanderlei Bonato[1], Eduardo Marques[1], and George A. Constantinides[2]

[1] Institute of Mathematical and Computing Sciences
The University of São Paulo
São Carlos - BR
{vbonato,emarques}@icmc.usp.br
[2] Department of Electrical and Electronic Engineering
Imperial College London
London - UK
g.constantinides@imperial.ac.uk

Abstract. This paper presents a real time parallel hardware architecture for image feature detection based on the SIFT (Scale Invariant Feature Transform) algorithm. This architecture receives as input a pixel stream read directly from a CMOS image sensor and produces as output the detected features, where each one is identified by their coordinates, scale and octave. In addition, the proposed hardware also computes the orientation and gradient magnitude for every pixel of one image per octave, which is useful to generate the feature descriptors. This work also presents a suitable parameter set for hardware implementation of the SIFT algorithm and proposes specific hardware optimizations considered fundamental to embed whole system on a single chip, which implements in parallel 18 Gaussian filters, a modified CORDIC (COordinate Rotation DIgital Computer) algorithm version and a considerable number of fixed-point operations, such as those involved in a matrix inversion operation. As a result, the whole architecture is able to process up to 30 frames per second for images of 320×240 pixels independent of the number of features.

1 Introduction

Image feature detection has received for many years a considerable attention from the scientific community. One of the first widely used feature detection algorithms for image matching purpose was proposed by Harris and Stephens [1] extended from the Moravec corner detector [2], which extracts interest points from edge and corner regions based on gradient magnitude information. Shi and Tomasi have also proposed a system where good features are detected by analysing the pixel intensity behavior of the feature regions during the tracking operation [3]. From these important contributions there has been a continuous effort in to develop robust algorithms to detect features invariant to scale, affine transformations, rotation and change in illumination [4] [5]. Among these proposals, Lowe [6] has presented one of the most complete and robust results, which has been named SIFT.

R. Woods et al. (Eds.): ARC 2008, LNCS 4943, pp. 137–148, 2008.

In [7] a partial implementation of the SIFT algorithm on FPGA for stereo calibration is demonstrated. It presents an architecture to detect feature candidates, which operates at 60 frames per second. However, the work does not state the image resolution or discuss FPGA resource architecture. Another FPGA-based system for SIFT is presented in [8], which needs 0.8ms to process an image of 320×240 pixels. However, again little information about the architecture has been provided. In contrast, we present the architecture for all phases of the original SIFT algorithm needed to detect a feature along with its descriptor information. Our architecture requires 33ms per 320×240 frame and is completely embedded on an FPGA (Field-Programmable Gate Array). It processes pixel stream read directly from a CMOS image sensor, and returns the detected features represented by their coordinates, scale, and octave. It also returns the orientation and gradient magnitude of every pixel of one image per octave. The coordinates represent the feature location in an image and the scale and octave represent the image frequency and the image resolution from where the feature was detected (see [6] for more details). The main contributions of this work are: it identifies appropriate hardware optimizations to embed whole architecture on-a-chip and, differently from other papers mentioned, it provides the implemented hardware details.

The paper is organized as follows. Section 2 presents our own hardware-orientated architecture of the algorithm, along with a detailed description of the architecture developed. In Section 3, experimental results are presented in order to verify the system performance. In addition, the FPGA resources and the processing performance are also presented. Finally, Section 4 concludes the work.

2   The Proposed Parallel Hardware Architecture

In this section we present a System-on-a-Programmable-Chip (SOPC) to detect features at 30 frames per second independent of the number of features. Fig. 1 shows a block diagram of the proposed architecture, featuring three blocks in hardware and one in software. The hardware blocks detect the features and compute the orientation and gradient magnitude for every pixel of one image per octave. The software block is only used to read data from the hardware blocks, which is prepared to be used for additional functionalities, such as the feature descriptor association by using the BBF algorithm [9] suggested in the original SIFT paper.

2.1   The System Configuration

The SIFT algorithm has parameters and functionalities that directly affect the complexity and the performance of the hardware architecture. To identify a suitable configuration for hardware implementation, Fig. 2 shows 16 configurations and their influence on the feature matching reliability. The first parameter determines whether the orientation and gradient magnitude are computed from an

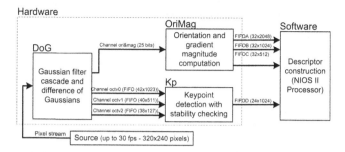

Fig. 1. Block diagram of the implemented system, composed of three hardware blocks, used to extract features from the images and to pre-compute data for the descriptors, and one block in software, which associates descriptors to features. The blocks are connected using dedicated channels, where each one, except the channel between DoG and OriMag, has internal FIFOs used as buffer while a receiver block is temporarily unavailable.

image chosen by the feature scale or from a pre-defined image scale. The second parameter gives the option to either duplicate the image size used as input or to keep the original size. The other two parameters are related to feature stability checking; the first one activates the keypoint (candidate to feature) location and the second one verifies the contrast threshold and the edge response.

The features used in the matching test were generated from two sets of ten images each, where the second set is a transformation of the first one in relation to scale, rotation and viewpoint. As seen in Fig. 2, the configuration options from 12 to 16 produce a very similar rate of incorrect matching (false positive). Based on this information the proposed architecture has been developed using option 12 because this configuration allows the gradient magnitude and orientation to be computed in parallel while the keypoint is been detected and reduces the on-chip memory needs by processing the input image in its original size. Another motive is that most computations in the threshold and the edge response functions are reused from the keypoint location function.

The system has been configured for three octaves (octave 0 to 2) with five scales (scale 0 to 4) in each one. This number of octaves is sufficient for images of 320×240 pixels, since a fourth octave would produce small and blurred images, resulting in a remote chance of detecting features. However, the number of scales has been chosen based on [6], where it has demonstrated that this number has the highest feature repeatability rate.

2.2 Gaussian Filter Cascade and the Difference of Gaussian

A simple approach to implement a Gaussian filter is through convolving a two-dimensional Gaussian kernel with the image. However, this method is computationally inefficient where the complexity to filter an image is given by $\Theta(n^2 m^2)$, where n and m are the kernel and image dimensions, respectively. Considering that this kernel K is separable, i.e. $K = kk^t$ for some vector k, representing

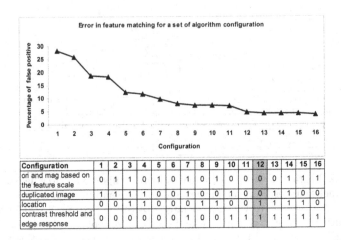

Fig. 2. An analysis showing the feature matching error in relation to the system configuration

a unidimensional Gaussian distribution, the filter can be implemented in optimized manner by convolving the input image I in row order with vector k and then convolving the result H in column order with vector k again. Equations (1) and (2) present these operations. In this case the computational requirements is reduced to $\Theta(nm^2)$.

$$H(x, y) = k(x) * I(x, y) \qquad (1)$$
$$G(x, y) = k^T(x) * H(x, y) \qquad (2)$$

Fig. 3 shows a pipeline architecture for the optimized Gaussian filter using a 7×7 kernel. The left side shows the convolution in row and the right in column. In this implementation we also take the advantage of the kernel symmetry and save two multipliers on the left side by reusing data from the multiplication result at k_1 and k_2. On the right side the same number of multipliers can be saved, however, for this case, as the convolution is performed in column order, it is necessary a buffer of size 6×w to store the data to be reused, where w is the image width. This architecture is again optimized so as to save more four multipliers by assuming that the kernel vector has always the values one or zero at position 1 and 7 and consequently avoid the multiplications at those points. It is possible to keep this pattern for kernels generated with any σ values by simply multiplying it by a constant. As the proposed system has 18 Gaussian filters working in parallel these optimizations strongly reduce the hardware resources necessary for the implementation. Another optimization is also obtained by connecting the filters in cascade in order to reduce the kernel dimension for higher image scales.

The next operation computes the difference of Gaussian D_i by subtracting pairs of Gaussian smoothed images (G_i, G_{i+1}) synchronized by internal buffers. Each octave produces five D_i in parallel totaling fifteen for the three octaves, which are sent to the Kp hardware block (see Fig. 1). Fig. 4 shows three graphs

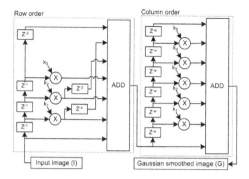

Fig. 3. An pipeline architecture for the optimized Gaussian filter version

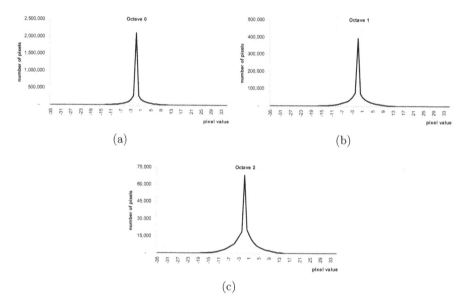

Fig. 4. Pixel range for fifty D_i images, where the image resolution for (a) is 320×240, (b) 160×120 and (c) 80×60

generated from 50 D_i images, demonstrating that most D_i pixel values are located in the range from -15 to +15. These three graphs also show that the range for the higher octaves is slightly bigger as a consequence of the accumulative smoothed level caused by the Gaussian filter cascade.

As the G_s images use 8 bits to represent one pixel, 9 bits would be sufficient to store the D_i pixels with the sign. However, a considerable amount of FPGA resources is saved by taking into account the distribution for the D_i pixel values shown in Fig. 4. Thus, in the proposed system we have used five bits (without the sign) to store D_i as it is highly unlikely to have its value bigger than 2^5.

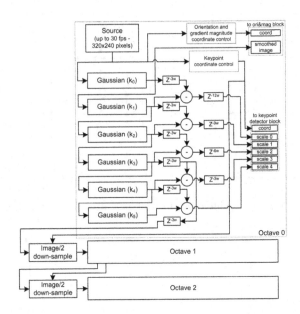

Fig. 5. A pipeline architecture implementing the Gaussian filter cascade and the difference of Gaussian function

Finally, Fig. 5 presents the proposed architecture for whole DoG block. In addition to the functions previously described, this architecture also down-samples the images for the octaves and generates the coordinate references for the pixels used in the forward blocks.

2.3   Orientation and Gradient Magnitude Computation

In this work we propose an architecture for pre-processing the orientation and gradient magnitude of every pixel for one image per octave independent of whether or not it lies inside a keypoint neighbourhood. These images are taken from scale zero of each octave after being Gaussian blurred, which is different from the original algorithm where the images are chosen according to the keypoint scale. However, our solution provides a significant hardware complexity reduction while it maintains a similar system robustness, as demonstrated in Fig. 2. The purpose of computing the orientation and gradient magnitude in advance is to exploit parallelism, as this operation can be carried out while features are being detected.

The trigonometric operation *atan2* and the square root are performed in hardware using an adapted version of the CORDIC algorithm in vector mode [10]. One of the standard function of the CORDIC algorithm is to compute *atan*, where each algorithm iteration is performed according to Equations (3), (4) and (5). Given the coordinates of a pixel $< x_0, y_0 >$, the rules for iteration transition and the initial rotation z_0 set to zero, the values from Equations (3) and (5) at iteration n correspond to the square root and *atan*, respectively.

$$x_{i+1} = x_i - s_i y_i 2^{-i} \tag{3}$$
$$y_{i+1} = y_i + s_i x_i 2^{-i} \tag{4}$$
$$\theta_{i+1} = \theta_i - s_i atan(2^{-i}) \tag{5}$$

where: $s_i = +1$ whether $y_i < 0$, $s_i = -1$ otherwise.

The *atan* is given in the range of $[0, \pi]$. However, as in this system the orientation is computed for *atan2* the range is $[-\pi, \pi]$. Considering that CORDIC rotates up to π in any direction the initial rotation to compute *atan2* needs to be no further than π from the final rotation (result). Hence, a new initial rotation has been proposed as follows, where not only x_0 is considered as in the *atan* operation, but also y_0 value is taken into account in order to know in which of the four quadrants of the arctangent the pixel belongs.

$$x_0 = s_0 x_0$$
$$y_0 = s_0 y_0 \tag{6}$$
$$\theta_0 = \alpha$$

where:
$$s_0 = -1 \text{ if } x_0 < 0$$
$$s_0 = +1 \text{ otherwise}$$
$$\alpha = 17 \text{ if } s_0 = -1$$
$$\alpha = 0 \text{ if } s_0 = 1 \text{ and } y_0 \geq 0$$
$$\alpha = 35 \text{ if } s_0 = 1 \text{ and } y_0 \leq 0$$

As in the original version, the proposed system represents $[-\pi, \pi]$ in the range of $[0, 35]$. When s_0 is negative *atan2* can be in either quadrant 2 or 3 (range $[9, 23]$) and when is positive it can be in either 1 $[0, 8]$ or 4 $[24, 35]$, being therefore defined by the $< x_0, y_0 >$ values.

Computation architecture. The proposed architecture, which is shown in Fig. 6, implements the CORDIC algorithm to compute the orientation and gradient magnitude of the pixels for three octaves in parallel. This architecture embeds two identical hardware blocks of the CORDIC algorithm, where the first one is dedicated to process data for octave 0 and the second one is shared between octaves 1 and 2. The input for the CORDIC blocks are the pixel difference in x and y directions directly computed from the pixel stream received from the DoG block. As seen in the figure, the pixel differences are performed by a simple circuit composed by synchronization buffers and subtractors.

Internally, the CORDIC represents data in fixed-point (11.8) format with 11 bits for the integer part since the maximum internal value is 594, which is given by the maximum value of the gradient magnitude multiplied by the CORDIC gain 1.647, and with 8 bits for the fraction part as, empirically, this resolution is sufficient for the application. However, the final results are given using integer

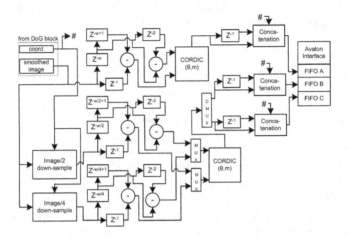

Fig. 6. Orientation and gradient magnitude computation architecture based on the CORDIC algorithm

number format where the magnitude is represented by 10 bits and the orientation by 6. In this architecture each CORDIC iteration needs 3 clock cycles and, as it has been configured to run five iterations for each pixel computation, the final result is given in 15 clocks. The result is then sent to the software block (NIOS II processor) via an Avalon bus using a DMA (Direct Memory Access) channel. To optimize the use of the data bus each word sent through the DMA channel has 32 bits allowing the concatenation of the magnitude and orientation of two pixels per word. The results in Section 3 demonstrate the performance and the necessary FPGA resources to implement this architecture.

2.4   Keypoint Detection with Stability Checking

This section presents an architecture for keypoint detection from three octaves, along with stability checking in relation to location, contrast and edge responses. The proposed hardware, shown in Fig. 7, receives as input fifteen pixel streams in parallel from the DoG block and gives as a result the features location given by the $< x, y >$ coordinates and the octave and scale numbers.

Each pixel stream is temporarily stored in on-chip memory banks in order to keep in memory the latest five image lines received from the DoG block, which is utilized to form a 5×5 image region (neighbourhood) needed for the keypoint computation. Having the image regions in memory, the first step is to analyse whether the DoG pixel located at the centre is a candidate keypoint. It is positive only if it has either the minimum or the maximum value in relation to its neighbourhood defined by a 3×3 window located at the same scale space and at the upper and lower adjacent scales (total 26 pixels). This architecture has been developed to identify candidate keypoints for an entire octave in parallel, which is performed by the *Extreme* blocks presented in Fig. 7. For every positive candidate keypoint the next step is to perform the location refinement for the coordinates $< x, y >$ and scale s, in a 3D dimensional space delimited by the neighbourhood regions located at the current keypoint scale and at one scale above and one below, which is implemented in the *Location* block. If the final location is still between scale one and three and inside of the 5×5 neighbourhood region, then the contrast and edge response functions are applied. Finally, if the candidate keypoint has been approved in all previous phases it is classified as a feature, and their coordinates, scale and octave are sent to the NIOS II processor via the Avalon bus.

The location, contrast threshold and the edge response functions were implemented using fixed-point representation (20.8). The 20 bits integer part is needed to store the intermediate values in a matrix inversion operation and the 8 bits fraction part was adopted since it provides a good balance for the application between hardware requirement and result precision. Fixed-point format allows more operations to be processed in parallel than would have in the case of using a floating-point approach in single precision as the FPGA resources needed to implement fixed-point hardware are considerably lower than the second alternative. This information is based on the fixed and floating-point libraries provided by the DK development environment from Celoxica [11]. Although we have adopted fixed-point, the high level of parallelism needed to achieve high performance has consequently increased the hardware cost for the implementation, using approximately 50% of whole system hardware. To have a feasible solution for embedding whole system on-a-chip this *Kp* hardware block is shared between the three octaves.

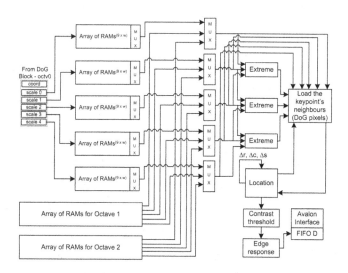

Fig. 7. Architecture for keypoint detection with stability checking

Table 1. Operational frequency and throughput for each hardware block

Hardware blocks	Function	Clock cycles per result	Freq (MHz)
DoG	all	1	pixel rate
OriMag	all	21	100
kp	keypoint detection	4 to 9	50
	stability checking	44 to 132	
	total	4 to 141	

3   Experimental Results

The hardware blocks were developed to process up to 2.3M pixels per second, which corresponds to 30 fps of 320×240 pixels each. Table 1 shows the operational frequency and throughput obtained for each block in order to achieve this performance. The DoG block is the only one that works in a pipeline mode, producing one result per clock cycle, which is given by the pixel rate. OriMag generates one result for every 21 clock cycles as the CORDIC algorithm needs five iterations to compute its results. Hence, its clock must be at least 21 times faster than the pixel rate; 100MHz is used in these experiments. For the Kp block, the throughput does not depend only on the pixel rate, it also depends on the image feature number. The fastest case is 4 clock cycles which happens when the data to be processed (DoG pixel) are located at the border region. An intermediate point is when the DoG pixel is on the image active region and is not a keypoint candidate. Another level is when the DoG pixel is a keypoint candidate and the stability checking is carried out. In this case the time varies from 44 to 132 clock cycles, depending on whether the keypoint is rejected during the checks and on how many times the location correction is realised. In the worst case, the whole operation takes 141 clocks.

If the system had been developed only for the worst case, the minimal frequency for the Kp block should be 2.3M times 141, resulting in 327MHz. For FPGA technology, such frequency for the Kp hardware is difficult to achieve. To tackle this problem the system has internal buffers to retain data whenever the Kp hardware needs to perform a stability check operation. The current block frequency is 50MHz, which is 21.7× faster than the DoG pixel rate. As a DoG pixel is rejected or classified as a keypoint candidate in 9 clocks, the remaining time is then used to compute those data from the buffers. On average fewer than 2% of the image pixels are classified as keypoints, so this solution has been implemented using internal buffer to store 1023 DoG pixels for octv0, 511 for octv1 and 127 for octv0 (see Fig. 1), and with these parameters an overflow has not occurred during our experiments.

The hardware blocks are implemented in Handel-C [11] and the Avalon components (DMA channels, FIFO controls and camera interface) and the camera interface are in VHDL. Table 2 presents the resources used to implement the system on an Altera Stratix II 2S60 FPGA [12]. Note that *whole system* in the table adds also the NIOS II processor, the camera interface and the Avalon components.

Table 2. FPGA (Altera Stratix II EP2S60F672C3) resources for each hardware block and for the whole system together

EP2S60	DSP blocks (9 bits)	RAM (Mbits)	Reg.	LUT	Max. F. (MHz)
DoG	0	0.91	7256	15137	149
OriMag	0	0.03	670	1863	184
Kp	48	0.20	2094	14357	52
Whole system	64 (22%)	1.32M (52%)	19100 (37%)	43366 (90%)	-

As can be seen, the whole system uses approximately all FPGA resources. This is because the DoG block has 18 Gaussian filters using 7×7 kernels and also because the Kp block implements in fixed-point format a considerable number of operations for the stability checking, such as the 3×3 matrix inversion. For the current FPGA practically no extra logic elements have been left for another applications. Nonetheless, it is necessary to consider that nowadays there are newer FPGAs with $3 \times$ more elements than this one.

As the DoG block implements highly customized Gaussian filters and its throughput is one pixel per clock, the DoG block can process 1940 fps of 320×240 pixels. However, when whole system is connected together the performance is limited to the slowest block and to the internal buffer overflows. Hence, these performance bottlenecks were considered in order to support 30 fps by balancing the desired performance and hardware resources.

4 Conclusion

The optimizations proposed in the hardware blocks were fundamental to allow the whole system to be embedded on-chip. Other decisions, such as the use of the CORDIC algorithm and the fixed-point format have also a significant influence in the hardware resource optimization. As a result, the system, fully embedded on an FPGA (Field-Programmable Gate Array), detects features up to 30 frames per second (320×240 pixels) and has a result quality similar to the original SIFT algorithm. The hardware blocks were developed to support any number of features per frame. The only parameter that needs to be adjusted is the internal buffer size between DoG and Kp blocks so as to avoid overflow. The proposed system has been applied to our simultaneous localization and mapping system for autonomous mobile robots [13], where robot navigation environment maps are built based on features extracted from images.

Acknowledgments

The authors would like to thank CAPES (Ref. BEX2683/ 06-7), FAPESP (Ref. 2005/02007-6) and EPSRC (Grant EP/C549481/1 and EP/C5125 96/1) for the financial support given to develop this research project.

References

1. Harris, C., Stephens, M.J.: A combined corner and edge detector. In: Avley Vision Conference, pp. 147–152 (1988)
2. Moravec, H.P.: Obstacle avoidance and navigation in the real world by a seeing robot rover. Stanford University (PhD Thesis) (1980)
3. Shi, J., Tomasi, C.: Good Features to Track. In: IEEE Conference on Computer Vision and Pattern Recognition, pp. 593–600 (1994)
4. Shokoufandeh, A., Marsic, I., Dickinson, S.J.: View-based object recognition using saliency maps. Image Vision Computing 17(5-6), 445–460 (1999)
5. Mikolajczyk, K., Schmid, C.: Scale and affine invariant interest point detectors. International Journal of Computer Vision 60(1), 63–86 (2004)
6. Lowe, D.: Distinctive image features from scale-invariant keypoints. International Journal of Computer Vision 60(2), 91–110 (2004)
7. Pettersson, N., Petersson, L.: Online stereo calibration using FPGAs. In: Proceedings of the IEEE Intelligent Vehicles Symposium, pp. 55–60 (2005)
8. Chati, H.D., Muhlbauer, F., Braun, T., Bobda, C., Berns, K.: Hardware/software co-design of a key point detector on FPGA. In: Proceedings of 15th IEEE Symposium on Field-Programmable Custom Computing Machines, pp. 355–356 (2007)
9. Beis, J.S., Lowe, D.G.: Shape Indexing Using Approximate Nearest-Neighbour Search in High-Dimensional Spaces. In: Proceedings of the Conference on Computer Vision and Pattern Recognition, pp. 1000–1006 (1997)
10. Andraka, R.: A Survey of CORDIC Algorithms for FPGA Based Computers. In: Proceedings of the ACM/SIGDA Sixth International Symposium on Field Programmable Gate Arrays, pp. 191–200 (1998)
11. Celoxica: Handel-C Language Reference Manual (User guide) (2005), http://www.celoxica.com
12. Altera: Stratix II Device Handbook (User guide) (2007), http://www.altera.com/literature/hb/stx2/stratix2_handbook.pdf
13. Bonato, V., Holanda, J.A., Marques, E.: An Embedded Multi-Camera System for Simultaneous Localization and Mapping. In: Bertels, K., Cardoso, J.M.P., Vassiliadis, S. (eds.) ARC 2006. LNCS, vol. 3985, pp. 109–114. Springer, Heidelberg (2006)

Reconfigurable HW/SW Architecture of a Real-Time Driver Assistance System

Josef Angermeier[1], Ulrich Batzer[1], Mateusz Majer[1], Jürgen Teich[1], Christopher Claus[2], and Walter Stechele[2]

[1] University of Erlangen-Nuremberg
[2] Technical University of Munich

Abstract. Driver assistance systems significantly increase the driving comfort and can prevent accidents. On the other side, they require high performance and computations need to adopt to the environment to reach their goals. Reconfigurable architectures offer the requested flexibility and performance, if care is taken to partition the tasks in hardware and software parts. Elsewise, real-time requirements can't be fulfilled. In this paper, the implementation and a hardware/software partitioning of a driver assistance system for a reconfigurable architecture are presented. The assistance system detects taillights of ahead moving vehicles in dark environments or in tunnels and visualizes the results. A detailed description of the implementation on a reconfigurable platform is given. Furthermore, the experimental results demonstrate the effectiveness of the approach.

1 Introduction

Driver assistance systems are gaining increased importance in the automotive sector. Cars get equipped with additional sensors and displays in order to, e.g., help the driver to smoothly back into a parking space. Real-time processing is an important requirement in most driver assistance systems, as the driver needs an immediate response to his actions. Furthermore, driver assistance is a highly performance-sensitive task, especially if image processing is involved. In video-based driver assistance systems, a camera records the view seen from the front window, performs certain computation steps on the images, and returns the driver a visualization of the results on a display. This visualization may significantly contribute to a higher level of driving comfort and prevent serious accidents. What kind of assistance is be appropriate depends on the driving context, e.g., when moving on the highway, no parking assistance is needed. Furthermore, driving by night or by day, through a tunnel or in the countryside, all may require different pattern recognition algorithms to detect, e.g., cars moving in front or sign-postings besides the lane. In short, the driving assistance systems must adapt to the environment along the road.

Reconfigurable systems, like FPGAs-based platforms, may be engaged to fulfill all the above mentioned requirements. They combine performance and flexibility. Tasks implemented in hardware can be loaded and executed in parallel on

R. Woods et al. (Eds.): ARC 2008, LNCS 4943, pp. 149–159, 2008.

the dynamically partially reconfigurable hardware and thus achieve a high performance. In contrast, control-sensitive tasks are rather implemented as software tasks and executed on the control CPU of the applied reconfigurable platform. Thus, to effectively use reconfigurable architectures for driver assistance, the tasks must be wisely partitioned in software and hardware parts in the design phase.

In this paper, we concentrate on one specific problem in driver assistance: detecting vehicles in dark environments in real-time. This will help a driver at night or in a tunnel to recognize moving cars ahead more quickly. Our approach is based on gray-scale images taken by a low-cost camera mounted in the driver's vehicle. A self-developed taillight-recognition algorithm is used on these video images. Thus, moving cars in front are detected by their taillights. The detected cars and lights, respectively, are presented to the driver on a display.

In the following section, related image recognition approaches for driver assistance systems are presented. In Section 2, the taillight recognition algorithm is explained shortly. In Section 4, the applied reconfigurable platform is introduced. In Section 5 a HW/SW partitioning of the algorithm on the specified platform is proposed. In Section 6, the implementation details of the taillight algorithm and required platform extensions are given. In the final section, this paper is summarized and an outlook is given.

2   Related Work

Many authors have described their work on hardware acceleration for image processing. Venkatesan et. al describe in [1] the implementation of a hardware accelerator for Edge detection based on the Canny edge filter. Compared to a PC based solution running on a PentiumIII with 1.3 GHz the processing could be accelerated by a factor of 20. In [2] the authors present an implementation for image segmentation algorithm that was compared against a software solution running on a PentiumIV with 2.4 GHz. Although running at a system frequency of only 66 Mhz, a performance improvement between 22% and 57% is reported. Benkrid et. al published an FPGA implementation of Connected Component Labeling in [3] which took 1.57 seconds to label an image (1024x1024 resolution). Compared to the equivalent software realization running on a 1.6 GHz Pentium-IV PC which took 18.17 seconds the FPGA-based solution is more than ten times faster. This publications prove that hardware acceleration in the field of image processing is meaningful and necessary especially for image pre-processing steps (e.g. segmentation). The authors in [4] describe the Hardware/Software Co-Design of a tracking system on an FPGA. The portions of the algorithm most appropriate for hardware were identified and implemented. A meaningful HW/SW partitioning of an algorithm to detect cars by their taillights as well as a detailed description of the algorithm itself is presented in [5]. This algorithm, which is part of the Autovision project [6] was modified and implemented on the ESM platform to benefit from its slot-based architecture which is suitable for dynamic partial reconfiguration.

3   Taillight Recognition

In order to understand the behaviour of the TaillightEngine the algortihm is described briefly. A detailed version can be found in [5]. First, the input data is extracted from the video stream received from the camera mounted at the own vehicle. In the next step, a pattern matching is done by the so-called *Spotlight-Engine* module. It identifies the light sources in the pictures. Based on these, the *LabelingEngine* performs a segmentation of the recognized light sources. The result is a list of lights. In a next step, the static light sources, e.g., street lanterns, are determined and sorted out of the light list. In the following step, light pairs are build out of the list of non-static lights. Then, the probability of the pair being a taillight of an ahead moving vehicle is analyzed. Finally, a list of valid taillights is sent to the visualization module in order to signal the driver the detected vehicles moving ahead. A complete overview of the data flow of the *TaillightEngine* is shown in Figure 3.

3.1   SpotlightEngine

In the first processing step of the *TaillightEngine*, the *SpotlightEngine* module performs a pattern matching in which the individual light sources in the image are identified. Thus, the *SpotlightEngine* recognizes taillights in a picture by finding bright pixels within a roughly square shape surrounded by distinctly darker pixels. The general form of the pattern is illustrated in Figure 1a). P_O denotes the mask for the brightness range of possible lights, P_U the mask of the dark environment. This pattern is applied to every pixel in the current image, and the darkest pixel in P_O is determined. If there is no brighter pixel in P_U, P_O is marked as a light source.

A demonstration of this approach is illustrated in Figure 1b). Hereby, a car taillight pattern is detected. In Figure 1c) a lane is not recognized as light since the lane is bright in the area of P_O and exhibits the same brightness in P_U.

3.2   LabelingEngine

In the second step of the processing chain, segmentation is done by the *LabelingEngine*. Light points are grouped together to regions and based on these a summary list is compiled. Each region data consists of the coordinates of the included pixels and their overall brightness. The regions are recognized in a pixel-based manner, similar as in the *SpotlightEngine*. This approach is also known as "Connected Component Labeling" [3].

3.3   Determination of Static Lights

The aforementioned processing of the *SpotlightEngine* and the *LabelingEngine* result in a list of light sources. In the next step, the static lights, e.g., idle vehicles, roadway lighting or reflections of roadway restrictions, are filtered out of the list. Previous images and light sources lists, respectively are used to determine a

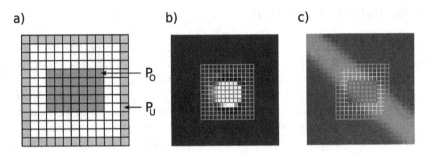

Fig. 1. a) Light pattern in *SpotlightEngine*, b) applied to taillight in image and c) applied to lane

motion vector for each light source. The apparent movement of a static light is obviously not caused by a motion of the static light, but by the movement of the own vehicle and the camera, respectively. Thus, the light's motion vector can be used to find out, whether it is static or not. Furthermore, direction changes of the road or fluctuating lighting can lead to motion vectors of static objects, which don't exactly point in the opposite direction of the vanishing point. Therefore, more than just two subsequent images are considered to determine the motion vector. The experiments proofed that this increases the accuracy of the results.

3.4 Determining Light Pairs

The second processing step on the light sources list examines the relationship between two or more individual lights. Our objective is to find light pairs, which correspond to the taillights of a moving vehicle. There are initially $\binom{n}{2} = \frac{n!}{2!(n-2)!}$ light pairs from the n lights in the list. Each light pair is evaluated according to a sum of criteria, resulting in a value between 0 (worst value) and 1000 (best value). This indicates the probability that the light pair in the image corresponds to a taillight of a moving vehicle.

4   Architecture

For the implementation of the drive assistance system, we apply a self-developed, dynamically partially reconfigurable platform called *ESM* [7,8]. The platform is centered around an FPGA serving as the main reconfigurable engine and an FPGA realizing a crossbar switch, see Fig. 2. They are separated into two physical boards called BabyBoard and MotherBoard and are implemented using a Xilinx Virtex-II 6000 and a Spartan-II 600 FPGA [9], respectively. The slot-based architecture of the ESM consists of the Virtex-II FPGA on the BabyBoard, the so-called *Main FPGA*, local SRAM memories, configuration memory, and a reconfiguration manager. In Figure 2 the two connected boards of the platform are shown. Additionally, there exists a control CPU, a PowerPC MPC875, which schedules the configuration of the *Main FPGA*.

The main idea of the ESM architecture is to accelerate application development as well as research in the area of partially reconfigurable hardware. The advantage of the ESM platform is its unique slot-based architecture which allows to configure individual hardware modules independently of their peripheral needs at run-time arranged in 1-D vertical slots. A separate crossbar switch is in charge of routing dynamically the data from the periphery, e.g., a video input signal, to the current position of the responsible hardware module. We decided to implement the crossbar off-chip on the Motherboard in order to have as many resources free on the FPGA for partially reconfigurable modules.

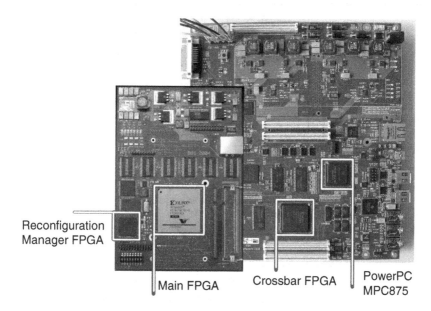

Fig. 2. Implementation of the ESM BabyBoard and MotherBoard. Technical data sheets are available at http://www.r-space.de

Thus, the ESM architecture is based on the flexible decoupling of the FPGA I/O-pins from a direct connection to an interface chip. This flexibility allows the independent placement of application modules in any available slot at run-time. As a result, run-time placement is not constrained by physical I/O-pin locations as the I/O-pin routing is done automatically in the crossbar.

5   HW/SW Partitioning

On the one side, the taillight recognition system consists of image processing operations on each camera image. On the other side, more complex operations must be applied for processing a list of recognized lights. Different criterions are evaluated to differentiate between static lights and vehicle taillights. The pixel-level image operations are simple and may be executed in parallel. Therefore,

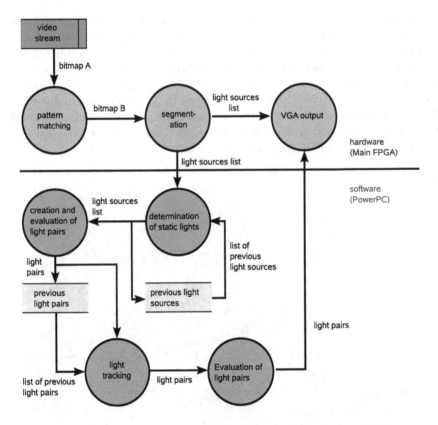

Fig. 3. HW/SW partitioning of the *TaillightEngine* on the ESM

they should be implemented in hardware. The operations on the light lists are more complex and include control-intensive steps. Therefore, these operations should be partially or completely implemented on the ESM in software. Hereby, our decision was based on two measurements. First, we investigated the data transfer rate between a hardware task and a software task on the *ESM* platform. Secondly, we evaluated the control CPU performance with a prototype algorithm of the light list processing steps. Based on these results, we decided to completely implement those tasks in software (see Figure 3, because it allows the extension and modification of those tasks in a very short time.

6   Implementation

The implementation of the *TaillightEngine* on the ESM corresponds to the hardware/software partitioning described in Figure 3. The data transfer between the control CPU and the hardware modules on the *Main FPGA* required a new hardware/software communication module. This is presented in the following subsection 6.1. The actual implementation of the hardware and software components of the *TaillightEngine* is given in subsection 6.2.

6.1 HW/SW Communication

The *Main FPGA* and the control CPU can only communicate via the crossbar, as they do not share any common clock, memory or signals. The control CPU is connected to the crossbar FPGA with its full 32 bit address and data bus. The crossbar contains a register bank that is transparently mapped into the PowerPC address space. Access to these registers is implemented through simple memory I/O read or write functions. The software drivers are implemented as Linux character device drivers. They control the access to the crossbar register bank and are responsible for read and write access to the memory mapped I/O registers. After successful driver installation a custom file descriptor */dev/hwswcom* is available for any software application. In order to ease the software interface, a custom software library is provided, named *libhwswcom*. This library implements functions necessary for sending or receiving whole data buffers to and from the *Main FPGA*.

The communication between the *Main FPGA* and the crossbar is realized with asynchronous FIFOs. These use a four-way handshake as the *Main FPGA* and the crossbar do not have a common clock. The FIFO implemented for the crossbar to *Main FPGA* communication can store 4096 words of 32 bits. The FIFO of the control CPU can store 2048 words of 32 bits. Both FIFOs are realized using BlockRAMs but can also be implemented using distributed RAM. In order to minimize the number of used I/O pins on the *Main FPGA* the communication channel is realized with a 2 bit wide data bus pair with the aforementioned four-way handshake.

6.2 Taillight Engine

The pattern matching of the *SpotlightEngine* is realized by a hardware module for the *Main FPGA*. The brightness of each pixel in the current frame is compared to the border of the 11x11 pattern matrix (see Figure 4a)). This processing step is based on fast access to the image data. Due to the differing memory architecture of the ESM, a new memory interface and a new addressing sequence of the image data was required.

One option is to store the current image in the external single-ported SRAMs of the ESM. A bandwidth saving method of loading the pixel matrix has to be used for fast processing. In each step, the matrix is shifted vertically by one pixel (see Figure 4b)). By doing so, per pixel only the first line of the matrix has to be loaded from the SRAM. The pixels in the outer columns and in the last line are made available by shift registers or FIFO buffers (see Figure 4b)). Still, this method requires several clock cycles per pixel.

Another option was to use the internal BlockRAMs on the Xilinx Virtex-II 6000 FPGA [9], which has a capacity of 2592 Kbit. This size is sufficient to store a grayscale image also in full VGA resolution ($640 \cdot 480 \cdot 8$ bit $= 2457$ Kbit).

Furthermore, BlockRAMs offer a higher bandwidth and also supports dual-port access. This enables the loading of the first and the last line of pixels in a single clock cycle (see Figure 4c)). The first, fifth and eleventh column of pixels can be contained in shift registers.

Due to the increased performance of the BlockRAMs, the latter approach was applied. Thus, a BlockRAM controller with a bandwidth of 128 bit is implemented to read 80 bits of each line in the matrix. In fact, 16 internal BlockRAMs are cascaded to to store the pixel data required by the matrix. Thus, the memory interface allows a byte-by-byte addressing and may also be used with other pattern matrices.

Furthermore, the actual implementation uses images with a size of $384 \cdot 288 \cdot 8$ bits = 110592 bits (QVGA). Therefore, each BlockRAM contains 110592/16 bits = 6912 bit. Based on the new memory interface, the pattern matrix can be applied in each clock cycle. The brightness of the pixel in the middle of the matrix is compared with the brightest pixel at the border. First, the maximum brightness of the 40 pixels at the border is determined and afterwards compared with the middle point. A pipeline architecture is applied to increase the execution time. A maximum number of pixel comparisons is performed in each pipeline stage. With a total of 40 pixels, the pipeline consists of $\lceil ld(40) \rceil = 6$ stages. Furthermore, extra effort is spent to handle pixels at the border of the image. Thus, also lights in these regions are now recognized.

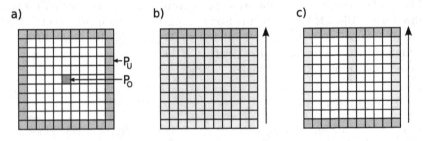

Fig. 4. Efficient pattern matching sequence with the new memory interface

Another BlockRAM is used to store the results of the pattern matching. For each pixel a zero is written to the corresponding position in this buffer, if the pixel in the image is darker than these at the border of the matrix. Elsewise, the difference in their brightness values is saved.

The *LabelingEngine* processes the output buffer of the *SplotlightEngine*. Regions with a similar positive difference value are grouped together to light regions. Only minor modifications on the original VHDL sources were required for the implementation on the ESM. A list of light sources is created as a result.

The new hardware-software communication module (see the section above) is used to transfer this list to the external control CPU. There, all possible light pairs are created and the valid taillights are filtered out. Afterwards, this list of detected taillights is sent back to the *Main FPGA*. The original C sources of these

Fig. 5. ESM platform visualizing detected static lights by green boxes and taillights by red boxes in the video output stream

algorithms were adopted to use the hardware-software communication module and ported to the ESM control CPU. Based on the results of the software, the visualization module draws green boxes around static light pairs and red boxes around taillights in the input image (see Figure 5).

7   Experimental Results

Runtime analysis and worst-case tests were performed on video data with a frame rate of 25 frames per second. The image resolution of each video frame is 384x288 pixels. Thus, the hardware and software components have to finish each execution run within 40 ms.

The hardware runtime can be calculated accurately. Both *SpotlightEngine* and *LabelingEngine* are working at 50 MHz. The *SpotlightEngine* is based on a hard real time clock. It calculates one pixel per clock. An exceptionally low amount of only four clocks is needed at the start of each column. During this time, the pixel matrix is initialized with the proper values. There is no additional wait time at the end of a column, neither is there a wait time at the end of an image. This is obtained by starting the *LabelingEngine* while the *SpotlightEngines* pipeline is still filled up. The resulting runtime for the *SpotlightEngine* can be calculated by:

$$t_{Spotlight} = \frac{w \cdot (h + (\lceil N/4 \rceil) + 1)}{f_{HW}}$$

With h, w representing height and width of the image, N being the dimension of the pixel matrix. For an image size of 384x288 and a 11x11 pixel matrix, the runtime can be calculated by $t_{Spotlight} = 2.23$ ms.

The runtime of the *LabelingEngine* is limited by an absolute upper bound of four clocks per pixel. The needed time depends on the amount of white pixels, i.e. lights recognized by the *SpotlightEngine*. There is no additional time needed for initialization, neither to finish the calculation.

$$t_{Labeling} = \frac{h \cdot w \cdot (4 \cdot p + 2 \cdot (1 - p))}{f_{HW}}$$

With h, w representing the image size. p is the probability for each pixel to be a light pixel extending an existing light region. As experience shows, p is lesser than 0.01 in common video data. The obtained runtime at $p = 0.01$ is $t_{Labeling} = 4.46ms$.

The total hardware runtime is the sum of $t_{Spotlight}$ and $t_{Labeling}$. With the data being used, an upper bound of $t_{HW} = t_{Spotlight} + t_{Labeling} \leq 2.23ms + 4.46ms = 6.69ms$ can be given. The maximal clock speed is at 52,1 Mhz, 90% of the BlockRAMs and 30% of the FPGA logic resources are currently used.

8   Conclusion

In this paper, we present an efficient, reconfigurable HW/SW architecture for a real-time vehicle recognition system. Ahead moving vehicles are recognized in the dark or in a tunnel by their taillights. We propose HW/SW partitioning in which the simple image operations are implemented in hardware. Based on results of prototype implementations and performance measurements, all complex operations evaluating the light sources are covered in our approach by software parts. The experimental results demonstrate the effectiveness of this partitioning. Furthermore, they show that the real-time requirements can be met.

In further work, additional assistance modules, e.g., lane detection for bright or dark environments, may be integrated in the current work. Dynamic reconfiguration can be applied to switch between the assistance modules, depending on the current environment. For example, the driver assistance system could be aware of a nearby tunnel entrance by corresponding maps and GPS-coordinates, and thus trigger the reconfiguration of the taillight module.

References

1. Venkatesan, M., Rao, D.V.: Hardware acceleration of edge detection algorithm on fpgas. Celoxica Inc. research papers (2004),
   http://www.celoxica.com/techlib/files/CEL-W040414XRZ-282.pdf

2. Bannister, R., Gregg, D., Simon Wilson, A.N.: Fpga implementation of an image segmentation algorithm using logarithmic arithmetic. In: 48th Midwest Symposium Circuits and Systems, vol. 1, pp. 810–813, August 7-10 (2005)
3. Benkrid, K., Sukhsawas, S., Crookes, D., Benkrid, A.: An fpga-based image connected component labeller. In: Y. K. Cheung, P., Constantinides, G.A. (eds.) FPL 2003. LNCS, vol. 2778, pp. 1012–1015. Springer, Heidelberg (2003)
4. Schlessman, J., Chen, C.Y., Wolf, W., Ozer, B., Fujino, K., Itoh, K.: Hardware/software co-design of an fpga-based embedded tracking system. In: CVPRW 2006: Proceedings of the 2006 Conference on Computer Vision and Pattern Recognition Workshop, p. 123, IEEE Computer Society, Washington (2006)
5. Alt, N., Claus, C., Stechele, W.: Hardware/software architecture of an algorithm for vision-based real-time vehicle detection in dark environments. In: DATE 2008: Proceedings of the conference on Design, automation and test in Europe, Munich, Germany (2008)
6. Claus, C., Stechele, W., Herkersdorf, A.: Autovision - a run-time reconfigurable mpsoc architecture for future driver assistance systems. Information Technology 49(3), 181–186 (2007)
7. Bobda, C., Majer, M., Ahmadinia, A., Haller, T., Linarth, A., Teich, J., Fekete, S., van der Veen, J.: The Erlangen Slot Machine: A Highly Flexible FPGA-Based Reconfigurable Platform, Napa, CA, USA, pp. 319–320 (2005)
8. Angermeier, J., Göhringer, D., Majer, M., Teich, J., Fekete, S.P., der Veen, J.V.: The erlangen slot machine - a platform for interdisciplinary research in dynamically reconfigurable computing. Information Technology 49, 143–148 (2007)
9. Xilinx, Inc.: Virtex-II Platform FPGAs: Complete Data Sheet (2005), http://www.xilinx.com/

A New Self-managing Hardware Design Approach for FPGA-Based Reconfigurable Systems

S. Jovanović, C. Tanougast, and S. Weber

Université Henri Poincaré - Nancy 1
Laboratoire d'instrumentation et électronique (LIEN)
54506 Vandoeuvre lès Nancy, France
slavisa.jovanovic@lien.uhp-nancy.fr

Abstract. Given the scale and complexity of today's systems, it is of increasing importance that they handle and manage system's problems on their own in an intelligent and autonomous way. To cope with all non-deterministic changes and events that dynamically occur in a system's environment, a new "self-managing based" design approaches must be developed. Within this framework, an architectural network-based approach can be a good solution for the high demanding computation and self-managing needs. In this paper, we present the basic concept of such a design approach, its main properties and uses. A case study that proves the feasibility of this approach is demonstrated and validated on a small image-processing application.

1 Introduction

In literature, we can find lots of terms and definitions relative to a system that exhibits a form of a life-like system. This system is characterized by intelligent and autonomous way of the system handling and managing itself. Within this framework, the term of self-organization appears. Finding a clear definition of this term that would satisfy everyone is extremely difficult because the concepts behind it are still only partially understood. However, one considers that the self-organizing systems are the systems that try to behave like natural systems whose behaviour emerges and evolves without an outside intervention or programming [1]. The main properties of these systems are high degree of robustness, flexibility and adaptability allowing tackling problems far more complex than any computer system ever made. They are also characterized by: interactivity, dynamic, decentralized control, increase in order of their internal structure and autonomy.

Another more restrictive and less general term relative to self-organization that we can find in literature is the term of autonomic computing [2]. The autonomic computing systems function largely independently of their human supervisors, adapting, correcting and repairing themselves whenever a problem

R. Woods et al. (Eds.): ARC 2008, LNCS 4943, pp. 160–171, 2008.

occurs. They called them autonomic, referring to the autonomic nervous system which controls bodily functions such as respiration and heart rate without requiring any conscious actions by the human being.

Implementation of self-* properties in technical domains presents a great challenge. This work seems more probable and realistic with the advent of FPGA reconfigurable technology. To face all non-deterministic (wished or unwished) events without the external control, such systems must have possibilities to evolve and adapt their functionality by changing their hardware structure. Some advantages of the FPGA reconfigurable technology, such as a spatio-temporal allocation by a run time reconfiguration and a partial reconfiguration match very well to these dynamically changing environments [8, 7]. Within this framework, we present our new design approach which allows us to design a system exhibiting a sort of self-managing properties.

This paper is organized as follows. In the Section 2 we present some related work on architectural concepts for autonomic computing systems. Section 3 details our design approach. The basic concept of this approach and its main properties are presented. Section 4 proves the feasibility of this approach on an image-processing application. At the end, in Section 5 some conclusions are given.

2   Background and Related Work

The Autonomic Computing was presented as an IBM initiative to face the growing IT (*Information Technology*) complexity crisis [2, 9]. As a result of this initiative, the four main areas of self-management, as an essence of the autonomic computing, are defined:

- Self-configuration : automatically configure components according to high-level policies to adapt them to different environments
- Self-optimization: Automatically monitor and adapt resources making appropriate choices to ensure optimal functioning regarding the defined requirements
- Self-healing: Automatically detect, diagnose, and repair hardware and software faults.
- Self-protection: Anticipate, identify, and prevent from arbitrary attacks and systemwide failures

IBM has expanded these autonomic and self-management concepts with the following additional criteria [4, 5, 6]:

- The system must perform something like healing - recovering from routine and external events
- The system continually optimizes, never maintaining the status quo
- The system requires self-knowledge of the whole and the components of the system

The basic building block of an autonomic system is the *autonomic element*. It consists of a managed element and its autonomic manager that controls it in accordance with defined policies. The managed element can be either a hardware or software resource or a combination of both. Essentially, an autonomic element consists of a closed control loop which can theoretically can control a system without an external intervention.

In [12], the authors describe behavioural properties of the autonomic elements, their interactions and how to build an autonomic system starting from a collection of the autonomic elements. They define some required behaviour of the autonomic elements. The autonomic element must handle problems locally, whenever possible. Its services must be defined accurately and in a transparent way to the other neighbouring elements. It must reject any services that would violate its policies or agreements. They also define different forms of policy at different level of specifications that the autonomic elements must respect in order to ensure desired behaviour. An overview of the policy management for the Autonomic Computing is given in [10].

In [11], the authors state that the core problems still remain. Those are the lack of appropriate standards and a precise definition describing self-managing system, the absence of mechanism for rendering self-managing systems adaptive and capability to learn . They expect the other scientific disciplines such as biology, physics and sociology to contribute towards vital concepts enabling the current systems to overcome existing problems of self-management.

An autonomic system by these definitions is highly desirable in the context of either software or hardware applications or a combination of both. For designing a hardware autonomic computing system with above mentioned properties, some aspects regarding the real-time constraints, failure-detection and fault-tolerance must be considered. Some works on failure-detection have already been done [3]. In contrast with these previous works based generally on software approaches, we focus on hardware self-management approach that realize the self-* properties without a closed control loop.

3   Architectural Design Approach for Self-management

3.1   Introduction

We apply a classic reductionist approach for a better understanding of functioning of how the whole system functions. Let us suppose that there is a system S which is composed of N modules E_i, $0 < i < N$, that can communicate and exchange data with each other. Each module E_i carries out a function e_i at a given time. Each module's function presents a part of a set of the available functions (or services) that could be accomplished by the given module, S_i, and contributes to the system's global function e_g. Defined that way, the system can be described by the following set of expressions:

$$e_1 \in S_1, S_1 = \left\{ e_{1_1}, e_{1_2}, ..., e_{1_{n_1}} \right\}$$

$$e_2 \in S_2, S_2 = \left\{ e_{2_1}, e_{2_2}, ..., e_{2_{n_2}} \right\}$$

$$\vdots \tag{1}$$

$$e_N \in S_N, S_N = \left\{ e_{N_1}, e_{N_2}, ..., e_{N_{n_N}} \right\}$$

$$e_g \in S_g, S_g = \left\{ e_{g_1}, e_{g_2}, ..., e_{g_{n_g}} \right\}$$

$$e_g = \cup_{i=1}^{N} e_i$$

where $n_g = n_1 n_2 \ldots n_N$ is the maximal number of different functions that this system can perform with a guaranteed service quality. Some functions of the system can be performed with a smaller number of modules to the detriment of the system's performances.

Let us also suppose that for each module's function e_i exists a set of the other modules' functions $\{e_{i_1}, e_{i_2}, \ldots, e_{i_r}\}$ ($i \neq i_1 \neq i_2 \neq \ldots \neq i_r$ and $r \geq 3$) that can at the same time successfully replace the function concerned and perform their own functions, as it presented by expression 2:

$$e_i \subset (e_{i_1} \cup e_{i_2} \cup \ldots e_{i_r}) \tag{2}$$

Without a loss of generality, we limit the set of the modules' functions to three and consider that the modules whose functions are in the given set of functions present direct neighbouring modules. This means for each group of 4 neighboring modules of the system, the statement described by the expression 2 is always valid. For a rectangular structure of modules $n_c \times n_r$, where n_c and n_r are numbers of columns and rows respectively, and for a module E_{ij} with (i, j) coordinates ($0 < i < n_c, 0 < j < n_r$), there exist 4 sets of functions which can replace functionally the concerned module (see Figure 1).

3.2   Modules Awareness - Flux

To make all modules aware of their neighbours and their states, we have introduced a dynamic data stream called *flux*. This is the main originality of our work. The main objective of this data stream is to gather information about the states of the modules and to inform the modules about the states of their neighboring modules.

The flux circulates through the module, gathers information about its function, current functioning mode, states and then informs the other modules about it. The flux is not a control structure. It does not impose any decisions on the module. Its main role is gathering and informing. On the other hand, the flux helps modules to make decisions taking into account agreements with their direct neighbours and their states.

Neither of the modules can make a decision before it informs its direct neighbours and gets from them a sort of agreement for the wished decision. Whenever a change of some parameters occurs, each module "proposes" its solution and

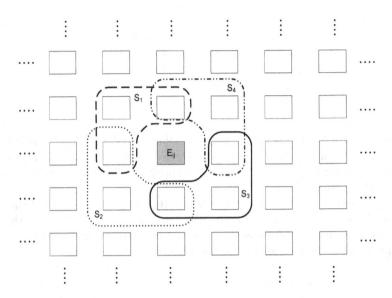

Fig. 1. For module E_{ij} there exist 4 sets of functions with which it can be replaced

through the flux informs other modules about the change and action that it is going to perform. Other modules analyse the flux, become aware of the changes and give a (dis)agreement for the proposed actions and eventually if they agree with the actions that will be taken, complement them with their own actions. Each module updates the flux about its intentions and actions that it will take.

If we compare our module and the *autonomic element* as defined in autonomic computing [2, 9], the "module's *manager*" makes decisions in accordance with the neighbouring modules. This is the consequence of its continuous monitoring and controlling by the other modules through the flux. That way the module cannot make a decision that would violate its own and policies and agreements of the other modules.

Moreover, the flux allows the system to handle the problems locally, whenever it is possible. For example, it can happen that a module discovers that its neighbouring modules which is on the way of the flux cannot perform the demanding services. In that case, it tries with the other modules affected by the same flux, to resolve the existing problem. If they do not succeed in it, there are three more fluxes comprising the same module and their modules will try to resolve the problem as well. In the worst case, if the problem cannot be solved locally, the rest of the system will become progressively aware of it. This is presented in Figure 2. The direct neighbouring modules of the module E_{ij} with the problem are shaded and surrounded by the first dotted circle. If they do not succeed in solving of the problem, the other modules (between two dotted circles) become aware of it and so on for the rest of the system.

3.3   Flux Structure

Figure 3 details a structure of the flux affecting 4 modules. The number of fields corresponds to the number of modules affected by the flux and it can be extended. Each module has its field in the flux. Each module's field contains several subfields. The number of subfields is not limited and it can be extended depending on designer's concepts. Each subfield refers to a module's parameter. These parameters give information about the functional correctness, the intention of module removing (for reconfigurable systems), the module's current functioning mode and wished functioning mode. The current functioning mode is the function which the module executes at given time. The wished functioning mode is the future functioning mode that will be executed by the module and it presents a result of an analysis of functioning modes of other modules affected by the same flux. This is more detailed in the next section. In Figure 3, the first subfield denotes the functional verification information. If this subfield is set, the module executes correctly its function otherwise its function is corrupted and it must be replaced. If a module must be replaced because of its corrupted function or from another reason (i.e. defragmentation of a reconfigurable area), the second subfield called "Presence" indicates these information. The current functioning mode is contained in this subfield whereas the wished functioning mode is placed in the last one (see figure 3).

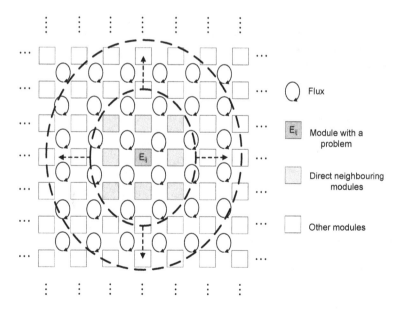

Fig. 2. The system solves the existing problem locally, if it is possible, if not, the rest of the system becomes aware of it. The first neighouring modules, if they cannot solve the problem, through the fluxes inform progressively the rest of the system. The arrows indicate the sense of the system's awareness for the existing problem.

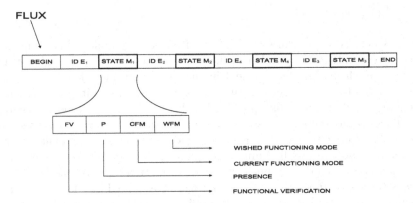

Fig. 3. An example of the flux in the case when it covers a group of 4 modules

3.4 Modules Descriptors

To ensure establishing and maintening relationships with the other modules through the flux, the module uses *descriptors*. The descriptor is defined as a static structure that is used to describe the module in an accurate way.

Each descriptor gives a faithful image of the module. It contains module's functioning modes, services that it can deliver, the ways how the services can be replaced and all information that could be useful for the other modules.

The descriptor is created at the system's designing phase but can be updated at run-time, if the concerned module would like to add some additional services to its basic set of services. The descriptor of a module is placed in its first neighbouring module in the way of circulation of the flux. That way, in the

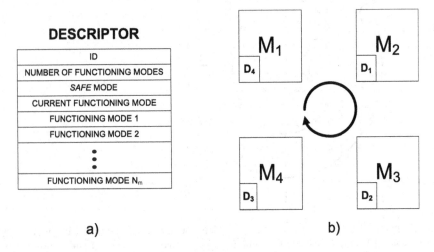

Fig. 4. a) Descriptor b) Placement of descriptors in a group of 4 modules affected by the same flux

case of the complete failure of the concerned module, the neighbouring modules have the "recipe" to recover its services and thus the global system function. This mechanism is presented in Figure 4b on the example of 4 modules. Each module contains its own descriptor and the descriptor of its direct neighbour. In Figure 4a is presented the descriptor which contains only functioning modes of other modules. The module's descriptor can be changed at the run-time, if the concerned module changes its structure or gets some "new functions" that are not previously described by the descriptor.

3.5   Self-management through the Flux Verification

Figure 6 shows the control flow graph of the flux verication block. Each module contains this block in which the received flux is analysed and treated. Firstly, each module verifies the states of other modules affected by the flux. Secondly, it updates its own states taking into account the states of other modules. For example, in the case of 4 modules covered by the flux, each module verifies the states of 3 others (see Figure 5).

The flux verification part is presented in Figure 6 with the dotted block called "Verification". Each subfield of each module's field is analysed. For instance, if the functional verification field of a module refers to a functional corruption of the module, the module that analyses the flux must take some actions and must adapt its functioning to the occurred problem. If it has not the descriptor of the faulty module, it waits for it from the direct neighbouring module placed in the sense of circulation of the flux. If the module has the descriptor of the faulty module, it will send it with the flux to other modules. Once the descriptor is received, the module compares its own descriptor with the one of the faulty module and it takes a decision. It chooses another functioning mode in which it will cover its own function and a part of the function of the faulty module. This phase is presented with the "Decision making" block in Figure 6. After having verified all modules' states, the flux verification block of the module updates its own states and sends the flux and eventually the descriptor to other modules.

Each module except the faulty one carries out the same procedure and after one flux circulation tour is finished, the faulty module module should be replaced by other modules. Of course the modules take also into account the changing of the flux circulation path which will not take anymore the faulty module.

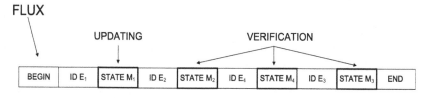

Fig. 5. Each module verifies the fields of the flux corresponding to the states of other modules affected by the flux and updates only the field corresponding to its own states

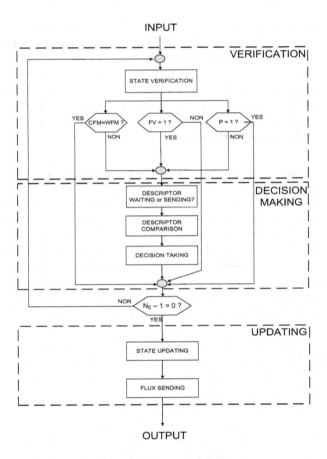

Fig. 6. Flux verification

This self-managing of the modules is possible if we have only one failure or another demand at the time. This approach can be simply extended to cover other cases but that will cause large system area overheads.

4   Case Study

We have implemented the flux on the example of an edge-detection image-processing application. This application is composed of an averaging filter followed by two spatial edge detectors and a final gradient computing [13]. The data-flow graph of this application is divided in four parts, each part is carried out in one module (see Figure 7a). For each module we have added some additional resources in order to respect the statement 2 from Section 3. That means, each of the 4 presented modules can be replaced with 3 others in the detriment of system's performances. These additional logics are presented with the M_{1p}, M_{2p}, M_{3p} and M_{4p} respectively for the M_1, M_2, M_3 and M_4 modules

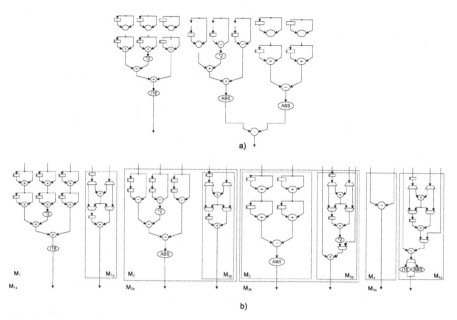

Fig. 7. Case study: an edge-detection image-processing application implemented on the CuNoC using proposed design approach: a) DFG of the application before and b) after applying proposed design approach

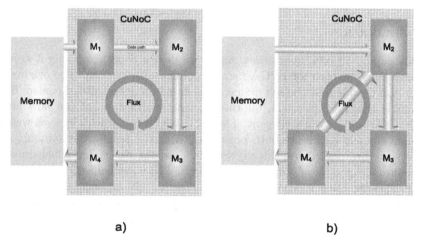

Fig. 8. Simulation cases before (a) and after (b) the failure of the module M_1

(see Figure 7b). We have used the descriptors which contain only the modules' functioning modes. As a communication medium for the modules, we have used the 4×4 CuNoC communication approach [15, 14]. The flux also circulates via the CuNoC.

We have simulated the complete failure of each module of the system at different times. Figure 7a illustrates the applied procedure on the failure of the module $M1$.

At a given time, the problem occurs and the other modules ($M2$, $M3$ and $M4$) through the flux become aware of it and make some decisions. They chose another functioning mode which covers a part of the M_1 function. After a while when the flux accomplished the circulation tour and all modules became aware of the problem, all services of the module $M1$ are replaced. Then the global function of the system is established again. The system's response time to occurred problem is equal to a time needed to flux to accomplish the circulation tour. During this time, all modules keep running their previous services till they become aware of existing problem of one of the modules. For the M_1 failure simulation case, instead of the previous data path comprising the modules $M1$, $M2$, $M3$ and $M4$, the new data path comprises only of $M2$, $M3$ and $M4$ but in the sequence $M2 - M3 - M4 - M2 - M3 - M4$. The first sequence of the modules $M2$, $M3$ and $M4$ is used to replace the function of the module M_1, and second one for their own functions. This is the main reason for the system's response time after reestablishing the system's global function which is much bigger than before.

We have implemented the system on Xilinx Virtex IV technology [16]. The implementation results show an area overhead of about 40 % with regard to the system without self-managing properties. This overhead is mostly due to additional logics which were implemented (M_{1p},M_{2p},M_{3p} and M_{4p}) in order to respect the statement 2 from Section 3. The area overhead due to flux verification block per computing module is insignificant.

5   Conclusion

In this paper, we presented a new hardware design concept making a system self-managing adapted for FPGA based reconfigurable systems. The originality of our approach is that the self managing is based on decentralized control from a scalable stream data which inform only the specification of the new interactions between system's element. The basic concept of this design, as well as its main characteristics are both presented. We have defined the dynamic and static structures called respectively *the flux* and *the descriptor* which present the main mechanisms of our design approach. These mechanisms are validated on an edge-detection image-processing application. As an ongoing work, some learning mechanisms that allow learning from past experience and remember effective responses are about to be considered as well as failure-detection and fault-tolerance mechanisms.

References

[1] Wolf, T., De, H.T.: Emergence versus self-organisation: different concepts but promising when combined. In: Brueckner, S.A., Di Marzo Serugendo, G., Karageorgos, A., Nagpal, R. (eds.) ESOA 2005. LNCS (LNAI), vol. 3464, pp. 1–15. Springer, Heidelberg (2005)

[2] Kephart, J.O., Chess, D.M.: The Vision of Autonomic Computing. Computer 36-1, 41–50 (2003)

[3] Nordstrom, S.G., Shetty, S.S., Neema, S.K., Bapty, T.A.: Modeling Reflex-Healing Autonomy for Large-Scale Embedded Systems. IEEE Transactions on Systems, Man, and Cybernetics, 36(3) (May 2006)

[4] Norman, D., Ortony, A., Russell, D.: Affect and machine design: Lessons for the development of autonomous machines. IBM Syst. J. 42(1), 33–44 (2003)

[5] Pacifici, G., Spreitzer, M., Tantawi, A.: Performance management for cluster based web services. IBM Tech. Rep (2003)

[6] Boutilier, C., Das, R., Kephart, J.: Cooperative negotiation in autonomic systems using incremental utility elicitation. In: Proc. 19th Conf. Uncertainty in Artificial Intelligence (UAI-2003), Acapulco Mexico, August 2003, pp. 89–97 (2003)

[7] Xilinx XAPP290: Two Flows for Partial Reconfiguration: Module Based or Difference based, http://www.xilinx.com

[8] Compton, K., Hauck, S.: Reconfigurable computing: a survey of systems and software. ACM Computing Surveys (CSUR) 34(2), 171–210 (2002)

[9] Horn, P.: Autonomic Computing: IBM's Perspective on the State of Information Technology. IBM Corp. (2003), http://www.research.ibm.com/autonomic/research/papers/AC_Visi-on_Computer_Jan_2003.pdf

[10] Agrawal, D., Lee, K.W., Lobe, J.: Policy-based Management of Networked Computing Systems. IEEE Communications Magazine (2005)

[11] Herrmann, K., Mühl, G., Geihs, K.: Self Management: The solution to Complexity or Just Another Problem? IEEE Distributed Systems Online 6(1), 1541–4922 (2005)

[12] White, S.R., Hanson, J.E., Whalley, I., Chess, D.M., Kephart, J.O.: An Architectural Approach to Autonomic Computing. In: Proceedings of the International Conference on Autonomic Computing (ICAC 2004) (2004)

[13] Luk, W., Shirazi, N., Cheung, P.Y.K.: Modeling and Optimizing Run-time Reconfiguration Systems. Proc. IEEE Symposium on FPGAs for Custom Computing Machines (1996)

[14] Jovanovic, S., Tanougast, C., Bobda, C., Weber, S.: CuNoC: A Scalable Dynamic NoC for Dynamically Reconfigurable FPGAs. FPL, Amsterdam, Netherlands (August 2007)

[15] Jovanovic, S., Tanougast, C., Bobda, C., Weber, S.: A Scalable Dynamic Infrastructure for Dynamically Reconfigurable Systems. In: ReCoSoC07 Montpellier, France (june 2007)

[16] Virtex-4 Family FPGAs., http://www.xilinx.com

A Preemption Algorithm
for a Multitasking Environment on
Dynamically Reconfigurable Processor

Vu Manh Tuan[1] and Hideharu Amano[1]

Keio University, Hiyoshi, Kohoku, Yokohama, Kanagawa, 223–8522 Japan
vmtuan@am.ics.keio.ac.jp

Abstract. Task preemption is a critical mechanism for building an effective multitasking environment on dynamically reconfigurable processors. When being preempted, necessary state information of the interrupted task in registers and distributed internal memories must be correctly preserved. This paper aims at studying a method for saving and restoring the state data of a hardware task, executing on a dynamically reconfigurable processing array, taking into account the great amount and the distribution on different storage elements of data. Performance degradation caused by task preemption is minimized by allowing preemption only at predefined points where demanded resources are small. Specifically, we propose: 1) algorithms to insert preemption points subject to user-specified preemption latency and resource overhead constraints; 2) modification steps to incorporate the offered algorithms on the system design flow. Evaluation results on the NEC DRP architecture show that the proposed method achieves a reasonable hardware overhead (from 6% to 14%) while satisfying a given preemption latency.

1 Introduction

To make the best use of the flexibility of reconfigurable devices like FPGAs, operating systems for managing task allocation, scheduling and configuration have been researched. Although being studied and implemented in some experimental systems, hardware task preemption still accompanies problems such as how to stop hardware execution, how to efficiently save and restore hardware context.

Recently, dynamically reconfigurable processing arrays (DRPAs) have been developed and widely introduced such as DRP, FE-GA and SAKE. They consist of a coarse-grained processing element (PE) array, and exploit the multi-context architecture to reduce configuration overhead. By providing storage for multiple configurations in each PE and broadcasting a pointer to individual configuration, hardware configuration can be changed very fast within a single clock cycle.

Compared with fine-grained FPGAs, since the configuration data of such DRPAs and the time for setting configuration data from outside are small, the task switching involving preemption in such devices is much more realistic than those for FPGAs. However, only a few researches[1] to implement such functions into

R. Woods et al. (Eds.): ARC 2008, LNCS 4943, pp. 172–184, 2008.

DRPAs have been exerted. Toward an efficient task preemption mechanism on DRPAs, we propose an approach where hardware tasks can only be preempted at predefined points based on their resource usage. By inserting special states for capturing and restoring context data into the state transition graph of an application at states where requirements for resources are small, the impact of preemption on the performance and cost for task switching could be reduced.

2 Related Work

Hardware multitasking on FPGAs and other reconfigurable devices have been a challenging subject for many researches. [2] deals with the support of concurrent applications in a multi FPGA-system by reconfiguring entire FPGAs. A multitasking environment allowing several tasks, which do not require all FPGA resources, to run in parallel is mentioned in [3]. In a preemptive multitasking environment on DRPAs, several solutions for saving and restoring context data when a hardware task is preempted have been proposed.

- *Readback:* The solution is based on the configuration readback capability, which allows to read the content of both registers and memories[4][5][6][7]. Although requiring no extra hardware, the solution is slow due to a great amount of data and needs additional computation to get useful information.
- *State supervision:* By adding extra interface to registers and memories, it is possible to access these elements when saving and restoring context data. This solution could be implemented as a scan chain, a memory-mapping structure, or a scan chain with shadow registers [7][8][9][10]. The advantage of the approach is the data efficiency as only the required information are saved; but, it demands extra resources and design efforts to implement interfaces.

[1] proposes a systematic methodology for incorporating preemption constraints in application specific multi-task VLSI systems. By considering a predetermined set of applications, the method tries to insert preemption points taking into account both dedicated and shared registers in order to to minimize the context switch overhead.

3 Target Device

Although the preemption algorithms proposed here can be extended to apply on other reconfigurable devices, in this research, we focus on DRP-1 as the target model. Being a coarse-grain dynamically reconfigurable processor core released by NEC Electronics in 2002[11], DRP-1 carries an on-chip configuration data corresponding to multiple contexts, which are dynamically rescheduled to realize multiple functions with one chip.

The primitive unit of the DRP core is called a tile, and a DRP core consists of arbitrary number of tiles. The primitive modules of a tile are processing elements (PEs), a State Transition Controller (STC), a set of 2-ported vertical memory

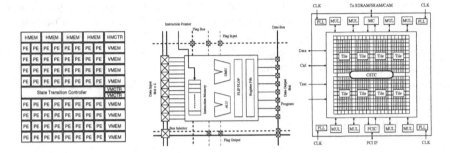

Fig. 1. Tile architecture   **Fig. 2.** PE architecture   **Fig. 3.** DRP-1

(VMEM) and 1-ported horizontal memory (HMEM). The structure of a tile is shown in Fig. 1. There are 64 PEs located in one tile. The architecture of a PE is shown in Fig. 2. It has an 8-bit ALU, an 8-bit data manipulation unit, sixteen 8-bit register file units, and an 8-bit flip-flop. As shown in Fig. 3, the prototype chip DRP-1 consists of a 8-tile DRP Core, eight 32-bit multipliers, and 256-bit I/Os. The maximum operation frequency is 100-MHz.

An integrated design environment called Musketeer, which allows applications described in a C-based hardware description language called Behavioral Design Language (BDL), is provided. Although BDL supports pointers, dynamically memory allocation is not allowed. All memory and register assignment as well as state registers allowing the DRP to transition from one state to another are determined at the compile time. The input/output interface of the DRP-1 is supported via two 64-bit separated channels. One input and one output operation can be executed concurrently in a clock cycle. Currently, the DRP has no multitasking capability. At one time, only one application can be configured and executed on the whole 8-tile reconfigurable array.

4   Preemption Analysis

4.1   Task Switch

In a preemptive multitasking environment on DRPAs, a typical task switching process can be illustrated on Fig. 4. While Task 1 is running, an interrupt signal, often caused by a system timer, indicating a possible task switch is generated. Before a new task (Task 2) can be executed, several preparing stages have to be done. First, an interrupt service is called to decide whether a task switch is necessary (Stage A). If it is, the

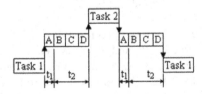

Fig. 4. Task switching

state data of Task 1 is saved in Stage B; and, that of Task 2 is loaded in Stage C. Furthermore, the configuration data of Task 2 is loaded in Stage D. (t_1) can

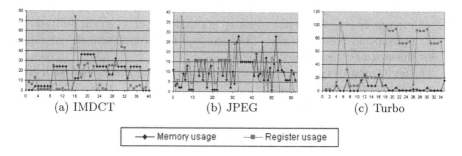

Fig. 5. Memory and Register usages vs. Computation States

be considered as interrupt latency; and, (t_2) is context switch latency. The sum $t = t_1 + t_2$ can be considered as preemption latency. Usually, Stage A does not take a long time for modern processors and operating systems. The information representing the context of of a hardware task is specific for a given task implementation and may scatter on different state-holding elements including registers, memories, and flip-flops.

4.2 Our Approach

During an execution, the amount of registers and memories for storing intermediate results is considerably varying over time. Most target applications of reconfigurable devices are stream processing, that is, data blocks to be processed are iteratively received in a certain interval. Between two data blocks, the required amount of state data is relatively small. This fact can be applied to build a preemption mechanism where preemption is allowed only at predefined steps called *preemption points*[12] or *switchpoints*.

Preliminary evaluation. Fig. 5 shows the memory and register usages in each computation state when an IMDCT, a JPEG encoder and a Turbo encoder are implemented on DRP-1. X ans Y axis show computation states and the amount of resources respectively. As seen from Fig. 5, the number of registers and memories for storing intermediate results and context switches greatly varies from state to state. For example, in IMDCT, states 0, 1, 2, 3, 4, 6, 13, 19, 22, 29 and 34 do not require too many memories and registers; in addition, states 10, 11, 23, 24 and 29 do not use a lot of memories through the number of registers is remarkable. Accordingly, by only allowing preemption at states where the requirement for resources is minimized, the amount of state data can be dramatically reduced.

Solution. Our proposed preemption method is based on the state transition graph and the resource examination of a particular application. The method could lead to the reduction of task switching overhead. The solution should be automatically done with a certain algorithm, since it must be combined into the design tool in the future.

- States where preemption is allowed are limited at predetermined points (pre-emption points) where resource usage is smaller than a certain limitation.
- At preemption points, special states tailored to current contexts are added for flushing and restoring state data.
- The performance degradation resulting from preemption is evaluated in order to optimize preemption points.
- The proposed algorithm are integrated into the system design flow.
- Algorithms for selecting and inserting preemption states are based on the design tools of DRP.

5   Preemption Algorithms

5.1   State Transition Graph

The homogeneous synchronous data flow [13] is used as the computational model for applications. The model iteratively processes semi-finite data blocks arriving in a certain interval. Stream applications, which are the main target of DRPAs, are suitable to be represented by this model. In this paper, an application is implemented and completely mapped onto on a DRPA for execution as a hardware task. In DPRAs, the behavior of a hardware task is often represented in the form of a State Transition Graph (STG) $G(N, E, START, END)$, where N is the set of nodes representing computation states; E is the set of edges showing the transition and data dependences between states; $START \in N$ is a distinguished start node with no incoming edges; and $END \in N$ is a distinguished end node with no outgoing edges Fig. 7 shows the STG of Task 1 and Task 2, where (a_i, b_i) $(i = 0 \ldots n)$ shows numbered states, arrows represents possible transitions from states to states, (a_0, b_0) and (a_9, b_6) are start and end states. Transition can be branched conditionally as in state a_2.

5.2   Metrics for Evaluating Preemption

In order to examine how a preemption mechanism affects the performance of an implementation, we define some metrics as follows.

- *Hardware overhead or context switch overhead H* specifies the amount of additional resources required by added preemption states. If H_{PE} and H_{PE}^* denote the number of required PEs in the original and modified implementations respectively, H can be represented by: $H = H_{PE}^* - H_{PE}$.
- *Preemption latency τ* can be defined as the time from a preemption request until a preempting task is ready to run. In this paper, we consider preemption latency as time for saving and restoring state data, and, τ can be computed as: $\tau = T_p + T_s + T_r$ where: T_p, T_s and T_r are time to reach the closest preemption point from the moment a preemption request is issued, time to save the state data of the preempted task, and time to restore the previously captured data of the preempting task respectively.

5.3   System Design Flow

The left part of Fig. 6 shows a typical design flow for the DRP. First, a source C-based program using BDL and an architecture description are taken as the input for the behavioral synthesis. The synthesis allocates operation resources and produces reports like required resources for reference or improvement. Next, the technology mapper actually produces HDL codes for STCs and PEs, and, an RTL functional simulation can be executed. The place-and-route compiles the HDL code into the netlist. Exact re-

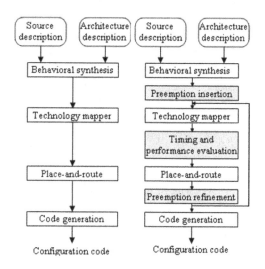

Fig. 6. System design flow

ports about the resource usage and the critical path can be achieved at this step. Finally, the code generator produces the configuration code for the underlying reconfigurable hardware.

The right part of Fig. 6 presents the modified design flow with the proposed preemption algorithm. Since, the DRP development environment does not support dynamic memory allocation, the resource report produced by the behavioral synthesis could describe quite exactly how temporary variables are allocated and which registers are necessary for context switches. This is the basic for preliminary analyzing preemption points and inserting preemption states at the step *preemption insertion*. The *evaluation* step is based on the RTL simulation for evaluating how added preemption states affect the implementation. The last step is the *preemption refinement* where preemption points are modified according to the exact report of resource usages and the evaluation result. Modified source will be fed back to the technology mapper for re-compiling.

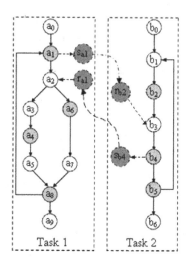

Fig. 7. Proposed solution

5.4   Example

Fig. 7 shows an example with the STGs of Task 1 and Task 2. The preemption algorithm traverses the STG to find out the states where used resources are

Saving states	Restoring states

reg(0:16) r[4];
mem(0:16) m0[8], m1[8];
mem(0:16) m2[8], m3[8];
...
dout = r[3]::r[2]::r[1]::r[0];
DataOut(dout);
m3[0]; m2[0]; m1[0]; m0[0];
$
dout = m3[0]::m2[0]::m1[0]::m0[0];
DataOut(dout);
m3[1]; m2[1]; m1[1]; m0[1];
$
...
	reg(0:16) r[4];
	mem(0:16) m0[8], m1[8];
	mem(0:16) m2[8], m3[8];
	...
	din = DataIn();
	r[3]::r[2]::r[1]::r[0] = din;
	
	$
	din = DataIn();
	m3[0]::m2[0]::m1[0]::m0[0] = din;
	
	$
	...

Fig. 8. Example code

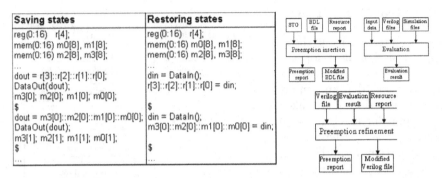

Fig. 9. Proposed method

smaller than a certain limit; for example, states (a_1, a_4, a_6, a_8) of Task 1 and (b_2, b_4, b_5) of Task 2 with gray circles are such states. These states are marked as preemption points, where special states for saving (states s_{ai}, s_{bj}) and restoring (states r_{ai}, r_{bj}) data are inserted and the STG is modified. These inserted states are assumed to be executed only when their coupled states are preempted. For example, when Task 1 is executing at state a_0, a preemption request occurs. Since a_0 is not a preemption point, Task 1 is not interrupted but continues to run. When the execution reaches a_1, which is a preemption point, Task 1 is stopped after a_1, and the execution is transferred to the correspondent state for saving state information of a_1 (state s_{a1}). After state r_{b2}, which restores the state data of b_2, is executed, the execution is moved to Task 2, and Task 2 starts to run from b_3 (assume that Task 2 was preempted before at b_2). Switching from Task 2 back to Task 1 is handled in the similar way, for instance, when Task 2 is preempted at b_4.

The example code in Fig 8 illustrates how state data can be saved and restored by states s_{ai}, s_{bj} and r_{ai}, r_{bj}. The example is coded in NEC's BDL, which is a C-based language. r, m_i (i = 0, 1, 2, 3) are arrays of *register* and *memory* types, which represent hardware registers and memories respectively, with the bit width of 16 bits. Symbol :: shows a concatenation operator, which links variables together to form a larger bit width result. For example, the statement $r[3]::r[2]::r[1]::r[0]$ concatenates four 16-bit elements of array r to create an output of 64 bits. *DataOut* and *DataIn* are output and input functions working with 64-bit output/input interfaces via 64-bit variables *dout* and *din*. Symbol $ presents a timing descriptor to manually divide the codes into different states.

The example shows that by modifying source programs at high level to insert preemption states, we can avoid the details of the underlying hardware architecture such as the exact place of a register variable.

5.5   Preemption Algorithm

In this research, the DRP is assumed to be a part of a system consisting of an outside general-purpose processor and an operating system for managing run-time environment on the device. The proposed method will be supported by the underlying hardware architecture for task preemption (stopping a hardware task at a preemption point according to a request, and transferring execution to saving and restoring states), and be integrated into the operating system to be a part of the task management module.

The proposed algorithm achieves the target of minimizing context switch overhead by: 1) allowing preemption only at computation states where used resources are small, and, 2) inserting special states for saving and restoring state data. They include just input/output instructions, so require small number of PEs, and no extra register files as well as memories.

The algorithm proposed here is consisting of three stages: inserting preemption states into the original STG, evaluating, and refining. Each stage requires different inputs and produces correspondent results as shown on Fig. 9.

Inserting preemption states. Using the resource report generated by the behavioral synthesis as an estimation, the insertion algorithm tries to find out potential preemption points.

- *Loop detection:* At the beginning, the algorithm detects all computation loops $L = l_1, l_2, ..., l_n$ using the given STG. Each loop l_i contains a number of states $l_i = s_{ij}, s_{ij+1}, ...$ The detection of computation loops is important since they are likely to take a considerable amount of time. Taking into account preemption latency, a loop without any preemption points inserted could violate a required preemption latency. Fortunately, instead of analyzing a complicated source program, it is more convenient to deal with the STG represented in the form of a flowgraph. Applying a loop detection algorithm[14] on the STG of an implementation, all loops are identified and marked in order that the insertion algorithm will analyze and insert at least one preemption point among states constituting a loop.
- *Sorting:* Using a suitable sort algorithm, loops l_i are sorted incrementally according to numbered states, i.e. $\forall s_u \in l_i$ and $s_v \in l_k : s_u \leq s_v$ $(i < k)$.
- *Preemption point finding:* Based on the resource report generated by the behavioral synthesis, loops are searched for possible preemption points where used resources are within a given threshold θ. States that do not belong to any computation loops are also investigated to find out preemption points using the threshold θ.
- *New states insertion:* At preemption points, new states are inserted for transferring necessary resources to outside. Since the input/output interface of the DRP uses 64 bits, resources are grouped into packets of 64 bits for output. Depending on the amount of resources and how memories are allocated, it would take a number of clock cycles for transferring. This contributes to the preemption latency and affects the overall performance of the task.

Refining preemption points. To prepare for refining preemption points, it is critical to quantitatively evaluate how preemption states inserted affect the implementation. This can be done by executing simulations on the original and modified implementations. Using design tools of DRP-1, the RTL simulation can be performed in order to obtain the critical path and the used resources at the technological mapping. With suitable computations, other parameters such as the throughput and the preemption latency at a given state can be determined.

Preemption points generated by the previous step may be improved since the insertion algorithm often generates more than necessary. Moreover, the estimation of the critical path at the early stage of the design flow, which is basic for computing the preemption latency, is usually larger than the real one. Therefore, based on the resource reports of the place-and-route phase and the evaluation results, redundant preemption points could be eliminated. Different requirements for the preemption mechanism could become criteria for removing preemption points from the list. In the simplest case when the preemption latency can be tolerated, the refining algorithm just tries to eliminate preemption states consuming a larger number of clock cycles. In many cases, a user specified constrain on preemption latency may be given. The following refining algorithm uses the input preemption latency as a criterion for optimize preemption points.

- *Preemption point scanning:* First of all, the algorithm scans the list of preemption points P generated at the previous stage to find out if the condition $\forall i : \tau_i \leq \psi_{given}$ $(i = 0..n)$ is satisfied. If not, extra preemption points are inserted at states where required resources are small.
- *Unnecessary preemption point elimination:* The algorithm tries to remove unnecessary preemption points using the given preemption latency ψ_{given}. Any preemption points in the list P between two points t_1 and t_2 that satisfies $\forall p_i \in P : \tau_{pi} \leq psi_{given}$, will be eliminated.
- *Preemption state modification:* Next, preemption states for saving and restoring context data are inserted or modified based on the accurate resource report generated by the place-and-route tool.
- *Management structure:* A structure should be defined for correctly managing data when saving and restoring, and for the outside operating system to control and schedule tasks. Therefore, while inserting extra states, for each preemption point, a data structure containing information such as the amount and the order of data saved and restored must be defined. The outside controller does not need to know about where data come from (registers or memories), and if values are 8, 16 or 32 bits. What it has to do is to allocate 64-bit buffers to hold data, to maintain the order of saving data, and to send in exactly the same amount in the type of 64-bit packets and order of data when data are restored.

6   Evaluation

The proposed preemption algorithm in this paper was evaluated on a number of real applications shown in Table 1. For each application, different cases are implemented and shown in column *Version*. Cases include implementations when no preemption points are inserted (A_0), when preemption points are inserted without any constrain on preemption latency (A_1), when the latency is specified

Table 1. Target applications and evaluation results

Applications	Abbr.	Version	Node	Edge	τ_{input} [ns]	Delay [ns]	Preemption latency		Used PEs
							τ_{min} [ns]	τ_{max} [ns]	
Discrete Cosine Transform	DCT	A_0	28	32	-	67.3	-	-	1105
		A_1	-	-	-	-	0	431.2	1197
		A_ψ	-	-	300	-	67.3	296.6	1218
		A_n	-	-	-	-	0	180	1459
Inverse Modified DCT	IMDCT	A_0	40	48	-	129.5	-	-	2582
		A_1	-	-	-	-	18.0	827.5	2854
		A_ψ	-	-	500	-	54.0	478.5	2820
		A_n	-	-	-	-	18.0	612.0	3714
Viterbi decoder	Viterbi	A_0	10	10	-	30.4	-	-	843
		A_1	-	-	-	-	0	182.4	843
		A_ψ	-	-	200	-	67.3	186.8	958
		A_n	-	-	-	-	0	828.0	1371
JPEG encoder	JPEG	A_0	62	76	-	54.7	-	-	1851
		A_1	-	-	-	-	18.0	436.9	2078
		A_ψ	-	-	250	-	72.7	344.1	2052
		A_n	-	-	-	-	18.0	378.0	2742
Turbo encoder	Turbo	A_0	35	41	-	77.8	-	-	3008
		A_1	-	-	-	-	18.0	712.4	3169
		A_ψ	-	-	400	-	18.0	314.4	3287
		Ao_n	-	-	-	-	18.0	324.0	4232
MPEG-2 decoder	MPEG	A_0	89	101	-	67.9	-	-	2787
		A_1	-	-	-	-	18.0	751.0	3200
		A_ψ	-	-	350	-	78.9	293.7	3052
		A_n	-	-	-	-	0.0	288	4431
G721 encoder	G721	A_0	12	17	-	93.6	-	-	1085
		A_1	-	-	-	-	111.6	392.6	1126
		A_ψ	-	-	300	-	111.6	295.2	1150
		A_n	-	-	-	-	18.0	252.0	1376

(A_ψ) (the proposed algorithm), and when preemption is allowed at every states (A_n). Columns 4 and 5 show the number of nodes and the number of edges in the STG of each application. Columns 6-10 denote the given preemption latency (τ_{input}), the critical path $(Delay)$, the minimum and maximum preemption latency of each implementation $(\tau_{min}$ and $\tau_{max})$, and the total number of used PEs $(Used\ PEs)$ respectively.

All implementations do not pack multiple states into a single context in order to see the impact of inserted states on the performance. Although this prevents implementations with more than 16 contexts from executing on the real chip, it is still possible to complete the place-and-route phase, to execute simulations and to achieve suitable reports.

The result of preemption latency is computed using formula in Section (5.2). In a multitasking environment, the calculation of preemption latency depends on

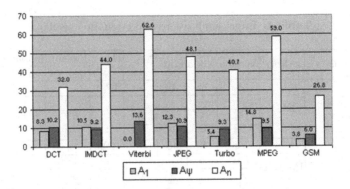

Fig. 10. Hardware overhead

the set of running applications, and the combination of saving/restoring states of preempted and preempting applications. The former is difficult to determine and depends on specific scenarios; and, the latter causes preemption latency to vary even if there are only two applications executing in a system. In this paper, the calculation of preemption latency is performed at every state on the STG of a single application with the assumption that the same set of resources is applied for both saving and restoring. Though not being the exact situation in a real system, this gives us a relative overview on how preemption latency may vary.

The delay shown in Table 1 is the critical path of implementations. Since the option to pack multiple states into a context is not used, added states containing only input/output instructions do not have any influence on the critical path mainly formed by other main computation states. Furthermore, additional states are assumed to be executed with a different operating frequency. This is reasonable since in a real device, the input and output of state data could be done independent from the main task on preemption.

6.1   Hardware Overhead

Although containing only input/output instructions, saving and restoring states still use PEs for concatenating data into 64-bit packets. Column $Used\ PEs$ in Table 1 shows the required hardware resource in term of PEs. Using implementations without preemption points (A_0) as the basic, Fig. 10 presents how the hardware overhead varies when preemption points are inserted. The hardware overhead varies from 0% to 15% for the A_1 case, from 6% to 14% for the A_ψ case, and from 27% to 63% for the A_n case. The hardware overhead of 0% for the A_1 Viterbi implementation comes from the fact that preemption points in the implementation are at states that do not use any registers or memories.

The hardware overhead of implementations according to the proposed algorithm is not large. More importantly, it is even smaller than the correspondent A_1 implementations in some cases (IMDCT, JPEG and MPEG). This results from the optimization performed by the refining algorithm to eliminate redundant preemption points using the given preemption latency as a criterion. Although some additional preemption points need to insert in order to satisfy the given preemption latency, other unnecessary preemption points could be removed. Therefore, the hardware overhead could become smaller.

6.2   Preemption Latency

For each specific implementation, as shown on Table 1, it is possible to compute the minimum and maximum preemption latency. In some cases, the minimum preemption latency become zero since there is nothing to be saved and restored when preemption occurs at certain points (DCT and Viterbi with A_1, A_n versions, and MPEG with A_n version).

In many implementations (IMDCT, Viterbi, JPEG and Turbo) the preemption latency τ_{max} of the A_ψ version is even smaller than that of the A_n although the latter has no delay for reaching a preemption point (all states in A_n versions can be preempted). This means in those cases, time to save and restore state data at some points dominates the total preemption latency.

7   Conclusion

A preemption method that allows task preemption at predetermined states where required resources are small is proposed to reduce the downside effects of preemption on hardware tasks in a multitasking environment on dynamically reconfigurable devices. Evaluation results on the DRP architecture show that the proposed method achieves a reasonable hardware overhead while satisfying a user-specified preemption latency.

Acknowledgments

The authors sincerely express their gratitude to NEC Electronics and NEC laboratories.

References

1. Kim, K., Karri, R., Potkonjak, M.: Micropreemption Synthesis: An Enabling Mechanism for Multitask VLSI Systems. IEEE Transactions on Computer-Aided Design of Integrated Circuits and Systems 25(1), 19–30 (2006)
2. Jean, J.S.N., Tomko, K., Yavagal, V., Shah, J., Cook, R.: Dynamic reconfiguration to support concurrent applications. IEEE Trans. on Computers 48(6), 591–602 (1999)
3. Brebner, G.: The Swappable Logic Unit: A Paradigm for Virtual Hardware. In: IEEE Symposium on FPGAs for CCMs, pp. 77–86 (1997)
4. Simmler, H., Levinson, L., Manner, R.: Multitasking on FPGA Coprocessors. In: Proc. of the 10th International Workshop on FPGA, pp. 121–130 (2000)

5. Levinson, L., Männer, R., Sesler, M., Simmler, H.: Preemptive Multitasking on FPGAs. In: Proc. of the 2000 IEEE Symposium on FCCM (2000)
6. Guccione, S.A., Levi, D., Sundararajan, P.: JBits: A Java-based interface for reconfigurable computing. In: Proc. of Second Annual MAPLD (September 1999)
7. Kalte, H., Porrmann, M.: Context Saving and Restoring for Multitasking in Reconfigurable Systems. In: Proc. of 15th FPL, vol. 228, pp. 223–228 (August 2005)
8. Koch, D., Haubelt, C., Teich, J.: Efficient hardware checkpointing: concepts, overhead analysis, and implementation. In: Proc. of FPGA, pp. 188–196 (February 2007)
9. Jovanovic, S., Tanougast, C., Weber, S.: A Hardware Preemptive Multitasking Mechanism Based on Scan-path Register Structure for FPGA-based Reconfigurable Systems. In: Proc. of NASA/ESA Conference on Adaptive Hardware and Systems (AHS), pp. 358–364 (August 2007)
10. Ullmann, M., Hübner, M., Grimm, B., Becker, J.: An FPGA Run-Time System for Dynamical On-Demand Reconfiguration. In: Proc. of 11th RAW (April 2004)
11. Motomura, M.: A Dynamically Reconfigurable Processor Architecture. Microprocessor Forum (October 2002)
12. Simonson, J., Patel, J.H.: Use of Preferred Preemption Points in Cache-Based Real-Time Systems. In: Proc. of International Computer Performance and Dependability Symposium, pp. 316–325 (April 1995)
13. Lee, E.A., Messerschmitt, D.C.: Static Scheduling of Synchronous Data flow Programs for Digital Signal Processing. IEEE Trans. on Computers 36(1), 24–36 (1987)
14. Aho, A.V., Sethi, R., Ullman, J.D.: Compiler: Principles, Techniques, and Tools. Addison-Wesley, Reading (1986)

Accelerating Speculative Execution in High-Level Synthesis with Cancel Tokens

Hagen Gädke[1] and Andreas Koch[2]

[1] Integrated Circuit Design (E.I.S.)
Technische Universität Braunschweig, Germany
gaedke@eis.cs.tu-bs.de
[2] Embedded Systems and Applications Group (ESA)
Technische Universität Darmstadt, Germany
koch@esa.informatik.tu-darmstadt.de

Abstract. We present an improved method for scheduling speculative data paths which relies on cancel tokens to undo computations in mis-speculated paths. Performancewise, this method is considerably faster than lenient execution, and faster than any other known approach applicable for general (including non-pipelined) computation structures. We present experimental evidence obtained by implementing our method as part of the high-level language hardware/software compiler COMRADE.

1 Introduction

Many compilers for compilation from C to hardware have been developed in the last few years; the following list is far from complete: GarpCC [1], NIMBLE [2], CASH [3], SPARK [4], ROCCC [5], Tartan [6], COMRADE [7,8]. All of these compilers make use of speculative execution to produce efficient hardware realisations of sequential code. Speculative execution in hardware means the technique of computation without knowing if such precomputed data will actually be needed for successive computations. Applying this concept to if statements results in computing both, the then and the else block in parallel, as soon as data dependencies are fulfilled. Analogously, all cases of a switch statement would also be computed in parallel. In the literature, this approach is referred to as an upward code motion before the condition [9], or a weakening of guards, in the extreme case: the complete removal of guards or replacement of all predicates by **true** [10]. Such speculative data paths are combined in multiplexers. Only one of the computed values, depending on the result of the control condition or predicate, flows through the mux to subsequent data paths, the others are discarded. In many cases these parallel, speculative data paths have different lengths, resulting in different computation time periods or numbers of cycles. Control conditions, often being composed of simple comparisons, are typically computed much faster than the longest speculative data path. Assuming that the result of the short data path in Fig. 1 as well as the control condition cond are already available, and cond is true, then the value of x2 will pass the mux,

R. Woods et al. (Eds.): ARC 2008, LNCS 4943, pp. 185–195, 2008.
© Springer-Verlag Berlin Heidelberg 2008

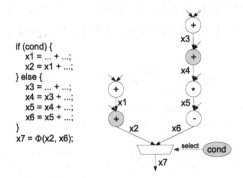

Fig. 1. Speculative data paths of different length. Gray highlighted operations denote currently available results.

while the current computation of the **else** block must be discarded to prevent erroneous results.

Section 2 outlines related work and motivates our approach of using *cancel tokens*. After describing the intermediate representation that we use to implement cancel tokens (Sec. 3), we present details on their functionality (Sec. 4) and give a solution for the problem of control redundancy (Sec. 5), which is inherent in cancel tokens. Section 6 summarises the advantages of cancel tokens, before we conclude with experimental results.

2 Related Work

The trivial approach for discarding speculated computations is to wait until *all* speculative data paths have finished their computation and only then forwarding the valid result through the mux.

The problem of waiting for the critical speculative data path is irrelevant if the traditional approach of *hardware loop pipelining* is used (such as in the StReAm compiler [11]). Short data paths can simply be extended with flipflops to match the length of critical paths. As long as the pipeline is efficiently used, computing multiple loop iterations at the same time, the length of the pipeline itself does not affect the throughput. However, if the loop contains a loop-carried dependency (LCD), the associated computation for iteration $n+1$ cannot start before the value from iteration n has been computed. In such a situation, a pipelined solution suffers from the same latencies as the trivial approach.

Lenient execution is used by Pegasus/CASH [3]. This method allows an operator to compute its result and forward it to successive operators, although not all data inputs are available yet. Typical examples are lenient ANDs, ORs and multiplexers. Note that lenient execution does not cancel any mis-speculated inputs.

Styles and Luk [12] present a method to accelerate the execution of loop nests, which contain an inner loop with LCDs while the outer loop is a non-LCD loop. During cycles in which the pipeline inputs of the inner loop are stalled (waiting for the LCD data to appear), an new iteration of the outer loop is executed in an overlapped fashion. Sequencing tokens are attached to the data items generated in the outer loop, identifying the loop iteration. Using these sequencing tokens later allows the correct ordering of data commits.

Our approach, which we briefly outlined already in [8], is even able to accelerate LCD loops *without* the presence of an enclosing non-LCD outer loop. We explicitly cancel mis-speculated operators using cancel tokens. In Fig. 1, x2 would then flow through the multiplexer in the next cycle, while a cancel token would be created at the node which computes x6. The cancel token would then move backwards along incoming data edges and finally cancel the mis-speculated computations. Thus, the runtime delays of the trivial approach are eliminated, while mis-speculated results are deleted. This methodology is not only able to accelerate LCD loops — it performs very well in designs employing non-pipelined operators, too: Cancelling a non-pipelined high-latency operator for a mis-speculation in the current iteration allows this operator to start the computation for the next loop iteration earlier. Furthermore, if speculative, cached memory accesses are used (something we intend to tackle next), cancel tokens can remove mis-speculated accesses from the load/store queue before they are actually executed. This increases the cache efficiency, both by reducing the general demand on cache bandwidth (fewer loads/stores in general) as well as limiting the cache thrashing (fewer mistakenly evicted lines due to mis-speculated loads).

A similar methodology for killing selected computations before they are completed has first been presented by Brej [13] (later extended by Ampalam [14], who correctly addresses metastability issues), but at the lower level of asynchronous gates in ASIC designs. Our own, independently developed approach for performing such actions on the higher-level of synchronous operators was first introduced in [7] and explained in more detail in [15]. The novel techniques we present in this work refine that scheme to handle cancellation of nested conditional constructs, which requires the construction of an efficient forwarding mechanism for cancel tokens along control edges.

3   CMDFGs

Before the functionality of cancel tokens is explained (Sec. 4), we describe the *CMDFG* (Control Memory Data Flow Graph), the intermediate representation (IR) we use to support cancel tokens in the COMRADE compiler.

Fig. 2(a) shows a C code sample which will be referred to as *test* throughout the paper. Fig. 2(b) shows the corresponding control flow graph (CFG) in static single assignment-form (SSA), Fig. 2(c) depicts a section of the resulting CMDFG. The CMDFG is a low-level, fine-grain IR similar to the program dependence graph (PDG) [16]. Its nodes are HW operations (arithmetic, logic, mux, registers, I/O), connected by three different types of edges that represent data, control and memory dependencies. The latter, being out of scope of this paper, guarantee the correct execution order of memory access nodes. Without memory edges, the CMDFG is somewhat similar to the dependence graph as used in [10]

```
unsigned int i, s;
s = 0;
for (i = 0; i < 6; i++) {
  if (i > 0) {
    if (i == 5) {
      s = s / i;
    } else {
      s = s + i;
    }
    s = s + i;
  }
}
printf("s = %d\n", s);
```

(a)

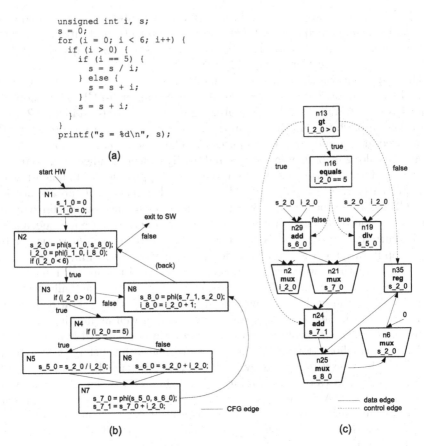

(b)

(c)

Fig. 2. *test* — (a) sample C source code; (b) SSA form CFG; (c) CMDFG for the loop body (redundancy not yet removed)

as well as the program dependence web (PDW) [17]. However, CMDFG nodes do not contain complete data flow graphs like in this prior work, but single HW operators (similar to Pegasus [3] and HCDG [9]). Compared to the PDW, the CMDFG contains neither γ and β functions, nor data flow switches. Instead it employs a more hardware-centric view by relying on multiplexers, whose predecessor nodes (and, for loop-carried values: successor nodes) are targets of control edges. In this model, mis-speculated and superfluous values can be cancelled (described in Sec. 4).

4   Activate and Cancel Tokens

CMDFGs operate in the data flow paradigm: as soon as all data predecessor nodes of a node provide a datum, the node starts its computation (i.e., CMDFGs use a self-timed scheduling). For a mux, this condition is somewhat altered in that the mux computes (i.e. passes on) the datum already if the *selected* datum

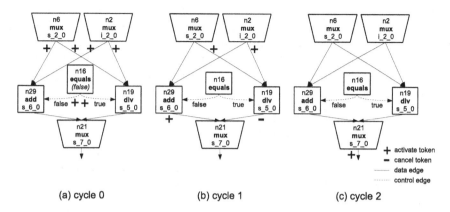

Fig. 3. Activate and cancel token flow

is available, the others are not required to be present. For any computing node that is also the target of a control edge, its result is not considered valid until the associated control condition is *also* fulfilled. A valid result of a CMDFG node corresponds to a so-called *activate token*, depicted as '+' in Fig. 3. An activated node holds one activate token per outgoing edge, the tokens each moving along their edges to the successor nodes. Conversely, cancel tokens usually (there are exceptions, see Section 5) move *backwards*, erasing data incoming from edges determined to have been mis-speculated.

In Fig. 3(a), both the activate token associated to the edge (n6, n29) of node n6 and the one associated to edge (n2, n29) of node n2 move forward along the data edges to n29, which means that n29 holds a valid result at its data output in cycle 1 (Fig. 3(b)). The figure also shows how mux predecessors are controlled via control edges. Node n16 is false in cycle 0, i.e. the left speculative data path is valid; thus, the value computed by n29 is valid in cycle 1. At the same time, a cancel token is created in n19, because it is the target of a control edge, whose control condition is *not* fulfilled. By causing these two actions, n16's two activate tokens are consumed in cycle 1. While the valid result of the adder moves *forward* to the mux in cycle 2, the cancel token moves *backwards* along n19's incoming data edges, killing the two activate tokens remaining in the mis-speculated path.

5   Removing Control Redundance and the Control Redundance Frontier

Similar to [10], we connect nested conditionals via control edges, e.g. edge (n13, n16) in Fig. 2(c). This is reasonable in context of cancel tokens: If an outer condition has already established that the entire subgraph is not to be executed, that subgraph can be *completely* cancelled. This is achieved by making cancel tokens move *forward* along control edges. Thus, a cancel token in a control node higher up in the hierarchy is propagated down to all sub-control nodes, which then cancel all the subgraph computations.

With this approach, however, a difficulty becomes apparent: In the initial model described so far, too many cancel tokens are generated at outer levels of the control hierarchy. For example, if $i\_2\_0 \not> 0$ in Fig. 2(c), a cancel token created in n16 by n13 to disable inner conditionals cancels n29 and n19. However, the outer cancel token sent to n24, now no longer *has* a result to delete: While n2 *does* supply data (and an activate token) to the left input of n24, no data (and activate token) is forthcoming from n21, since both of that mux' inputs have already been cancelled by the inner condition. Without a datum to neutralise, the cancel token itself remains here indefinitely.

In this situation, we term n24 to be *redundantly controlled*. In order to avoid such a creation of excess cancel tokens, which do not have a corresponding activate token to neutralise, we have to remove such redundancies. One solution would be the removal of the control edge (n13, n24) and the addition of an edge (n13, n2), which would lead to the neutralisation of the activate token coming into n24 from n2.

We now describe an algorithm that can solve this problem in the general case. First, we define that x, y and c are nodes in a CMDFG T. x is termed to be *controlled by* c (written as $x \in C(c)$) if there exists a control edge $(c, x) \in T$ **or** there exists a direct data or control predecessor z of x which is not a mux and is itself controlled by c. x is *redundantly controlled* by c (written as $x \in R(c)$) if there exists a control edge $(c, x) \in T$ **and** there exists a direct data predecessor z of x with $z \in C(c)$. In order to remove the redundancy, we define the *c-control redundance frontier* of x as $F(c, x)$, being the set of direct data predecessors z of x, with $z \notin C(c)$. Token imbalances can thus be avoided by removing all redundant control edges (c, x) with $x \in R(c)$, and adding instead non-redundant edges (c, z) for $z \in F(c, x)$. This is precisely the solution we used in the example described in the last paragraph.

6   Advantages of Cancel Tokens

Cancel tokens avoid delays due to waiting for the results of mis-speculated branches of the computation. However, this applies to non-pipelined computations. In pipelined computations, it is not possible to cancel a branch (sub-pipeline), since this would alter the latency of this computation path. That is of course not acceptable in a pipelined compute unit where merging paths must all be balanced to have the same latency from the input nodes. Here, mis-speculated results are always fully computed, just not used afterwards.

However, since we are aiming for the compilation of general C code, possibly with irregular control flow in loops and loop-carried dependencies (as shown for the variable s in Fig. 2(a)), we cannot always generate strictly pipelined compute units (the next set of input data cannot enter the pipeline before the previous result has been computed by the pipeline). In order to handle even the non-pipelined case efficiently, we rely on the cancel mechanism.

Another advantage of cancelling non-pipelined multi-cycle operators (e.g. div, transcendental functions, etc.) is that the next computation — typically corresponding to the next loop iteration — of such operators can start earlier, reducing the execution time for the correlated loop iterations. The advantages to cancelling mis-speculated memory operations were already pointed out in Sec. 2.

7 Experimental Results

To evaluate the practical impact of our approach, we extended the COMRADE compiler appropriately. COMRADE creates combined HW/SW solutions for *adaptive computing systems* (consisting of both a software-programmable processor and a reconfigurable compute unit, [18]). After HW/SW partitioning the input C program, COMRADE transforms the HW-suitable pieces of the code to SSA form and creates a CMDFG for each HW kernel. For each CMDFG operator node, our module generator library GLACE [19] creates an optimised, pre-placed netlist. Furthermore, a central controller is generated as a Verilog netlist. It holds the token registers for each HW operator (an activate and a cancel bit per outgoing edge) and dynamically controls the data flow.

This initial implementation of the controller synthesis is not yet optimal: A target node of a control edge starts its computation only *after* the control condition has been computed; a better design would be to start computation as soon as all data dependencies are fulfilled (cf. Sec. 4). Also, all operators are currently registered, i.e. we have not exploited chaining yet. However, despite these deficiencies, we can already measure the impact of the cancel mechanism.

While we can demonstrate the actual system-level execution of COMRADE-generated HW/SW applications on a Xilinx Virtex-II Pro-based hardware platform, our techniques are applicable to all fined-grained reconfigurable devices. For the experiments, we consider HW kernels from different benchmark suites (mostly from MediaBench and MiBench), as well as three additional synthetic HW kernels of our own design: the *parallel* kernel computes 100 iterations of 50 independent additions contained in the body of an if statement; *test* corresponds to the code in Fig. 2(a); *test_unrolled* refers to the same code with the loop unrolled. After using COMRADE for compilation to HW, we obtained the values listed in Table 1 by post-place&route analysis. For checking the feasibility of the approach in actual hardware, the most demanding (in terms of token amounts) parallel kernel was also successfully executed on a prototype HW platform, achieving the 100 MHz clock frequency required for this reference design [20].

The adpcm, des and pegwit kernels contain memory loads and stores. These are currently executed non-speculatively and serialised, because COMRADE does not exploit its memory dependence analyses during hardware generation yet. While not critically relevant in context of this paper (we have not discussed the memory-dependence handling parts of the CMDFG IR here), we give some performance numbers for reference: Accesses to the DDR-DRAM-based main memory are routed through a fully-associative 4 KB cache running at 100 MHz, provided by the configurable MARC memory system [21]. For a hit, the read/write latency is 1 cycle; a miss takes 45 cycles to load a cache line of 128 bytes. Also, all HW operators are currently non-pipelined (a new GLACE version currently under development will change this, too).

Table 1. Benchmarks obtained from simulating selected kernels; #lines: number of C source code lines (HW relevant part only), excluding comments, declarations, constant array definitions and white space; #cycles: HW computation cycles only, without SW/HW transfer of live variables; DOP (degree of parallelism): max. number of parallel computing operations; #AT: max. number of activate tokens; #CT: max. number of cancel tokens; #Op: total number of HW operators.

	#lines	#cycles	DOP max	#AT max	#CT max	#Op
adpcm	79	4497	4	101	7	123
bitcount	5	99	2	12	1	12
des	7	437	6	57	1	74
pegwit	9	797	4	70	6	96
parallel	55	398	50	256	50	315
test	11	77	2	21	5	21
test_unrolled	57	64	7	77	12	60

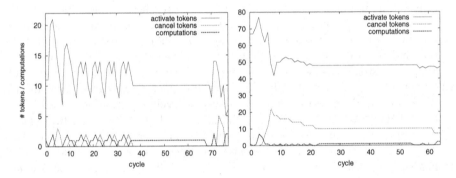

Fig. 4. *test* (left) and *test_unrolled* (right): tokens and parallel computations over time

The DOP value of the `parallel` kernel in Table 1 reveals that all data-independent computations are actually done in parallel. The number of activate tokens (AT) in flight exceeds the operator parallelism, since each operator stores an AT per *outgoing* CMDFG edge. Thus, an increase of operator dependencies directly translates into an increase of ATs. The number of cancel tokens (CT) is much smaller, which means that only a relatively small number of operations had to be cancelled due to mis-speculation.

The left graph of Fig. 4 shows the AT, CT and DOP values for `test` over time. The peaks are correlated to new loop iterations. The first five iterations (6 or 9 cycles each) are much faster than the last iteration (40 cycles), because the data path containing the high-latency divider was cancelled in all but the last iteration, demonstrating the efficiency of cancel tokens.

As the `test` example contains a loop-carried dependency (variable s), unrolling the for-loop achieves only a relatively small performance gain (64 instead of 77 cycles), at the large expense of tripling the number of HW operators. This shows

Table 2. Measured and calculated execution times for the separate iterations of the test example. The number of cycles per iteration corresponds to the number of cycles needed to compute a new value for variable s_2_0 (see Fig. 2(b,c)).

Iteration	trivial approach	lenient execution (non-pipelined div)	lenient execution (pipelined div)	cancel tokens
	#cycles (calc.)	#cycles (calc.)	#cycles (calc.)	#cycles (meas.)
$i = 0$	40	6	6	6
$i = 1$	40	36	36	9
$i = 2$	40	36	6	6
$i = 3$	40	36	35	6
$i = 4$	40	36	6	6
$i = 5$	40	72	41	40
Total	240	222	130	73

a typical situation where pipelining would be similarly inefficient. Here, it would be more efficient to omit the unrolling and execute the loop in a non-pipelined fashion, relying instead on our cancel mechanism for speed-ups.

For the test example, Table 2 compares our cancel token approach to the trivial approach and lenient execution. The values shown are actual measurements for the cancel-token approach using non-pipelined operators. The trivial approach and lenient execution values had to be manually calculated, since no corresponding compiler implementations are available. To calculate these numbers, we assume the same operators and data flow as used by the cancel token approach.

Assuming the trivial approach, *each* iteration would require 40 cycles since the merge points in the data path would *always* have to wait for the slowest branch (the divider). Because of the LCD, this holds for both using a pipelined or a non-pipelined divider.

Lenient execution with a non-pipelined divider computes the first iteration in only 6 cycles, but consecutive iterations have to wait for the divider, resulting in 36 cycles per iteration. In the last iteration, the divider first has to finish its computation for $i = 4$ and after that additionally computes the value for $i = 5$, which results in 72 cycles.

A pipelined divider significantly increases the performance of the lenient execution version. But there are still long delays every two iterations arising from the fact that the multiplexer for s_7_0 (the successor of the divider in the data flow) cannot forward a value before the divider has completed its computation of the previous iteration (i.e., the multiplexer cannot store the information that two or more values from one of its inputs have to be discarded).

In the cancel token approach, the divider being non-pipelined, the time-consuming data flow branch containing the divider is cancelled in the first five iterations, thus its latency affects only the iteration for $i = 5$. Here, a pipelined divider wouldn't increase performance due to the LCD.

In summary, Table 2 shows that cancel tokens can achieve significant improvements of runtime compared to the other approaches. These gains are due to the differing lengths of data path branches, which of course vary between different applications. Note that we did not yet consider the impact of reduced memory traffic due to cancelling of mis-speculated memory accesses. This will be evaluated in future work.

8   Conclusion and Future Work

We have presented a method for dynamically scheduling speculative data paths using cancel tokens, which allow the explicit cancelling of mis-speculated paths at run-time. We have already implemented cancel tokens in the hardware generation passes of the compiler COMRADE, and have thus practically demonstrated their feasibility and measured their effect on several benchmark kernels. Our method leads to significantly faster hardware than the trivial and lenient execution approaches commonly used today. The impact of cancelling in-flight memory accesses has not even been considered here yet. Future work will concentrate on implementing the mechanisms (both in the compiler as well as in the hardware memory system) allowing this cancelling of mis-speculated memory operations.

References

1. Callahan, T., Hauser, J., Wawrzynek, J.: The Garp architecture and C Compiler. IEEE Computer 33(4), 62–69 (2000)
2. MacMillen, D.: Nimble Compiler Environment for Agile Hardware. Storming Media LLC, USA (2001)
3. Budiu, M.: Spatial Computation. Ph.D. Thesis, Computer Science Department, Carnegie Mellon University, Pittsburgh, PA, USA (December 2003)
4. Gupta, S., et al.: SPARK: A High-Level Synthesis Framework for Applying Parallelizing Compiler Transformations. In: Intl. Conf. on VLSI Design (VLSI), New Delhi, India (January 2003)
5. Guo, Z., Buyukkurt, B., Najjar, W., Vissers, K.: Optimized Generation of Datapath from C Codes for FPGAs. In: Intl. Conf. on Design, Automation, and Test in Europe (DATE), Munich, Germany (March 2005)
6. Mishra, M., Callahan, T., Chelcea, T., Venkataramani, G., Budiu, M., Goldstein, S.: Tartan: Evaluating Spatial Computation for Whole Program Execution. In: Intl. Conf. on Architectural Support for Programming Languages and Operating Systems (ASPLOS), San Jose, California, USA (October 2006)
7. Koch, A., Kasprzyk, N.: High-Level-Language Compilation for Reconfigurable Computers. In: Intl. Conf. on Reconfigurable Communication-centric SoCs (ReCoSoC), Montpellier, France (June 2005)
8. Gädke, H., Koch, A.: COMRADE: A Compiler for Adaptive Computing Systems Using a Novel Fast Speculation Technique. In: Intl. Conf. on Field Programmable Logic and Applications (FPL), Amsterdam, Netherlands (August 2007)
9. Kountouris, A., Wolinski, C.: Efficient Scheduling of Conditional Behaviors for High-Level Synthesis. ACM Transactions on Design Automation of Electronic Systems (TODAES) 7(3), 380–412 (2002)

10. Gong, W., Wang, G., Kastner, R.: A High Performance Application Representation for Reconfigurable Systems. In: Intl. Conf. on Engineering of Reconfigurable Systems and Algorithms (ERSA), Las Vegas, NEV, USA (June 2004)
11. Mencer, O., Hubert, H., Morf, M., Flynn, M.: StReAm: Object-Oriented Programming of Stream Architectures using PAM-Blox. In: IEEE Symposium on Field-Programmable Custom Computing Machines (FCCM), Napa Valley, CA, USA (April 2000)
12. Styles, H., Luk, W.: Pipelining Designs with Loop-Carried Dependencies. In: IEEE Intl. Conf. on Field-Programmable Technology (FPT), Brisbane, Australia (December 2004)
13. Brej, C., Garside, J.: Early Output Logic using Anti-Tokens. In: Intl. Workshop on Logic Synthesis (IWLS), Laguna Beach, CA, USA (March 2003)
14. Ampalam, M., Singh, M.: Counterflow Pipelining: Architectural Support for Preemption in Asynchronous Systems using Anti-Tokens. In: Intl. Conf. on Computer Aided Design (ICCAD), San Jose, CA, USA (November 2006)
15. Kasprzyk, N.: COMRADE - Ein Hochsprachen-Compiler für Adaptive Computersysteme. Ph.D. Thesis, Integrated Circuit Design (E.I.S.), Tech. Univ. Braunschweig, Germany (June 2005)
16. Ferrante, J.: The Program Dependence Graph and Its Use in Optimization. ACM Transactions on Programming Languages and Systems (TOPLAS) 9(3), 319–349 (1987)
17. Campbell, P., Krishna, K., Ballance, R.: Refining and Defining the Program Dependence Web. Technical Report TR 93-6, Department of Computer Science, University of New Mexico, Albuquerque, NM, USA (March 1993)
18. Koch, A.: Advances in Adaptive Computer Technology. Habilitation, Integrated Circuit Design (E.I.S.), Tech. Univ. Braunschweig, Germany (December 2004)
19. Neumann, T., Koch, A.: A Generic Library for Adaptive Computing Environments. In: Intl. Conf. on Field-Programmable Logic and Applications (FPL), Belfast, Northern Ireland, UK (2001)
20. Lange, H., Koch, A.: An Execution Model for Hardware/Software Compilation and its System-Level Realization. In: Intl. Conf. on Field-Programmable Logic and Applications (FPL), Amsterdam, Netherlands (August 2007)
21. Lange, H., Koch, A.: Memory Access Schemes for Configurable Processors. In: Intl. Conf. on Field-Programmable Logic and Applications (FPL), Villach, Austria (August 2000)

ARISE Machines: Extending Processors with Hybrid Accelerators

Nikolaos Vassiliadis, George Theodoridis, and Spiridon Nikolaidis

Electronics and Computer Section, Physics Department, Aristotle University of
Thessaloniki, Greece
nivas@physics.auth.gr

Abstract. ARISE introduces a systematic approach to extend once a
processor to support thereafter the coupling of an arbitrary number of
Custom Computing Units (*CCUs*). A CCU, hardwired or reconfigurable,
can be utilized in a hybrid, tight and/or loose, model of computation. By
selecting the appropriate model for each part of the application, the complete application space can be considered for acceleration, resulting to
significant performance improvements. To support these features ARISE
proposes: i) a machine organization, ii) a set of Instruction Set Extensions (*ISEs*), and iii) a micro-architecture. To evaluate our proposal, a
MIPS processor is extended with the ARISE infrastructure and implemented on an FPGA. Results show that the ARISE infrastructure can
easily fit into the timing model of the processor. A set of benchmarks is
mapped on the evaluation machine and it is proved that exploiting the
hybrid model of computation, performance improvements of up to 68%
are achieved compared to the case when only one model is supported.
This results to significant application speedups from 2.4x up to 4.8x.

Keywords: reconfigurable instruction set processor, coprocessor, custom unit, FPGA.

1 Introduction

Extending a general purpose processor with CCUs is an effective way to meet
the computational demands of modern applications. In such systems, the base
Instruction Set Architecture (*ISA*) of the processor serves as the bulk of flexibility to execute any algorithm, while the CCUs are exploited through ISEs to
accelerate the execution of computational-intensive parts. Furthermore, providing the CCUs with the capability to reconfigure their functionality, high degrees
of flexibility are gained. Reconfigurable CCUs provide dynamic ISEs offering the
adaptation of the system to the target application.

In the majority of existing systems the CCUs are coupled to the processor
following either a tight (as a functional unit) or a loose (as a co-processor) model
of computation. Each of these models exhibits advantages and disadvantages
making it preferable for specific type of applications. Thus, supporting only one
model may lead to unexploited performance gains. To address this drawback

R. Woods et al. (Eds.): ARC 2008, LNCS 4943, pp. 196–208, 2008.

we introduce the Aristotle Reconfigurable Instruction Set Extensions (*ARISE*) framework. ARISE proposes a systematic approach to extend once a processor to support thereafter any number and type of CCUs. ARISE is comprised of: i) a machine organization that allows the co-operation of the CCUs and processor, ii) an one-time extension of the ISA of the processor with eight new instructions, called *ARISE ISEs*, to control the CCUs, and iii) an efficient micro-architecture implementation. After an ARISE-aware machine has been developed, arbitrary number and types of CCUs can be coupled to the processor and utilized following any model of computation to meet the specifications of the target application.

To evaluate our proposal a MIPS-I processor core is extended and an ARISE machine is developed. The machine is implemented on a Xilinx FPGA and validate that the performed extensions do not affect the timing model of the processor. A set of benchmarks is implemented on the machine and experimental results prove that ARISE combines the tight and loose model of computations to achieve important performance improvements.

The rest of the paper is organized as follows. Section 2 discusses related work. In Section 3 the general overview of ARISE machine is given. Section 4 presents the development of the evaluation ARISE machine, its synthesis and performance experimental results. Finally conclusions are drowned in Section 5.

2 Related Work

Over the last years a number of academic (e.g. [17], [18]) and commercial (e.g. Xtensa, ARC) configurable systems have been introduced that extend a core processor with application-specific CCUs. As these systems supports CCUs of small or none reconfigurability they lack flexibility. Reconfigurable technology offers a lot of advantages to meet the computational demands of modern application. Thus, a number of commercial processors supporting the coupling of reconfigurable CCUs became available. Such processors are available as soft-cores (e.g. NIOS II, microBlaze) or hard-cores (e.g. Xilinx PowerPC APU, Stretch S6000).

Based on the approach followed to couple the CCUs to the processor, the existing systems can be divided in two categories. In the first one, the CCUs are loosely-coupled to the processor following a co-processor model of computation, like [1]-[4]. In these systems, the CCUs undertake the execution of computational-intensive parts that loosely interact with the remaining parts of the application. Due to the loose interaction between them, the processor and the CCUs can operate concurrently resulting in high performance. However, the control of the CCUs and the data communication between the CCUs and the processor are done explicitly through a number of instructions. This results in a communication and control overhead, which may eliminate the performance gains if autonomous tasks can not be found.

In the second category, the CCUs are tightly-coupled as functional units of the processor's pipeline (e.g. [5]-[8]). In these systems the CCUs execute fine-grain tasks that strongly interact with the execution flow of the processor. The communication of operands between the processor and CCUs is performed through the register file. Operations that are executed by the CCUs are identified and controlled via opcodes encoded in the instruction word. Thus, the communication and control overheads are reduced. However, the size of the instruction word limits the number of different operations and the number of operands supported per operation resulting in unexploited performance improvements.

It is clear that each of the above models of computation exhibits advantages and disadvantages. Thus, a hybrid approach supporting both models can increase the efficiency of the machine. For example in [18] a methodology to generate and select hybrid CCUs targeting at a configurable Xtensa processor was presented. Experimental results proved that a hybrid approach achieves better area/performance tradeoffs than using only one of them.

In contrast to the presented related work, ARISE proposes a systematic approach to extend once any typical embedded processor with the necessary infrastructure to support thereafter the coupling of any number of reconfigurable CCUs. The CCUs can then be exploited using any computational model or even a hybrid combination of them, to satisfy the needs of the target application. This results to significant speedup improvements and reduction of area requirements.

3   Overview of ARISE Machines

Our approach assumes that several computational-intensive parts of the application have already identified and each of them can be more efficiently executed on a CCU as a single operation called *ARISE operation*. Such an operation may be as simple as a few nodes of the application's DFG or as complex as a kernel.

3.1   Machine Organization and Instruction Set Extensions

An ARISE machine, depicted in Figure 1, consists of: a) the Core Processor (CP), b) the ARISE instruction decoder, c) the ARISE interface, and d) the CCU wrappers. The interface is further divided into: i) the control unit, ii) the Opcode-to-Id table, and ii) the Input/Output Buffer (IOB).

The extension of the processor with the interface is performed once. Then, an arbitrary number of CCUs can be attached, via the interface, employing a wrapper for each CCU. To provide CCUs with configuration bits and data, the memory is accessed through the memory ports of the processor. Additionally, dedicated configuration memory and memory ports can be used to increase memory bandwidth. To utilize the CCUs, the processor's ISA is extended once with a set of specific instructions, called *ARISE instructions*, which control: 1) the execution of the ARISE operations on the CCUs, 2) the data communication between the CP and the CCUs, and 3) the configuration of the CCUs.

All ARISE instructions have the same format that includes three fields defining: i) the type of the ARISE instruction (*instr*), ii) the opcode (*opc*) of an ARISE operation, and iii) the operands (*operands*) of the instruction. To extend the CP's ISA with ARISE instructions these fields are encoded into the instruction word of a CP as shown in Figure 2. As an example, a typical format of a processor's instruction word is assumed of which only one *opcode* is reserved

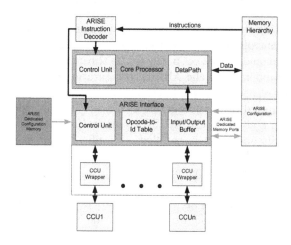

Fig. 1. Organization of an ARISE machine

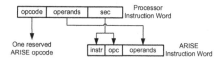

Fig. 2. Encoding the ARISE instruction word into a processor's instruction word

for all ARISE instructions. The secondary field, *sec*, is used to encode both the *instr* and *opc* fields, while the *operands* fields are the same. The operands of an ARISE instruction are accessed via the register file of the CP.

Instructions are pre-decoded by the ARISE Instruction Decoder to determine their type (CP or ARISE instructions) and they are issued accordingly to the CP or to interface. On the Opcode-to-Id Table the *opc* field, which has limited bit-width, is assigned to a unique identifier, Id, which can be of arbitrary size. The Id identifies an ARISE operation implemented on a CCU. The table also allows the dynamic (at execution time) re-assignment of the *opc* to an Id. Thus, the same *opc* in an ARISE instruction can be assigned to different ARISE operations. In that way the number of different ARISE operations is not constraint by the limited bit-width of the *opc* field. Also, the assignment of *opc* to operations is not fixed. Thus, new CCUs and ARISE operations implemented on them can be easily ported providing them with an Id.

The IOB provides temporary storage space for the operands of an ARISE operation. It is exploited (through a sequence of move instructions) to support operations with more operands than the CP's register file provides/accepts per instruction. It is also configured to utilize the complete bandwidth of the register file (i.e. all register file ports) and it is implemented to do the above without extra latency. The IOB is not exposed to the architecture meaning that its registers are not addressable. Operands of an ARISE operation are stored and accessed from consecutive places in the IOB. Exploiting the IOB the operand limitation problem is alleviated with the minimum communication overhead (without considering the case of increasing the register file ports).

The wrapper controls the configuration and execution of an ARISE operation. It also serves the memory accesses of the CCUs through the CP's memory ports. Moreover, the wrapper stores the ARISE configuration bitstream for each operation. Two types of configuration bitstreams exist in an ARISE machine. The first is the one required by reconfigurable CCUs and it is provided by the CCU's vendor tools. The second, is the ARISE configuration bitstream that specifies the way an ARISE operation is handled . Specifically, for each operation the ARISE configuration bitstream defines: 1) if it accesses the data memory, 2) if its latency is known or not at compile time, 3) its latency (CP cycles), and 4) its exception policy. With this information the wrapper controls the execution of the ARISE operation transparently to the processor architecture.

ARISE instructions are configured at design time to match the characteristics of the CP. The typical configuration presented below assumes that the register file provides at least two read and one write port, which is a typical case for embedded processors. It can be also configured to utilize register files with more ports. The typical configuration contains the following ARISE instructions:

confopc2id <**opc**>, <**id**>: The "*configure opcode-to-id*" instruction assigns the opcode of an ARISE operation to a unique identifier Id. This assignment is stored in the Opcode-to-Id table.

confld <**opc**>, <**start_addr**>, <**end_addr**>: The "*load configuration*" instruction is responsible for the loading of the ARISE and CCUs (if reconfigurable CCUs are used) configuration bitstreams. The loading is performed for the operation assigned to the <opc> value. The <start_addr> and <end_addr> operands determine the memory space where the bitstreams are placed. During the execution of this instruction the CP is stalled. An extra instruction, the confld_conc ("*load configuration in concurrent mode*") is included to perform the same operation without stalling the CP.

movta <**src1**>,...., <**srcM**>: The "*move to ARISE*" instruction transfers the contents of registers src1...srcM to the Input Buffer. <srcM> corresponds to the m-th read port of the register file of the CP. A sequence of movta instructions stores the input operands of an ARISE operations in consecutive places in the Input Buffer.

movfa <**dest1**>, ..., <**destN**>: The "*move from ARISE*" instruction moves the results of an ARISE operation from the Output Buffer to registers dest1 ...destN. <destN> corresponds to the n-th write port of the register file. A sequence of movfa instructions reads the output operands of an ARISE operations from consecutive places of the Output Buffer.

execa <**opc**>, <**dest1**>,.., <**destN**>, <**src1**>, .., <**srcM**>: The "*execute ARISE*" instruction initiates the execution of the ARISE operation defined by the <opc> field. The input operands are moved from the src1srcM registers of the CP's register file to the Input Buffer, while the output operands are moved from the Output Buffer to the dest1destN registers. Until the completion of the ARISE operation the CP is stalled. The **execa_conc** <**opc**>, <**src1**>,..,

<srcM> ("*execute ARISE in concurrent mode*") that performs the same operation without stalling the CP, is also supported. It does not contain destination operands, while the results of the ARISE operation are returned to CP explicitly through *movfa* instructions. Fetching a *movfa* instruction before the completion of an *execa_conc* instruction breaks the concurrent operation of CP and CCU to ensure data coherency.

checka <dest>: The "*check ARISE status*" instruction returns the ARISE Status Register (ASR), which encodes the current status of the ARISE (error, configuring, executing etc) to the register <dest> of the CP register file.

For all the aforementioned instructions the operands are accessed through the register file. The only exception is the <opc> that is encoded in the opc field of the ARISE instruction word. A more detailed description of the machine organization, the ARISE ISEs, and the programming of an ARISE machine exist in [14], which also includes a version of ARISE instructions that support one operand per instruction.

In an ARISE machine, a CCU is tightly integrated in the processor's architecture. However, this CCU can execute operations in a loose computational model by operating concurrently with the CP while direct memory access is provided to the CCU through the wrapper. Furthermore, using the *execa* instruction the same CCU can execute operations in a tight computational model with minimum communication and control overhead. Concluding, the proposed machine organization and ISEs can exploit a CCU in a hybrid, loose or tight, computational model based on the characteristics of the target application.

3.2 Micro-architecture Implementation

The block diagram of Figure 3, presents the micro-architecture of an ARISE machine, which is composed of the CP and the ARISE interface. The interface is organized in a pipeline structure, which designed to easily extent the pipeline of the CP. As an example, a single-issue in-order processor with five pipeline stages is used. The interface consists of three pipeline stages, which are: 1) the pre-processing (PRE), in which the instructions are decoded and the operands are fetched, 2) the processing (PRO), in which the operands are processed, and 3) the post-processing (POST) stage, which returns the result of the processing. To incorporate the ARISE interface the pipeline of the CP is augmented with a number of well-defined extensions, which have been marked with circled numbers in Figure 3. In addition, the interface can stall the CP.

To pre-decode the fetched instruction, the IF stage of the CP is extended by the ARISE instruction decoder. This decoder produces the ARISE and CP instruction words and forwards them to the PRE and ID stages, respectively. At the PRE stage, based on the received *instr* value, the ARISE Control Unit generates the control signals for all ARISE components. Also, based on the executed ARISE instruction, the Opcode-to-Id table provides the Id that already has assigned to the *opc* of the executed instruction or performs a new assignment. The Id is forwarded to the CCU wrapper at stage PRO to define the ARISE operation.

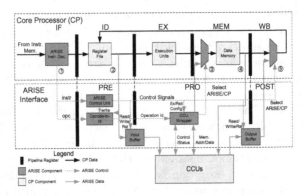

Fig. 3. Micro-architecture of an ARISE machine

The second extension point (2) is a link from the read ports of the CP's register file to the PRE stage of the interface. This link is used for providing the operands of an ARISE instruction from the register file. The operands of an ARISE operation are temporary stored into the Input Buffer that operates as a pipeline register between the PRE and PRO stages. Thus, an *execa* instruction reads the input operands at the PRE stage and initiates the execution of the ARISE operation without extra latency.

The interface access the data memory through points (3) and (4). The wrapper controls the multiplexer at point (3) for sharing the memory between the CP and CCUs. If both request access to memory the wrapper stalls the CP. Afterward, via the link (4) the data are accessed by the CCUs. The results of an ARISE operation are stored in Output Buffer, which operates like a pipeline register between the PRO and POST stages. At the POST stage, the results of the ARISE operation are returned to the register file via the multiplexer at point (5) which is controlled by the ARISE control unit.

Since ARISE is tightly integrated to the processor, modifications on the processor's micro-architecture are needed. However, the control of the processor remains unchanged. The only, requirement is that the ARISE interface should be able to stall the CP and block interrupts/exceptions. Also, ARISE is organized into a pipeline that operates in parallel to the CP's pipeline. The implementation (see next section) shows that ARISE fits in the CP's timing model without degrading its performance.

4   Experimental Results

To evaluate our proposal, we experimented with a MIPS processor that was extended with the ARISE components. Specifically, the MIPS-I ISA and its R3000 implementation was used. This is an in-order, five-stage pipelined, 32-bit RISC processor, featuring a three-address ISA similar to that used in Section 2. Thus, all conclusions presented in Section 2, are applicable and no any further consideration is required concerning the extension of the MIPS core. The configuration

Table 1. ARISE configuration

Feature	Configuration
opc length	6-bit; 64 opcodes
Id length	7-bit; 128 operations
# of configurations in wrapper	32
ARISE Configuration bitstream	24 bits
Input Buffer size / write ports	16 registers/2 ports
Output Buffer size / read ports	8 registers/1 port

Table 2. ARISE machine synthesis results

		FPGA Slices	fmax (MHz)
CP	MIPS-I	2788[1]	103
ARISE	Wrapper	722	416
	Instruct. Decoder	36	457
	Input Buffer	319	537
	Output Buffer	218	510
	Opcode-to-Id	418	361

[1] Including 2 DSP Blocks

selected for the various features of the ARISE machine is shown in Table 1. Furthermore, the CCUs access the data memory through the standard memory port of the processor that provides a bandwidth of 32-bits per cycle.

4.1 Synthesis Results

This ARISE machine was implemented on a Xilinx xc4vlx25 device (speed grade 12) and synthesis results are presented in Table 2. Results indicate that the ARISE components consume a reasonable amount of resources. The remaining FPGA resources were used to implement a CCU on which the ARISE operations are executed. The frequency values were derived measuring the critical-path of the whole ARISE machine (CP extended with the ARISE components) that each component contributes to. Results prove that the ARISE infrastructure easily fits into the timing model of the processor. For the rest of the experiments the ARISE machine was clocked at the operation frequency of the MIPS processor, namely at 103 MHz.

4.2 Performance Study

In the following we study the performance improvements when a loose, tight, or hybrid computational model is adopted. As mentioned, ARISE offers the capability to support both these models allowing some parts of the application to be accelerated under the loose and some other parts under the tight model. To the best of our knowledge ARISE is the only machine in the field that supports such a hybrid model.

The compiler of the ARISE machine is based on the GNU tool-chain. The GNU compiler was cross-built targeting at MIPS-I, while its assembler was extended to support the interpretation of the ARISE instructions. The ArchC [9] MIPS processor model was also modified to implement the ARISE infrastructure and used as simulation and evaluation platform. It must be stressed that this platform is cycle accurate ensuring the correctness and accuracy of the results presented bellow. To evaluate performance we experimented with a set of benchmarks derived from the MiBench [10] (adpcm.enc, adpcm.dec) and Motorola Powerstone [11] (crc, jpeg, des, pocsag) benchmarking suites.

Loose model of computation. In this model, the parts of the application that are considered for acceleration as ARISE operations are coarse-grain computational-intensive parts (kernels) that weakly interact with the rest of the control flow of the application. Usually, they are identified as application's procedures. Thus, the benchmarks were first compiled for MIPS-I and the GNU *gprof* tool was used to identify such kernels for each benchmark. The SPARK [15] high-level synthesis tool was then used to generate VHDL code for each kernel. The kernels were implemented on the FPGA and the synthesis results are presented in Table 3. The second column of the table presents the kernel percentage of the total workload, while column three shows FPGA resources consumed by each kernel. Column four, reports the latency (in terms of processor cycles) required by each kernel to execute on the FPGA. Average latencies are reported for the cases when execution time is not known at compile time. For all following experimental results, the complete ARISE machine and ARISE operations were concurrently implemented on the FPGA.

The source code of each benchmark was modified to configure and execute the ARISE operations and the ARISE configuration bitstreams for each operation was produced and included in the source code. Furthermore, the source code was configured to execute the ARISE operation in concurrent mode, thus maximizing the performance improvements. Figure 4, specifically the second bar for

Table 3. Kernels synthesis results

Benhmark/Kernel	Workload (%)	FPGA Slices	Latency (Cycles)
adpcm_coder/ adpcm.enc	99.9	588	12361^2
adpcm_decoder/ adpcm.dec	99.9	406	10355^2
icrc1/crc	72.1	218	12
set_key/des	60.8	1021	224
encrypt/des	32.9	1120	206
fast_idct_8/jpeg	56.3	973^1	20
find_syndromes/pocsag	39.3	149	95
comp32/pocsag	29.7	169	7
alpha_proc/pocsag	4.6	562	7
num_proc/pocsag	2.5	125	14

[1] Including 24 DSP Blocks   [2] Average

Table 4. Speedup comparison for ARISE and co-processor approaches

Benchmark	Co-Processor	ARISE	Differ.(%)
adpcm.enc	4.0	4.0	0.0
adpcm.dec	3.7	3.8	2.7
crc	2.3	2.8	21.7
des	4.6	4.8	4.3
jpeg	2.0	2.1	5.0
pocsag	1.7	2.2	29.4

each benchmark, shows the speedups achieved for each benchmark for the loose model of computation. The speedup is calculated by comparing the number of cycles required to execute the benchmarks with and without support of ARISE operations. In all cases, overhead cycles required to configure ARISE for execution were included in the results. As presented, significant speedups ranging from 2.1x to 4.8x are achieved.

A key-feature of ARISE machines is that they effectively address the communication overhead between the CP and CCUs. To evaluate this for the case of loose model of computation, we compared the ARISE machine against an alternative approach which follows a typical co-processor programming paradigm. To accomplish this, the above kernels were coupled to the CP as memory-mapped co-processors. This means that the CP and the co-processors are exchanging control and data values via memory. The memory latency for each exchange was assumed to be one cycle. Speedup comparisons are shown in Table 4. Results indicate that when the time required to execute a kernel on the CCU/co-processor (see Table 3) is high the impact of the communication overhead is negligible. Thus, performance is not affected in this case. Therefore, the two *adpcm* benchmarks achieve the same speedup for both approaches. However, as the execution time reduces the impact of the communication overhead increases. As shown in Table 4, this affects mainly the co-processor approach. Since ARISE alleviates this limitation performance improvements up to 29.4% are achieved compared to co-processor approach.

Tight model of computation. In this model, the parts of the application which are considered for acceleration as ARISE operations are simpler than those of loose model. Specifically, they are acyclic sub-graphs of the application's DFG and consist of a few nodes collapsed into a single operation. They do not access the data memory, while due to their tight interaction with the application's flow they cannot benefit by concurrent execution. Therefore, such operations may provide smaller performance improvements compared to the loose model. However, a wider range of the application's space, rather than only the kernels, can be considered for acceleration.

To identify such operations and evaluate the performance of the ARISE machine, the following were performed. First, the MaxMISO [12] (Maximal Multiple-Input Single-Output) algorithm was implemented into the Harvard Machine SUIF [13] back-end compiler framework. This algorithm identifies the

Table 5. MaxMISO operations results

Benchmark	Operations	FPGA Slices
adpcm.enc	7	116
adpcm.dec	7	148
crc	15	318
des	46	1410
jpeg	42	888[1]
pocsag	10	164

[1] Including 24 DSP Blocks

maximum non-overlapping connected sub-graphs of the basic blocks that produce a single result. Then, it was used to automatically identify such sub-graphs for each benchmark. The obtained sub-graphs implemented on the FPGA as ARISE operations and synthesis results are presented in Table 5.

Speedup results achieved for each benchmark operating under the tight model of computation are shown in Figure 4 (first bar for each benchmark). As expected the achieved speedups are significantly smaller compared to the loose model. They are ranging from 1.2x for the two *adpcm* benchmarks, to 1.9x for the case of *des*. It must be noticed that the tight model of computation and the corresponding operations cannot be supported by machines developed only for a loose computational model. This happens because in the tight model each operation contributes a small number of cycle count reduction. Therefore, if the communication overhead is high this contribution is eliminated. To prove this statement we re-performed the experiments comparing against the memory mapped co-processor used before. For all benchmarks the co-processor approach failed to deliver any performance improvements.

Hybrid model of computation. In an ARISE machine the two models of computation can be combined into a hybrid model to achieve better performance improvements. That is, the kernels of the application are accelerated following a loose model, while the reaming part of the application is accelerated based on a tight model. Since, the whole application space is improved, high performance gains are expected. To evaluate this feature we combined the two previously presented experiments into one that exploits both models. Specifically, it was assumed that the benchmarks are first implemented following a loose model while the remaining parts of the benchmarks are considered by the MaxMISO algorithm to produce the operations corresponding to the tight model. For the hybrid model case speedups are reported for each benchmark by the third bar in Figure 4. The two *adpcm* and the *des* benchmarks were not benefited from the hybrid model, since almost the complete application workload is consumed into kernels. However, for the other benchmarks the ARISE machine operating in hybrid model, efficiently combines the advantages of tight and loose models to achieve impressive performance improvements. Thus, for the *crc* and *jpeg* benchmarks speedup is improved by 68% and 62% respectively, compared to the loose model of computation. For the *pocsag* the limited performance from the MaxMISO operations resulted to only 10% speedup improvement.

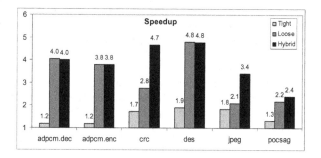

Fig. 4. Speedup results for ARISE machine operating in various models of computation

5   Conclusions

A systematic approach to extend a typical processor once to support thereafter the coupling of arbitrary hardware accelerators was presented. It was proved that the extensions can be easily fit into the timing model of a processor without degrading its performance. Then, it was demonstrated how the resulting machine exploits a hybrid, loose or tight, model of computation to increase the performance. Performance results showed an improvement of up to 68% compared to a typical approach that utilizes only one of the two models.

Acknowledgments. This work was supported by PENED 2003 programme of the General Secretariat for Research and Technology of Greece and the EU.

References

1. Hauser, J.R., Wawrzynek, J.: Garp: A MIPS Processor with a Reconfigurable Co-processor. In: FCCM, pp. 12–21 (1997)
2. Goldstein, S.C., et al.: PipeRench: A Coprocessor for Streaming Multimedia Acceleration. In: ISCA, pp. 28–39 (1999)
3. Singh, H., et al.: MorphoSys: an Integrated Reconfigurable System for Data Parallel and Computation-Intensive Applications. IEEE Trans. on Comp. 465–481 (2000)
4. Vassiliadis, S., et al.: The Molen Polymorphic Processor. IEEE Trans. on Comp. 53(11), 1363–1375 (2004)
5. Clark, N., et al.: An Architecture Framework for Transparent Instruction Set Customization in Embedded Processors. In: ISCA, pp. 272–283 (2005)
6. Vassiliadis, N., et al.: A RISC architecture extended by an efficient tightly coupled reconfigurable unit. Int. Journal of Electronics 93(6), 421–438 (2006)
7. Lodi, A., et al.: A VLIW Processor with Reconfigurable Instruction Set for Embedded Applications. IEEE Journal of Solid-State Circuits 38(11), 1876–1886 (2003)
8. Hauck, S., et al.: The Chimaera Reconfigurable Functional Unit. In: FCCM, pp. 87–96 (1997)
9. The ArchC Website: http://www.archc.org
10. Guthausch, M.R., et al.: Mibench: A free, commercially representative embedded benchmark suite. In: IEEE 4th Annual Workshop on Workload Characterization, pp. 3–14 (2001)

11. Scott, J., et al.: Designing the Low- Power MoCORE Architecture. In: Int'l. Symp. on Comp. Arch. Power Driven Microarch. Workshop, pp. 145–150 (1998)
12. Alippi, C., et al.: A DAG Based Design Approach for Reconfigurable VLIW Processors. In: IEEE DATE, pp. 778–779 (1999)
13. Machine-SUIF research compiler,
    http://www.eecs.harvard.edu/hube/research/machsuif.html
14. Vassiliadis, N., et al.: The ARISE Reconfigurable Instruction Set Extensions Framework. In: Proc. of IC-SAMOS, pp. 153–160 (2007)
15. Gupta, S., et al.: SPARK: A High-Level Synthesis Framework for Applying Parallelizing Compiler Transformations. In: Int. Conf. on VLSI Design, pp. 461–466 (2003)
16. Goodwin, D., Petkov, D.: Automatic generation of application specific processors. In: Proc. of CASES, pp. 137–147 (2003)
17. Atasu, K., et al.: Automatic application-specific instruction-set extensions under micro-architectural constraints. In: Proc. of DAC, pp. 256–261 (2003)
18. Sun, F., et al.: Automatic generation of application specific processors. IEEE TCAD 26(11), 2035–2045 (2007)

The Instruction-Set Extension Problem: A Survey

Carlo Galuzzi and Koen Bertels*

Computer Engineering, EEMCS
Delft University of Technology, The Netherlands
{C.Galuzzi,K.L.M.Bertels}@ewi.tudelft.nl

Abstract. Over the last years, we have witnessed the increased use of Application-Specific Instruction-Set Processors (ASIPs). These ASIPs are processors that have a customizable instruction-set, which can be tuned towards specific requirements. The identification, definition and implementation of those operations that provide the largest performance improvement and that should be hardwired, extending in this way the Instruction-Set, constitutes a major challenge. The purpose of this paper is to investigate and study the issues regarding the customization of an Instruction-Set in function of the specific requirements of an application. Additionally, the paper provides an overview of all relevant aspects of the problem and compensates the lack of a general view of the problem in the existing literature.

1 Motivation

Electronic devices are very common in everyday life. It's enough to think about mobile phones, digital cameras, etc. This great variety of devices can be implemented using different approaches and technologies. Usually these functionalities are implemented using either *General Purpose Processors* (GPPs), or *Application-Specific Integrated Circuits* (ASICs), or *Application-Specific Instruction-Set Processors* (ASIPs). GPPs can be used in many different applications in contrast to ASICs which are processors designed for a specific application such as the processor in a TV set top box.

The main difference between GPPs and ASICs is in terms of flexibility. The programmability of GPPs supports a broad range of possible applications but usually leads to more power consumption due to the inefficient units consumption. On the other hand, ASICs are able to satisfy specific constraints such as size, performance and power consumption using an optimal architecture for the application, but today designing and manufacturing an ASIC is a long and expensive process [1]. This design complexity grows exponentially due to shrinking geometries and the high mask and testing costs constitute a significant part of the manufacturing cost.

---

* This work was supported by the European Union in the context of the MORPHEUS project Num. 027342.

R. Woods et al. (Eds.): ARC 2008, LNCS 4943, pp. 209–220, 2008.

Over the last years, we have witnessed the increased use of GPPs that are combined with ASIPs. These ASIPs are processors situated in between GPPs and ASICs that have a customizable instruction-set, which can be tuned towards specific requirements. Time-to-market and reduced development costs have became increasingly important and have paved the way for reconfigurable architectures. These combine the flexibility of SW with the performance of HW. The higher cost/performance ratio for ASIPs have led researchers to look for methods and properties to maximize the performance of these processors. Each particular configuration can then be seen as an extension of the instruction-set. The identification, definition and implementation of those operations that provide the largest performance improvement and that should be hardwired, constitutes a major challenge.

The issues involved at each step are various and range from the isomorphism problem and the covering problem, well known computationally complex problems, to the function's study necessary for the guide function and the cost function, involved in the generation step and in the selection step respectively. Beside these, all the issues involved in this problem will be analyzed and studied in detail.

The customization of an instruction-set can be categorized in two main approaches. As the name suggests, complete customization involves the whole instruction-set which is tuned towards the requirements of an application [2,3,4,5], while partial customization involves the extension of an existing instruction-set by means of a limited number of instructions [6,7,8,9,10,11,12,13,14]. In both cases the goal is to design an Instruction-Set containing the most important operations needed by the application to maximize the performance. Besides providing an overall account, we also address considerations such as scalability, how to deal with overlapping instructions and how to address the complexity of the problem at hand.

The instruction-set customization problem represents a well specified topic where results and concepts from many different fields, such as engineering and graph theory are required. Especially the latter is the dominant approach and seems to provide the right analytical framework. Every application is thus represented by a directed graph and the required new complex instructions are seen as subgraphs having particular properties. The problem then translates into recognizing isomorphic subgraphs. Equally important are the covering and the selection problem. These are addressed by different techniques such as branch-and-bound, dynamic programming, etc. The proposed solutions are either exact, mathematical models whenever appropriate and possible or, given that the problem involved is known to be computationally complex, heuristics that are used in those cases where the mathematical solution is not computable.

The purpose of this paper is to investigate and study the issues regarding the customization of an instruction-set in function of the specific requirements of an application. The main goal of the paper is to provide a critical and detailed overview of all the aspects involved in instruction-set customization. The contribution of the paper is twofold: firstly, it provides an overview of **all relevant aspects** of the problem. Secondly, it compensates for the **lack** of a general view of the problem in the existing literature which only consists of **sporadic comparison** limited to isolated issues involved.

The paper is structured as follows. In Section 2, an introduction to the problem is presented. Section 3, 4 and 5 present the subproblems involved in the instruction-set customization, namely instruction generation and selection and the guide/cost function respectively. Section 6 presents an analysis of the type of instructions which is possible to generate. Concluding remarks and an outline of research conducted are given in Section 7.

2   Introduction to the Problem

Typically we start with a high level code, like C, that specifies the application and we manually specialize the embedded processor in a way that performance and cost constraints are satisfied. Irrespective of the type of customization, complete or partial, we can distinguish two approaches related to the level of abstraction on which we operate, i.e. the granularity at which code is considered: *fine-grained* and *coarse-grained*. The first one works at the operation level and implements small clusters of operations in HW [7,10,12,13,14,43,59,44]; the second one operates at the loop or procedure level and identifies critical loops or procedures in the application, and displaces them from SW to HW as a whole [16,17,18,19,20,21]. The main differences are in terms of speedups and flexibility: although a coarse-grained approach could produce a large speedup, its flexibility is limited, given that this approach is often performed on a per application basis and it is difficult that other applications have the same loop or procedure as critical part. Consequently many authors prefer either a fine-grained approach, even if it limits the achievable speedup compared to the coarse-grained one, or a mix of coarse and fine-grained techniques, since they operate at different levels and do not interfere with each other.

Basically the target is the identification of the operations that should be implemented in HW and the ones that have to be left for SW execution to achieve the requirements of the application. For this reason many authors naturally define this problem as a *HW-SW codesign problem* or *HW-SW partitioning* [22,23,24,25,26] which consists of concurrently balance at design time, the presence of HW and SW. The operations implemented in HW are incorporated in the processor either as new instructions and processor capabilities, in the form of special functional units integrated on the processor or implemented as peripheral devices. The interface between these systems parts is usually in the form of special purpose instructions embedded in the instruction stream. These HW components are more or less tightly coupled to the processor and involve different synchronization costs. Thus it becomes necessary also to select an appropriate communication and synchronization method within the architecture. The implementation of clusters of operations in HW as new complex operations, whatever nature they have, will benefit the overall performance only if the time the HW platform takes to evaluate them is less than the time required to compute the same operations in SW. As a result, compilation time and initialization time of the reconfigurable resources have to be considered as well.

At first, we profile the application SW looking for computation intensive segments of the code which, if mapped on HW, increases performance. The processor is then manually tailored to include the new capabilities. Although human ingenuity in manual creation of custom capabilities creates high quality results, performance and time-to-market requirements as well as the growing complexity of the design space, can benefit from an automatic design flow for the use of these new capabilities [28,29,12,30,31,32,13,14,60]. Moreover the selection of multiple custom instructions from a large set of candidates involves complex tradeoff and can be difficult to be performed manually.

There is a huge number of different interpretations and possible solutions to the instruction-set extension problem. Many authors adopt a graph theoretical approach in their work. Graph theory has became the dominant approach and seems to provide the right analytical framework. In this context the code of the application is represented with a directed graph, called the subject graph, and the intensive segments of the code to map on HW are subgraphs of the subject graph [12,14]. Depending on the level of abstraction on which we operate, nodes represent basic operations as well as entire procedures, functions or loops; edges represent data dependencies.

The extension of an instruction-set with new complex instructions can formally be divided into instruction generation and instruction selection. Given the application code, instruction generation consists of clustering of basic operations (such as add, or, load, etc.) or of mixed operations into larger and more complex operations. These complex operations are identified by subgraphs which can cover entirely or partially the subject graph. Once the *subgraphs* are identified, these are considered as single complex operations and they pass through a selection process. Generation and selection are performed with the use of a *guide function* and a *cost function* respectively, which take into account constraints that the new instructions have to satisfy to be implemented in HW. We now analyze instruction generation and instruction selection in more detail.

3   Instruction Generation

Instruction generation is mainly based on the concept of template. We call **template** a set of program statements that is a candidate for implementation as a custom instruction. Therefore a template is equivalent to a subgraph representing the list of statements selected in the subject graph, where nodes represent the operations and edges represent the data dependencies.

Instruction generation can be performed in two non exclusive ways: *using existing templates* or *creating new templates*. A collection of templates constitutes a **library of templates**. Many authors assume the existence of templates which are given as an input and which are identified inside the subject graph [33,6,31], however this is not always the case and many authors develop their own templates [16,17,34,7,10,35,14,43,59].

In the first case, instruction generation is nothing more than the identification of recurrences of specific templates from the library within the application. It is similar to the graph isomorphism problem [36,37,62]. In this case instruction generation can be considered as **template identification**. In the second case templates are identified inside the graph using a guide function. This function considers a certain number of parameters (often called constraints) and starting from a node taken as a seed, grows a template which respects all the parameters. Once a certain number of templates is identified the graph is usually reanalyzed to detect recurrences of the *built* templates.

The analysis of the application to identify instructions is often called design space exploration. We can detect a certain number of problems involved in instruction generation: (1) the complexity of the exploration, (2) the shape of the graph and (3) the overlapped templates.

A graph with n nodes contains 2^n subgraphs. Theoretically this means that there is an exponential number of possible new complex operations which can be selected inside a graph. This turns into an exponential complexity in the design space exploration. This problem can be avoided in two ways: reducing the design space explored, for example using heuristic instead of exact algorithms, or introducing more parameters into the guide function and introducing efficient bounding techniques. The use of heuristics, even though it reduces the design space explored, turns into the generation of non optimal solution or feasible ones, and they are often used with no theoretical guarantee. The introduction of additional parameters in the guide function can reduce the number of candidates for HW implementation, but has the drawback that every time a node is evaluated for a possible inclusion or not in the cluster, every parameter has to be satisfied and therefore the reduction of candidates turns into an increase of complexity of the approach due to the multiple analysis of the nodes.

A way to solve exactly covering problem is by using a **branch-and-bound** approach. This approach starts with a search space potentially exponential in size, and reduce step by step the search space using effective bounds and pruning techniques [38,39]. Other covering approaches use dynamic programming which is a way of decomposing certain hard to solve problems into equivalent formats that are more amenable to solution. A drawback of dynamic programming is that it can only operate on tree-shaped subject graph and patterns, excluding directed graph with cycles. Thus the non-tree-shaped graph has to be decomposed into sets of disjoint trees. Other approaches, like [10], are based on dynamic programming, without the requirement that the subject graph and the patterns are trees.

The second difficulty concerns the shape of the graph. First of all graphs can be divided in cyclic and acyclic graphs. Usually only acyclic graphs are considered during the analysis. This follows from the fact that acyclic graph can be easily sorted, for example by a topological ordering, whereas cyclic graph cannot. Therefore the trouble of defining a one-to-one order of the nodes to the complexity of the problem is added. Moreover a cyclic graph can be transformed into an acyclic one if, for example, the cycles are unrolled. An other problem is given by the management of disconnected graphs. Even though the study of the problem including disconnected graphs in the analysis allows for exploiting the parallelism provided by considering each connected components at the same time [40,12,14], in many cases the authors have taken up only the study of connected graphs [10,28,25,31,32,41], shifting the study of disconnected graph in the study of k graphs, where k is the number of connected components.

The last problem is the management of overlapped templates[1] [32,42]. This problem is mainly related to the case when templates are provided. Usually, when a template is grown, the nodes included in the template are removed from the nodes subject to further analysis and therefore two disjointed templates can not overlap. This problem which, for instance, can be solved with the replications of the common nodes between the overlapped template, is very important. By the replication of few nodes, the cost of the replicated nodes can be paltry compared to the gain in performance which it is possible to get implementing in HW all the overlapped templates, especially under tight area constraint. Although mainly related to instruction generation, overlapped templates are a problem which affects also instruction selection.

4   The Guide Function and the Cost Function

Instruction generation as well as instruction selection make use of a function to identify or select the most profitable instructions to hardwire. These functions are called **guide function** and **cost function** respectively. They are strictly related one another and both are used to help the search of new instructions.

The aim of the guide function in template generation is to help the identification of a certain number of templates inside the graph. The output of the guide function is a set P defined as follows: $P = \{T_i \subseteq G, \text{ with } i \in \mathbb{N}\}$, where G is the subject graph and T_i are the templates identified in G.

Instruction selection makes use of a cost function. This function, similar to the guide function, is used to prune the set of candidates P generated during instruction generation. The main goal of the cost function is the identification of an optimal subset $P_{Opt} \subseteq P$ of templates. These templates satisfy a certain number of constraints. This is usually reflected into a reduction of the execution time of the application, and/or into a properly filling of the available area on the reconfigurable component, and/or into a minimization of the delay, and/or of reduction the power consumption, etc. Clearly the bigger is the size of P, i.e. the greater is the number of templates identified inside the subject graph, the harder is the selection of $P_{Opt} \subseteq P$. Although this can be seen as an additional problem, it is not always the case. A big size of P in terms of candidates for HW implementation becomes useful when the constraints are changed, shrunk or relaxed allowing different choices of the subset P_{Opt} satisfying the new constraints. As a consequence, the reconfigurability of the approach benefits.

The guide function usually includes physical constraints as parameters like the number of inputs and outputs. Apart from that, the guide function can include more generally constraints which, if respected, allows the implementation

---

[1] For example two subgraphs with set of nodes $\{1, 2, 4\}$ and $\{1, 3, 5\}$ respectively overlap at node 2 and then only one of them is enumerated.

in HW. A cost function, however, reduces a big set and leaves those elements which increase performance. The two functions are often considered together since they have a similar use. When the functions are considered independently, a right division of the parameters taken into account by the functions can reduce the complexity of the approach limiting the number of checks. For example [12] describes an approach for the generation of convex MIMO operations. The new operations are grown from a single operation/node taken as a seed and the adjacent nodes are evaluated for inclusion in the cluster. Every time a node is analyzed for inclusion in the cluster, the node passes through a triple check: inputs, outputs and convexity. Using this approach to identify convex MISO operations the complexity can be reduced. This because a MISO operation is naturally a convex operation [14,43,44] and therefore a check on single outputs of the final cluster naturally implies that the cluster is convex.

The main metrics which usually are all or part of the parameters used by the guide and cost functions are the following :

- *number of inputs and outputs*, usually related to the type of architecture used. Although limitations on input and output result in reduced performance, many architectures impose severe limitations on the characteristic of the final cluster to implement in HW.

- *area*, although it is hardly related to the single instructions, each instruction occupies a certain area, hence the total area of the cluster is an important factor;

- *execution time*, even though not possible to obtain accurate estimates of the system's cycle time in all cases. Therefore *cycle count* is often used as a substitute for the execution time;

- *power consumption.*

Usually a subset of the above metrics is used to identify and select an optimal set of new instructions. An exhaustive outline of metrics can be seen in [2, Chap.4]. One of the main goals when designing an instruction-set is to make the design appropriate for an implementation on many different technologies.

The coming of new technologies, and especially the increased use of reconfigurable technologies in the last decade can therefore lead researchers to think about the design of an instruction-set technology independent and suitable for multiple reuses. Theoretically exact, this concept has to deal with the effective implementation of an instruction-set which includes compilation time, initialization time as well as time for loading and reading parameters from memory or registers. Since these metrics are strictly dependent on the effective implementation, the design of an optimal instruction-set cannot be completely independent of the effective architecture on which it is implemented. Additional metrics can be identified in specific properties that the final cluster has to satisfy, as graph properties (like convexity, a property which guarantees a proper scheduling, etc.). Additional properties can be seen as a metric but in this survey we make a distinction between metrics and graph properties like connection, convexity, etc.

5   Instruction Selection

The main goal of instruction selection is the identification of a set of optimal new instructions to hardwire from a superset of candidates generated by the instruction generation step. One of the main problem during the selection of the best candidates is the covering of the design space: exact algorithms can be too expensive in terms of computational cost. Heuristics alone do not guarantee optimality, or even feasibility of the solution. The selection can follow different policies. The elements of P_{Opt}[2] can be selected attempting to minimize the number of distinct templates that are used [7], or the number of instances of each template, or the number of nodes left uncovered in the graph [45,46], or in such a way that the longest path through the graph should have minimal delay. Other approaches select instructions based on regularity, i.e. the repeated occurrence of certain templates [47,48,49,40], or resource sharing [50,51], or considering the frequency of execution, or the occurrence of specific nodes [11,52]. Instruction selection, guided by the cost function, can take one or more of these targets as parameters for an optimal choice of the instructions.

A way to address instruction selection is by using Integer Linear Programming (ILP) and more generally Linear Programming (LP) in combination with efficient LP solver. Basically each instruction is associated to a variable which can have integer value (Integer Linear Programming, ILP), non integer value (Linear Programming, LP), or boolean value (0-1 Linear Programming). The instructions, and then the variables, have to satisfy a certain number of constraints which are expressed with a system of linear inequalities and the optimal solution is the one that maximize or minimize the, so called, objective function. Example of instruction selection by using LP can be seen in [53,22,13,14].

A way to solve exactly covering problem is by using dynamic programming or branch-and-bound methods. Exact solutions are proposed in [54,55]. Clearly a method is efficient if it is possible to prevent the exploration of unsuccessful branches at earlier stages of the search, and this relies on efficient bounding techniques [38,39,56,57].

6   The Type of Instructions

Basically, there are two types of clusters that can be identified, based on the number of output values: Multiple Input Single Output (MISO) and Multiple Input Multiple Output (MIMO). Clearly the set of MIMO graphs includes the subset of MISO graphs. We identify these two types of graphs for a specific reason: the sequence of instructions to shift from SW to HW can be seen as a multivalued function: given $n \geq 1$ input the function produces $m \geq 1$ outputs: $(Out_1, ..., Out_m) = f(In_1, ..., In_n)$, which can be written in a short way using a vector notation as $\underline{Out} = f(\underline{In})$.

Accordingly, there are two types of algorithms for instruction set extensions which are briefly presented in this section.

---

[2] In case an optimal solution is not feasible, P_{Opt} contains elements which are *close-to-optimal*.

For the first one, a representative example is introduced in [58,28] which addresses the generation of MISO instructions of maximal size, called MAXMISO. The proposed algorithm exhaustively enumerates all MAXMISOs. Its complexity is linear with the number of nodes. The reported performance improvement is of some processor cycles per newly added instruction. Access to memory, i.e. load/store instructions, are not considered.

The approach presented in [32] targets the generation of general MISO instructions. The exponential number of candidate instructions turns into an exponential complexity of the solution in the general case. In consequence, heuristic and additional area constraints are introduced to allow an efficient generation. The difference between the complexity of the two approaches in [32,58] is due to the properties of MISOs and MAXMISOs: while the enumeration of the first is similar to the subgraph enumeration problem (which is exponential) the intersection of MAXMISOs is empty and then once a MAXMISO is identified, it is removed generating a linear enumeration of them. A different approach is presented in [44] where, with an iterative application of the MAXMISO clustering presented in [58], MISO instructions called SUBMAXMISOs are generated with linear complexity in the number of processed elements. The iterative application of this algorithm allows the generation of MISO instructions of smaller size at each iteration when, for instance, tight limitations on the total number of inputs are applied.

The algorithms of second type are more general and provide more significant performance improvements. However they also have exponential complexity. For example, in [12] the identification algorithm detects optimal convex MIMO subgraphs based on Input/Output constraints but the computational complexity is exponential. A similar approach described in [41] proposes the enumeration of all the instructions based on the number of inputs, outputs, area and convexity. The selection problem is not addressed. Contrary to [12] which has scalability issues if the data-flow graph is very large or the micro-architectural constraints are too fine, this approach is quite scalable and can be applied on large data-flow graphs with relaxed micro-architectural constraints. The limitation to only connected instructions has been removed in [61], where the authors address the enumeration of the disconnected instructions.

In [13] the authors target the identification of convex clusters of operations given input and output constraints. The clusters are identified with a ILP based methodology. The main characteristic is that they iteratively solve ILP problems for each basic block. Additionally, the convexity is verified at each iteration increasing in this way the overall complexity of the approach.

In [14] the authors address the generation of convex MIMO operations in a manner similar to [13] although the identification of the new instructions is rather different. The authors construct convex MIMO based on MAXMISOs clustering in order to maximally exploit the MAXMISO level parallelism. The main difference between this approach and [13] is that the latter iteratively solves ILP problems for each basic block, while the former has one global ILP problem for the entire procedure. Additionally the convexity is addressed differently: in [13] the convexity is verified at each iteration, while in [14] it is guaranteed by construction.

An extension of the work in [14] is presented in [43]. In [43], the authors present a heuristic of linear complexity which address the generation of convex MIMO instruction. The key difference between the two solutions presented in [14] and [43] is the combination per levels. Since single MAXMISO execution in HW does not provide huge improvements in performance, the main idea is to combine, per levels, MAXMISOs available at the same level in the reduced graph, into a convex MIMO that is executed as a single instruction in HW where convexity is theoretically guaranteed. The idea of combining MAXMISO per level(s) has been further extended in [44,59] where linear complexity algorithms based on the notion of MAXMISO are presented.

7   Conclusions

In this paper, we presented an overview of the Instruction-Set extension problem providing an analysis of all relevant aspects involved in the problem. It compensates the lack of a general view of the problem in the existing literature which only consists of sporadic comparisons that address only a limited number of the issues involved. Additionally, we provided an in-depth analysis of all the subproblems involved. Therefore, our study benefits different kinds of readers ranging from the one simply interested in the issues involved in the problem, to the one interested in advancing the state-of-the-art and needs to know in detail the existing approaches and the open issues.

References

1. Keutzer,: From ASIC to ASIP: The next design discontinuity. In: ICCD 2002 (2002)
2. Holmer: Automatic design of computer instruction sets. PhD thesis (1993)
3. Huang: Generating instruction sets and microarchitectures from applications. In: ICCAD 1994, (1994)
4. Huang: Synthesis of instruction sets for pipelined microprocessors. In: DAC 1994, (1994)
5. Van Praet: Instruction set definition and instruction selection for ASIPs. In: ISSS 1994, (1994)
6. Liem: Instruction-set matching and selection for DSP and ASIP code generation. In: ED & TC 1994, (1994)
7. Choi,: Synthesis of application specific instructions for embedded DSP software. IEEE Trans. on Comp. 48(6), 603–614 (1999)
8. Faraboschi,: LX: a technology platform for customizable VLIW embedded processing. ACM SIGARCH Computer Architecture News, Special Issue. In: Proceedings of the 27th annual international symposium on Computer architecture (ISCA 2000) 28(2), 203–213 (2003)
9. Wang: Hardware/software instruction set configurability for System-on-Chip processors. In: DAC 2001 (2001)
10. Arnold: Designing domain-specific processors. In: CODES 2001(2001)
11. Kastner,: Instruction generation for hybrid reconfigurable systems. ACM TODAES 7(4), 605–627 (2002)
12. Atasu: Automatic application-specific instruction-set extensions under microarchitectural constraints. In: DAC 2003 (2003)

13. Atasu: An integer linear programming approach for identifying instruction-set extensions. In: CODES+ISSS 2005 (2005)
14. Galuzzi: Automatic selection of application-specific instruction-set extensions. In: CODES+ISSS 2006 (2006)
15. Alomary: A hardware/software codesign partitioner for ASIP design. In: ICECS 1996 (1996)
16. Athanas,: Processor reconfiguration through instruction-set metamorphosis. IEEE Computer 26(3), 11–18 (1993)
17. Razdan: PRISC software acceleration techniques. In: ICCS 1994 (1994)
18. Wirthlin: DISC: The dynamic instruction set computer. In: FPGAs for Fast Board Devel. and Reconf. Comp. vol. 2607, pp. 92–103 (1995)
19. Geurts: Synthesis of Accelerator Data Paths for High-Throughput Signal Processing Applications. PhD thesis (1995)
20. Geurts,: Accelerator Data-Path Synthesis for High-Throughput Signal Processing Applications. Kluwer Academic Publishers, Norwell (1997)
21. Hauser: GARP: a mips processor with a reconfigurable coprocessor. In: FCCM 1997 (1997)
22. Niemann: Hardware/software partitioning using integer programming. In: EDTC 1996 (1996)
23. Niemann,: An algorithm for hardware/software partitioning using mixed integer linear programming. ACM TODAES, Special Issue: Partitioning Methods for Embedded Systems 2(2), 165–193 (1997)
24. De Micheli,: Hardware/software co-design. Proc. of IEEE 85(3), 349–365 (1997)
25. Baleani, Sangiovanni-Vincentelli, A.: HW/SW partitioning and code generation of embedded control applications on a reconfigurable architecture platform. In: CODES 2002 (2002)
26. Arató: Hardware-software partitioning in embedded system design. In: WISP 2003 (2003)
27. Gschwind: Instruction set selection for ASIP design. In: CCODES 1999 (1999)
28. Pozzi: Automatic topology-based identification of instruction-set extensions for embedded processors. Technical Report CS 01/377, EPFL, DI-LAP, Lausanne (December 2001)
29. Clark: Automatically generating custom instruction set extensions. In: WASP 2002 (2002)
30. Peymandoust: Automatic instruction set extension and utilization for embedded processors. In: ASAP (2003)
31. Clark,: Processor acceleration through automated instruction set customization. In: MICRO 36
32. Cong: Application-specific instruction generation for configurable processor architectures. In: FPGA 2004 (2004)
33. Rao, S.: Partitioning by regularity extraction. In: DAC 1992 (1992)
34. Arnold: Automatic detection of recurring operation patterns. In: CODES 1999 (1999)
35. Kastner: Instruction generation for hybrid reconfigurable systems. In: ICCAD 2001 (2001)
36. Fortin: The graph isomorphism problem. Technical Report TR 96-20, Department of Computing Science, University of Alberta, Canada (July 1996)
37. Chen,: Graph isomorphism and identification matrices: Parallel algorithms. IEEE Trans. on Paral. and Distr. Systems 7(3), 308–319 (1996)
38. Coudert: New ideas for solving covering problems. In: DAC 1995 (1995)

39. Coudert: On solving covering problems. In: DAC 1996 (1996)
40. Brisk: Instruction generation and regularity extraction for reconfigurable processors. In: CASES 2002 (2002)
41. Yu: Scalable custom instructions identification for instruction-set extensible processors. In: CASES 2004 (2004)
42. Aletà,: Removing communications in clustered microarchitectures through instruction replication. ACM TACO 1(2), 127–151 (2004)
43. Vassiliadis, S., Bertels, K., Galuzzi, C.: A Linear Complexity Algorithm for the Automatic Generation of Convex Multiple Input Multiple Output Instructions. In: Diniz, P.C., Marques, E., Bertels, K., Fernandes, M.M., Cardoso, J.M.P. (eds.) ARCS 2007. LNCS, vol. 4419, pp. 130–141. Springer, Heidelberg (2007)
44. Galuzzi: A linear complexity algorithm for the generation of multiple input single output instructions of variable size. In: SAMOS VII Works
45. Liao: Instruction selection using binate covering for code size optimization. In: ICCAD 1995 (1995)
46. Liao,: A new viewpoint on code generation for directed acyclic graphs. ACM TO-DAES 3(1), 51–75 (1998)
47. Rao, S.: On clustering for maximal regularity extraction. IEEE Trans, on CAD 12(8), 1198–1208 (1993)
48. Rao, S.: Hierarchical design space exploration for a class of digital systems. IEEE Trans. on VLSI Systems 1(3), 282–295 (1993)
49. Janssen: A specification invariant technique for regularity improvement between flow-graph clusters. In: EDTC 1996 (1996)
50. Huang: Managing dynamic reconfiguration overhead in system-on-a-chip design using reconfigurable datapaths and optimized interconnection networks. In: DATE 2001 (2001)
51. Moreano: Datapath merging and interconnection sharing for reconfigurable architectures. In: ISSS 2002 (2002)
52. Sun: Synthesis of custom processors based on extensible platforms. In: ICCAD 2002 (2002)
53. Imai: An integer programming approach to instruction implementation method selection problem. In: EURO-DAC 1992 (1992)
54. Grasselli,: A method for minimizing the number of internal states in incompletely specified sequential networks. IEEE Trans. Electron. Comp. EC-14, 350–359 (1965)
55. Brayton: Boolean relations and the incomplete specification of logic networks. In: ICCAD 1989 (1989)
56. Liao: Solving covering problems using LPR-based lower bounds. In: DAC 1997 (1997)
57. Li: Effective bounding techniques for solving unate and binate covering problems. In: DAC 2005 (2005)
58. Alippi: A DAG-based design approach for reconfigurable VLIW processors. In: DATE 1999 (1999)
59. Galuzzi: The spiral search: A linear complexity algorithm for the generation of convex multiple input multiple output instruction-set extensions. In: ICFPT 2007 (2007)
60. Huynh: An Efficient Framework for Dynamic Reconfiguration of Instruction-Set Customizations. In: CASES 2007 (2007)
61. Yu: Disjoint pattern enumeration for custom instructions identification. In: FPL 2007 (2007)
62. Bonzini: A retargetable framework for automated discovery of custom instructions. In: ASAP 2007 (2007)

An FPGA Run-Time Parameterisable
Log-Normal Random Number Generator

Pedro Echeverría[1], David B. Thomas[2], Marisa López-Vallejo[1], and Wayne Luk[2]

[1] Dept. de Ingeniería Electrónica, Universidad Politécnica de Madrid (Spain)
{petxebe,marisa}@die.upm.es
[2] Dept. of Computing, Imperial College London (United Kingdom)
{dt10,wl}@doc.ic.ac.uk

Abstract. Monte Carlo financial simulation relies on the generation of random variables with different probability distribution functions. These simulations, particularly the random number generator (RNG) cores, are computationally intensive and are ideal candidates for hardware acceleration. In this work we present an FPGA based Log-normal RNG ideally suited for financial Monte Carlo simulations, as it is run-time parameterisable and compatible with variance reduction techniques. Our architecture achieves a throughput of one sample per cycle with a 227.6 MHz clock on a Xilinx Virtex-4 FPGA.

1   Introduction

The Log-normal random-walk is a key feature of many financial models, as it captures random changes in relative magnitude, rather than the absolute magnitude changes provided by the Gaussian random-walk. Using relative changes has two key benefits that match the behaviour of asset prices in the real-world: prices can never go negative, and the magnitude of price changes is proportional to the magnitude of the price.

While it is known that real-world asset prices do not actually follow Log-normal walks (usually very small and very large changes in price are more frequent than predicted), the approximation is sufficiently good for many applications, and it forms part of the Black-Scholes-Merton model which underlies much of modern financial theory [1, 2].

As its name implies, a Log-normal distribution is a probability distribution function whose logarithm is a normal distribution. We define the PDF (Probability Density Function) f and the CDF (Cumulative Distribution Function) F in terms of ϕ and Φ (the PDF and CDF of the standard Gaussian distribution) for $x > 0$, where μ and σ are respectively the mean and the standard deviation of the Log-normal distribution:

$$f(x; \mu, \sigma) = \frac{1}{x\sigma}\phi\left[\frac{\ln(x) - \mu}{\sigma}\right], \qquad \phi(x) = \frac{\exp(-\frac{x^2}{2})}{\sqrt{2\pi}} \tag{1}$$

$$F(x; \mu, \sigma) = \Phi\left[\frac{\ln(x) - \mu}{\sigma}\right], \qquad \Phi(x) = \int_{-\infty}^{x} \frac{1}{x\sigma}\phi(y)dy \tag{2}$$

R. Woods et al. (Eds.): ARC 2008, LNCS 4943, pp. 221–232, 2008.

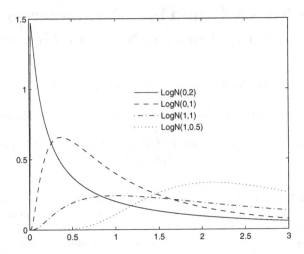

Fig. 1. Log-normal Distributions (PDFs)

Note that the Log-normal distribution has two parameters, μ and σ, that can cause great variation among Log-Normal distributions (see Figure 1, where the PDF of different distributions are plotted). In financial terms, these two parameters represent the estimated growth and volatility of an asset's price in the future. An established company's stock might have low μ and low σ (a low-return low-risk investment), while a new-technology startup might have high μ (good potential for growth) and high σ (uncertainty about that growth).

One of the benefits of the Log-normal distribution is that it allows one to easily explore the behaviour of future prices using Monte-Carlo simulation. Assume that we have a portfolio containing derivatives (e.g. futures or options) that depend on asset price S, and the value of the portfolio at any point is given by a pricing function $p(S)$. Given S_0, the initial price of an asset, and an estimate of μ and σ over a time period t, we can generate a random sample from the future price distribution as $S_t = S_0 x$, where x is a Log-normal sample[1] randomly generated. We can then estimate the value $\hat{p}$ of the portfolio at a given time t:

$$\hat{p} = \frac{1}{N} \sum_{i=1}^{N} p(S_0 x_i) \qquad (3)$$

where N is the number of individual simulations needed in the Monte Carlo stochastic approach.

This Monte-Carlo pricing approach is simple, but it has a number of problems, all relating to the random generation of the Log-normal samples $x_1..x_N$:

1. In general N might need to be very large to achieve sufficient accuracy, so a large number of independent Log-normal samples must be generated

---

[1] This is a slight simplification: the distribution parameters are actually chosen as a simple function of the time period, price growth and volatility.

and evaluated. However, each random trial can be evaluated independently, presenting huge amounts of parallelism with almost no I/O constraints.

2. Generating samples from the Log-normal distribution is very expensive, unless μ and σ are fixed. However, a financial application often requires multiple parameterisations of the distribution, as μ and σ will vary from asset to asset.

3. Methods exist for drastically reducing N while maintaining accuracy based on Variance Reduction techniques [3], but these require that $z_1..z_N$, where $z_i = \Pr[x_i \leq L]$, cover the range $(0..1)$ very uniformly. Generating such uniformly spaced samples is only possible using the inversion method [4], the most expensive generation method (see Section 2).

Since such Monte-Carlo applications present both huge amounts of parallelism, and compute-bound number-crunching, they are natural candidates for FPGA-based acceleration [5]. However, the missing component is the Log-normal random number generator (RNG), which is a key component for several financial Monte Carlo simulations. The software complexity of a Log-normal RNG makes it ideal for hardware acceleration, taking advantage of the excellent performance of the latest FPGAs.

In this work we present an FPGA design for such accelerator, with single precision floating point arithmetic and throughput of one random sample per cycle. This accelerator is also run-time parameterisable and compatible with Variance Reduction techniques.

The paper is organised as follows. Section 2 introduces the main characteristics of our Log-normal generator, while Section 3 describes its architecture. Section 4 details the experimental results, and finally Section 5 draws some conclusions.

2   Log-Normal RNG

As discussed in Section 1, the high speed generation of random samples from a Log-normal distribution is critical for hardware acceleration of Monte-Carlo pricing approach. What is needed is an FPGA Log-normal generator that meets the following requirements:

Fast and Efficient: It should generate one sample per cycle at high clock rates with low resource usage.

Parameterisable: The parameters μ and σ should be changed on a per-cycle basis.

Inversion Based: The generation method must be inversion-based so that Variance Reduction techniques can be used.

High Quality: The statistical quality of the overall distribution must be very high.

Previous methods for sampling from the Log-normal distribution meet some of these requirements, but none meet all. An efficient, high-quality inversion-based method has previously been presented [6], which uses a customized function-approximation technique to construct an approximation to F^{-1}. However, μ

and σ must be given as parameters to the function-approximation process, and cannot be changed without re-synthesizing the circuit from scratch.

A number of methods exist for approximating arbitrary distributions [7, 8], which offer fast and resource efficient circuits, and allow the distribution to be changed at run-time. However, per-cycle modification of μ and σ is not possible, as hundreds or thousands of cycles are needed to modify block-RAMs. Additionally, such generators cannot always provide high quality distributions, particularly when approximating the Log-normal distribution (due to the PDF shape near zero).

The only approach we know that provides a truly per-cycle parameterisable generator is to combine an exponential function unit with a Gaussian RNG. If X is a Log-normal distribution, then $Y = \ln X$ is a Gaussian distribution, and inversely X can be obtained from the Gaussian distribution: $X = e^Y$.

This way, using an exponential function unit, any $N(\mu,\sigma)$ can be transformed into a $LogN(\mu,\sigma)$. The introduction of the two parameters can be handled in the generation of $N(\mu,\sigma)$. Due to the mathematical properties of Gaussian distributions, variables from one distribution $N_1(\mu_1, \sigma_1)$ (v_1) can be transformed to variables from $N_2(\mu_2, \sigma_2)$ (v_2) directly:

$$v_2 = (v_1 - \mu_1) \times \frac{\sigma_2}{\sigma_1} + \mu_2 \tag{4}$$

Most Gaussian generation methods cannot provide the quasi-random point distribution required to apply Variance Reduction techniques, except the inversion method [4]. The inversion method is a general technique to generate non-uniform distributions using the inverse function of the corresponding cumulative distribution function (CDF) and a uniform distribution. Uniform variables correspond to values of the cumulative probability that are converted to the desired distribution through CDF^{-1}. Since CDF^{-1} conserves the properties of the uniform distribution, Variance Reduction techniques can be easily applied to the uniform distribution and in this way to the non-uniform distribution.

3   Hardware Architecture

As seen previously in Section 2, the Log-normal distribution with any mean, μ, or standard deviation, σ, can be generated from a Gaussian one with the same μ and σ just by applying an exponential operation to the Gaussian distribution.

Thus, the architecture of the parameterisable Log-normal RNG can be reduced to two main components: a parameterisable $N(\mu,\sigma)$ RNG, and an exponential unit. From formula (4) it is clear that the simplest way to generate the parameterisable $N(\mu,\sigma)$ is to use as base Gaussian RNG one with normal distribution, $N(0,1)$, so the previous transformation is reduced to:

$$v_2 = v_n \times \sigma_2 + \mu_2 \tag{5}$$

as $\mu_1 = 0$ and $\sigma_1 = 1$.

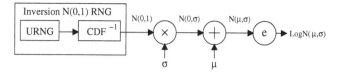

Fig. 2. Log-normal RNG Hardware Architecture

Figure 2 shows the complete architecture for the parameterisable LogN(μ,σ). It is composed of a Normal RNG based on the inversion method and three mathematical units: a multiplier, an adder/subtracter unit and an exponential unit. The Normal RNG with the multiplier and the adder form the parameterisable N(μ,σ) RNG, while the exponential unit transforms the previous distribution into the desired Log-normal distribution.

3.1 Arithmetic Considerations

Once the Log-normal RNG architecture has been designed, the next step is to determine what type of arithmetic suits the proposed generator. A key choice is to decide between fixed point arithmetic and a floating point arithmetic.

After analyzing the exponential function, it is clear that floating point arithmetic is needed to represent accurately a Log-normal distribution. The output range of the function, $(0,\infty)$ is achieved with a reduced input range, as it tends quickly to zero for negative inputs and to infinity for positive ones. A fixed point arithmetic would need a large number of bits to represent Log-normal variables with adequate resolution, or a large reduction of the input range to reduce the bit-width of the output.

When choosing between standard floating point arithmetic, single precision (32 bits) is appropriate since double precision (64 bits) requires a large amount of resources and more complex units. Additionally, we are not aware of any double precision exponential operator or Normal RNG in previous literature.

Using single precision for the exponential operator reduces its input range to (-103.98, 88.723) when denormalized numbers are considered at the output, or to (-87.337, 88.723) when only normalized numbers are considered. For larger negative numbers, the result is always zero, while for larger positive numbers the result is always ∞. Meanwhile, handling denormalized numbers in the output implies that the logic needed in the exponential unit increases considerably. We have chosen to round them to zero to reduce resources, thus considering only the (-87.337, 88.723) input range because the accuracy lost is very small as denormalized numbers are very close to zero ($< 2^{-126}$).

3.2 N(μ,σ) RNG

The components of the N(μ,σ) RNG follow the previous scheme, involving single precision floating point arithmetic without handling denormalized numbers, just rounding them to zero. This is because the exponential unit has no resolution for denormalized inputs: their results are always one, as for zero input. The single

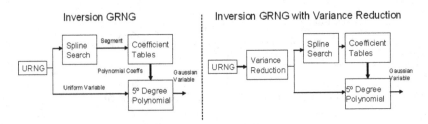

Fig. 3. Inversion Gaussian RNG

precision RNG is based on the inversion method, as we have previously developed an inversion-based N(0,1) RNG using quintic Hermite interpolation [9]. Our generator implements the Normal CDF^{-1} with a non-uniform, non-hierarchical segmentation (and a five degree polynomial as interpolation for each segment, using Hermite coefficients) that ensures the accuracy of the inversion with at least 21 bits accuracy (see in detail in [9]).

Figure 3 shows a simplified architecture for computing N(0,1). Our inversion N(0,1) RNG is composed of a base uniform RNG and three main units involved in the calculation of the CDF^{-1}: a spline search unit to determine the correct calculation spline for each uniform sample, the coefficient tables storing the polynomial coefficients for every spline, and the five degree polynomial unit (composed of five multipliers and five adders with a tailored arithmetic).

In addition to using accurate segment interpolation, this architecture employs a spline search algorithm. Non-uniform, non-hierarchical segmentation ensures high accuracy with a reduced number of segments, but it needs hardware to overcome the multicycle search of software algorithms. Taking advantage of the characteristics of current FPGAs with dual port RAM memory blocks, an adapted indexed searching method (using index and search tables) has been used.

$GCDF^{-1}$ is monotonically increasing and so will be the resulting segmentation. Thus, the index search method has been extended to ensure that the pointer obtained from an index table (constructed with a local search scheme based on fixed arithmetic and multiple local index tables) always points to the correct segment or the segment immediately below in the search table. This way, each search can finish with just one access to the indexed table to obtain the pointer, and another access to the search table reading simultaneously the segment starting points at pointer and pointer+1. A subsequent comparison of the searched value with the segment starting point at pointer+1 will determine to which of the two segments the searched value belongs.

In Figure 3 also shows the compatibility of the N(0,1) RNG with Variance Reduction techniques. Units implementing these techniques can be introduced immediately after the Uniform RNG (and both modules can be considered as a Uniform RNG itself). Meanwhile, the modules involved in the calculation of the CDF^{-1} (segment search, coefficients tables, and five degree polynomial) remain unchanged.

Another important feature of the architecture is that the multiplier and the adder/subtracter single precision units, used for transforming the N(0,1) RNG into an $N(\mu,\sigma)$ RNG (as well as the ones calculating the five degree polynomial), require fewer resources than the ones handling denormalized numbers, because the pre-normalization and post-normalization operations of both units are greatly simplified. In the standard units, most logic for those operations is needed for the case of a denormalized input or output [10].

3.3 Exponential Unit

The most complex of the three operators involved in the Log-normal RNG is the exponential unit. As shown in Section 3.1, this is also the operator that mainly determines the characteristics of the arithmetic needed.

Previous work either employs an algorithm that does not exploit FPGA characteristics [11], or tend to have a complex architecture [12]. Our design (depicted in Figure 4) is inspired by [12] but is simpler and faster. It combines an approximate calculation of the exponent of the result ±1 (k in the figure) with an input range reduction technique to obtain a smaller number range for the exponential computation:

$$x \approx k \ln 2 + y \;\rightarrow\; e^x \approx 2^k e^y$$

The calculation of e^y, that will generate the significand of the result, also involves a second range reduction as y can be splitted, $e^y = e^{y_1} e^{y_2}$. The calculation of both exponentials is based on a table-driven method and while e^{y_1} is calculated directly, e^{y_2} is calculated using the Taylor formula $T(y_2) \approx e^{y_2} - 1 - y_2$ (bottom part of the figure). Finally the exponent of the result is adjusted depending on the value of the significand. The innovative features of our design include:

Specialisation for single precision: our design is optimised specifically for single precision arithmetic. In particular, constant coefficient multipliers are used where appropriate; for instance, they are used in the calculation of the exponent for the result. The use of constant coefficient multipliers improves performance and reduces size.

Unsigned arithmetic: operations involving range reduction and calculation of the exponent for the result are signed. Some operations are, however, consecutive and related, and the sign of the result can be inferred from the input sign. For such operations signed arithmetic has been replaced by unsigned arithmetic with the corresponding logic reduction.

Improved pipelining: the speed of the exponential unit is enhanced by systematically introducing pipeline stages to the datapath of the exponential unit and its subunits.

4   Experimental Results

The architecture for the Log-normal RNG has been implemented on a Xilinx Virtex-4 XC4VF140-11 FPGA. The results are divided into two main parts. Firstly, the results for the exponential unit are described, focusing on the advantages and trade-offs of different possible configurations. Secondly, the results for the whole Log-normal RNG are discussed.

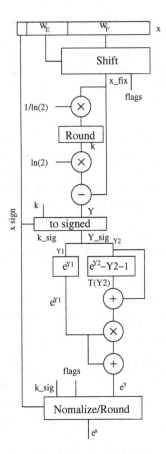

Fig. 4. Exponential Hardware Architecture

4.1   Exponential Unit

The results for the redesigned exponential unit are summarized in Table 1, where the base parameterisable exponential unit is compared with some configurations of our unit: V_1 employs a LUT based multiplier for the largest multiplication in algorithm [12], while in V_2 the embedded FPGA multipliers are used. The configurations in brackets correspond to the same implementations but replacing the largest LUT exponent table [12] by a block RAM.

As one can observe, the speed of the unit has been substantially increased by 67% although we have reduced the number of stages of the pipelined architecture (between two and four stages). This is due to the redesign of the datapath, and the use of unsigned arithmetic for consecutive operations instead of signed arithmetic in each operation, which eliminates unnecessary stages. This way the need for additional pipeline stages to enhance speed has been eliminated.

The resources required vary considerably depending on the configuration employed. When only LUTs are considered, our implementation increases the slices

Table 1. Exponential Units Comparison (Xilinx Virtex-4 XC4VF140 -11)

	Base [12]	V_1 (RAM)	V_2 (RAM)
Slices	1054	1226 (974)	726 (492)
18x18 Mult.	0	0	4
Block RAMs	0	0 (1)	0 (1)
Speed [MHz]	148.9	250.2	250.2
Samples/Cycles	1	1	1
Pipeline Stages	19	18	16

used by 16.5% with respect to the previous implementation [12], as the enhanced speed has been achieved by duplicating some resources and redesigning units with faster but more expensive architectures.

The LUT based multiplier mentioned above is responsible for almost half of the unit (592 slices). Replacing part of the multiplier logic with four 18x18 embedded multipliers reduces its slices to just 42 while also eliminating two pipeline stages. Finally, the largest exponent table is responsible for a large proportion of resources. Introducing a Block RAM eliminates completely the slices used by this table (approximately 270 slices). This way the number of slices used can be reduced up to 53% when both multipliers and a Block RAM are used.

4.2   Complete Log-Normal RNG

The implementation parameters are the following:

- Gaussian and Log-normal RNG periodicity of 2^{88}.
- Architecture with 65 pipeline stages.
- μ and σ with single precision floating point inputs.
- One 32 bit single precision floating point sample per cycle.

Table 2 shows the experimental results of the whole Log-normal RNG, and its corresponding elements. From the previous exponential unit configurations, we have selected the one using both multipliers and a Block RAM.

As one can observe, the $N(\mu, \sigma)$ RNG is the component that uses most resources: 79.5% of slices, 71% of Block Rams and 82% of the embedded multipliers. It also determines the throughput of the system as it is slower than the exponential unit. The complexity of the $N(0,1)$ RNG [9], involving a five degree polynomial and a search algorithm, is mainly responsible of these resources.

Moreover, most of the stages of this deeply pipelined architecture also correspond to the $N(0,1)$ RNG, which contains 39 stages. The design with 55 stages reported in [9], has been optimised by improving the polynomial adders and multipliers, eliminating two stages on the adders and one on the multipliers, while the remaining stage is eliminated in the search unit.

Table 3 compares the performance of our hardware with a comparable software implementation when random samples are taken at each stage of the generation

Table 2. Log-normal RNG Implementation results (Xilinx Virtex-4 XC4VF140 -11)

	Slices	Block RAMs	18x18 Mult	Speed [MHz]	Stages
LogN(μ,σ) RNG	2381	6	23	227.6	65
exp unit	492	1	4	250.2	16
N(μ,σ) RNG	1892	5	19	227.6	49
N(0,1) RNG	1473	5	15	236.8	39
x unit	118	0	4	242.2	4
+ unit	313	0	0	242.0	6

Table 3. Comparison of software and hardware generation rates (in MSamples/s)

	Uniform	Gaussian	Log-Normal
Pentium-4 2.4GHz	136.7	59.0	12.5
Opteron 2.2GHz	127.0	40.6	15.3
Virtex-4 XC4VF140	989.1	227.6	227.6

process. The software implementation uses the Ziggurat method to generate Gaussian samples, starting from a low quality but high speed uniform source. Then the Gaussian samples are converted to Log-normal using the C library function expf. Single precision is used throughout and the average generation rate in MSamples/s is measured on an otherwise unloaded machine for at least 10 seconds[2].

We see that although the software is able to generate uniform samples quickly, the generation rate rapidly declines when those samples must then be shaped. Both conversion stages reduce performance by two thirds, with the result that Log-normal generation is only about one tenth that of uniform generation. In contrast, the FPGA maintains a high clock rate for all stages as the conversion of the gaussian sample to a Log-normal one does not affect the generation rate. Even so, the Log-normal generator uses only a small amount of the resources on Virtex-4 XC4VF140 (11% of DSP, 3% of slices and 1.2% of Block RAMs) , leaving plenty of room for the logic that will consume the random numbers, whereas in software the consuming process would be interleaved with the generation process, reducing the generation rate even further.

Finally, Table 4 compares this LogN(μ,σ) RNG and previous implementations, in terms of the requirements in Section 2. We have compared against [6], which is also an inversion based RNG, but it is just designed for fixed μ and σ. Using different values for these parameters will require of a redesign of the whole RNG. Meanwhile [7, 8] are capable of run-time parameterisation using FPGA run-time reconfigurability to modify the values stored in block-RAMs. However, this solution is not reliable as it implies a huge amount of cycles to

---

[2] The code is compiled using gcc with the flags "-O3 -ffast-math -mfpmath=sse".

Table 4. Log-normal RNG requirements

	[6]	[7]	[8]	This work
Fast & Efficient	yes	yes	yes	yes
Run-time Parameterisable	no	yes	yes	yes
(per cycle)	(no)	(no)	(no)	(yes)
Inversion based	yes	no	no	yes
High Quality	yes	no	no	yes

complete the changing of memory values, while the statistical quality of the distribution achieved with these implementations is not very good.

In contrast, our LogN(μ,σ) RNG fulfills the four requirements in Section 2. The architecture achieves per cycle run-time parameterisation since only μ and σ must be fed to the adder and multiplier of the N(μ,σ) RNG. The use of the developed base N(0,1) RNG ensures the statistical high quality of the Log-normal distribution. Finally the combination of the high performance arithmetic units and the N(0,1) RNG designed produces a fast and efficient LogN(μ,σ) RNG that generates one sample per cycle.

As future work, a smaller and simpler implementation can be developed by improving the exponential unit works. Its input range is only (-87.337,88.723) and internally it transforms the single precision floating input into a signed fixed point number of 36 bits [12]. An alternative fixed point arithmetic can be adopted for the N(μ,σ) RNG, while μ and σ values should be restricted to fixed values.

5   Conclusions

This work presents an FPGA design and architecture of a parameterisable single precision floating point Log-normal RNG. The use of a base N(0,1) combined with a multiplier and an adder/subtracter unit achieves run-time parameterisation to form a N(μ,σ) RNG, while the use of a high-performance exponential unit transforms N(μ,σ) into LogN(μ,σ). The use of an inversion method for N(0,1) ensures the compatibility of the solution with advanced Monte Carlo simulation capabilities like the use of Variance Reduction techniques. Our hardware accelerator achieves high performance due to a pipelined architecture with a 227.6 MHz clock and a throughput of one sample per cycle on a Xilinx Virtex-4 FPGA.

Acknowledgements

This work has been partly funded by BBVA under contract P060920579, by the Spanish Ministry of Education and Science through the project TEC2006-00739, and by the UK Engineering and Physical Science Research Council grants EP/D062322/1, EP/D60569/1 and EP/C549481/1.

References

1. Black, F., Scholes, M.: The pricing of options and corporate liabilities. The Journal of Political Economy 81(3), 637–654 (1973)
2. Merton, R.C.: Theory of rational option pricing. The Bell Journal of Economics and Management Science 4(1), 141–183 (1973)
3. Gentle, J.E.: Random Number Generation and Monte Carlo Methods. Springer, Heidelberg (1998)
4. Bratley, P., Fox, B.L., Schrage, L.E.: A Guide to Simulation. Springer, Heidelberg (1983)
5. Zhang, G.L., et al.: Reconfigurable acceleration for Monte Carlo based financial simulation. In: Proc. IEEE International Conference on Field-Programmable Technology, pp. 215–222 (2005)
6. Cheung, R.C.C., Lee, D.-U., Luk, W., Villasenor, J.D.: Hardware generation of arbitrary random number distributions from uniform distributions via the inversion method. IEEE Transactions on Very Large Integration (VLSI) Systems 18(8), 952–962 (2007)
7. Thomas, D.B., Luk, W.: Non-uniform random number generation through piecewise linear approximations. IET Computers and Digital Techniques 1(7), 312–321 (2007)
8. ——, Efficient hardware generation of random variates with arbitrary distributions, In: Annual IEEE Symposium on Field-Programmable Custom Computing Machines, pp. 57–66 (2006)
9. Echeverría, P., López-Vallejo, M.: FPGA gaussian random number generator based on quintic hermite interpolation inversion. In: IEEE International Midwest Symposium on Circuits and Systems, pp. 871–874 (2007)
10. Govindu, G., Zhou, L., Choi, S., Prasanna, V.: Analysis of high-performance floating-point arithmetic on FPGAs. In: IEEE International Parallel and Distributed Processing Symposium, pp. 26–30 (2004)
11. Doss, C.C., Riley, R.L.: FPGA-Based implementation of a robust IEEE-754 exponential unit. In: IEEE Field-Programmable Custom Computing Machines, pp. 229–238 (2004)
12. Detrey, J., de Dinechin, F.: A parameterized floating-point exponential function for FPGAs. In: IEEE International Conference Field-Programmable Technology, pp. 27–34 (2005)

Multivariate Gaussian Random Number Generator Targeting Specific Resource Utilization in an FPGA

Chalermpol Saiprasert, Christos-Savvas Bouganis,
and George A. Constantinides

Department of Electrical & Electronic Engineering,
Imperial College London, Exhibition Road,
London SW7 2BT, United Kingdom
{cs405,christos-savvas.bouganis,g.constantinides}@imperial.ac.uk

Abstract. Financial applications are one of many fields where a multivariate Gaussian random number generator plays a key role in performing computationally extensive simulations. Recent technological advances and today's requirements have led to the migration of the traditional software based multivariate Gaussian random number generator to a hardware based model. Field Programmable Gate Arrays (FPGA) are normally used as a target device due to their fine grain parallelism and reconfigurability. As well as the ability to achieve designs with high throughput it is also desirable to produce designs with the flexibility to control the resource usage in order to meet given resource constraints. This paper proposes an algorithm for a multivariate Gaussian random number generator implementation in an FPGA given a set of resources to be utilized. Experiments demonstrate the proposed algorithm's capability of producing a design that meets any given resource constraints.

Keywords: Multivariate Gaussian Distribution; Random Numbers; FPGA; Resource Constraint.

1 Introduction

Financial applications are one of the fields that require computationally extensive simulations. Examples of these applications include equity returns modeling and portfolio optimization [1]. Many of these applications involve simulations for predicting the behaviour of stock prices in the stock market. Monte Carlo simulation is a well known technique that is widely used in order to realize these simulations [2]. A key component in a Monte Carlo simulation is a random number generator which generates random samples from a variety of distributions that model certain aspects in equity pricing. One of the most widely used distributions is the multivariate Gaussian distribution which is defined by its mean and covariance matrix. The function of the covariance matrix is to encapsulate correlation information of the random variables.

R. Woods et al. (Eds.): ARC 2008, LNCS 4943, pp. 233–244, 2008.
© Springer-Verlag Berlin Heidelberg 2008

In certain applications, such as calculating the value-at-risk, it can take up to a day to complete the simulation using a cluster of PCs due to its computationally demanding nature [3]. In order to accelerate this task, one possibility is to improve the speed of the random number generator. One way to achieve that is by dedicating a hardware device which implements the multivariate Gaussian random number generator. Often, this target device is a Field Programmable Gate Array (FPGA) due to its fine grain parallelism and reconfigurability properties.

In most applications, a random number generator module constitutes part of a larger application such as modeling equity returns and portfolio optimization. As the number of resources on a single FPGA is limited, it is essential to keep the number of resources dedicated to such a module as low as possible. Recently, Thomas and Luk [4] have proposed an architecture for generating multivariate samples from a Gaussian distribution. Their algorithm, however, does not have the flexibility to tune the number of resources required to implement the proposed architecture in hardware to a specific resource requirement. Moreover, since the covariance matrix is constructed empirically from historical data it is expected that its elements deviate by certain amount from the underlying values. Therefore, a certain degree of freedom is allowed in the search for a hardware design by allowing some deviation in the approximation of the original covariance matrix. In order to exploit this idea we require a methodology which produces a design that generates multivariate Gaussian random samples by permitting an approximation to the original covariance matrix. The quality of the approximation depends on the number of utilized resources when the design is mapped into hardware. This paper presents a novel architecture for the implementation of a multivariate Gaussian random number generator in hardware, with the ability to tune the resource usage to user's requirement.

The organization of this paper is as follows. The background theory involved in this paper is explained in Section 2, while a description of current related work concerning Gaussian random number generators is given in Section 3. Section 4 focuses on the detailed description of the proposed algorithm and on the hardware implementation. Results regarding the performance evaluation of the proposed architecture are presented in Section 5. Finally, Section 6 concludes the paper.

2   Background Theory

Many existing techniques are available in the literature for the generation of multivariate Gaussian random samples such as the Rotation method [5], the Conditional method [6] and the Triangular Factorization method [7]. One of the current techniques that researchers have heavily focused on is the Triangular Factorization method where multivariate Gaussian samples are generated based on univariate Gaussian random samples. This approach factorizes the covariance matrix $\mathbf{C}$ into a product of a lower triangular matrix $\mathbf{A}$ and its transpose, $\mathbf{C} = \mathbf{A}\mathbf{A}^T$. The required multivariate Gaussian random samples $\mathbf{x}$ are generated by multiplying a vector containing univariate Gaussian random numbers, $\mathbf{r} \sim N(O, \mathbf{I})$ with the lower triangular matrix **A** to achieve the desired correlation structure while a vector **m** is added to adjust the mean values as shown in (1).

$$\mathbf{x} = \mathbf{Ar} + \mathbf{m}. \tag{1}$$

3   Related Work

In the literature researchers have focused on various techniques to generate multivariate Gaussian random samples. In [8], three methods for generating multivariate Gaussian random vectors are reviewed. These are the Rotation method, the Conditional method and the Triangular Factorization method which are all based on univariate Gaussian random samples. The authors in [8] implemented these approaches in software and evaluation of results have shown that the Triangular Factorization method is the most preferable method out of the three approaches as it requires less processing time and memory.

Recent technological advances coupled with today's requirements have driven designers towards hardware implementation of these generators on digital circuits. Many architectures exist for the generation of univariate Gaussian random numbers on an FPGA platform. This includes the Ziggurat method [9], the Wallace method [10] and the Box-Muller method [11]. An extensive review of these techniques has been performed in [12] where it has been concluded that the Wallace method has the highest throughput while the Ziggurat method comes second. However, the Wallace method is susceptible to correlation problems. Although these three methods are capable of producing Gaussian random samples using an FPGA platform, their hardware architectures involve the use of embedded multipliers. An alternative approach is established by Thomas and Luk [13] targeting an architecture without multipliers. The piecewise-linear approximation technique enables the design to be pipelined easily in order to perform high speed operations. This is because the design does not require any multipliers but only a lookup table, a subtractor and a comparator are utilized instead.

In the case of a multivariate random number generator in hardware, designs can be classified into two major categories, serial and parallel. If a vector of N samples is to be generated then a serial generator outputs one element of the vector in every clock cycle requiring N clock cycles for creating a complete vector. On the other hand, a parallel generator produces a complete vector of size N every clock cycle. The parallel approach has a larger throughput than the serial approach requiring however many more resources than the serial design. Thus, a trade off between throughput and resource usage exists between the two approaches. The rest of the paper focuses on the class of serial designs.

Thomas and Luk [4] developed a hardware model to generate multivariate Gaussian random numbers based on the Triangular Factorization method. To date, this is the only hardware based approach to generate such samples where the design is mapped onto an FPGA. Their design is capable of producing a vector of length N which contains multivariate random samples for every N clock cycles. In terms of resource usage their approach requires N Multiply

Accumulate (MACC) Units which are directly mapped into DSP blocks on an FPGA.

If we consider a scenario where the number of available DSP blocks on an FPGA is fewer than the size of the output vector N then the number of available MACC units will not be adequate to implement Thomas and Luk approach [4] on to a single FPGA, maintaining the same throughput. In order to further illustrate this point, if a vector of 1000 multivariate samples is to be generated then a 1000x1000 covariance matrix is required resulting in 1000 DSP blocks to be implemented on an FPGA using Thomas and Luk architecture [4]. This amount exceeds the number of available DSP blocks available on a modern high-end FPGA. For example, a high-end FPGA such as a Xilinx Virtex-4 offers up to 512 available DSP blocks [14]. As a consequence, multiple FPGAs would be required to map this architecture. Thus, a drawback of this approach is the lack of flexibility to accommodate designs where the size of the output vector is larger than the available DSP blocks on a single FPGA or the case where the system designer does not want to allocate the required resources to this module. In order to address this problem, this paper proposes an approach that produces multivariate Gaussian random samples by utilizing only a certain number of available DSP blocks specified by the system designer by allowing some error in the approximation of the covariance matrix while maintaining the same throughput as Thomas and Luk approach [4].

4   Proposed Algorithm

The proposed algorithm is based on the Triangular Factorization method. According to this method, the covariance matrix $\mathbf{C}$ is decomposed into a product of a lower triangular matrix $\mathbf{A}$ and its transpose using Cholesky Decomposition [15]. This lower triangular matrix $\mathbf{A}$ is multiplied with a vector $\mathbf{r} \sim N(O, \mathbf{I})$ which contains univariate Gaussian samples in order to produce multivariate samples (2) which have zero mean and covariance matrix $\mathbf{C}$.

$$\mathbf{x} = \mathbf{Ar}. \tag{2}$$

For an $N \times N$ lower triangular matrix $\mathbf{A}$ the number of multiplications required to perform the computation in (2) is $N(N + 1)/2$ which corresponds to the number of non-zero elements in matrix $\mathbf{A}$. In the proposed algorithm, the lower triangular matrix $\mathbf{A}$ is approximated by applying the Singular Value Decomposition algorithm. The Singular Value Decomposition algorithm [16] or SVD is a technique where a matrix is decomposed into a product of an orthogonal matrix $\mathbf{U}$, a diagonal matrix $\mathbf{S}$ and the transpose of another orthogonal matrix $\mathbf{V}$. The diagonal matrix $\mathbf{S}$ contains only positive or zero elements in its main diagonal which are sorted in descending order, hence $s_{1,1} \geq s_{2,2} \geq s_{3,3}$ and so on. Essentially, the SVD algorithm expresses an initial matrix $\mathbf{A}$ as a linear combination of separable matrices using the least number of decomposition levels, K, as possible.

The result of applying the SVD algorithm to the lower triangular matrix $\mathbf{A}$ is shown in (3) where the original matrix multiplication can be expressed as vector multiplication. $\mathbf{u}_i$ denotes the $i^{(th)}$ column of matrix $\mathbf{U}$ while $\mathbf{v}_i$ denotes the $i^{(th)}$ column of matrix $\mathbf{V}$. K is the number of decomposition levels used by the algorithm. Using the SVD algorithm the number of general multiplications to achieve the same output is $2KN$ where K is the number of decomposition levels. Therefore, the number of required multiplications can be reduced if K is less than $N/2$ in comparison with Thomas and Luk approach [4].

$$\mathbf{x} = \mathbf{A}\mathbf{r} = \mathbf{U}\mathbf{S}\mathbf{V}^T\mathbf{r} = \left(\sum_{i=1}^{K} \mathbf{u}_i s_i \mathbf{v}_i^T \mathbf{r} \right) = \sum_{i=1}^{K} \mathbf{u}_i s_i \left(\mathbf{v}_i^T \mathbf{r} \right). \tag{3}$$

Due to the fact that most of the large covariance matrices are constructed empirically, it is expected that they deviate from the true underlying matrix. The proposed methodology exploits this fact by approximating the covariance matrix up to the appropriate precision level defined by the user.

The metric which is used to assess the quality of the approximation is the mean square error (MSE) between the original covariance matrix and its approximation using (4).

$$Err_K = \frac{1}{N^2} \sum_{i=1}^{N} \sum_{j=1}^{N} \left(\mathbf{C}_{i,j}^K - \widehat{\mathbf{C}}_{i,j}^K \right)^2. \tag{4}$$

$\mathbf{C}$ represents the original covariance matrix, $\widehat{\mathbf{C}}$ corresponds to the approximated covariance matrix after approximating matrix $\mathbf{A}$ through the SVD algorithm, N is the size of the output vector and K is the decomposition level. i and j are the row and column indices of the matrix respectively.

4.1   Generation of U and V Using the SVD algorithm

The proposed algorithm takes a covariance matrix $\mathbf{C}$ as an input and produces matrices $\mathbf{U}$ and $\mathbf{V}$ which contain the decomposition vectors $\mathbf{u}_q^i$ and $\mathbf{v}_q^i$ for each decomposition level i by applying the SVD algorithm. The subscripts q denotes the quantized version of the vectors. The decomposition can be driven either by the required MSE in the covariance matrix approximation or by the number of available resources.

In the proposed algorithm, fixed point number representation is used to store the matrix coefficients since fixed point arithmetic leads to designs which are smaller and have higher operating frequency in an FPGA compared to floating point arithmetic based designs. Thus, quantization error is introduced when the vectors are mapped into hardware. The proposed algorithm minimizes the inserted error in the system due to quantization effect by propagating it to the next level of decomposition [17]. Hence, the added error is taken into account in the remaining decomposition stages.

The pseudo-code that illustrates the outline of this operation is shown in Fig. 1. The first step of the proposed algorithm is to obtain the first level of the decomposition of the lower triangular matrix $\mathbf{A}$ resulting in the generation of vectors $\mathbf{u}$ and

---

Algorithm: Approximate a covariance matrix $\mathbf{C}$ given K DSP blocks and p bits precision

Calculate lower triangular matrix $\mathbf{A}$ using Cholesky Decomposition $\mathbf{A} = Chol(\mathbf{C})$

$\mathbf{A}_r = \mathbf{A}$

$N = \lceil \frac{K}{2} \rceil$

FOR $i = 1 : N$

    Calculate the first decomposition level of $\mathbf{A}$ using $[\mathbf{u}_i, s_i, \mathbf{v}_i^T] = \text{SVD}(\mathbf{A}_r, 1)$

    Transform $\sqrt{s}\mathbf{u}_i$ and $\sqrt{s}\mathbf{v}_i^T$ to be in the range [-1,1) using a power of 2 scaling

    Quantize $\sqrt{s}\mathbf{u}_i$: $\mathbf{u}_q^i \leftarrow \sqrt{s}\mathbf{u}_i$ with p bits precision

    Quantize $\sqrt{s}\mathbf{v}_i$: $\mathbf{v}_q^i \leftarrow \sqrt{s}\mathbf{v}_i$ with p bits precision

    $\hat{\mathbf{A}} = \sum_{K=1}^{i} \mathbf{u}_q^K (\mathbf{v}_q^K)^T$

    $\mathbf{A}_r = \mathbf{A} - \hat{\mathbf{A}}$

    Store $\mathbf{u}_q^i$ in a 2-dimensional array $\mathbf{U}(:,i)$

    Store $\mathbf{v}_q^i$ in a 2-dimensional array $\mathbf{V}(:,i)$

END LOOP

RETURN $\mathbf{U}$ and $\mathbf{V}$

Fig. 1. Outline of the algorithm

$\mathbf{v}$ and a scalar s. As the order in which the scalar s is multiplied to vector $\mathbf{u}$ and $\mathbf{v}$ has no effect on the resulting product, the coefficient $\sqrt{s}$ is multiplied to both $\mathbf{u}$ and $\mathbf{v}$. The two vectors are then transformed so that their coefficients lie in the range [-1,1) using a power of 2 scaling. This is to ensure that the range of numbers representable in hardware implementation is maximized. The vectors $\sqrt{s}\mathbf{u}$ and $\sqrt{s}\mathbf{v}$ are quantized to a user specified number of bits and an initial approximation of the $\mathbf{A}$ matrix is obtained. The two quantized vectors are now represented by $\mathbf{u}_q$ and $\mathbf{v}_q$ respectively. The entire process is repeated, having the remaining matrix $\mathbf{A}_r$ as a starting point, until the termination condition is met.

4.2   Hardware Implementation

Fig. 2 illustrates a high level hardware implementation of the multivariate Gaussian random number generator. In the figure, the circuit comprises of two computational blocks representing the two decomposition levels. In terms of the architecture the vectors $\mathbf{u}_q^i$ and $\mathbf{v}_q^i$ generated from the proposed algorithm are stored in the embedded block RAMs on the FPGA permitting parallel access to the data.

The inner structure of each computational block is illustrated in Fig.3. Both the MACC unit and the multiplier are mapped onto one of the available DSP blocks on the FPGA. The overall operation can be pipelined into two sections to achieve improved throughput. The first part performs the multiply-accumulate of the vector with univariate samples $\mathbf{r}$ and a vector $\mathbf{v}_q$ to produce a scalar quantity rv which is stored in a register. Note that the whole process of multiply-add requires one clock cycle as this function is realized using the MACC unit. For a vector of size N, it takes N cycles for the output in the register to be valid. The second part of the circuit multiplies rv with the vector $\mathbf{u}_q$ and N clock cycles are required in order to generate a complete output vector of size N. As both stages

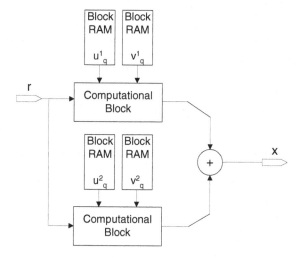

Fig. 2. High level hardware implementation

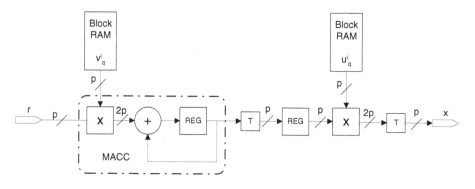

Fig. 3. Inner structure of the computational block

take N cycles to produce a valid output, the design is optimized by running the two modules in parallel. P denotes the precision of the system which is specified by the user, while the block denoted by T is a truncation block where the data is truncated to a specified precision. The final stage of the implementation is the summing stage where an adder tree structure is utilized for adding the outputs of K computational blocks to obtain an element in the output vector.

5   Performance Evaluation

In the hardware implementation, a Virtex-4 XC4VSX55 FPGA from Xilinx is utilized to map the design. A benefit for selecting the Virtex-4 model is that it provides DSP blocks which have the capability to perform a multiply-accumulate operation (MACC) in one clock cycle [14]. This is desirable since we would like to produce a sample per clock cycle and if the multiply-accumulate was not performed every clock cycle then two clock cycles would be required due to the feedback. In this work we adopt the method in [13] for the implementation of the univariate random number generator as it is the most efficient in terms of resources requirement in comparison to other techniques in the literature.

5.1   Impact of the Matrix Structure on the Proposed Algorithm

The eigenvalues of a matrix can provide a lower bound on the error of the approximation for a given number of decomposition levels. In order to demonstrate that we have selected, without the loss of generality, two lower triangular 30×30 square matrices $\mathbf{A}$ and $\mathbf{B}$ with different eigenvalue profiles to be applied with the proposed algorithm. The first ten eigenvalues of both matrices are plotted versus the level of decomposition in Fig. 4(a). From the graph, it can be seen that matrix $\mathbf{A}$ is more separable than matrix $\mathbf{B}$ since fewer decomposition levels are required before the eigenvalue drops to small values. Fig.4(b) illustrates the mean square error (MSE) of covariance matrices $\mathbf{C}_A = \mathbf{A}\mathbf{A}^T$ and $\mathbf{C}_B = \mathbf{B}\mathbf{B}^T$ for different decomposition levels. From the figure it is apparent that matrix $\mathbf{C}_A$ requires approximately 17 levels of decomposition to achieve an MSE of around 10^{-30} while 30 levels of decomposition are required for matrix $\mathbf{C}_B$ to approximately obtain the same MSE. Thus, it can be concluded that matrices with different separability properties require considerably different decomposition levels to achieve a certain error in the approximation. This provides a lower bound for the achieved error for a given decomposition level in the proposed algorithm since the quantization effect and truncation effect in the data path have not been considered. In summary, the above demonstrates that the performance of the proposed algorithm depends on the separability property of the matrix of interest.

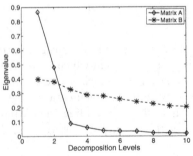

(a) Eigenvalue profiles of matrices $\mathbf{A}$ and $\mathbf{B}$.

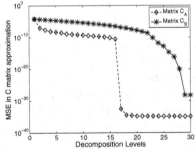

(b) MSE Comparison of matrices with different eigenvalue profile.

Fig. 4. Impact of different eigenvalue profiles to the approximation of a matrix

5.2   Evaluation of the Proposed Algorithm

The main idea behind this work is that by permitting a certain error in the approximation of the covariance matrix a reduction of the number of required DSP blocks on the FPGA can be achieved.

As illustrated in Section 4.2, the proposed algorithm employs two DSP blocks for every level of decomposition, one for the MACC unit and one for the multiplier. An experiment is performed where matrices **A** and **B** are used from the previous section to determine the achievable MSE given a range of resources. The calculated MSE is the error between the original covariance matrix $\mathbf{C_A}$ and the approximated covariance matrix $\widehat{\mathbf{C_A}}$. The same principle applies for matrix **B**.

The proposed algorithm is applied to matrices $\mathbf{C}_A$ and $\mathbf{C}_B$ with no quantization, 4 bits quantization and 18 bits quantization. In order to compare the

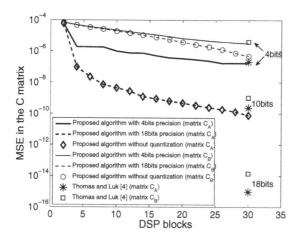

Fig. 5. Comparison of mean square error from two randomly generated matrices

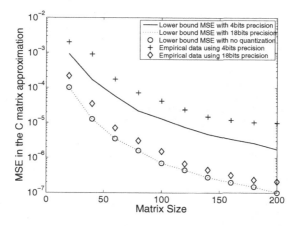

Fig. 6. MSE of covariance matrix approximation using empirical data

performance of the proposed algorithm with the technique proposed by Thomas and Luk [4], the MSE is also obtained from Thomas and Luk algorithm [4] where the algorithm is applied to the same matrices.

Fig. 5 illustrates the obtained results. The results show that regarding matrix **B** there is only a considerable difference in the obtained MSE between 4 bits quantization and 18 bits quantization when 10 or more DSP blocks are utilized using the proposed algorithm. However, the difference in MSE between 4bit and 18 bit precisions can clearly be seen for matrix **A** as shown in the graph. The difference in the patterns of the MSE plots between the two matrices is due to the different eigenvalue profiles. Moreover, for both matrices **A** and **B**, the MSE of the covariance matrix obtained using the proposed algorithm with 18 bits word-length is slightly higher than the optimum MSE obtained using the proposed algorithm without any quantization. The approach by Thomas and Luk [4] is only able to generate samples using a fixed number of resources as can be seen on the graph where three different MSE values are plotted that correspond to different level of precisions.

In addition, the results from the figure demonstrate that the proposed algorithm has the ability to produce designs across the available design space while the approach by Thomas and Luk [4] does not have this flexibility, with both approaches maintaining the same throughput.

In order to fully assess the functionality of the proposed algorithm, it is necessary to investigate the covariance matrix taking into account the quantization effects of the data path. An experiment is performed to calculate the MSE between the original covariance matrix and the empirical covariance matrix. The number of DSP blocks used is set to half of the size of the output vector N, thus, in all cases, the decomposition level K is equal to $N/2$. Fig. 6 illustrates the result of this experiment. As expected, it is apparent that the MSE obtained with 18bits precision is lower than that of 4bits precision. The graph also shows the lower bound of MSE for the 4 and 18 bits precision and the case where no quantization to the coefficients is performed. Moreover, a trend can be observed where the MSE decreases as the size of the matrix increases. This behaviour depends on the structure of the covariance matrix and it should not be generalized. Matrices with different eigenvalue profiles are expected to have different levels of approximation.

5.3   Hardware Synthesis

Table 1 illustrates the results of implementing the proposed algorithm onto a Virtex-4 FPGA. In this paper the design is synthesized into hardware using Handel-C. N denotes the size of the output vector while K represents the decomposition level. Note that this data does not include the resource usage of a univariate Gaussian random number generator, it solely considers the proposed architecture. It is apparent from the table that the number of slices utilized scales linearly with the levels of decomposition. The designs generated have 101.21MHz operating frequency. Moreover, the percentage of DSP block usage is calculated based on the fact that the Xilinx Virtex-4 XC4VSX55 contains 512 available

Table 1. Resource usage in the Virtex-4 architecture using the proposed algorithm

Configuration	Block RAM	DSP Block	Slices	DSP Blocks Usage
N=20, K=5	10	10	185	1.95%
N=50, K=10	20	20	402	3.91%
N=100, K=30	60	60	913	11.72%
N=150, K=50	100	100	1841	19.53%
N=300, K=100	200	200	3678	39.06%

DSP blocks [14]. The table clearly illustrates the linear dependency between the decomposition levels and the required Block RAMs, DSP blocks and slice usage. On the other hand, the same design mapped onto an FPGA using Thomas and Luk approach [4] requires N number of DSP blocks where N denotes the size of the output vector.

In addition, synthesis results have shown that the proposed algorithm is able to generate 1 sample every 9.88ns. Therefore, the throughput of the proposed architecture is $1.01 \times 10^8/N$ vectors per second where N denotes the size of the output vector.

6   Conclusion

In this paper, a novel hardware architecture to serially generate multivariate Gaussian random samples with the ability to control the resource usage in a modern FPGA is presented. The key idea is the approximation of the lower triangular matrix using the Singular Value Decomposition algorithm for the generation of multivariate Gaussian random samples. The motivation behind this work is the need to produce a design that generates multivariate Gaussian random samples given any number of available resources and the fact that a certain error in the approximation of the covariance matrix can be tolerated. For large covariance matrices, where the size of the output vector is larger than the available DSP blocks in a single FPGA, the proposed algorithm offers the flexibility to implement the design in a single FPGA which is not possible using the currently available approach [4]. Future work includes the investigation of the appropriate level of quantization precision given the separability of the matrix under consideration.

References

1. Verhofen, M.: Markov chain monte carlo methods in financial econometrics. Financial Markets and Portfolio Management 19, 397–405 (2005)
2. Brace, A., Gatarek, D., Musiela, M.: The market model of interest rate dynamics. Mathematical Finance 7, 127–155 (1997)

3. Glasserman, P., Heidelberger, P., Shahabuddin, P.: Variance reduction techniques for value-at-risk with heavy-tailed risk factors. In: Proceedings of the 32nd conference on Winter simulation, pp. 604–609 (2000), Society for Computer Simulation International, San Diego, CA, USA (2000)

4. Thomas, D.B., Luk, W.: Sampling from the multivariate gaussian distribution using reconfigurable hardware. In: Proceedings IEEE International Symposium on Field-Programmable Custom Computing Machines, pp. 3–12 (2007)

5. Graybill, F.A.: An Introduction to Linear Statistical Models. McGraw-Hill, New York (1961)

6. Scheuer, E.M., Stoller, D.S.: On the generation of normal random vectors. Technometrics 4(2), 278–281 (1962)

7. Graybill, F.A.: Introduction to Matrices with Applications in Statistics, Wadsworth, Belmont, CA (1969)

8. Barr, D.R., Slezak, N.L.: A comparison of multivariate normal generators. Commun. ACM 15(12), 1048–1049 (1972)

9. Zhang, G., Leong, P.H., Lee, D.-U., Villasenor, J.D., Cheung, R.C., Luk, W.: Ziggurat-based hardware gaussian random number generator. In: Proceedings IEEE International Conference on Field Programmable Logic and Applications, pp. 275–280 (2005)

10. Lee, D.-U., Luk, W., Villasenor, J.D., Zhang, G., Leong, P.H.: A hardware gaussian noise generator using the wallace method. IEEE Transactions on Very Large Scale Integration (VLSI) Systems 13, 911–920 (2005)

11. Lee, D.-U., Villasenor, J.D., Luk, W., Leong, P.H.W.: A hardware gaussian noise generator using the box-muller method and its error analysis. IEEE Transactions On Computers 55(6), 659–671 (2006)

12. Thomas, D.B., Luk, W., Leong, P.H., Villasenor, J.D.: Gaussian random number generators. ACM Comput. Surv. 39(4), 11 (2007)

13. Thomas, D.B., Luk, W.: Non-uniform random number generation through piecewise linear approximations. IET Computers & Digital Techniques 1, 312–321 (2007)

14. Xilinx, Virtex-4 family overview, 2007. [Online]. Available:
   `http://www.xilinx.com/support/documentation/data_sheets/ds112.pdf`.

15. Horn, R.A., Johnson, C.R.: Matrix Analysis. Cambridge University Press, Cambridge (1985)

16. Press, W.H., Teukolsky, S.A., Vetterling, W.T., Flannery, B.P.: Numerical Recipes in C. Cambridge University Press, Cambridge (1992)

17. Bouganis, C.-S., Constantinides, G.A., Cheung, P.Y.K.: A novel 2d filter design methodology for heterogeneous devices. In: Proceedings of the 13th Annual IEEE Symposium on Field-Programmable Custom Computing Machines, pp. 13–22. IEEE Computer Society Press, Washington DC, USA (2005)

Exploring Reconfigurable Architectures for Binomial-Tree Pricing Models

Qiwei Jin[1], David B. Thomas[1], Wayne Luk[1], and Benjamin Cope[2]

[1] Department of Computing, Imperial College, 180 Queen's Gate London SW7 2AZ,
UK
[2] Circuits and Systems Group, Department of Electrical and Electronic Engineering,
Imperial College London SW7 2AZ, UK
`qj04@doc.ic.ac.uk, db10@doc.ic.ac.uk, wl@doc.ic.ac.uk,`
`benjamin.cope@imperial.ac.uk`

Abstract. This paper explores the application of reconfigurable hardware to the acceleration of financial computations involving binomial-tree pricing models. A parallel pipelined architecture capable of computing multiple binomial trees is presented, which can deal with concurrent requests for option valuations. The architecture is mapped into an xc4vsx55 FPGA. Our results show that an FPGA implementation with fixed-point arithmetic at 87.4MHz can run over 250 times faster than a Core2 Duo processor at 2.2GHz, and more than two times faster than an nVidia Geforce 7900GTX processor with 24 pipelines at 650MHz.

1 Introduction

The binomial option pricing model is a numerical method that can be used to value and analyse financial options [5]. It is widely used within finance applications since it is simple, efficient, and can handle certain types of options that cannot be priced using Monte-Carlo methods. The model is often used to provide prices to a trader, but increasingly is also used as a component of larger applications, where the application may use the model to value hundreds or thousands of options.

Pricing a single option using the binomial model is relatively fast, and can typically be performed in milliseconds on a modern general-purpose processor. However, when huge numbers of options need to be valued, for example if the binomial pricing model is embedded in a Monte-Carlo simulation, or if a huge number of options are being revalued on a second-per-second basis, the pricing model can become the main computational bottleneck. This paper shows how Field Programmable Gate Arrays (FPGAs) can provide a viable method of accelerating binomial pricing computation, and how the proposed approach can be mapped effectively onto reconfigurable hardware.

The main contributions of this paper are:

- a parallel pipelined architecture capable of computing multiple binomial trees to support concurrent requests for option valuations,

R. Woods et al. (Eds.): ARC 2008, LNCS 4943, pp. 245–255, 2008.

- implementation of the architecture in reconfigurable hardware, exploiting on-chip resources to avoid re-computing costly calculations,
- evaluation of the proposed approach and comparison with alternative implementations based on general-purpose Intel processors and nVidia GPUs (Graphics Processing Units).

In the following, Section 2 states the motivation of this paper. Section 3 introduces the binomial option pricing model. Section 4 suggests an approach to develop hardware architectures for such model. Section 5 explains how the core evaluation computation of the binomial option pricing model can be implemented in reconfigurable hardware. Section 6 contains results and comparison of the proposed approach and other implementations in general-purpose processors and GPUs. Section 7 concludes the paper.

2   Motivation

Previous work on hardware acceleration of financial simulation has focused on Monte Carlo methods. Three examples are given below. First, a stream-oriented FPGA-based accelerator with higher performance than GPUs and Cell processors has been proposed for evaluating European options [6]. Second, an automated methodology has been developed that targets high-level mathematical descriptions of financial simulation to produce optimised pipelined designs with thread-level parallelism [7]. Third, an architecture with a pipelined datapath and an on-chip instruction processor has been reported for speeding up the Brace, Gatarek and Musiela (BGM) interest rate model for pricing derivatives [12]. All three approaches result in designs based on Monte Carlo methods. However, many financial simulations have closed-form solutions, for which techniques such as binomial trees will be more effective.

Binomial trees can be seen as a discrete-time approximation to the continuous-time Black-Scholes model [1]. We briefly explain the model in terms of an *American call option*. A *call option* is a contract that gives party A the right to buy some asset S from party B at a fixed price K (called the strike price). The important factor is that the option provides a right, not an obligation: party A can choose whether or not to exercise that right (i.e. to buy asset S at price K).

In general the option will only be exercised if $S_t > K$, i.e. the current price of the stock (S_t) is greater than the strike price, as party A can immediately sell the asset and realise a profit of $S_t - K$. If $S_t < K$ then party A will choose not to buy the asset and will neither gain nor lose money. By contrast party B has no control over the option, so in the first case will lose $S_t - K$, and in the second case will neither gain nor lose. Because party A only stands to gain, and B only stands to lose, B must be offered some kind of compensation. The point of an option pricing model is to determine how much A should pay B in order to create the option contract, or equivalently how much A can charge some third party for the option at a later date.

An *American* call option is one where party A can exercise the option at any time up until the option expires at time T. In contrast, a European option is one where the option can only be exercised at time T. All else being equal, an American option must be worth more than a European option with the same parameters, as party A has more flexibility. With the flexibility come more opportunities for profit, which translates to greater possible losses for party B, so more compensation is required for the option contract.

The American option is very common, but presents some difficulties in pricing due to the freedom to exercise the option before the expiry date. In particular it becomes very difficult to determine the option price using Monte-Carlo methods, another common method of option pricing mentioned earlier [7]. In contrast, techniques based on binomial trees are able to accurately price both European and American options.

3   The Binomial Option Pricing Model

The binomial model works by discretising both time and the price of asset S, and mapping both onto a binary tree. Each step from the root towards the leaves increases time by one step, and at each node one of the branches leads to an increase in S, while the other branch leads to a decrease in S. This is shown in Figure 1, with time along the horizontal axis, and asset price along the vertical axis.

At each node the upper branch increases the asset price by a factor u, while the lower branch decreases the price by a factor d. At the root of the tree the asset price is S_0, which is the asset price right now. At the leaves of the tree are the possible asset prices at time T, which are defined by S_0 and the path through the tree to the leaf. For example, the highest price in Figure 1 is reach by taking only upper branches from the root, so the asset price at that node is $S_0 u^3$. Note that the asset price can only take a fixed number of values, shown as a horizontal dashed lines. The tree also recombines, so the leaf node with value $S_0 u$ can be reached through three paths (uud, udu, or duu).

The idea behind binomial tree techniques is that we already know that the option is worth $\max(S_T - K, 0)$ at the leaves of the tree. Knowing the value at all the leaves of the tree enables us to work backwards to previous time steps,

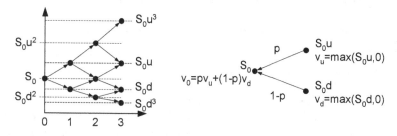

Fig. 1. The left-hand side shows the recombining binary tree of asset prices. The right-hand side shows the valuation of an option over one time period, with each node showing the asset price on top, and the option price below.

until eventually the root of the tree is reached. The right-hand side of Figure 1 gives a simplified example over just one time step. The node asset prices are already known (shown at the top of each node label), so the option values at the leaves (shown as v_u and v_d) can immediately be determined. To work back to v_0 we require another piece of information, which is the probability (p) that the asset price will move up. Given p, the expected value of the option at the first node can then be calculated.

Two further considerations are needed for practical use. The first is that interest rate evolution means that money earned in the future is worth less than money earned now. We handle this consideration by applying a discount factor r (where $r < 1$) to option values as we move backwards up the tree. The second is that at some nodes, early exercise may offer a better return than future exercise; so at each node we need to choose the higher of the discounted future payoff versus the payoff from early exercise.

From the above discussion, the pricing model can be described as:

$$v_{T,i} = \max(S_{T,i} - K, r) \tag{1}$$

$$v_{t,i} = \max(S_{t,i} - K, r(pv_{t+1,i+1} + (1-p)v_{t+1,i-1})) \tag{2}$$

$$S_{t,i} = \begin{cases} S_0 u^i, \text{ if } i \geq 0 \\ S_0 d^i, \text{ otherwise} \end{cases} \tag{3}$$

where i is an integer indicating the number of steps up or down from the initial asset price, and t is an integer indicating the number of time steps away from the root of the tree, with the leaves at time $t = T$. All other values are real numbers. The inputs to the model are T, S_0, K, u, d and r, and the output from the model is $v_{0,0}$, which is the estimated price for the option.

The model can be implemented in computational form as a recursive function; however a direct implementation of this function is inefficient unless memoisation is used. An efficient solution can be formulated in an iterative form, with an outer loop stepping t backwards from T to 0, and an inner loop calculating the price for each i at level t in the tree. A temporary array holds the intermediate values, and can be updated in place.

4   Mapping the Binomial Model to Hardware

In mapping the binomial model into hardware, we make two central assumptions:

- The trees use a non-trivial number of time-steps, so the amount of I/O per tree is small compared to the number of nodes that must be evaluated. The number of parameters needed for transfer is of order x, where x is the number of time-steps; this overhead is insignificant when compared with the number of computations, which is of the order the factorial of x. In our case I/O can be pipelined to take place concurrently with computation, hence further reducing the overhead.
- Requests for option valuations are received concurrently, so many individual trees can be valued in parallel.

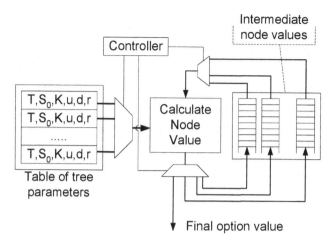

Fig. 2. System architecture for computing the binomial tree model

The first assumption means that we only need to consider evaluation when it is computationally bound, so we can largely ignore the performance of any software to hardware communications channels. The second assumption allows us to use high-latency pipelined functional units to achieve high clock rates while still achieving high throughput, by using the C-Slow approach [8].

Figure 2 shows our proposed architecture for mapping the binomial model into hardware. On the left is a bank of parameter sets, each of which describes a binomial tree which is currently in the process of being evaluated. In the center is a large pipelined block which takes two previously calculated option values and calculates the value of the parent node. To manage temporary storage, a set of buffers (shown to the right) are used; ideally they should be FIFO stream buffers which hold the option values until they are needed again. C-Slow operation can be achieved by modeling multiple trees in parallel: we continuously provide parameters into the pipeline to evaluate other trees while we are waiting for the results required for the next iteration of the current tree. The stream buffers are carefully designed for this approach. A controller manages the overall timing of the system, ensuring that the intermediate values are stored and retrieved correctly, and that the correct parameter set is selected on each cycle.

Figure 3 shows an example of the hardware design of the evaluation core. For each tree it evaluates, it takes in a set of parameters that are shipped over by the controller from the tree parameters table. To optimise performance, a lookup table is initialised with all possible asset strike prices. The architecture takes from the stream buffers three parameters: the two previous tree node values, and i, the price offset. Using the price offset i the current strike price $S_{t,i}$ can be retrieved from the lookup table.

With all the parameters ready, the Algorithmic Core in Figure 3 computes the option price $v_{t,i}$ for the current tree node. The result is then shipped back to the stream buffers for later use. The C-Slow method can be implemented here if:

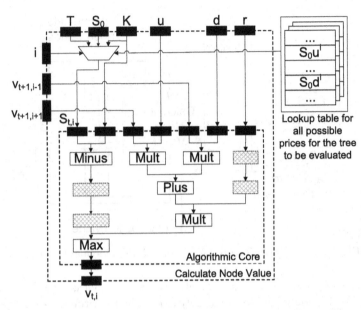

Fig. 3. Hardware design for the block *Calculate Node Value* in Fig. 2. The solid black boxes denote registers and the dotted grey boxes denote pipeline balancing registers that are allocated automatically by HyperStreams.

- The outside controller is able to ship over the correct parameters.
- The lookup tables in need are initialised.
- The controller is able to store the result into the right buffer.

So far the evaluation core would be the largest component that calculates the next node value as specified by Equation 2. In the asymptotic case we would expect the overall performance to be dominated by the size and speed of this block, as the other components consist of a small amount of memories and selection logic. In the next section we examine the implementation of this block in hardware.

5   The Option Update Pipeline

Our FPGA implementation of the node evaluation logic to support the binomial option pricing model is based on *HyperStreams* and the *Handel-C* programming language.

HyperStreams is a high-level abstraction based on the *Handel-C* language [6]. It supports automatic optimization of operator latency at compile time to produce a fully-pipelined hardware implementation. This feature is useful when implementing complex algorithmic calculations in FPGAs. In addition, *HyperStreams* also provides various means of connecting to FPGA resources such as block RAMs.

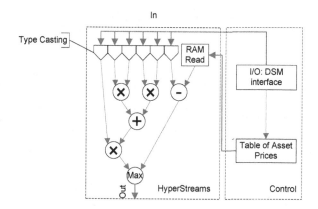

Fig. 4. The data flow of the hardware part of the binomial tree model implemented on FPGA; note the separation of control and pipelined data flow

Figure 4 shows a fully pipelined FPGA implementation of the node evaluation logic indicated in Equation 2. Each symbol shown in a *"HyperStreams"* block in Figure 4 refers to a *HyperStreams* operator: for example, $\oplus$ for *HsAdd*, RAMRead for *HsRAMRead* and so on. Each arrow from *DSM* (Data Stream Manager), the interface used for hardware-software communication, indicates a stream data element received as an unsigned integer. The inputs are cast to desired internal representation, for example *HS_DOUBLE*, at the top of the HyperStreams block. Once all the computations are finished, the output stream is then cast back to the desired output format using the *HsCast* operator.

The control logic, which is used to send and retrieve data from pipelines, is written in the *Handel-C* language.

We use block RAMs to implement a lookup table for $S_{t,i}$ (see Equation 2), which is initialized at the beginning of each tree-evaluation run, to get around expensive exponential calculations in hardware. Once the evaluation is finished, the result is then shipped back to software via the *DSM* interface.

The tool flow is as follows. *Handel-C* source code is synthesised to EDIF using the Celoxica DK5 suite which supports *HyperStreams*. Xilinx ISE 9.2 project navigator is used to place and route the design.

The target device on our Celoxica **ADMXRC4SX** platform is an xc4vsx55 FPGA [9] from the Xilinx Virtex 4 family, but it would be simple to re-target our design to some other FPGAs supported by DK5.

6   Results

The American put option benchmark has been calculated using three different FPGA implementations in different numerical representation as well as a reference PC implementation. All the FPGA implementations are compared to software implementations on a PC which provide the reference. The reference

Table 1. Performance/area results for xc4vsx55 FPGA, Geforce 7900 GPU, Intel Core2 Duo and Pentium4 processors; note that acceleration is compared with the reference Intel PC1

	FPGAs			GPU	Intel PC1	Intel PC2
	Double	Single	Fix	Single	Double	Double
Slices	8,270 (33%)	4,194 (17%)	1,980 (8%)	-	-	-
FFs	6,882 (14%)	3,366 (6%)	1,888 (3%)	-	-	-
LUTs	8,968 (18%)	4,821 (9%)	1,242 (2%)	-	-	-
SRLs	8,270 (33%)	4,194 (17%)	1,980 (8%)	-	-	-
BRAMs	20 (6%)	18 (5%)	18 (5%)	-	-	-
DSPs	48 (9%)	12 (2%)	12 (2%)	-	-	-
MHz	67.3	75.4	87.4	650	2200	3200
Replication (cores/chip)	3	5	12	24 Pipelines	1	1
Processing Speed (M nodes/sec)	67.3	75.4	87.4	477	4.2	1.1
Least^2 Error	0	4×10^{-3}	6×10^{-3}	4×10^{-3}	0	0
Acceleration	16×	18×	21×	–	1×	0.26×
Acceleration (replicated cores)	48×	90×	252×	114×	1×	0.26×

Intel PC1 implementation is based on C++ code fully optimized for local hardware profile running on a 2.2GHz Core2 Duo processor with 1GB of RAM and Windows XP pro operating system. The reference Intel PC2 is a 3.2GHz Pentium4 processor with 1GB of RAM; this implementation is fully optimised C++ code with *Intel SSE3* enabled.

The GPU design is implemented on an nVidia Geforce 7900GTX device with 512MB of on board RAM. The stated clock rate is the peak rate specified by nVidia. Double-precision floating-point arithmetic is unavailable in the current generation of GPUs [6]. The device utilization figures are shown in the upper part of Table 1. The results indicate that none of the FPGA device is fully occupied in all three cases involving double-precision, single-precision and fixed-point arithmetic. Hence performance improvement can be achieved by replicating the evaluation core in a single device. Although only nodes on the same level of a binomial tree can be computed simultaneously, acceleration can be achieved by evaluating several trees in parallel.

The lower part of Table 1 shows the acceleration results for different precision implementations, including core replication that can be done on a single device to gain further performance. The speed benchmark for both reference PCs and GPU is to evaluate a 1×10^3 step binomial tree for 2^{20} times.

First consider the acceleration of the FPGA over the Intel PC1 and PC2 benchmarks. From the results, it can be seen that the 32-bit 16.16 fixed-point implementation offers a 21 times acceleration, while the 32-bit single precision floating-point and the 64-bit double precision version offer 18 times and 16 times speedup respectively.

Not surprisingly, fixed-point arithmetic is faster and smaller than floating-point arithmetic in an FPGA. For instance, 3 cores can be implemented on a single xc4vsx55 device if double precision arithmetic is adopted, which leads to a 48 times speedup over optimized software running on a Core2 Duo processor. In contrast, 12 cores in fixed-point arithmetic can be implemented in an xc4vsx55 FPGA, indicates a 252 times acceleration for multiple binomial trees evaluated in parallel.

It is interesting to see that the floating-point implementation on GPU is faster than the single precision implementation on FPGA with replicated cores. However it is worth noting that the difference is within a factor of 2, therefore not significant.

Both the GPU and FPGA approaches are based on straightforward implementations without including further parallelism and optimisation. For instance, the GPU can potentially be made 4 or 5 times faster with higher parallelism. Our GPU is a Geforce 7900GTX, which is close to obsolescence. A significant performance improvement can be expected if the latest Geforce 8800 class GPU is adopted: 2.5 times speedup can be gained from clock speed increases (from 650MHz to 1.5GHz) and a further 1.5 times speedup from increased parallelism (128 stream scalar processors versus 24 fragment 4-vector processors) plus possible improvement in instruction-level parallelism. However, since our problem is compute bound, there will be no benefit from the Geforce 8800 memory system unless the new CUDA technology [3] is deployed. However, we believe that the Virtex-4 FPGA and the Geforce 7900GTX GPU are broadly comparable, since both are based on 90 nm technology. Similarly, single precision operators in FPGAs can run at a clock rate of up to 322MHz [10]; our current implementation at 75.4MHz has much scope for improvement. From experience, additional acceleration of up to 4 times can be achieved if optimised manually. Furthermore, if we are able to reduce device utilization to half of the original size with manual optimisation, that would enable us to put twice as many evaluation cores on the FPGA, producing a further 2 times speedup.

The speed benchmark is purely for the purpose of measuring maximum evaluation speed, hence we choose to measure 1024^2 trees to achieve maximum parallelism. In reality, it is rarely the case that 1024^2 options will be changing price at the same time. Therefore the GPU implementation will not have significant advantage in the real world where only hundreds of options will be needed for parallel evaluation. The justification for this is that the node count will be much less than the thread batch size of the GPU, which is predicted by Mark Harris (from nVidia) on the nVidia forum to be 1000-2000 concurrently live threads. In addition the requirement of varying tree depths for neighbouring nodes would map inefficiently to the GPU SPMD (single program multiple data) programming model. An FPGA implementation can be designed with data path flexibility to alleviate this restriction.

The results show that there is a tradeoff when using *HyperStreams* between the development time and the amount of acceleration that can be achieved. Although we are able to implement complex algorithms easily in FPGAs with

HyperStreams, the highest possible performance and utilisation of FPGA resources is not guaranteed. The balance between development time and performance needs to be explored with further research and experiment. However our *HyperStreams* implementation still gives a satisfactory result with significant acceleration over the software implementations. Hence *HyperStreams* is useful particularly for producing prototypes rapidly to explore the design space; once promising architectures are found, further optimisations can be applied. The data also indicate that the FPGA implementations have advantages in terms of processing speed and flexibility in implementing variable tree depths for computing option pricing in parallel over other implementations. While further comparison with nVidia's new CUDA [3] technology is desirable, so far FPGA implementations have produced satisfactory results.

7   Conclusion

This paper describes a novel architecture for accelerating option pricing models based on binomial trees. The proposed design involves a highly pipelined datapath capable of supporting multiple binomial tree calculations in parallel, which can deal with concurrent requests for option valuations. We have implemented our design onto an xc4vsx55 FPGA, and demonstrate that our implementation can run more than 250 times faster than a Core2 Duo processor, and more than 2 times faster than an nVidia GPU.

Further work is planned to carry out a complete hardware implementation of the binomial tree model, with various speed and area optimisations based on hardware cores with the highest performance. An important omission in our current study is power consumption. Since both pipelining [11] and word-length optimization [4] can improve performance and reduce power consumption, it would be worthwhile to investigate how these two techniques can be used in automating domain-specific strategies for producing binomial tree designs which best meet user requirements in speed, area and power consumption. More sophisticated comparisons with nVidia's new CUDA technology, AMD/ATI GPUs, Altera FPGAs and the Cell Broadband Engine are also planned.

Acknowledgement

The support of Celoxica, Xilinx and UK Engineering and Physical Science Research Council grants EP/D062322/1, EP/D60569/1 and EP/C549481/1 is gratefully acknowledged.

References

1. Black, F., Scholes, M.S.: The pricing of options and corporate liabilities. Journal of Political Economics 81, 637–659 (1973)
2. Celoxica, http://www.celoxica.com
3. nVidia, http://developer.nvidia.com/object/cuda.html

4. Constantinides, G.A.: Word-length optimization for differentiable nonlinear systems. ACM Trans. on Design Automation of Elect. Sys. 11(1), 26–43 (2006)
5. Hull, J.C.: Options, Futures and Other Derivatives, 6th edn. Prentice-Hall, Englewood Cliffs (2005)
6. Morris, G.W., Aubury, M.: Design space exploration of the European option benchmark using hyperstreams. In: Proc. Int. Conf. on Field Programmable Logic and Applications, IEEE, Los Alamitos (2007)
7. Thomas, D.B., Bower, J.A., Luk, W.: Automatic generation and optimisation of reconfigurable financial Monte-Carlo simulations. In: IEEE Int. Conf. on Application-Specific Systems, Architectures and Processors (2007)
8. Weaver, N., Markovskiy, Y., Patel, Y., Wawrzynek, J.: Post-placement C-slow retiming for the Xilinx Virtex FPGA. In: Proc. Int. Symp. on FPGAs, pp. 185–194. ACM Press, New York (2003)
9. Xilinx Inc. Virtex 4 FPGA handbook (2004)
10. Xilinx Inc. Floating-point operator v3.0 manual (2006)
11. Wilton, S.W., et al.: The impact of pipelining on energy per operation in Field-Programmable Gate Arrays. In: Becker, J., Platzner, M., Vernalde, S. (eds.) FPL 2004. LNCS, vol. 3203, pp. 719–728. Springer, Heidelberg (2004)
12. Zhang, G.L., et al.: Reconfigurable acceleration for Monte Carlo based financial simulation. In: Proc. Int. Conf. on Field-Programmable Technology, pp. 215–224. IEEE, Los Alamitos (2005)

Hybrid-Mode Floating-Point FPGA CORDIC Co-processor

Jie Zhou, Yong Dou, Yuanwu Lei, and Yazhuo Dong

Department of Computer Science,National University of Defense
Technology,Changsha, P.R.China 410073
{zhoujie,yongdou,yuanwulei,dongyazhuo}@nudt.edu.cn

Abstract. This paper presents a 32-bit floating-point CORDIC co-processor on FPGA, providing all known CORDIC functions. Firstly, we propose a hybrid-mode algorithm, combining hybrid rotation angle methods with argument reduction algorithm to reduce hardware area usage and meanwhile keep unlimited convergence domain for any floating-point inputs. And according to algorithm, the hybrid-mode CORDIC co-processor is organized into three phases, argument reduction, CORDIC calculation and normalization with 34 pipeline stages for FPGA implementation. The synthesis results show the clock frequency can reach 217MHz on Xilinx Virtex5 FPGA. Comparing to general-purpose microprocessor in three scientific program kernels, the CORDIC co-processor can guarantee at least 23-bit precision and achieve a maximum speedup of 47.6 times, 35.2 times in average.

1 Introduction

The CORDIC (COordinate Rotation Digital Computer) was originally introduced by Volder.J [9] in 1959 and later was bought into light again by J.S.Walther [10] in 1971. Now, all kinds of CORDIC processors have been widely used in signal processing [4] and matrix operations [11] , such as in FFT, DCT, matrix decomposition, etc. With the rapid development of large-scale integrated circuit technology, FPGA chips have been used to accelerate scientific applications.

This paper presented a hybrid-mode CORDIC algorithm, which consists of three phases: argument reduction, CORDIC calculation and normalization. Based on the algorithm above, we implemented a 32-bit hybrid-mode CORDIC co-processor on FPGA, which is organized as three modules according to three phases of hybrid-mode CORDIC algorithm respectively. To achieve 23-bit precision and improve the clock frequency, we partition the CORDIC co-processor into 34 pipeline stages. Synthesis and experimental results shows that the hybrid-mode CORDIC co-processor can reach the clock frequency of 217MHz on Virtex5 FPGA.

2 Background and Related Works

The basic CORDIC iteration equations are [10]:

R. Woods et al. (Eds.): ARC 2008, LNCS 4943, pp. 256–261, 2008.
© Springer-Verlag Berlin Heidelberg 2008

$$\begin{cases} X_{i+1} = K_i(X_i - m\sigma_i 2^{-S(m,i)}Y_i) \\ Y_{i+1} = K_i(Y_i + \sigma_i 2^{-S(m,i)}X_i) \quad \sigma_i \in \{-1,1\}, i = 0,1,...n-1 \\ Z_{i+1} = Z_i - \sigma_i \alpha_{m,i} \end{cases} \quad (1)$$

where the coordinate parameter m defines the coordinate system (circular, linear, and hyperbolic coordinate for m equal to 1, 0, and -1 respectively). The rotation angle is $\alpha_{m,i} = m^{-1/2}\tan^{-1}(m^{1/2}2^{-i})$ and the scaling factor is $K_m = \prod_i K_i = \prod_i \sqrt{1 + m\sigma_i^2 2^{-2S(m,i)}}$. The rotation sequence S(m,i) is defined as follows:

$$S(m,i) = \begin{cases} 0,1,2,3,4,5,6\ldots n,\ldots & m=1, m=0 \\ 1,2,3,4,4,5,\ldots,13,13,14,...,40,40,41,... & m=-1 \end{cases}$$

There are plenty of researches on CORDIC algorithm to enhance its performance. Most of them are focused on CORDIC calculation time, hardware cost and convergence domain.

Reducing the latency iteration and decreasing the iteration number are two basic methods to accelerate the CORDIC algorithm. Redundant CORDIC [6] is the main method to reduce the latency of each iteration in VLSI. And for reducing the number of iterations, lots of techniques have been presented, such as Unidirectional CORDIC [5] , Scaling-free CORDIC [3] and so on.

To solve the limited convergence domain, repetition of certain iteration steps [2] and argument reduction [10] are different kind of approaches, which can be employed to expand the range of convergence.

Recently, there are some CORDIC researches based on FPGA, such as literature [1] [8] and [7]. But all researches on FPGA either implemented the traditional CORDIC or the elementary function respectively, and did not present an integrated CORDIC algorithm for FPGA implementation.

3   Hybrid-Mode CORDIC Algorithm

As shown in Figure 1, the hybrid-mode CORDIC algorithm consists of three phases: argument reduction, CORDIC calculation and normalization. Argument reduction phase transforms the inputs from floating-point format into fixed-point format and expands the convergence range of hybrid-mode CORDIC algorithm. All CORDIC functions computations are accomplished in the CORDIC calculation phase. Normalization phase performs the outputs transformation from fixed-point format into floating-point format and standardized them into ANSI/IEEE Std 754-1985 format.

The intention of hybrid rotation angle method is reducing the hardware cost of CORDIC calculation phase implementation on FPGA. In this method, different rotation angle is employed during the calculation.

Hybrid rotation angle method consists of three data paths-X, Y and Z, as shown in (b) of Figure 2. In hybrid rotation angle method, $\alpha_{m,i} = 2^{-S(m,i)}$ [6] holds when the rotation sequence $S(m, i) \geq n/3$. Therefore, $\alpha_{m,i}$ can be replaced by $2^{-S(m,i)}$ as rotation angle for $\alpha_{m,i} = 2^{-S(m,i)}$. That can be used to optimize Z-path of CORDIC calculation phase iin rotate and vectoring mode.

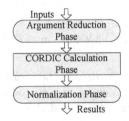

Fig. 1. Main phases of hybrid-mode CORDIC algorithm

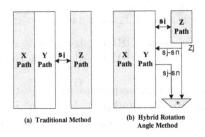

(a) Traditional Method   (b) Hybrid Rotation
                                     Angle Method

Fig. 2. Traditional and hybrid rotation angle methods

4   Implementation of Hybrid-Mode Floating-Point CORDIC Co-processor

The hybrid-mode 32-bit floating-point CORDIC co-processor includes pre-process module, CORDIC process module and post-process module, which corresponds to the argument phase, CORDIC calculation phase and normalization phase depicted in section 4 respectively. More detailed pipeline structures are shown in Figure 3. Sub-figure (c) is the pre-process module; Sub-figure (c) is one pipeline of X and Y data path and (d) is Z's; Sub-figure (e) is the pipelines of post-process module. In more details, the stages are arranged as follows:

S1: Converting the floating-point format of inputs into fixed-point format.

S2-S3: Scale factor compensation operations and angle mapping in argument reduction.

S4-S5: Calculation mapped angle in argument reduction.

S6: Selecting the inputs of the CORDIC process module according to the mode selecting sign Mode_sel and the coordinate selecting sign CO_sel.

S7-S14: The first part of CORDIC calculation phase.

S15-S31: The second part of CORDIC calculation phase.

S32: Finishing the calculation of corresponding functions.

S33: Counting leading zeros

S34: Normalization of output. X, Y, Z, and ex are shifted to the left according to the number of the leading zeros and then are truncated to form the mantissas of the outputs respectively.

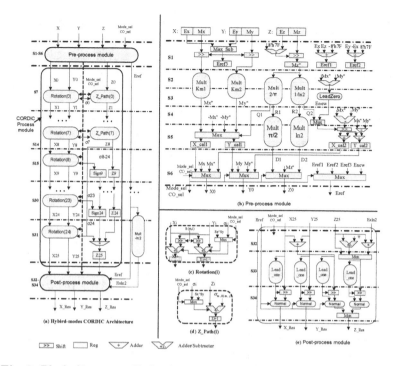

Fig. 3. Block diagrams of hybrid-mode floating-point CORDIC co-processor

Table 1. Synthesis results of various CORDIC calculation modules

FPGA	Item	Tradition	Ours	Rotation	Vectoring	RV-Mode
StratixII	frequency	210.79	211.60	226.81	223.86	223.58
	LUT	3342	2776	2276	2218	4591
	Reg	2500	2522	1550	2217	3829
Virtex5	frequency	285.50	285.61	278.07	311.19	275.34
	LUT	2475	1947	1654	1545	3281
	Reg	2527	2542	1786	2226	4116

5 Experimental Results

The first experiment aims to select the best approach to implement the module of CORDIC calculation for the 32-bit floating-point hybrid-mode CORDIC co-processor. We map different improvement methods advanced in [2] and section 4 on FPGAs of StratixII and Virtex5, and then show the synthesis results in Table 1. Here, the RV-Mode is the integration of Rotation's and Vectoring's.

In experiment 2, we synthesized our hybrid-mode floating-point CORDIC co-processor on FPGAs of StratixII and Virtex5 respectively and the results are summarized in Table 2. As shown in Table 2, 32-bit floating-point hybrid-mode CORDIC co-processor occupy a little area of FPGA and several copies of this architecture can be integrated in a single FPGA chip to compute several different transcendental functions concurrently to accelerate the computation of scientific.

Table 2. Synthesis results of 32-bit floating-point hybrid-mode CORDIC co-processors

FPGA	Pre-Process		CORDIC-Process		Post-Process		Total		Frequency (MHz)
	LUT	Reg	LUT	Reg	LUT	Reg	LUT	Reg	
StratixII	2135	2244	2776	2522	1008	558	6469(4.5%)	5372(3.7%)	195.08
Virtex5	2039	2037	1947	2531	1211	569	5412(2.6%)	5130(2.5%)	217.24

Table 3. Execution results of scientific program slices

Prog ram	Pentium 4(μs)	Single-CORDIC		Mult-CORDICs		
		Time(μs)	Speedup	Time(μs)	Speedup	Num_C
Slice1	293.02	42.17	6.9	6.16	47.6	8
Slice2	181.65	52.71	3.4	6.50	27.9	10
Slice3	179.22	21.17	8.5	5.95	30.1	4
Average	217.96	38.68	5.6	6.20	35.2	7.3

In experiment 3, we chose three program slices from two scientific computation programs. One is UZ1 used to solve the Ordinary Differential Equations. The other is UE2 used to solve Unbalance Stiff Equations. The three program slices are executed in three different platforms. One is Pentium 4 CPU with 2.80GHz clock frequency, where the source code is written in VC++ 6.0 environment and compiled into release version. Another is a FPGA chip using only single multifunctional floating-point CORDIC processor and the third is also a FPGA chip using multiple CORDIC processors to parallel the computation. The test results, as depicted in Table.3, demonstrate that parallel CORDIC processors can be used to enhance the speed of scientific computation more, achieving a maximum speedup of 47.6 times, 35.2 times in average.

6   Conclusion

In this paper, we presented a hybrid-mode CORDIC algorithm, which can provide all known CORDIC functions calculation and allows all floating-point values be its inputs. And then, we implemented a 32-bit floating-point hybrid-mode CORDIC co-processor on FPGA and organized it into three modules according to the three phases of the proposed algorithm with 34 pipeline stages. Synthesis results tell us that the clock frequency of our 32-bit hybrid-mode CORDIC co-processor reaches 217MHz on Virtex5 and 195MHz on StratixII.

Acknowledgments

This work is supported by NSFC of China under the NO. 60633050.

References

1. Andraks, R.: A survey of cordic algorithm for fpga based computers. In: Proceedings of the 1998 ACM/SIGDA Sixth International Symposium on Field Programmable Gate Arrays, pp. 191–200 (1998)

2. Xiaobo, H., Ronald, G.H., Steven, C.B.: Expanding the range of convergence of the cordic algorithm. IEEE Transactions on Computers 40, 13–21 (1991)
3. Maharatna, K., Troya, A., Banerjee, S., Grass, E.: Virtually scaling-free adaptive cordic rotator. Computers and Digital Techniques, IEE Proceedings 151, 448–456 (2004)
4. Maharatna, K., Dhar, A.S., Banerjee, S.: A vlsi array architecture for realization of dft, dht, dct and dst. Signal Process 81, 1813–1822 (2001)
5. Ravichandran, S., Asari, V.: Implementation of unidirectional cordic algorithm using precomputed rotation bits. Circuits and Systems 3, 453–456 (2002)
6. Timmermann, D., Hahn, H., Hosticka, B.: Low latency time cordic algorithms. IEEE Trans. Computers 41, 1010–1015 (1992)
7. Vadlamani, S., Mahmoud, D.W.: Comparison of CORDIC Algorithm Implementations on FPGA Families. System Theory [e]. Tennessee Technol, Univ. USA (2002)
8. Valls, J., hlmann, M., Parhi, K.: Efficient mapping of cordic algorithm on fpga. In: Signal Processing Systems, pp. 336–345 (2000)
9. Volder, J.E.: The cordic trigonometric computing technique. IRE Trans. Electron. Comput. 8, 330–334 (1959)
10. Walther, J.S.: A unified algorithm for elementary functions. In: Proc. AFIPS Conf., vol. 38, pp. 389–395 (1971)
11. Hu, X., Bass, S.C., Harber, R.G.: An efficient implementation of singular value decomposition rotation transformations with cordic processor. J. Parallel Distrib. Comput. 17, 360–362 (1993)

Multiplier-Based Double Precision Floating Point Divider According to the IEEE-754 Standard

Vítor Silva[1], Rui Duarte[1], Mário Véstias[2], and Horácio Neto[1]

[1] INESC-ID/IST/UTL, Technical University of Lisbon, Portugal
[2] INESC-ID/ISEL/IPL, Polytechnic Institute of Lisbon, Portugal

Abstract. This paper describes the design and implementation of a unit to calculate the significand of a double precision floating point divider according to the IEEE-754 standard. Instead of the usual digit recurrence techniques, such as SRT-2 and SRT-4, it uses an iterative technique based on the Goldsmith algorithm. As multiplication is the main operation of this algorithm, its implementation is able to take advantage of the efficiency of the embedded multipliers available in the FPGAs. The results obtained indicate that the multiplier-based iterative algorithms can achieve better performance than the alternative digit recurrence algorithms, at the cost of some area overhead.

1   Introduction

FPGAs are becoming a commonplace in the design of computational units to accelerate many applications. Some of these applications require the use of single or double floating point arithmetic. Therefore, hardware designers are looking for efficient solutions to implement floating point arithmetic in FPGAs using the available resources of the programmable hardware units. The works from [1], [2] and [3] are some of the first approaches implementing single precision (or lower) floating-point division in FPGA. [4] extended the previous work with a floating-point divider. [9] presents a divider core for both single and double precision. [10] describes a double precision floating-point core for division and other operations, that supports the complete IEEE-754 standard.

In the case of the floating point division operation, most implementations are based on the well-known digit recurrence algorithms. However, today's FPGAs include a significant number of built-in multipliers, which makes multiplication-based division algorithms increasingly interesting.

In this paper, a new architecture to calculate the division of the significands of a double precision floating point divider according to standard IEEE-754 is presented. The architecture is completely pipelined and is based on the Goldsmith method for the calculation of division, instead of the more usual NRD or SRT4 algorithms. The method is based on successive iterations and calculates the division with better performance than previous approaches.

Section 2 describes the Goldsmith iterative division algorithm. Section 3 is concerned with the generation of the seed. Section 4 presents the architecture

R. Woods et al. (Eds.): ARC 2008, LNCS 4943, pp. 262–267, 2008.

of the divisor. Section 5 describes the implementation results. Finally, section 6 ends the document with the conclusions.

2   Iterative Algorithm for Division

The Goldsmith method for division uses the Taylor series expansion to calculate the reciprocal of the denominator (divisor), that is, $q = \frac{N}{D} = N \times g(y)$, such that $g(y)$ may be efficiently calculated using an iterative method.

A straightforward approach is to consider $g(y) = 1/y$ with $p = 1$ and then calculate the series. However, it is computationally more efficient to consider the Maclaurin series $g(y) = 1/(y+1)$ (with $p = 0$). In this case, $g(y)$ is given by

$$g(y) \approx \frac{1}{(1+y)} = 1 - y + y^2 - y^3 + y^4 + \cdots \tag{1}$$

To obtain $\frac{1}{D}$ from $g(y)$, y must be replaced by D - 1, with D normalized such that $0,5 \le D$ and $|y| \le 0,5$. In this case, the quotient is given by:

$$q = N \times [(1 - y)(1 + y)^2(1 + y)^4(1 + y)^8...] \tag{2}$$

This equation can be calculated iteratively, considering that an approximation to the quotient can be calculated from $q_i = \frac{N_i}{D_i}$, where N_i and D_i are the values of the numerator and the denominator after iteration i of the algorithm.

The Goldsmith algorithm starts with $N_0 = N$ and $D_0 = D$. Then, in the first iteration both N_0 and D_0 are multiplied by $R_0 = 1 - y = 2 - D$ to generate a new approach for the numerator, N_1, and for the denominator, D_1.

Generically, the iterative process calculates the following recurrent equations:

$$N_{i+1} = N_i \times R_i, D_{i+1} = D_i \times R_i, R_{i+1} = 2 - D_{i+1} \tag{3}$$

where N and D have quadratic convergence to q and 1, respectively.

To reduce the number of iterations needed to achieve a certain precision, a better precision for R_0 may be used, which is usually designated seed. Based on this idea, [6] proposed a modified Goldsmith algorithm that uses an initial seed with enough precision to guarantee that a single iteration is sufficient to obtain double precision. In this case, equations (3) are replaced by the equations,

$$\mathbf{G} = R_0 \times N_0, \mathbf{V} = 1 - R_0 \times D_0, \mathbf{Q} = G + G \times V \tag{4}$$

which are mathematically equivalent but computationally more efficient.

3   Seed Generation

The seed is computed using an efficient algorithm based on a second degree polynomial approximation, similar to the one proposed by Piñeiro [7] with the modifications proposed by Muller [5]. The seed is calculated using second order polynomial approximations calculated with the *Minimax* technique. The domain of the reciprocal is first divided into a power of two number of intervals and then the two order polynomial approximation is found for each interval.

Assuming all operands are in IEEE-754 normalized form, in order to implement the 2nd degree minimax polynomial approximation the significand of the input of the seed generator is split into an upper part $X_1 = [1.x_1x_2..x_{m1}]$, a middle part $X_2 = [x_{m1+1}..x_{m2}] \times 2^{-m_1}$ and a lower part $X_3 = [x_{m2+1}..x_n] \times 2^{-m_2}$.

An approximation to the reciprocal in the range $X_1 \leq X < X_1 + 2^{-m_1}$ can be found by evaluating the polynomial:

$$X^p \approx C_0 + C_1 \times X_2 + C_2 \times X_2^2 \tag{5}$$

The coefficients C_0, C_1 and C_2 are computed for each of the 2^{m_1} intervals. So, a different polynomial is used for each interval. X_3 does not play any part in the computation of the approximation.

The coefficients are then are stored in three lookup tables, each with 2^{m_1} entries, one for each of the above mentioned segments. Each table is addressed by the m_1 most significant bits of the fractional part of the significand.

To determine the set of coefficients, the following steps are considered:

1. Step 1 - Given the desired precision (ϵ_d) the space of the 2nd degree minimax polynomials approximation must be swept to find a good candidate for the number of segments that the approximation function must be split into.
2. Step 2 - Find the appropriate word length for C_0, C_2, X_2, and the number of bits of X_2 used as inputs to the squarer unit.
3. Step 3 - Fill in the tables of coefficients.

Step one. uses a semi-automatic iterative procedure in which a script is executed with the following inputs:

1. Word length of C_1, denoted k from now on.
2. Number of bits used to address the tables, m_1.

For each pair (k,m_1), the algorithm determines the coefficients C_0, C_1, and C_2 with the computer algebra system Maple, which performs the minimax approximations using the Remez algorithm. Then the Partially Rounded (PR) approach from Muller is applied. According to PR, C_1 is rounded to k bits and, from $C_{1rounded}$, the new values of C_0, and C_2 are found as follows [5]:

$$C_{0new} = C_0 + (C_1 - C_{1rounded}) \times 2^{-m_1-3} \tag{6}$$
$$C_{2new} = C_2 + (C_1 - C_{1rounded}) \times 2^{m_1} \tag{7}$$

The difference between the polynomial approximation with both sets of values is the error of the approximation with the pair of values (k,m_1).

The script is run as many times as needed to find a good candidate, that is, a tuple (k,m_1) for which the accuracy found with the PR approach is greater than the desired accuracy, ϵ_d.

Step two. consists in finding the appropriate word length for the parameters of the polynomial. Once the value for the tuple (k,m_1) and the accuracy (ϵ_{pr})

for the PR approximation is computed, the missing parameters may be easily figured out. Due to the rounding of C_0, C_2 and X_2 in the PR approximation, the final accuracy is lower than ϵ_{pr}. Therefore, we try to achieve an accuracy $(\epsilon'_{pr}) = (\epsilon_{pr}) - 1$, that is, an error less than $2^{-\epsilon'_{pr}}$. Formally, we want an error on the computation of $C_{0new} + C_{2new} \times (X - X_1)^2 \leq 2^{-\epsilon'_{pr}}$ (from now on we will refer to $(X - X_1)$ as h). Algebraically, we want to guarantee that

$$\left| C_{0new} - C_{0newRounded} \right| + \left| C_{2new} \times h^2 - C_{2newRounded} \times (h + h_{error})^2 \right| \leq 2^{-\epsilon'_{pr}}$$

(8)

Given that $h \leq 2^{-m_1}$ then the word lengths of C_0 (C_{0WL}), C_2 (C_{2WL}), h (h_{WL}), and X_2 (X_{2WL}) are as follows:

$$C_{0WL} = \epsilon'_{pr} + 1 \tag{9}$$
$$C_{2WL} = \epsilon'_{pr} + 2 - 2 \times m_1 \tag{10}$$
$$C_{hWL} = \epsilon'_{pr} + 4 - 2 \times m_1 \tag{11}$$
$$X_{2WL} = \epsilon'_{pr} + 2 - m_1 \tag{12}$$

C_0 will have 1 bit for the integer part and C_{0WL} for the fractional part.

Step three. A script in Maple receives the size of the tables (m_1), and the word length of C_0, C_1 and C_2 and generates the tables.

4   Architecture to Calculate the Significand

The architecture to calculate the significand consists in the unit to determine the seed and the unit to calculate the significand with double precision.

Using the rounding criteria defined in [8] and knowing that the Goldsmith algorithm has quadratic convergence, we conclude the seed must have at least 29 bits of precision so that a single iteration is enough to complete the division.

Figure (1) shows the hardware structure of the circuit used to calculate X^{-1}. The circuit has three coefficient tables, two multipliers, one squarer, one adder and one subtractor. The size of each coefficient and of the arithmetic units were obtained with the process described previously with $\epsilon'_{pr} = 29$.

From the seed, equations (4) are used to calculate the significand. Figure (2) shows the structure of the unit to calculate the significand. As shown, the Add/Sub operator implements an adder/subtractor controlled by bit 28 of V. If V< 28 > is '0' then the adder unit is used. Otherwise, the operation is a subtraction. Thus, it was possible to reduce the size of the operands of (4) and the product $G \times V$, that appears at the second term of equation (4). This is due to the fact that the seed has 29 bits of precision, which guarantees that $|V| \leq 2^{-29}$ and,therefore, at least the most significant 29 bits from the equation (4) are fixed. Hence, it is possible to reduce 28 bits in the two's complement operator and, in the case of the multiplication $G \times V$ it allows the replacement of a 57×57 multiplication for a 57×28 multiplication.

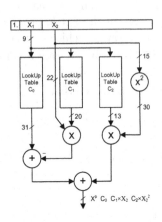

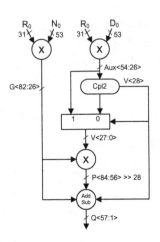

Fig. 1. Hardware to compute the seed

Fig. 2. Hardware to compute Q

5   Implementation and Results

The architecture was specified in VHDL, synthesized with Xilinx ISE8.2 and then implemented in a Xilinx Virtex-2 6000 FPGA [13] with 144 multipliers included in a Celoxica ADMXRC2 board.

From Table 1 we observe that our circuit calculates the significand in 33 cycles at more than 350 MHz. Also observing the results of a straightforward approach for the pre and postprocessing circuits we conclude the complete circuit can achieve a frequency of 325 MHz in about 70 cycles. The performance of the circuit is very good when compared to other recent approaches (see table 2).

Table (2) includes the works from [9], [10], [11] and [12]. The first two were obtained with a Virtex 2/2P, while the others were obtained with a Virtex-4. All algorithms use the digit-recurrence technique to calculate the significand, except ours and the Xilinx IP core 1.0, which are iterative.

When compared to the works of [9] and [10], ours is much faster with about the same number of cycles. While the former approach does not support exceptions and only supports rounding to nearest, the second one supports the complete standard. The main difference to our approach has to do with the algorithm used to calculate the significand.

Table 1. Implementation of our circuit in a Virtex2^{TM} post-$P\&R$

Stages	Slices	FFs	MULT18×18s	Mhz	Latency
Preprocessing	1922	3220	0	325 MHz	12
Seed	2170	3802	3	372 MHz	11
Significand	6900	12331	28	361 MHz	22
Post processing	1549	2635	0	372 MHz	18

Table 2. Comparison with our approach

Author	Algorithm	Mhz	Latency
Underwood	RD	83	67
Prasanna	RD	140	68
Xilinx Div 1.0	Iter	284	99
Xilinx FP 3.0	RD	266	57
Ours	Iter	325	70

6   Conclusions

The significand divider implemented in this work based on the Goldsmith algorithm is very competitive when compared to algorithms based on digit recurrence. The proposed circuit achieves higher frequencies than previous works with a similar number of cycles.

The next step of the project is to optimize the architecture to reduce the latency of the circuit. Also, the complete double precision floating point divider according to standard IEEE-754 is already being tested in a Virtex-II platform.

References

1. Wang, X., Leeser, M.: Variable Precision Floating Point Division and Square Root. In: 8th Annual High Performance Embedded Computing Workshop (October 2004)
2. Lienhart, G., Kugel, A., Manner, R.: Using floating-point arithmetic on FPGAs to accelerate scientific N-body simulations. In: FCCM 2002 (April 2002), pp. 182–191
3. Liang, J., Tessier, R., Mencer, O.: Floating point unit generation and evaluation for FPGAs. In: FCCM 2003 (April 2003)
4. Daga, V., Govindu, G., Prasanna, V.K., Gangadharpalli, S., Sridhar, V.: Floating-point based block LU decomposition on FPGAs. In: ERSA 2004(June 2004)
5. Muller, J.-M.: Partially rounded. Small-Order Approximations for Accurate Hardware-Oriented, Table-Based Methods, Reserach Report 4593, INRIA (2002)
6. Piñeiro, J.A., Bruguera, J.D.: High-Speed Double-Precision Computation of Reciprocation and Division. In: DCIS 2001 (November 2001)
7. Piñeiro, J.A., Bruguera, J.D., Muller, J.M.: Faithful Powering Computation Using Table Look-Up and a Fused Accumulation Tree. In: ARITH 2001 (June 2001)
8. Stuart, F.: Oberman and Michael J. Flyn, Fast IEEE rounding for division by functional iteration, TR CSL-TR-96-700, DEECS, Stanford University (1996)
9. Underwood, K.: FPGA vs. CPUs: Trends in Peak Floating Point Performance. In: FPGA 2004 (February 2004)
10. Govindu, G., Scrofano, R., Prasanna, V.: A Library of Parameterizable Floating-Point Cores for FPGAs and Their Application to Scientific Computing. In: ERSA 2005 (June 2005)
11. www.xilinx.com/bvdocs/ipcenter/data/_sheet/div/_gen/_ds530.pdf
12. http://www.xilinx.com/bvdocs/ipcenter/data_sheet/floating_point_ds335.pdf
13. ADM-XRC-II Reconfigurable Computer Documentation, Alpha-Data (2002), http://www.alphadata.com/adm-xrc-ii.html

Creating the World's Largest Reconfigurable Supercomputing System Based on the Scalable SGI® Altix® 4700 System Infrastructure and Benchmarking Life-Science Applications

Haruna Cofer, Matthias Fouquet-Lapar, Timothy Gamerdinger,
Christopher Lindahl, Bruce Losure, Alan Mayer,
James Swoboda, and Teruo Utsumi

SGI, 1140 E. Argues Avenue, Sunnyvale, CA 94085, USA
{haruna,mfl,timg,lindahl,blosure,ajm,swoboda,teruo}@sgi.com

Abstract. FPGA accelerated systems in High Performance Computing are typically limited to single digit numbers of FPGAs in a Single System Image (SSI). However, SGI has built an SSI system with 70 FPGAs to study the feasibility of running real-world customer test cases on such a large scale system. This paper will detail the system architecture, the implementation, and the results of performing both a real-world bioinformatics benchmark and a synthetic global bandwidth test where all 70 FPGAs were driven by a single process.

1 Introduction

As part of our on-going engineering and application development focused on applied heterogonous supercomputing, the SGI RASC Engineering and Manufacturing teams assembled a test system consisting of:

- 32 CPU blades, each blade featuring a dual core Intel® Itanium® Montecito processor running at 1.6GHz
- 35 RC100 RASC blades, each blade featuring two Xilinx Virtex 4 LX200 FPGAs
- 256 GB of physical and globally addressable cache-coherent memory

The system was built within two days using off-the-shelf SGI parts from SGI's SGI® Altix® 4700 series. We were able to boot our standard Linux OS, SUSE Enterprise Server 10 SP1 (kernel version 2.6.16.46-0.12), running our latest RASC Abstraction Layer (RASCAL) release without any modifications.

About one-half day was used to run standard diagnostic tests as part of SGI's Quality Process, and no problems were found.

We performed functional testing of the new features in the next RASCAL release and ran a real-world benchmark using the popular bioinformatics application called BLAST. The BLAST implementation used was Mitrion Accelerated BLAST 1.0 [3], which is based on NCBI BLAST 2.2.13 [4]. The same BLAST benchmark was also run on a typically used AMD Opteron cluster for comparison.

R. Woods et al. (Eds.): ARC 2008, LNCS 4943, pp. 268–273, 2008.

2 SGI Altix 4700 System Overview

The SGI Altix 4700 computer system is based on a distributed shared memory (DSM) architecture. The system uses a global-address-space, cache-coherent multiprocessor that scales up to sixty-four Intel 64-bit processors in a single rack. Because the architecture is modular via the NUMAflex and NUMAlink™ technologies, the DSM combines the advantages of lower entry cost with the ability to scale processors, memory, and I/O independently to a current maximum of 1024 processor sockets (2,048 processor cores) in a single-system image (SSI). Larger SSI configurations may be offered in the future.

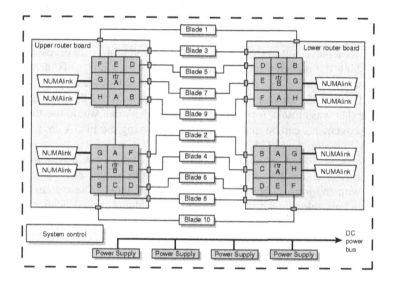

Fig. 1. Functional Block Diagram of the Individual Rack Unit (IRU)

2.1 The SGI® RASC™ RC100 Blade

The SGI® RASC™ RC100[1] blade is our fourth FPGA based acceleration product and has been in production for more than two years. Its architecture is well balanced to suit a large set of applications and is tightly integrated into the SGI Altix 4700 system infrastructure.

The RC100 blade uses two Xilinx Virtex 4 LX200[2] FPGAs, each with five 36-bit wide independent SRAM banks supporting ECC.

2.2 RASCAL Software Overview

SGI's RASCAL software stack provides an extremely flexible and powerful API to the application. This software stack provides, in addition to the administrative commands and low level driver, a resource manager which has shown to work well with this large configuration. The RASCAL software performs the device allocation, the reconfiguration of FPGAs, the automatic wide scaling across multiple FPGAs, the management of data movement to or from the FPGAs, and the exception handling for error conditions in the algorithms. The software also provides the interface for an FPGA aware version of gdb and configures the hardware abstraction layer for the algorithm block.

3 Observations

The test we used to verify bandwidth scaling was a very simple bitstream that pulled data off the data channel as fast as possible, incremented each word of the data, then pushed the data back into the data channel. The data channel moves data at 6.4 GB/sec theoretical peak. This is bi-directional throughput, with 3.2 GB/sec in each direction, simultaneously. The application bitstream was fully capable of driving the data at rated speed.

In order to achieve full performance in a NUMA system, it is necessary to avoid oversubscribing the memory and processor resources on a node. To achieve this, it was necessary to make the RASCAL libraries (RASClib) aware of the system topology. Once RASClib was aware of the topology, it could then allocate memory on the node that was closest, topologically, to the FPGA that would use that memory. Further improvements can be made if the threads driving the FPGA are pinned to the node that is closest to the FPGA.

We built the 70 FPGA system in order to verify that we could boot and run on a system of this size and to verify that the bandwidth would also scale. We were successful with the former, but disappointed with the latter. The system booted and ran with standard, released software without any problems or modifications. We were able to run the test applications on all 70 FPGAs concurrently. We were quite pleased with the performance of the BLAST-N application. However, the bandwidth bound application showed disappointing results with large numbers of FPGAs.

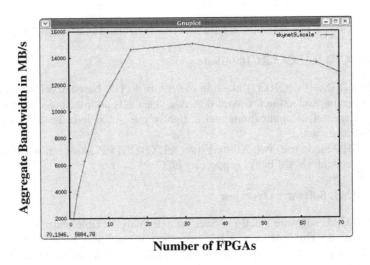

Fig. 2. High Bandwidth Test with 16MB Data Transfers on 70 FPGA System

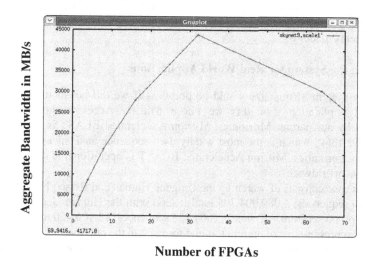

Number of FPGAs

Fig. 3. High Bandwidth Test with 256MB Data Transfers on 70 FPGA System

As can be seen from the plot in **Fig. 2**, the ability to scale dropped off dramatically at about 16 FPGAs.

The above data was generated using a bandwidth limited application that did data transfers of 16 MB. We ran the same application again, using 256 MB data transfer sizes with the results in **Fig. 3**.

These were better results, but there was still that precipitous drop-off at about 32 FPGAs. Instrumentation showed that series of relatively minor issues with pthread jitter and another with a spin lock in the Linux kernel when pinning the huge page into memory in preparation for the data transfer to or from the FPGA contributed to each FPGA running at only 80% of theoretical peak of network bandwidth.

Unfortunately, we did not have sufficient time to implement the fixes in software during our allotted time on the system. We were, however, able to reproduce the scaling issues on a smaller 16 FPGA system, to continue development. To handle the bandwidth limitations observed in the 70 FPGA system, an additional CPU blade per RC100 blade was added to bring this smaller system to 16 CPU blades and 16 FPGAs.

There were two issues associated with the use of pthreads. In the first case, a worker thread would fully utilize the processor core being used by the control thread. This was fixed with a call to pthread_cond_broadcast() to allow the control thread to complete prior to waking the worker threads. In the second case, two or more worker threads would contend for the same processor core despite having ample resources. This problem was alleviated by pinning the worker threads to specific processor cores on the node.

Finally, there was a kernel lock issue that was fixed by putting the important work that the kernel call get_user_pages() did in the RASC driver without the lock. In the specific case the driver did not require the lock since the data structure the lock was protecting was not used.

After this work, we ran tests on the smaller, 16 FPGA, system and achieved nearly linear scaling results. Future work will include runs on a large machine to verify the improvements made.

3.1 Using the System for Real World Applications

Building a system of this size would be pointless if we did not include the test of a real-world application. For this we chose Mitrion Accelerated BLAST 1.0[3], developed by our partner Mitrionics. Mitrion Accelerated BLAST is based on NCBI BLAST 2.2.13[4], which is the most widely used sequence analysis application in the area of bioinformatics. Mitrion Accelerated BLAST is operational at several customer installations worldwide.

The test case consists of searching the Unigene Human and Refseq Human databases (6,733,760 sequences; 4,089,004,795 total letters) with the Human Genome U133 Plus 2.0 Array probe set from Affymetrix (604,258 sequences; 15,106,450 total letters). This test case is representative of current top-end research in the pharmaceutical industry.

To run this test case on 70 FPGAs, the input queries were initially split into 169 chunks to utilize the maximum total query length supported by Mitrion BLAST 1.0. Each chunk was then processed by one of the FPGAs using Mitrion Accelerated BLAST. The 169 chunks were distributed to the 70 FPGAs in 3 separate groups consisting of the first 70 chunks, followed by the next 70 chunks, and finally the remaining 29 chunks. The total wall clock time of running the test case on 70 FPGAs was 32 minutes 29 seconds.

To run this test case on a typically used AMD Opteron cluster, the input queries were divided into 16 chunks (to use 16 AMD Opteron cores). Each chunk was then processed by one of the cores using NCBI BLAST 2.2.13. The total wall clock time of running the test case on a 16-core 2.8GHz AMD Opteron 8220 SE cluster was more than 4 days (101h:45m:48s).

Therefore, the speedup of running this BLAST benchmark on the 70-FPGA system versus the 16-core Opteron cluster was 188x. The magnitude of this speedup in BLAST processing speed is significant because scientists worldwide are being challenged by the exponential growth in genomic sequence data.

Given a fairly complex job mix, we found that additional scheduling mechanisms would be required to guarantee optimal resource allocation. We believe that such an implementation would be straightforward to interface with our RASCAL devmgr tool that controls total device allocation and would further improve the production throughput benchmark.

4   Conclusions

We conclude that a large, production FPGA system can be built, tested, and deployed in a short period of time. We also find that an application that is bandwidth limited can be scaled, nearly linearly, with the system bandwidth scaling to reduce computation time. We have shown that applications can make use of 64 or more FPGAs in a single system image to solve a common problem, and we have shown that the SGI Altix architecture and RASC software can handle this scaling with minimal effort on the part of the algorithm developer.

References

1. SGI® RASC™ RC100 User's Guide,
   http://techpubs.sgi.com/library/tpl/cgi-
   bin/download.cgi?coll=hdwr&db=bks&docnumber=007-4718-006
2. Xilinx Vitrex 4 User's Guide.
   http://www.xilinx.com/support/documentation/virtex-4.htm#19324
3. BLAST-N project, http://mitc-openbio.sourceforge.net/blast_blastn.html
4. National Center for Biotechnology Information, http://www.ncbi.nlm.nih.gov

Highly Efficient Structure of 64-Bit Exponential Function Implemented in FPGAs

Maciej Wielgosz[1,2], Ernest Jamro[1,2], Kazimierz Wiatr[1,2]

[1] AGH University of Science and Technology,
Al. Mickiewicza 30, 30-059 Kraków
[2] Academic Computer Centre Cyfronet AGH,
ul. Nawojki 11, 30-950 Kraków
{wielgosz,jamro,wiatr}@agh.edu.pl

Abstract. This paper presents implementation of the double precision exponential function. A novel table-based architecture, together with short Taylor expansion, provides low latency (30 clock cycles) which is comparable to 32-bit implementations. Low area consumption of a single *exp()* module (roughtly 4% of XC4LX200) allows implementation of several parallel modules on a single FPGAs. The exp() function was implemented on the SGI RASC platform, thus external memory interface limitation allowed only a twin module parallelism. Each module is capable of processing at speed of 200 MHz with max. error of 1 ulp, RMSE equals 0,62. This implementation aims primarily to meet quantum chemistry's huge and strict requirements of precision and speed.

Keywords: HPRC (High Performance Reconfigurable Computing), FPGA, elementary function, exponent function.

1 Introduction

The HPRC (High Performance Reconfigurable Computing) has important advantages over HPC (High Performance Computing) like significantly lower power consumption and more efficient silicon coverage. Unfortunately conducting floating-point operation within FPGA absorbs much more area than fixed-point calculations, therefore for a long time, FPGAs had not been employed to support double precision operation. Nowadays, there are some implementations of single precision floating-point operations[1,2,3]. Since the proposed *exp()* module aims to speed up HPC chemistry and physics calculations, it has to be compatible with the data format employed so far. Consequently, the IEEE-754 double precision standard is adopted.

2 Architecture of *Exp* Module

To evaluate *exp* function the following commonly known mathematical identities are employed:

$$e^x = 2^{x \cdot \log_2 e} = 2^{x_i} \cdot e^{x - x_i / \log_2 e} \tag{1}$$

R. Woods et al. (Eds.): ARC 2008, LNCS 4943, pp. 274–279, 2008.
© Springer-Verlag Berlin Heidelberg 2008

$$e^{x+y} = e^x \cdot e^y \tag{2}$$

where x_i is an integer part of $x \cdot log_2 e$.

The equation (1) is employed to separate input argument into the integer part x_i and fractional part x_f. Integer part x_i is used directly to evaluate the exponent part of the final result 2^{xi}. Therefore the main problem is evaluation of the fractional part $exp(x_f)$.

The proposed architecture of the *exp* function evaluation employs two methods to evaluate the fractional part:

- Look-Up Table (LUT) based architecture
- polynomial approximation.

The partial results of these two methods are combined employing equation (2). Furthermore, (2) can be also used to divide one large LUT memory into several smaller LUT memories. Therefore employment of (2) is the main idea of the proposed architecture.

The mixed method adoption always leads to the dilemma of the trade-off between LUT memories' size and polynomial part evaluation cost. In the case of *exp* function implementation, increase of LUT memory size results in a decrease of the multiplication area. Nevertheless, analysis of the resources occupied by multipliers and LUT memories has led to the conclusion that employment of Block RAMs (BRAMs) embedded in the FPGAs would be the best solution. Replacement of floating-point multipliers with fixed-point ones further reduces occupied FPGA resources. It is possible because the input data was previously converted into a fixed-point format. Furthermore input data smaller than 2^{-60} may be neglected during the calculation as they have unnoticeable impact on the final result.

In the proposed architecture the polynomial approximation is significantly simplified. According to Taylor-Maclaurin exp(x) can be evaluated as follows:

$$e^x = 1 + x + x^2/2 + x^3/6 + \dots \tag{3}$$

In order to disregard $x^2/2$ and higher degree expressions, the input argument must be very small to satisfy maximum mantissa error $< 2^{-54}$ for double precision format. This is satisfied for $x < 2^{-27}$. Consequently the most significant 27 bits of input x_f are calculated employing LUT-based methods, the reset less-significant bits are calculated using Taylor-Maclaurin expansion limited to: $e^x \approx 1 + x$. To obtain the final result, the results of the LUT-based algorithm and polynomial approximation are multiplied according to (2). It should be noted that (2) allows to use only LUT-based method, nevertheless employment of the polynomial approximation results in a significant decrease of the number of multipliers and LUTs.

Summing up, the input argument x after conversion to fixed-point format is divided into 5 sections:

1. integer part (11-bit), x_i, which evaluates 2^{Xi} (exponent part of the result),
2. fractional MSB part, x_M, bits $2^{-1} \div 2^{-9}$,
3. fractional middle-bits part, x_D, bits $2^{-10} \div 2^{-18}$,
4. fractional LSB part, x_L, bits $2^{-19} \div 2^{-27}$,
5. fractional Taylor part, x_T, bits $2^{-28} \dots$

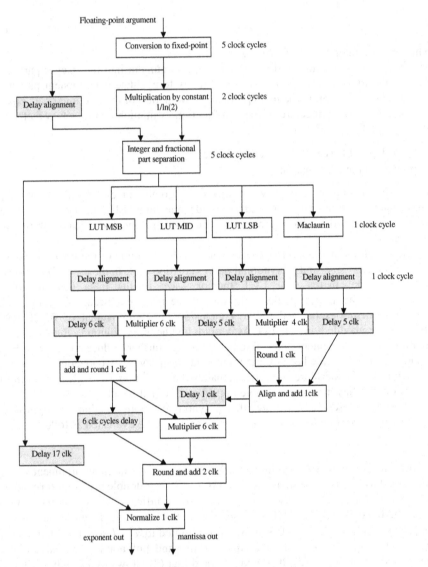

Fig. 1. Exp() module block diagram and its pipeline latency

Afterwards the following mathematical operations are employed:

$$x_I = \lfloor x \cdot \log_2(e)) \rfloor \tag{4}$$

$$x_F = x_M \,\&\, x_D \,\&\, x_L \,\&\, x_T = x - x_I \cdot (\log_2(2))^{-1} \tag{5}$$

$$y = 2^{x_I} \cdot e^{x_M} \cdot e^{x_D} \cdot e^{x_L} \cdot (1 + x_T) \tag{6}$$

where: & - bit concatenation, $\lfloor x \rfloor$ - rounding to the greatest integer x_I such that $x_I \leq x$.

Using (4) and (5) enables separation of the integer and fractional parts. This step can be considered to be a scaling process that transforms input data to interval of boundaries at 0 and ln(2). It should be noted that x_I is a small integer represented on 10 bits, otherwise $exp(x)$ results in infinity. Therefore this approach in practice replaces a large multiplication (required by identity $e^x = 2^{X/ln(2)}$) with two smaller multiplications, one to compute inaccurately x_I according to (4), second to compute (accurately but with reduced width) $x_I \cdot ln(2)$ according to (5).

2.1 Error Analysis

In the proposed architecture the following sources of errors can be distinguished:

1. Taylor series expansion,
2. multiplier (and LUT) width limitation.

The Taylor series expansion is limited only to: $e^x \approx 1 + x$. For $x \to 0$ the expansion error can be approximated by the next omitted expression, i.e. $x^2/2$. As input argument $x_T < 2^{-27}$ the Taylor series expansion error is limited roughly by 2^{-55}. It should be noted that the input value is $x_T \geq 0$, thus the result $y_T = 1 + x_T \geq 1$. Consequently relative error is also $\leq 2^{-55}$. Summing up, Taylor series expansion error is much lower than the double precision format accuracy.

The multiplier inputs are roughly 54-bit wide, therefore the product width is 108-bit wide. Such a bit-width is far beyond the required precision, therefore the LSBs of the product are usually disregarded. As a result, in the proposed architecture, some of the LSBs logic is not implemented at all. Unfortunately, calculation error is much greater for the given architecture. To decrease this error, some additional guard bits are provided. i.e. calculations are carried out on 62-bits. Similarly LUT memory bit-width is extended by additional guard bits, as a single calculation error generated by LUT memory is within required double precision format, nevertheless aggregate whole system error can be outside requirements.

3 Implementation Results

The *exp* function was implemented on SGI Reconfigurable Application-Specific Computing (RASC) platform [4]. The presented in Tab. 1 and Tab. 2 implementation results contain *exp* module logic consumption together with RASC core services, essential to provide compatibility with Altix 4700. The RC100 Blade is connected using the low latency NUMALink interconnect to the SGI Altix 4700 Host System, for a rated peak bandwidth of 6.4GB per second.

The RASC RC100 Blade consist of two Virtex-4 LX 200 FPGAs, with 40 MB of SRAM logically organized as two 16MB blocks and an 8MB block. The SRAM are 36-bit QDR devices, thus transferring 128-bit data every clock cycle.

128-bit data vectors are read from one SRAM bank, spread into two substreams consisting of 64-bit each. Every clock cycle (due to pipelining) data is processed by two exponential modules and results are concatenated to 128-bit vector which is finally written to the second SRAM bank. Afterwards the result is transferred through the NUMAlink to the rest of the system.

Table 1. Implementation results

Implementation results	# 4-input LUT	# flip-flops	# 18-Kb BRAMs
Single exp() module	13,614 (7%)	19,704 (11%)	29 (8%)
Twin exp() module	17,897 (10%)	25,461 (14%)	35 (10%)

Table 2. The RASC system parameters

Max. frequency	200 Mhz
Max. error	1 ulp
Root mean square error	0,6186052
Pipeline latency	30 clk

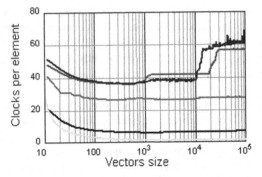

1) *   X87 code for all processors
2) **   Pentium III processor
3) ***   Pentium 4 processor
4) ****   Itanium / Itanium 2 processors
5) ○○○○○ RASC (2 exp() per FPGA)

Fig. 2. Exp calculation on different platforms

Table 3. Average calculation time [ns] per an exp calculation

	Pentium 4	Itanium / Itanium 2	RASC
Exp()	13.65	3.08	2.5

To compare the calculation speed-up achieved by the RASC, average double precision calculation time per single *exp* function [5] is given in Tab. 3 for Pentium 4 and Itanium processors. It is assumed that processors (Table 3) work at 2 GHz while single FPGA was clocked at 200 MHz. The RASC platform provides two FPGA chips (Xilinx Virtex 4 LX200), that allows to double the calculation rate by employing the second FPGA (this is not taken into account in Fig. 2 and Tab. 3).

The calculation speed-up achieved by the RASC is not significant, nevertheless it should be noted that the throughput can be doubled by employing two FPGAs. Secondly, the calculation throughput is limited by external memory transfers and only 10% of FPGA resources are occupied. Thus additional arithmetic functions can be incorporated in the same FPGA. Besides, by improving external memory interface, the number of parallel *exp* modules can be increased.

It should be noted from Fig. 2 that for general-purpose processors, the calculation time decreases with increasing vector size only up to a curtain limit. Then the calculation time rapidly increases. Probably the reason of this increase is that input or output data cannot be incorporated into internal processor cache memory, and external memory transfers significantly influence the whole system throughput. Summing up, both FPGA and general-purpose processors throughput degradation is caused by external memory access. Nevertheless, this degradation is not taken into account for the general-purpose processors in Tab.3.

4 Summary

This paper describes a novel architecture of double precision exponential function implemented in FPGAs and SGI RASC platform. The presented *exp* architecture introduces several novel hardware solutions never used for *exp* function: a) 3 independent LUTs and Taylor series expansion for *exp* function, b) sign-migration to integer part x_I, fractional part x_F is always positive, c) optimized reduce-width multipliers.

There are two improvements considerations worth introducing. Source code of quantum – chemistry software application can be substantially investigated in the future in order to eliminate a precision overhead. There is still a lot of silicon space on the FPGA (approximately 80%) that can easily fit addition logic. Investigations are being conducted to expand *exp()* function with additional logic of the hot spots found in quantum chemistry application source code.

References

[1] Doss, C.C., Riley Jr., R.L.: FPGA-Based Implementation of a Robust IEEE-754 Exponential Unit. In: 12th Annual IEEE Symposium on Field-Programmable Custom Computing Machines (FCCM 2004), pp. 229–238 (2004)

[2] Bui, H.T., Tahar, S.: Design and Synthesis of an IEEE-754 Exponential Function. In: 1999 IEEE Canadian Conference on Electrical and Computer Engineering Shaw Conference Center, Edmonton, Alberta, Canada, May 9-12, 1999 vol. 1, pp. 450–455 (1999)

[3] Detrey, J., de Dinechin, F.: A parameterized foating-point exponential function for FPGAs. In: IEEE International Conference on Field-Programmable Technology (FPT 2005), Singapore, pp.27–34, December 2005 (2005)

[4] Silicon Graphics, Inc. Reconfigurable Application-Specific Computing User's Guide, Ver. 004, March 2006, SGI

[5] The University of Texas in Austin, TACC Intel Math Kernel Library (November 22, 2007), http://www.tacc.utexas.edu/services/userguides/mkl/functions/exp.html

A Framework for the Automatic Generation of Instruction-Set Extensions for Reconfigurable Architectures

Carlo Galuzzi and Koen Bertels*

Delft University of Technology, The Netherlands
{C.Galuzzi,K.L.M.Bertels}@ewi.tudelft.nl

Abstract. In this paper we present a framework for the automatic identification and selection of convex MIMO instruction-set extensions for reconfigurable architecture. The framework partitions the analysis of the problem into phases of different computational complexity and it generates instruction-set extensions of different granularity. The framework is retargetable and additional clustering policies can be added with just small modification on the design.

1 Introduction

In the past decade we have witnessed a general shifting from the use of general-purpose computing systems to systems able to perform only a limited number of tasks but more efficiently. Although general-purpose systems can execute a broad range of applications making them extremely flexible, the power consumption is relatively high. A good trade-off between flexibility and power consumption is represented by reconfigurable systems. A simple reconfigurable system can be realized, for instance, by coupling a General Purpose Processor (GPP) and a reconfigurable hardware like an FPGA. When an application is executed on a general system, a certain number of instructions are executed in hardware, namely the ones that belongs to the Instruction-Set, whereas the rest of the instructions is executed in software. If the same application is executed on a reconfigurable system, we can use the reconfigurable hardware to execute additional more complex instructions, application-dependent, so that to extend the Instruction-Set and speed up the execution of the application on the system. The identification of those instructions suitable for hardware implementation represents the so called *Instruction-Set Extension (ISE) problem* [2].

Taking into account the data-flow or control-flow graph of an application, it is easy to understand that the parts of the application suitable for hardware implementations correspond to subgraphs of the graph representing the application. The subgraph enumeration problem is a well known problem which is computationally complex and requires exponential time to provide an exhaustive enumeration of all the subgraphs. Since not all subgraphs are suitable for a hardware

---

* This work was supported by the European Union in the context of the MORPHEUS project Num. 027342.

R. Woods et al. (Eds.): ARC 2008, LNCS 4943, pp. 280–286, 2008.

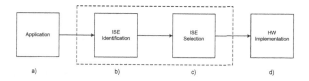

Fig. 1. The main parts of the ISE creation process: a) application to analyze, b) extension identification c) extension selection and d) hardware implementation of the selected new instructions

implementation[1], the problem becomes the design of efficient algorithms for the identification of only instructions suitable for a hardware implementation.

Figure 1 depicts a general flow for ISE identification: once the application is selected (Figure 1a), the application is analyzed to discover a certain number of candidate instructions for hardware implementation (Figure 1b), the identified instructions pass through a selection process which identify the most suitable ones to hardwire usually based on hardware limitations (Figure 1c) and finally the selected instructions are implemented in hardware (Figure 1d).

In this context, we present *a framework for the automatic identification and selection of Multiple Input Multiple Output Instruction-Set extensions*. The proposed design targets the Molen organization [1] which allows for a virtually unlimited number of new instructions without limiting the number of input/output values of the new instruction to be executed on the reconfigurable hardware. More specifically the main contributions of this paper are the below listed:

- a framework for the automatic identification and selection of Instruction-Set extensions which partitions the analysis into phases of different granularity and computational complexity;
- an analysis of the main issues to export the presented framework, designed for the Molen architecture, to general reconfigurable architectures.

The reminder of the paper is the following: in Section 2, a description of the framework in detail together with a computational complexity analysis and an analysis of the issues to improve the presented framework and extend it to a general reconfigurable architectures are presented. Finally, in Section 3, we present concluding remarks and an outline of future work.

2   Description of the Framework

In Figure 2, we present an overview of the framework proposed in this paper. For more technical details about definitions and concepts addressed in the following,

---

[1] Depending on the target architecture, the new instructions can have limitations on the total number of inputs and/or outputs, or on the area they occupy when implemented on the reconfigurable hardware, etc.

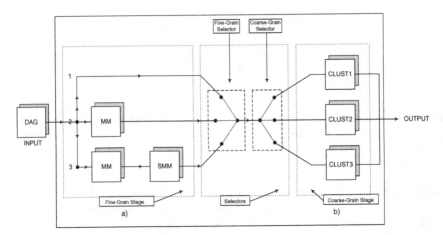

Fig. 2. The Framework for the Automatic Generation of Instruction-Set extensions

the interested reader can refer to [5,6,4,7]. The main idea behind the design of such a framework is the generation of convex MIMO instruction-set extensions with multiple steps of different granularity and complexity. More specifically the design can be split in two parts: the first part concerns a fine-grain clustering (Figure 2a) and the second one concerns a coarse-grain clustering (Figure 2b). The framework has three main stages: the fine-grain stage, the selector stage and the coarse-grain stage described in the following. We assume the Molen architecture as the target reconfigurable architecture. Some issues concerning how to export the framework to general reconfigurable architecture and possible extensions and improvements for the framework are addressed later in the paper.

One of the strengths of such a framework is the convexity guarantee of the clusters generated. Traditional methods for convex instruction identification usually perform a check for the convexity of the cluster at each inclusion of a node in the cluster. This affects the overall complexity of the solution which increases. With our clusterings, the selected nodes do not have to be tested for convexity since the convexity of the cluster is theoretically guaranteed by construction.

STEP 1: Fine-Grain Stage. The input of the framework is given by the DAG $G = (V, E)$ that represents the application to be analyzed where the nodes represent primitive operations and the edges represent the data dependencies. The focus of the analysis is on which parts of the code are suitable for a software implementation and which ones are suitable for a hardware implementation to increase the overall performance of execution of the application onto the reconfigurable architecture. We have three different paths that the input can follow before arriving to the selector stage:

- PATH 1: The nodes of G are convoyed directly to the selector step;
- PATH 2: The nodes of G are partitioned in MAXMISOs [3];
- PATH 3: The nodes of G are firstly partitioned in MAXMISOs and subsequently every MAXMISO is partitioned in SMMs [4].

In PATH 3, from the definition of SMM [4], we know that the SMM partitioning depends on the choice of the bereaved node[2] and this node can be selected in n different ways, where n is the order of G. In all the cases the output is a minimal cover of convex non-overlapping MISO elements[3]. We remind that a *minimal cover* is a cover for which removal of one member destroys the covering property of the graph. *We note that in all cases convexity is guaranteed theoretically by construction* while in general, other approaches perform an additional analysis on the clusters to test the convexity. We remark that, in PATH 3, the algorithm for SMM generation can also be used iteratively to generate MISO instructions of relatively smaller size when tight constraints on the inputs are imposed.

STEP 2: Coarse-Grain Stage. Based on the output of the fine-grain stage (more specifically on the input selected by the fine-grain selector) there are three possible ways to generate convex MIMO instructions depending on the shape of the graph in terms of depth and width of the graph[4].

CASE 1: $w > d$. (CLUST 1, Figure 2) Let us consider a partitioning of the nodes of G in levels. When two nodes n_1 and n_2 with latency in hardware l_1 an l_2 at the same level are selected for hardware execution, if they are implemented as separate instructions we have a performance loss, which can be roughly estimated as $l_1 + l_2 - \max(l_1, l_2)$. An optimal selection of which nodes to select at the same level to implement in parallel in hardware can then provide a considerable speed up estimated as $\sum_i l_i - \max_i(l_i)$. An algorithm for the optimal selection of convex MIMO ISE based on an ILP formulation, more suitable for graphs wider than deeper, has been proposed in [5]. Although the algorithm has been designed for an optimal selection through the levels of MAXMISOs at the same level, it is possible to generalize the result to every minimal cover with non-overlapping elements.

CASE 2: $w < d$. (CLUST 2, Figure 2) When a graph is deeper than wider, a heuristic clustering algorithm of linear complexity in the number of processed elements is proposed in [6]. Similarly to the previous case, the result is applicable to every minimal cover with non-overlapping elements. This algorithm starts from a node at a certain level and moving vertically through the levels it identifies nodes to include in the cluster. Clustering is performed up to when there is available area left on the reconfigurable hardware.

CASE 3: $w \propto d$. (CLUST 3, Figure 2) When clustering is performed on graph with comparable width and depth, an extended version of the algorithms proposed in the previous cases is presented in [7]. This paper present a clustering method of linear complexity based on a spiral search through the levels of a

---

[2] The choice of the node can be random or directed by specific properties defined by the user.

[3] We note that a single node is trivially a convex subgraph and a MISO.

[4] The depth, d, of a graph is defined as the maximum number of the levels of its node, while the width, w, of a graph is defined as the maximum number of nodes belonging to the same level through the levels.

graph. Contrary to the previous two algorithms which select nodes favoring a specific direction (horizontal CASE 1 and vertical CASE 2), this algorithm clusters nodes following a spiral search centered in the initial node selected and expanding the search through the levels in both directions: vertical and horizontal. Also in this case clustering is performed up to when there is available area left on the reconfigurable hardware. Similarly to the previous cases, the result is extendible to every minimal cover with non-overlapping elements.

These algorithms perform instruction generation and selection at the same time based on a certain number of parameters: hardware and software latency of the generated instructions, total area occupied by the generated instructions when implemented in hardware and total area available on the FPGA. Additionally, while the first clustering produces an optimal solution, the other clusterings are heuristics. We remark that although the algorithms are more suitable in specific cases than others, there is no limitation in the use of any of them for any graph.

Fine- and Coarse-Grain Selector Stage. In Figure 2 two selectors are depicted: a fine-grain and a coarse-grain selector. The former, a 3-1 selector, forwards the output of one of the PATH 1-3 to the latter, a 1-3 selector, which directs the data to one of the coarse-grain clustering algorithms. We have 3×3 possible combinations, which means that we can have up to 9 possible different instruction-set extensions of different granularity. Additionally the framework can be extended with additional algorithms for clustering in both stages, the fine-grain and the coarse-grain stage, with small adjustments on only the selectors to include more inputs or outputs for the additional clustering algorithms.

The Complexity of the Framework. As described before, the framework produces an ISE depending on the input and output of the selectors. All the clustering algorithms presented in the framework but one have linear complexity in the number of processed elements. Only the clustering algorithm CLUST 1 has exponential complexity but it provides an optimal solution. This means that when in the coarse-grain stage it is selected the first algorithm for the generation of convex MIMO instruction set extensions, the overall complexity of the process is exponential. In the remaining cases the overall complexity is linear in the number of processed elements.

Additionally, the SMM clustering, CLUST 2 and 3 generate clustering based on the initial selection of a node, which can be random or directed by specific properties defined by the user. This means that keeping variable the selection of the node, for each choice of the node it is possible to generate a different instruction-set extension with the same computational complexity.

Extensions and improvements for the Framework. The framework presented in this paper has a flexible design: additional clustering algorithm can be integrated into the design with modifications of only the selectors in principle. As mentioned before, our target architecture is the Molen architecture. When the present design is exported on different architectures, additional constraints on number of I/O have to be usually introduced during the clustering in the fine- and coarse-grain clustering step.

Hardware reuse can be considered to further speed up the overall execution time of the application onto the reconfigurable architecture, implementing in hardware only the unique instructions and saving area for additional ones. This can be done with an isomorphism check strategically positioned into the design. On one side, an isomorphism check for hardware reuse can save area and increase the speed up using the saved area for additional new complex operations. On the other side, no polynomial solution is known for the graph isomorphism problem. This means that the inclusion into the design of an isomorphism check will increase the overall complexity of the solution. Efficient algorithms for graph isomorphism are available in literature, which represents a good trade-off between their complexity and the quality of their solution [8].

Additionally, CLUST 2 and CLUST 3 perform selection of the clusters based on the total available area left. An optimal selection of which are the instructions suitable for hardware implementation based on latency and area can be obtained formulating the selection as an ILP problem and using efficient solver to find the solution. This can be solved as in [5] without the requirements that the selected clusters belong to specific levels. This will provide a better selection of the instruction but it will increase the overall complexity of the generation process as well. This means that all the clusters will be first generated, giving a minimal cover of the graph and then the ones belonging to the optimal solution will be implemented in hardware based on the total available area on the reconfigurable component.

3   Conclusions

In this paper we presented a framework for the automatic identification and selection of convex MIMO instruction-set extensions for reconfigurable architecture. The framework partitions the analysis of the problem into phases of different computational complexity and granularity. The framework is retargetable and additional clustering policies can be added with just small modification on the design. In our future work we intend to verify with experimental results the benefit of the insertion of such a framework into the design for automatic instruction set extension. Preliminary results presented in [5] and [6] have shown the benefit of the insertion of part of the algorithms presented in this paper.

References

1. Vassiliadis: The molen polymorphic processor. IEEE Trans. on Comp. 53(11) (2004)
2. Galuzzi: The Instruction-Set Extension Problem: A Survey. In: ARC 2008 (2008)
3. Alippi: A dag-based design approach for reconfigurable vliw processors. In: DATE 1999 (1999)
4. Galuzzi: A linear complexity algorithm for the generation of multiple input single output instructions of variable size. In: SAMOS VII

5. Galuzzi: Automatic selection of application-specific instruction-set extensions. In: CODES+ISSS 2006 (2006)
6. Galuzzi: A linear complexity algorithm for the automatic generation of convex multiple input multiple output instructions. In: Inter. J. of Elec. (2008) (to appear)
7. Galuzzi: The spiral search: A linear complexity algorithm for the generation of convex multiple input multiple output instruction-set extensions. In: ICFPT 2007 (2007)
8. Bonzini: A retargetable framework for automated discovery of custom instructions. In: ASAP 2007 (2007)

PARO: Synthesis of Hardware Accelerators for Multi-dimensional Dataflow-Intensive Applications

Frank Hannig, Holger Ruckdeschel, Hritam Dutta, and Jürgen Teich

Hardware/Software Co-Design, Department of Computer Science
University of Erlangen-Nuremberg, Germany

Abstract. In this paper, we present the PARO design tool for the automated hardware synthesis of massively parallel embedded architectures for given dataflow dominant applications. Key features of PARO are: (1) The design entry in form of a compact and intuitive functional programming language which allows highly parallel implementations. (2) Advanced partitioning techniques are applied in order to balance the trade-offs in cost and performance along with requisite throughputs. This is obtained by distributing computations onto an array of tightly coupled processor elements. (3) We demonstrate the performance of the FPGA synthesized hardware with several selected algorithms from different benchmarks.

1 Introduction and Related Work

The rising complexity of embedded digital applications and the growing importance of time-to-market require powerful modeling methods and tools to automate the design and implementation process. Whereas software compilers have reached a mature level, there still exist only few and restricted tools for the synthesis of hardware implementations from high-level algorithm descriptions. Commercial examples of such systems are Catapult-C from Mentor Graphics [9], Forte Cynthesizer [4], or PICO Express by Synfora [11]. Apart from commercial systems, there exist several C-based synthesis approaches for reconfigurable systems in academia. For instance, the SPARK [6] synthesis methodology which is particularly targeted to control-intensive signal processing applications. However, SPARK can handle only one dimensional arrays. The aforementioned design tools start from a subset of C, C++, or SystemC code. However, starting with sequential languages has the disadvantage that their semantics force a lot of restrictions on the execution order of the program. Most of the parallelism contained in the original mathematical model of the algorithm is lost during the transformation to sequential code. One option is to directly start from a functional language as for instance Haskell [13]. However, also Haskell has only restricted abilities to handle true multi-dimensional arrays (i.e., arrays in which every dimension is treated as equivalent). Other approaches try to avoid the restrictions of sequential languages by using different programming and execution models. For instance, the MMAlpha system [5] is based on loop parallelization in the polytope model similar to our approach. In previous work, we used our methodology only for handcrafted mapping of certain algorithms [3] or presented the generation of dedicated FPGA hardware accelerators for one parameterizable digital signal processing application [10]. Whereas, in this paper we present

R. Woods et al. (Eds.): ARC 2008, LNCS 4943, pp. 287–293, 2008.

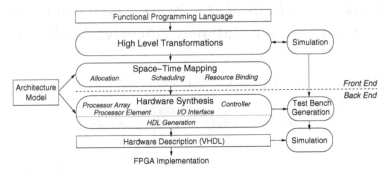

Fig. 1. PARO design flow trajectory for the generation of hardware accelerators

for the first time the PARO design tool for the automated generation of highly parallel hardware accelerators for a broad variety of multi-dimensional dataflow dominant applications selected from different benchmarks.

2   Description of the Front End

An overview of our tool's design flow is depicted in Fig. 1. As design entry we developed a functional programming language. The class of algorithms that can be expressed by a PARO program is based on the mathematical model of *dynamic piecewise linear/regular algorithms (DPLA)* [7]. The language consists of a set of recurrence equations defined for a multi-dimensional iteration space as it occurs in nested loop programs. When modeling signal processing algorithms, a designer naturally considers mathematical equations. Hence, the programming is very intuitive. To allow irregularities in a program, an equation may have iteration and run-time dependent conditionals. Furthermore, big operators (also often called reductions) which implement mathematical operators such as $\sum$ or $\prod$ can be used. In contrast to the common mathematical notation, the iteration space is not required to be 1-dimensional, as the following image processing code fragment of a 2-D Gaussian window filter demonstrates

```
w[0,0] = 1; w[0,1] = 2; w[0,2] = 1;
w[1,0] = 2; w[1,1] = 4; w[1,2] = 2;
w[2,0] = 1; w[2,1] = 2; w[2,2] = 1;
h[x,y] = SUM[i>=0 and i<=2 and j>=0 and j<=2](pic_in[x+i,y+j] * w[i,j]);
pic_out[x,y] = h[x,y] >> 4;   // divided by 16
```

Based on a given algorithm, various source-to-source compiler transformations and optimizations can be applied within the design system. Among others, these transformations include: Constant and variable propagations, common sub-expression elimination, loop perfectization, dead-code elimination, affine transformations of the iteration space, strength reduction of operators (usage of shift and add instead of multiply or divide), and loop unrolling. Algorithms with non-uniform data dependencies are usually not suitable for mapping onto regular processor arrays as they result in expensive global communication or memory. For that reason, a well known transformation called *localization* exists which replaces affine dependencies by regular dependencies.

For such a regular algorithm, the data dependencies can be visualized as reduced dependence graph (RDG), which contains one node for each variable. If there are several equations defining the same variable due to iteration dependent conditionals, there is

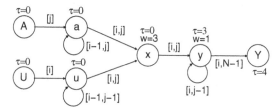

Fig. 2. Reduced dependence graph with annotated schedule for an example FIR filter algorithm

only one node for the corresponding variable in the graph. So, the terms variable and node may be used synonymously in the following. The data dependencies are annotated to the edges. Figure 2 shows the RDG after localization of data dependencies of an FIR filter initially described by the equation $Y(i) = \sum_{j=0}^{N-1} A(j) \cdot U(i-j)$ with $0 \leq i < T, N$ denoting the number of filter taps, $A(j)$ the coefficients, $U(i)$ the filter input, and $Y(i)$ the filter result.

Partitioning is a well known transformation which covers the index space of computation using congruent hyperplanes, hyperquaders, or parallelepipeds called *tiles*. Well known partitioning techniques are multiprojection, LSGP (local sequential global parallel, often also referred as clustering or blocking) and LPGS (local parallel global sequential, also referred as tiling). Partitioning is employed in order to match an algorithm to given architectural constraints in functional resources, memory and I/O bandwidth. Hierarchical partitioning methods apply multiple hierarchies of tiling [2].

Allocation and Scheduling. An important step in our design flow is the *space-time mapping* which assigns each iteration point $I \in \mathcal{I}$ a processor index $p \in \mathcal{P}$ (allocation) and a time index $t \in \mathcal{T}$ (scheduling) as given by the following affine transformation:

$$\begin{pmatrix} p \\ t \end{pmatrix} = \begin{pmatrix} Q \\ \lambda \end{pmatrix} \cdot I + \begin{pmatrix} q \\ \gamma \end{pmatrix} \tag{1}$$

with $I \in \mathcal{I}, Q \in \mathbb{Z}^{s \times n}, \lambda \in \mathbb{Z}^{1 \times n}, q \in \mathbb{Z}^s$, and $\gamma \in \mathbb{Z}$. $\mathcal{T} \subset \mathbb{Z}$ is called *time space*, that is the set of all time steps where an execution takes place. $\mathcal{P} \subset \mathbb{Z}^s$ is called *processor space*. Q is called *allocation matrix* and determines the processor that executes an iteration point I. λ is called *schedule vector* and provides the start time of each iteration point I.

Having hardware implementation in mind, it is not enough to assign a start time to each iteration point. In lieu thereof, one must determine the start time of each operation in the loop body. Therefore, we extend the time mapping in order to include the offset for the computation of each left hand side variable in the loop body and each node in the RDG, respectively. For node v_i, let this offset be $\tau(v_i)$. The overall start time of node v_i at iteration point I is: $t(v_i(I)) = \lambda \cdot I + \gamma + \tau(v_i)$.

The purpose of *scheduling* is to determine the optimal schedule vector λ (global scheduling), and the value of $\tau(v_i)$ for each node v_i (local scheduling). The purpose of *binding* is to assign each node a functional unit (*resource*) which can execute the node functionality. After binding is done, each node is associated an execution time which is denoted by $w(v_i)$. The problem of resource constrained scheduling and binding is solved by mixed integer linear programming (MILP) similar as in [12,7].

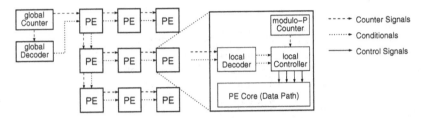

Fig. 3. Overview of control architecture. The data path interconnect is not shown.

3   Hardware Synthesis

This section describes the synthesis of hardware accelerators in form of a processor array. The synthesis both of the array generates a completely platform and language independent register transfer level (RTL) description of the hardware as intermediate representation. This representation is subsequently retargeted to HDL code (e.g., VHDL). The synthesis of a regular processor array consists of several steps: synthesis of processor elements, the array interconnection structure, and the control path.

Synthesis of Processor Elements. A processor element (PE) consists of the processor core and a local controller. The processor core implements the data path where the actual computations are performed. The synthesis of the processor requires a scheduled reduced dependence graph. During the binding phase, each operation in the loop body was assigned a functional unit (resource) that executes the operation. These functional units are instantiated in the processor core. In case of reuse of functional units, input multiplexers may be required in order to select the correct operands in every time step. The interconnection between the functional units can be directly derived from the reduced dependence graph.

Synthesis of Interconnection Structure. In order to synthesize the processor interconnection structure, one must analyze the data dependencies of the program and use the scheduling and placement information. Therefore, given the following equation of an input specification, $x_i[I] = \mathcal{F}_i(\ldots, x_j[I+d_{ji}], \ldots)$ if $\mathcal{C}_i^l(I)$ and a space-time mapping as in Eq. (1). The synthesis of processor interconnection for the data dependency $x_j[I+d_{ji}] \longrightarrow x_i[I]$ is done by determining the *processor displacement* as $d_{ji}^p = Q \cdot (I+d_{ji}) - Q \cdot I = Q \cdot d_{ji}$. For each pair of processors p_t and $p_s = p_t + d_{ji}^p$ with $p_s \in \mathcal{P} \wedge p_t \in \mathcal{P}$, a corresponding connection is drawn from the source processor p_s to the target processor p_t. The *time displacement* denotes the number of time steps that the value of $x_j[I+d_{ji}]$ must be stored before it is used to compute $x_i[I]$. In processor arrays, the time displacement is equal to the number of delay registers on the respective processor interconnection. The time displacement is given by $d_{ji}^t = \lambda \cdot (I+d_{ji}) + \tau(x_j) + w(x_j) - \lambda \cdot I - \tau(x_i) = \lambda \cdot d_{ji} + \tau(x_j) + w(x_j) - \tau(x_i)$. Here, $\tau(x_j)$ is the offset of the calculation of x_j, and $w(x_j)$ is the execution time of the associated operation. If the number of delay registers is large or the delay registers are only filled sparsely, FIFOs, or embedded memories are selected instead.

Synthesis of Control Structure. In the context of regular processor arrays, synthesis of efficient control structures is of utmost importance for producing control signals to

Table 1. Experimental results

Algorithm	No. of PEs	No. of LUTs	No. of FFs	No. of MULTs	No. of BRAMs	max. Clock (MHz)	Exec. Time (cycles)	avg. Output Interval (cycles)
Edge Detection								
– 100×100 image, partitioned	1×4	2962	1455	0	4	143	$7.7 \cdot 10^3$	3
– 1000×1000 image, partitioned	1×4	2997	1913	0	44	120	$7.5 \cdot 10^5$	3
Gaussian Filtering								
– 100×100 image, 3x3 mask	3×3	655	1439	9	2	171	$1.0 \cdot 10^4$	1
– 1000×1000 image, 3x3 mask	3×3	683	1463	9	2	171	$1.0 \cdot 10^6$	1
– 2000×2000 image, 3x3 mask	3×3	696	1472	9	4	169	$4.0 \cdot 10^6$	1
– 1000×1000 image, 5x5 mask	5×5	1538	3909	25	4	171	$1.0 \cdot 10^6$	1
FIR Filter								
– 64 Taps, partitioned	1×4	773	834	4	0	125	71	16
– 64 Taps, partitioned	1×8	1915	1014	8	0	132	71	8
– 64 Taps, projected	1×64	5782	9089	64	0	167	68	1
Matrix Multiplication								
– 6x6 matrix size, sequential	1	204	157	1	0	131	250	6
– 6x6 matrix size, partitioned	2×2	829	795	4	0	115	72	1.5
– 6x6 matrix size, projected	6×6	1888	4067	36	0	166	20	0.28
Discrete Cosine Transformation	2	1754	1152	8	1	130	94	0.65
Elliptical Wave Digital Filter	1	1169	624	1	0	94	$2.5 \cdot 10^5$	1
Partial Differential Equation Solver	1	619	502	1	0	128	$1.2 \cdot 10^5$	(1 result)
MPEG2 Quantisizer	1	637	1190	1	0	141	222	2.95
JPEG Loop 1	1	82	79	0	0	224	63	1
JPEG Loop 2	1	570	1139	0	0	158	126	1

orchestrate the correct computation of the algorithm. The size of the control path should be as independent of the problem size and the processor array size as possible in order to ensure the high scalability of regular arrays. The key characteristic of our control methodology as depicted in Fig. 3 is the use of combined global and local control facilities. All control signals that are common for all processor elements are generated by global control units and propagated through the array, whereas local control is only necessary for signals that differ among the processor types. This strategy reduces significantly the required area and improves the clock frequency [1]. The central component of the control architecture is a global counter which generates the non-constant parts of the iteration vector. The counter signals are taken to compute the iteration dependent conditionals. Here, one can identify conditionals which are independent of the current processor index and can thus be evaluated by a global decoder unit. Only the processor dependent conditionals are subject to evaluation by per-processor local decoders. The globally evaluated conditionals are propagated as Boolean signals along with the counter signals with the appropriate delay through the processor array. Furthermore, several operations scheduled at each iteration (with offset $\tau(v_i)$), so additional logic is required to assure the correct execution behavior. During every iteration of an iterative schedule the same sequence of control signals must be generated. Thus, the control functionality can be implemented by a modulo counter whose output is connected to a decoder logic along with globally and locally evaluated iteration dependent conditionals. This decoder generates the control signals for the functional units and multiplexers.

4   Case Studies

We have synthesized several algorithms from various application domains, some of which are taken from the well-known MediaBench suite [8]. We profiled the JPEG and MPEG2 algorithms and identified some of the most computational intensive loop kernels. The results, and the results from some more algorithms, are shown in Table 1. All algorithms were implemented using 16-bit integer or fixed point arithmetics, respectively, and synthesized using the *Xilinx ISE 6.3i* toolchain targeting a *Virtex-II 8000* FPGA.

For each example, the table shows the dimension of the processor array, the cost in terms of FPGA primitives, the maximum clock frequency, the total execution time for the algorithm in clock cycles, and the average number of clock cycles between the availability of two successive output instances (for example samples, pixels). The latter is the inverse of the throughput, that is, a smaller number denotes a higher throughput. An initial latency does not affect the throughput. Note that an output interval less than 1 means that more than one output instances are available per clock cycle. The Gaussian filter was partitioned such that implementation costs remain mostly constant for larger image sizes — of course, the latency raises. For the FIR filter, we used partitioning to trade throughput and cost at constant latency. The projected implementation is fast but very expensive, whereas partitioning allows for a fine-grained design space exploration. Similar are the results for matrix multiplication but partitioning was applied in a way that the total execution time can also be selected according to the user's requirements.

5   Conclusions

In this paper we presented PARO, a novel tool for the continuous design flow for the mapping of computationally intensive nested loop programs onto parallel processor arrays that are implemented in FPGAs. Starting point of our approach is a functional programming language which preserves the inherent parallelism of a given application. Partitioning is used as a core transformation in order to match a given algorithm to hardware constraints and user requirements. For the first time, hierarchical partitioning is supported in the whole design flow, that is, during high-level transformations, allocation, scheduling, hardware synthesis, and HDL generation phases.

References

1. Dutta, H., Hannig, F., Ruckdeschel, H., Teich, J.: Efficient Control Generation for Mapping Nested Loop Programs onto Processor Arrays. Journal of Systems Architecture 53(5–6), 300–309 (2007)
2. Dutta, H., Hannig, F., Teich, J.: Hierarchical Partitioning for Piecewise Linear Algorithms. In: Proceedings of the 5th International Conference on Parallel Computing in Electrical Engineering (PARELEC), Bialystok, Poland, September 2006, pp. 153–160 (2006)
3. Dutta, H., Hannig, F., Teich, J., Heigl, B., Hornegger, H.: A Design Methodology for Hardware Acceleration of Adaptive Filter Algorithms in Image Processing. In: Proceedings of IEEE 17th International Conference on Application-specific Systems, Architectures, and Processors (ASAP), Steamboat Springs, CO, USA, pp. 331–337 (September 2006)
4. Forte Design Systems, http://www.forteds.com

5. Guillou, A., Quinton, P., Risset, T.: Hardware Synthesis for Multi-Dimensional Time. In: Proceedings of IEEE 14th International Conference on Application-specific Systems, Architectures, and Processors (ASAP), pp. 40–50, The Hague, The Netherlands (June 2003)

6. Gupta, S., Dutt, N., Gupta, R., Nicolau, A.: SPARK: A High-Level Synthesis Framework for Applying Parallelizing Compiler Transformations. In: Proceedings of the 16th International Conference on VLSI Design, pp. 461–466 (January 2003)

7. Hannig, F., Teich, J.: Resource Constrained and Speculative Scheduling of an Algorithm Class with Run-Time Dependent Conditionals. In: Proceedings of the 15th IEEE International Conference on Application-specific Systems, Architectures, and Processors (ASAP), Galveston, TX, USA, pp. 17–27 (September 2004)

8. Lee, C., Potkonjak, M., Mangione-Smith, W.H.: MediaBench: A Tool for Evaluating and Synthesizing Multimedia and Communicatons Systems. In: International Symposium on Microarchitecture, pp. 330–335 (1997)

9. Mentor Graphics Corp, http://www.mentor.com

10. Ruckdeschel, H., Dutta, H., Hannig, F., Teich, J.: Automatic FIR Filter Generation for FPGAs. In: Hämäläinen, T.D., Pimentel, A.D., Takala, J., Vassiliadis, S. (eds.) SAMOS 2005. LNCS, vol. 3553, pp. 51–61. Springer, Heidelberg (2005)

11. Synfora, Inc., http://www.synfora.com

12. Teich, J., Thiele, L., Zhang, L.: Scheduling of Partitioned Regular Algorithms on Processor Arrays with Constrained Resources. J. of VLSI Signal Processing 17(1), 5–20 (1997)

13. Thompson, S.: Haskell: The Craft of Functional Programming. Addison Wesley, Reading (1999)

Stream Transfer Balancing Scheme Utilizing Multi-path Routing in Networks on Chip

Piotr Dziurzanski and Tomasz Maka

Szczecin University of Technology,
Zolnierska 49, 71-210 Szczecin, Poland
{pdziurzanski,tmaka}@wi.ps.pl

Abstract. A novel technique for balancing streams of data transferred in every cycle in the wormhole routing dedicated for Networks on Chip architectures is presented in this work. The influence of the traditional and the proposed techniques over the total network flow is computed for popular multimedia stream-based algorithms. The experimental results confirming the proposed approach are provided.

Keywords: Networks on Chip, stream-based processing, wormhole routing, tapeworm routing, Ford-Fulkerson method.

1 Introduction

Since today single-processor computers are considered insufficiently powerful to deal with demanding multimedia applications, the Multi Processor Systems on Chips (MPSoCs) are often viewed as their natural successors in this domain [2]. However, contemporary MPSoCs, whose connections are either bus-based or point to point, do not scale well enough to maintain the foreseen growth of the number of intellectual property (IP) cores in a single chip [1]. It is one of the reasons of the mounting popularity of the Network-on-Chip-based (NoC-based) connections in the contemporary designs. The popularity of this on-chip commu-nication scheme is caused with the lower contention level in a chip with a large number of cores, where traditional on-chip buses are considered as the main obstacle in the MPSoC efficiency. The performance of both dedicated wiring and buses has been reported as inferior to NoCs due to their worse reusabil-ity, scalability, higher latency and noise [2]. The NoC architectures offer high bandwidth and good concurrent communication capability, but an effective flow control mechanism has to be applied to avoid resource starvation and conges-tion [1]. As an MPSoC includes a set of IP cores, it usually exploits the tiled architecture where the tiles comprise of (i) the core realizing the functionality of the algorithm given with the high-level description and (ii) the router which is typically connected to four neighboring tiles.

As a large number of popular multimedia applications make usage of the streaming approach, e.g. MPEG, WiMax, DVB, etc., it may be important to consider the data-flow management in a NoC dedicated to streaming data trans-fer. In these applications, there are relatively large amount of data transmitted

R. Woods et al. (Eds.): ARC 2008, LNCS 4943, pp. 294–299, 2008.

between predefined computing cores with a fixed time frame. Similarly, the efficiency of these algorithms' implementations raises if a pipeline scheme is applied as the cores may work in parallel on subsequent amount of data. The data streams are usually large, but fixed for relatively long time and the computation expenditures of particular cores are equal for each sample. These properties of data-flow streams, which are important to the efficiency of the proposed technique, are well characterized in [3].

2   NoC Routing Issues

One of the most popular packet switching techniques used in NoC is the wormhole routing [1], where a packet is split into smaller units, flits. The first flit usually contains the destination address, whereas the second one keeps the information about the payload data length.

After obtaining the first flit, a router selects the next-hop router (using a routing algorithm). This path is used for the remaining flits of the package. Then, a package to be transferred between two non-adjacent cores has to cross a number of connections and, consequently, uses these connections in an exclusive manner and does not allow other transfers to use this link simultaneously. As the result, the second transfer is blocked as long as the first is not finished. The described situation is referred to as contention. In stream-based applications the situation is even worse in comparison with other algorithms, as the same transfers appear in every clock cycle and, consequently, it is hampered to compensate the contention at further stages.

In the popular XY routing algorithm, a flit is firstly routed according to the X axis as long as the X coordinate is equal to the X coordinate of the destination core, and then the flit is routed vertically. Although being deadlock-free, this algorithm does not adapt to the temporary dataflow and even two data-flows to be transmitted by one link result in contention. Thus, the mapping of IP cores into tiles in a NoC structure influences the level of contention.

3   Proposed Approach

The first stage of the proposed approach is to construct a flow network for a given stream-based algorithm. The processing blocks of the algorithm are identified and the transfers between them are computed. Then, we have to determine the mapping of the cores into the mesh structure leading to the improved performance of the NoC structure.

The impact of the mapping on the final implementation properties is very significant in case of the traditional wormhole XY routing approach. For the example of MPEG-4 decoder [5], the difference between the required capacity and the best and the worst mappings is about 203.04 per cent.

For example, the XY algorithm applied to the H.264 video decoder [4] for core permutation 0-2-3, 7-8-4, 1-6-5 in the first, second, and the third row, respectively, leads to the transfers presented in Fig. 2c. In this situation, the maximal transfer between adjacent cores is relatively high being equal to 2240 Mbit/s. It means that in every second such amount of data is to be transferred between cores 8 and 7, so that the NoC infrastructure has to offer capacities large enough to cope with this transfer. Assuming the most popular regular NoC mesh architecture, all the links have to have equal capacities, so all of them have to be capable of transferring 2240 Mbit/s. However, the majority of the remaining links are utilized in small percentage of this maximal value. It may be expressed with the standard deviation value, which is equal to about 598.36 Mbit/s. Thus, we assumed that the standard deviation express the transfer balancing level. The smaller the standard deviation, the transfers are closer to each other. Moreover, only 13 links out of 24 are utilized, which results in unbalanced transfers and poor utilization of the available resources.

This is our main motivation to introduce a routing scheme we named *tapeworm routing*. We propose this name due to the similarity with the anatomy of a tapeworm - both its body and a package body are split into segments; segments are comprised of a number of flits, the first two flits of the segment forms a header. In this approach, we modified the standard XY algorithm in the following way.

Having selected an appropriate mapping, it is important to balance transfers between each path in a NoC structure. The algorithm (Fig. 1.) needs on its input a complete list of data transfers in the network flow built at the previous stage. We describe T_i, i.e., the i-th transfer, as a triplet (S_i, D_i, A_i), where S_i and D_i denote the source and the destination nodes, and A_i is the size of the data stream transferred between these nodes. The proposed technique takes advantage of the well-known Ford-Fulkerson method for determining maximal throughput of the network between a set of cores.

The decomposition of the package into segments is performed by a router in the following way. Each router has a routing table that enlists all the routes to a destination core sorted with respect to the length of the route and the equal-length routes are sorted according to the XY rule. Consequently, the first route is obtained with the traditional XY algorithm. In the second route the flit is routed horizontally as long as the X coordinate of the router is lower by 1 than the X coordinate of the destination core. Then, the flit is routed vertically by 1 link and further according to the standard XY algorithm. In the next path, the

```
1. for a given permutation p
2.    Max = ∑_i A_i
3.    Min = 0
4.    while (Max > Min)
5.        create flow network G for the appropriate NoC
6.        for each transfer i
7.            find all paths P_j between S_i and D_i
8.            sort P_j with respect to the paths length
9.            sort the paths in P_j of equal lengths according to XY rule
10.           determine minimal flow c_min utilizing Ford-Fulkerson method
11.               A_i = A_i - c_min
12.               if (A_i > 0)
13.                   Max = Average(Min, Max) - 1
14.               else
15.                   Min = Average(Min, Max) + 1
```

Fig. 1. Pseudo-code of the proposed algorithm for transfer balancing

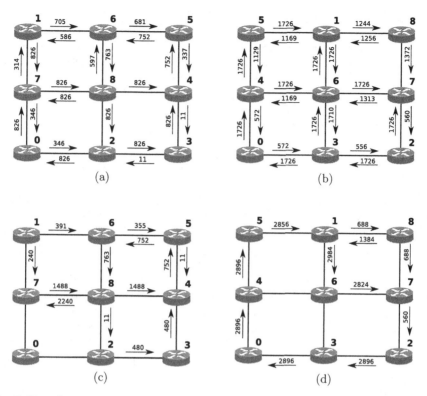

Fig. 2. Transfers comparison for the following decoders and routing algorithms: H.264, Tapeworm (a); MPEG-4, Tapeworm (b); H.264, XY (c); MPEG-4, XY (d)

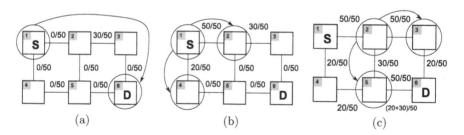

Fig. 3. Successive steps of the tapeworm algorithm

flit is routed according to the X axis as long as the X coordinate of the router is lower by 2 than the X coordinate of the destination core, and so on.

The example of the three successive steps of the tapeworm algorithm is presented in Fig. 3. In this figure, the numbers written above links mean a flow and a remaining available capacity. The data length to be sent between cores S and D is equal 70 bits. At the first stage, 30 bits of the link between routers 2 and 3 have been already allocated. As the available capacity between routers 1 and 2 (i.e., the link selected by the XY rule) is only 50 bits, 50 bits are sent by this link, and the remaining 20 bits are sent by the alternative route to the 4th router. In router 2, the package is further segmented: 20 bits follow the path to the router 3, whereas 30 bits are sent to router 5. Thus, the total data length sent between routers 5 and 6 is equal to 50 bits.

4   Experimental Results

We have implemented the tapeworm algorithm, described earlier in this paper for H.264 and MPEG-4 decoders. Using exhaustive set of permutations, the average throughputs for the whole population have been obtained. We have measured that these values are about 2431.6251 Mbit/s (H.264) and 3903.1804 Mbit/s (MPEG-4) for the traditional XY algorithm, whereas for the tapeworm routing we have obtained about 1303.1422 Mbit/s (H.264) and 2597.4315 Mbit/s (MPEG-4). It means the proposed algorithm gains respectively about 46.41 (H.264) and 33.45 (MPEG-4) per cent of the overall transfers.

The total transfers by this routing technique for the same decoder, as described in Section 3 for the XY algorithm, is shown in Fig. 2a. In this case, the standard deviation is equal to 308.95 Mbit/s and only two links are not utilized. Similarly, we utilized the proposed approach for MPEG-4 decoder and obtained the transfers presented in Fig. 2b. For comparison, the XY algorithm leads to the standard deviation of 1295.73 Mbit/s, whereas the tapeworm approach resulted in 514.25 Mbit/s.

According to our test, performed as an area and critical path estimation for the models synthesized into a cycle-accurate logic network, an implementation of the router needs 102258 NAND gates and 2628 flip flops[1]. It has been shown in [2] that the area and time requirements for NoC-based communication scheme is similar to bus-based realizations and considerably less in comparison with point-to-point (P2P) connections, whereas the performance scaling rate is quite similar to the P2P approach. Moreover, these requirements are the result of trade-off between the target chip area and efficiency; as five loop bodies have been replicated 51 times each as the result of the unrolling operation, and five others - 6 times each. Besides, each of the five router's ports includes a relatively large buffer that can store 30 flits. Thus it is possible to decrease the target area significantly by eliminating some loop optimizations.

5   Conclusion and Future Work

In this paper, we have proposed an approach for balancing streams in multimedia applications realized in a Network on Chip environment. Our routing technique allows a segmentation of packages in comparison with the wormhole XY algorithm. Having applied this technique, we have diminished the average

---

[1] The estimation has been performed with Celoxica Agility software, for Xilinx XC3S1500FG320-4.

transfers by about 33 and 46 per cent for MPEG-4 and H.264 decoders, respectively, taking into account all possible core mapping permutations. The transfer overhead for transferring additional headers caused by an implementation of the wormhole scheme is negligible (less than 10^{-6} per cent of all transferred flits). Our balancing technique decreases the standard deviation by about 60 and 48 per cent respectively for MPEG-4 and H.264 decoders.

The obtained results confirm the advantage of the proposed technique over the XY routing algorithm, which is one of the most widely-used routing schemes in the Network on Chip architectures.

The research work presented in this paper was sponsored by Polish Ministry of Science and Higher Education (years 2007-2010).

References

1. Bjerregaard, T., Mahadevan, S.: A Survey of Research and Practices of Network-on-Chip. ACM Computing Surveys (CSUR) 38 (2006) (Article 1)
2. Lee, H.G., Chang, N., Ogras, U.Y., Marculescu, R.: On-chip communication architecture exploration: A quantitative evaluation of point-to-point, bus, and network-on-chip approaches. ACM Transactions on Design Automation of Electronic Systems (TODAES) archive 12(3) (2007)
3. Smit, G.J.M., et al.: Efficient Architectures for Streaming DSP Applications, Dynamically Reconfigurable Architectures. In: Internationales Begegnungs- und Forschungszentrum fuer Informatik (IBFI), Schloss Dagstuhl, Germany (2006)
4. van der Tol, E.B., Jaspers, E.G.T., Gelderblom, R.H.: Mapping of H.264 decoding on a multiprocessor architecture. Image and Video Communications and Processing 5022, 707–718 (2003)
5. van der Tol, E.B., Jaspers, E.G.T.: Mapping of MPEG-4 Decoding on a Flexible Architecture Platform. vol. 4674, pp. 362–363, Media Processors (2002)

Efficiency of Dynamic Reconfigurable Datapath Extensions – A Case Study

Steffen Köhler, Jan Schirok, Jens Braunes, and Rainer G. Spallek

Institute of Computer Engineering
Technische Universität Dresden
D-01062 Dresden, Germany
stk@ite.inf.tu-dresden.de

Abstract. In this paper, we examine the efficiency of the ARRIVE architecture, a coarse-grain reconfigurable datapath extension to an embedded RISC microprocessor. It is considered platform specific, optimized for the media and communication processing domain. Detailed chip area requirements are obtained through the mapping to an UMC 0.18μm standard cell ASIC process layout. Furthermore, we present hardware utilization and power simulation results of six media/communication benchmark applications based on post-layout process information. As a result, we can recognize increased area efficiency ($\frac{operations}{mm^2 \cdot s}$) and power efficiency ($\frac{operations}{mW \cdot s}$) of the reconfigurable datapath extended RISC microprocessor.

1 Introduction

SIMD datapath extensions commonly known as multimedia extensions have been available for DSP algorithm acceleration in embedded microprocessors for several years. Its main advantage is the low implementation effort required to extend the core datapath. As a drawback, the utilization of the SIMD datapath is comparatively low in most cases. This disadvantage can be overcome by coarse-grain reconfigurable datapath extensions, since they provide a higher degree of flexibility. On the other hand, the flexibility gained from reconfiguration causes additional hardware costs. The configuration memory and the interconnect network consume a significant amount of chip area. Also, in many cases a not negligible number of reconfigurable elements may remain fully or partially unutilized because of application irregularity or resource constraints. Thus, a reconfigurable datapath architecture is only beneficial compared to its hard-wired counterpart, when it gains an increased flexibility at a comparable functional execution density and an acceptable cost vs. performance ratio. Previous work has mainly focused on performance gain through hardware reconfiguration. It is interesting to note that area and power efficiency of reconfigurable datapath extensions have rarely been addressed as an embedded processor design issue [1]. In this paper, we explore the efficiency of an 0.18μm CMOS ASIC implementation of the ARRIVE architecture [2], a coarse-grain reconfigurable datapath extension to an embedded RISC microprocessor. A detailed cost/benefit analysis is given based on chip area requirements and power consumption.

R. Woods et al. (Eds.): ARC 2008, LNCS 4943, pp. 300–305, 2008.

2   Datapath Architecture

The ARRIVE architecture extends an ARMv4 compatible RISC core [3] by two coarse-grain reconfigurable functional units (RALU/VLSU) as illustrated in Fig. 1. All units share the lower eight mode-independent registers of the RISC core through a separate read/write port, which provides an efficient datapath-coupling in case of a simultaneous operation of all units. To avoid transfer bottlenecks, the RFUs are also connected to a parallel accessible local register file not visible from the RISC core. The ARRIVE architecture is not an ISA extension, since the processing operations of the RFUs are controlled by a context configuration manager (CCM) in accordance with the RISC instruction pointer.

The Reconfigurable ALU Array is composed of coarse-grain processing elements (PEs), which can be controlled by 32 loadable contexts. Horizontal routing is provided through dedicated busses. The inputs of the PEs are connected to the source registers or the previous row via configurable switches. Vertical routing is maintained only through the PEs. The PEs can be configured to execute 48 different arithmetic, logic, shift and conditional selection functions. Each PE also includes a pipeline data register. For maximum performance, the adders of adjacent PEs are conflated horizontally and implemented using fast carry look-ahead logic. Isolated operation of the PE adders is possible through dedicated configurable separation bits. This technique significantly reduces the combinatorial path delay compared to carry chains often found in FPGA devices. The outputs of the bottom row interface to the destination register bus. The size of the array is currently assigned - but not limited to - 4×4 16-bit PEs, as it was most suitable for our benchmark applications. For the same reason, multipliers are only integrated into the PEs of the first row, since they can hardly be utilized in the other rows.

The Vector Load/Store Unit (VLSU) provides a flexible and scalable interface to dedicated local memories. It enables parallel data load/store of the

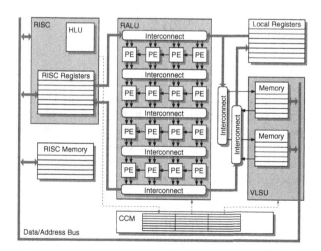

Fig. 1. ARRIVE Overview

RISC core registers or the RALU/VLSU local registers through the source and destination register busses. Through special address registers the VLSU supports typical DSP memory transfers including post-increment/-decrement, write-back and offset address modes. Independently to the RALU array, the VLSU implements its own 32 loadable configuration contexts.

The Context Configuration Manager (CCM) activates the configuration contexts in the RALU/VLSU. Its 64 entries define the relation of RISC PC addresses to the context numbers to be activated accordingly. In each clock-cycle, the RISC fetch address register is compared against all CCM address entries simultaneously. In case of a match, the specified RALU/VLSU context numbers are transfered to the RFUs through separate context configuration busses. Hence, the context numbers directly address the RALU/VLSU operations stored in the local configuration memories. The configuration memories are pre-loaded by the RISC core on a per-application basis. According to the RISC pipeline, the context activation process is implemented as a triple-stage pipeline, achieving activation of the RFU functions exactly in the execution-stage of the RISC core-pipeline.

3   ASIC Core Layout

The design of a standard-cell ASIC layout of the ARRIVE architecture was created using an UMC 6 metal-layer 0.18μm 1.8V CMOS process [4] and the UMC 0.18μm VST standard cell library [5] made available to universities through *Europractice IC Service*. The VHDL RTL model of the ARRIVE architecture was previously tested and evaluated by the mapping to a FPGA prototype [2]. Since the selection of SRAM modules available through *Europractice* is limited, the entire chip layout had to be aligned to the geometry of the available SRAM modules, which are oversized in the current implementation. The ASIC layout was obtained using *Cadence SoC Encounter v5.2* design environment. Table 1 summarizes the chip area of the ARRIVE components.

4   Efficiency Evaluation

In this section, we discuss the mapping of six significant DSP algorithms onto the ARRIVE architecture. Further, we show the increase of area efficiency E_A (performance per chip-area) and power efficiency E_P (performance per mW) compared to an original 200MHz ARM922T embedded core [6], which has a comparable core size and is also implemented in a 0.18μm CMOS process. A detailed comparison of both cores is shown in table 2.

$$G_A = \frac{E_{A_{ARRIVE}}}{E_{A_{ARM922T}}} = \frac{OP_{ARRIVE} \cdot A_{ARM922T} \cdot t_{ARM922T}}{OP_{ARM922T} \cdot A_{ARRIVE} \cdot t_{ARRIVE}}$$

$$G_P = \frac{E_{P_{ARRIVE}}}{E_{P_{ARM922T}}} = \frac{OP_{ARRIVE} \cdot P_{ARM922T} \cdot t_{ARM922T}}{OP_{ARM922T} \cdot P_{ARRIVE} \cdot t_{ARRIVE}}$$

Table 1. Chip Area Consumption of the ARRIVE Core

CCM	0.325 mm^2
LR	0.100 mm^2
RISC	0.480 mm^2
ARRAY_IN	0.225 mm^2
RALU Row 0	0.750 mm^2
RALU Row 1	0.525 mm^2
RALU Row 2	0.525 mm^2
RALU Row 3	0.525 mm^2
ARRAY_OUT	0.400 mm^2
VLSU 0	0.300 mm^2
VLSU 1	0.300 mm^2
VLSU_OUT	0.030 mm^2
I/O & Debug	1.000 mm^2
ARRIVE Core total	5.485 mm^2

Table 2. Chip Area Comparison of the ARRIVE and ARM922T Core

ARRIVE SoC Layout	Chip Area
ARRIVE Core total	5.49 mm^2
Memory 3 × 16384 × 32	9.86 mm^2
ARRIVE total	15.35 mm^2

ARM922T SoC Layout	Chip Area
ARM9TDMI Core total	6.87 mm^2
Cache 2 × 2048 × 32	1.23 mm^2
ARM922T total	8.10 mm^2

Table 3. Benchmarks: Cycle Counts and Power Consumption

Benchmark	Cycle Count ARM922T	ARRIVE	Power consumption ARRIVE (mW)
FFT Radix-2 (512pt.)	99608	4996	592
FIR Filter (Tap)	9.5	0.25	541
DCT (2D, 8pt.)	5213	149	589
IIR Filter (Biquad)	59.7	3	536
Viterbi (Symbol)	212	10	460
Turbo Decoder (Symbol)	4648	216	566

For the calculation of the functional efficiency, both chip area values A include the memory areas. The power efficiency evaluation is based on an averaged power consumption P obtained by a post-layout power simulation of the particular benchmark application using *Synopsys PrimePower* software. Additionally, the ARRIVE implementation has been verified to meet the timing requirements for a 100MHz operation in conjunction with our benchmark applications. Table 3 shows the achieved cycle counts and the power consumption of the AR-RIVE ASIC implementation. Fig. 2 summarizes the increase of area and power efficiency of the 100MHz ARRIVE implementation compared to the 200MHz ARM922T processor consuming 1mW/MHz [6]. Further, a detailed RFU datapath utilization is given in Fig. 3 for the pipelined and non-pipelined mappings of the benchmark algorithms.

FIR Filter. The implemented FIR uses the direct-form structure and operates on 16-bit fractional input, output and coefficient values. The intermediate results are 32 bit wide. In each iteration, two consecutive output values are calculated in parallel.

IIR Filter. The implemented IIR filter can be considered a cascade of IIR filter blocks with an order of two. A direct-form-II structure was chosen for the filter block implementation as it requires less delay stages. 16-bit fixed-point

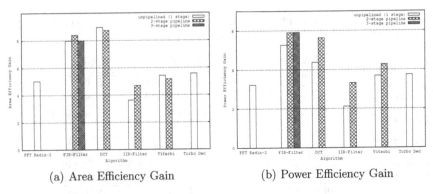

(a) Area Efficiency Gain   (b) Power Efficiency Gain

Fig. 2. Efficiency Gain of the ARRIVE processor compared to the ARM922T processor

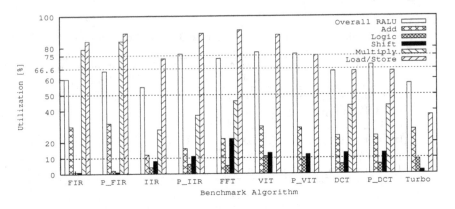

Fig. 3. RFU Utilization

numbers are used for the input values, output values and coefficients, and 32-bit values for the intermediate results.

Fast Fourier Transform. The FFT is computed in-place and uses a radix-2 butterfly decomposition. The implementation is based on 16-bit fixed-point numbers for the real and imaginary values. The addressing scheme was laid out for parallel calculation of two butterfly operations.

Viterbi Decoder. For the Viterbi algorithm implementation we chose the "class 1" polynomial of the GSM standard [7] with a code-rate of 1/2 and a trellis graph with 16 states. Soft-decision is used for the input stream to achieve higher decoding gain.

Discrete Cosine Transform. The DCT is decomposed into two blocks with N one-dimensional DCTs [8]. The schedule is optimized for 8×8 points as it can be often found in digital image processing. Each one-dimensional eight-point DCT operates on 16-bit integer data.

Turbo Decoder. The chosen Turbo code [9] following the 3GPP-standard consists of two parallel concatenated convolutional codes with 8 states and a code rate of 1/2. The overall code rate is 1/3, since systematic information is transmitted only once. The SISO decoders uses the Max-LogMAP algorithm and 8 decode iterations. A forward-backward-forward recursion was selected in the current algorithm implementation.

5 Conclusions

In this paper, we have shown the area and power efficiency of a coarse-grain reconfigurable datapath extension for DSP algorithm acceleration. As a result of a chip-area comparison, we estimated the ARRIVE core area size lower than the core area size of a less powerful, but entirely hard-wired ARM922T processor core. Further, we have shown that it is possible to integrate a reconfigurable datapath extension using an industry-standard ASIC design flow. This makes reconfigurable datapath extensions a considerable alternative in embedded system design. It is interesting to note, that through increased pipeline depth, the power efficiency increases compared to the single-stage versions. Obviously, the amount of toggling signals within the array decreases due to the insertion of pipeline registers, which eventually reduces ripple on combinatorial paths inside the RALU array. Further improvements are required to reduce the global routing effort by the implementation of a more efficient RISC/RALU communication mechanism since the available bandwidth of the chosen tight register-set coupling was not utilized in any of the considered applications.

References

1. Veredas, F.J., Scheppler, M., Moffat, W., Mei, B.: Custom Implementation of the Coarse-Grained Reconfigurable ADRES Architecture for Multimedia Purposes. In: International Conference on Field Programmable Logic and Applications, pp. 106–111. IEEE Press, Los Alamitos (2005)
2. Köhler, S., Zimmerling, M., Zabel, M., Spallek, R.G.: Prototyping and Application Development Framework for Dynamically Reconfigurable DSP Architectures. In: Grass, W., Sick, B., Waldschmidt, K. (eds.) ARCS 2006. LNCS, vol. 3894, Springer, Heidelberg (2006)
3. Furber, S.: ARM System-on-Chip Architecture. Addison-Wesley, Reading (2000)
4. United Microelectronics Corporation: The UMC 0.18μm CMOS SoC Process, http://www.umc.com/English/process/d.asp
5. Faraday Technology Corporation: UMC Free Library, http://freelibrary.faraday-tech.com/ips/018library.html
6. AMI Semiconductor: AMI Semiconductor to License ARM7 and ARM9 Microprocessor Cores, Provide Foundry Services. Design & Reuse Headline News (2001), http://www.us.design-reuse.com/news/news605.html
7. Redl, S., Weber, M., Oliphant, M.W.: An Introduction to GSM. Artech House Inc. (1995)
8. Chen, W.H., Smith, C.H., Fralick, S.: A fast computational algorithm for the discrete cosine transform. IEEE Transactions on Communications 2, 1004–1009 (1977)
9. Berrou, C., Glavieux, A., Thitimajshima, P.: Near Shannon Limit Error-correcting Coding and Decoding: Turbo-Codes. In: 1993 IEEE International Conference on Communications, Geneva, Switzerland, pp. 1064–1070 (1993)

Online Hardware Task Scheduling and Placement Algorithm on Partially Reconfigurable Devices

Thomas Marconi, Yi Lu, Koen Bertels, and Georgi Gaydadjiev

Computer Engineering Laboratory, EEMCS
TU Delft, The Netherlands
{thomas,yilu}@ce.et.tudelft.nl, k.l.m.bertels@tudelft.nl,
g.n.gaydadjiev@ewi.tudelft.nl
http://ce.et.tudelft.nl

Abstract. In this paper, we propose an online hardware task scheduling and placement algorithm and evaluate it performance. Experimental results on large random task set show that our algorithm outperforms the existing algorithms in terms of reduced total wasted area up to 89.7%, has 1.5 % shorter schedule time and 31.3% faster response time.

1 Introduction

Reconfigurable devices with partial reconfigurable capabilities allow partial update of their hardware resources without interrupting the overall system operation [1]. Embedded applications which have exploited this capability include: neural network implementation [2], video communication [3], cryptography [4], crossbar switches [5], image processing [6], and more. Such functionality also allows multitasking applications on a single chip. However to fully exploit the advantages of such platforms the scheduling and placement problems are to be considered. This is to use the limited hardware resources as efficient as possible.

Our approach focusses on a number of shortcomings of existing algorithms in order to improve the FPGA resources utilization and improve the overall execution times. The main contributions of this paper are:

- a novel online scheduling and placement algorithm, called "Intelligent Stuffing";
- careful experimental evaluation of our and other existing algorithms based on statistically large 100k task sets randomly generated;
- improvements of up to 89.7% in terms of reduced total wasted area, 1.5% in schedule time and 31.3% shorter response time.

The remainder of this paper is organized as follows. The problems of scheduling and placement in dynamic reconfigurable devices is introduced in Section 2. In Section 3, we briefly discuss the previous art. Details of our algorithm are depicted in Section 4. In Section 5, we present the evaluation of the algorithm. Finally, we conclude the paper in Section 6.

R. Woods et al. (Eds.): ARC 2008, LNCS 4943, pp. 306–311, 2008.

2 Problem of Scheduling and Placement in Dynamic Reconfigurable Devices

Given a task set representing a multitasking application with their arrival times a_i, execution times e_i and widths w_i[1] , online scheduling and placement algorithms have to determine placements and starting times for the task set such as there are no overlaps both in space and time among all tasks. The goals of the algorithms are: a) to utilize effectively the available FPGA resources (referred as minimize wasted area in this paper); b) to run the overall application on FPGA faster (minimize schedule time); c) to shorten waiting time of the tasks to be executed on the FPGA (minimize response time) and d) to keep the runtime overhead low (minimize the algorithm execution time).

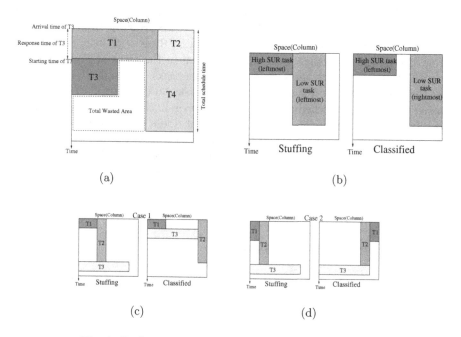

Fig. 1. Performance parameters and previous algorithms

We define total wasted area as the overall number of space-time units that are not utilized as shown in Figure 1(a). Total schedule time is the total number of time units for the execution of all tasks. Response time is the difference between starting and arrival times for each task (in time units). Total response time is the sum of response times for all tasks. The overall algorithm execution time is the cumulative time needed to schedule and place all the tasks.

---

[1] We use 1-D model for the FPGA as more representative for the current technology.

3   Previous Algorithms

In [7] [8], Steiger et al. proposed the Stuffing. It schedules tasks to arbitrary free areas that will exist in the future, including areas that will be used later by tasks currently in its reservation list. It always places a task on the leftmost of its free space as shown in the left of Figure 1(b). Because the Stuffing algorithm always places tasks on the leftmost edge of the available area, it places tasks T1 and T2 as shown in the left of Figure 1(c). These placements block task T3 to be scheduled earlier. In this case, it fails to place task T3 earlier.

In [9], Chen and Hsiung proposed the Classified Stuffing to solve the drawback of the Stuffing in case 1 (Figure 1(c)). The main difference between the algorithm and the Stuffing is the classification of tasks. It can place a task on the leftmost or rightmost of its free space based on the task Space Utilization Rate (SUR). SUR is the ratio between the number of columns required by the task and its execution time. High SUR tasks (SUR > 1) are placed starting from the leftmost available columns of the FPGA space, while low SUR tasks (SUR ≤ 1) are placed from the rightmost available columns as shown in the right of Figure 1(b). In case 1, it can recognize the difference between tasks T1 (high SUR task) and T2 (low SUR task), so it places successfully tasks on different placements. This makes task T3 earlier scheduling possible. However in case 2 (Figure 1(d)), it fails to solve the problem of the Stuffing. Because it doesn't recognize the difference between tasks T1 and T2 (both of the tasks are low SUR tasks), it fails to place tasks on different placements. These placements block task T3 to be scheduled earlier. Therefore in case 2, both of the previous algorithms fail to schedule task T3 earlier. Total wasted area, total schedule time, and total response time will increase as a consequence.

4   The Proposed Algorithm

Figure 2(a) (top) shows an empty FPGA and a leftmost alignment status is defined, e.g. a new free space always will be allocated at the leftmost position. At this point, the free space list SL contains only a single free space (FS_1) defined by its leftmost column (CL_1), its rightmost column (CR_1) and free time FT_1.

When a new task $T1$ arrives, the algorithm searches the free space list SL and places it on the leftmost edge of FS_1 (according to its alignment status). This action reduces the size of FS_1 as shown in the middle of Figure 2(a), toggles the alignment status of FS_1 from leftmost to rightmost, and creates a new free space FS_2. FS_2 has (CL_2, CR_2) dimension and its free time is FT_2 and leftmost alignment status.

Assume there is another task $T2$ simultaneously arriving with $T1$ the free space list SL will be processed again. Because the alignment status of FS_1 was changed to rightmost, $T2$ will be placed on rightmost edge of FS_1. This action reduces the FS_1 size as shown in Figure 2(a) (bottom) and again toggles the alignment status of FS_1 to leftmost. The size of FS_2 is also adjusted and a new free space FS_3 (CL_3,CR_3) is created with free time FT_3 and leftmost alignment

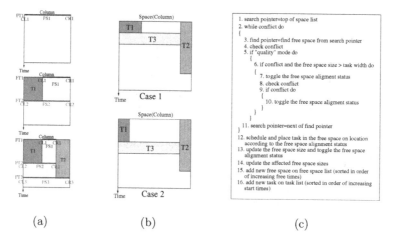

Fig. 2. Our algorithm

status. By keeping tasks $T1$ and $T2$ on the edges, the largest space possible is created, so future tasks can be scheduled earlier and we can address the problem of previous algorithms for both case 1 and case 2 as shown in Figure 2(b).

Our algorithm maintains two linked lists: a free space list (SL) and a task list (TL). The SL contains all free spaces FS_i with their previous pointers PP_i, dimensions $(CL_i$ and $CR_i)$, free times FT_i, alignment statuses AS_i and next pointers NP_i. The free time is the time when the corresponding free space can be used. The alignment status is a boolean determining the placement location of the task (leftmost or rightmost) within this free space segment. The new list entries of SL are inserted in order of increasing free times.

The TL stores all scheduled tasks with their previous pointers PP_j, start times ST_j, task dimensions (CL_j, CR_j), task execution times ET_j and next pointers NP_j. The start time is the time that the task initiates execution on the FPGA. The column left (CL_j) and right (CR_j) determine the FPGA area that is used by the task. The new list entries of TL are inserted in order of increasing of start times.

There are two operating modes: *speed* and *quality*. In the speed mode, the algorithm execution time is more important than the quality of scheduling and placement. While the quality mode is designed for higher utilization of the resources. The pseudocode of our algorithm is presented in Figure 2(c). When a new task arrives, our algorithm walks through the SL to find a first fit free space avoiding conflicts with the scheduled tasks in the TL (line 1 to 11). The first fit free space has the earliest free time which enough columns of reconfigurable units to fit the task.

If quality mode is chosen, lines 6 to 10 are executed for better quality (in speed mode those lines are skipped to reduce the algorithm execution time). In lines 6 to 8, a placement of the task at the opposite position to the alignment status is attempted. This action increases the quality, but it requires additional algorithm time. If the task still conflicts with the currently scheduled tasks in the TL (line 9), the alignment status of the corresponding free space is set to its initial condition (line 10).

In line 12, the first fit free space without conflicts with the TL list is found, however this space may be wider than that the task requirements. The task is placed on the FS_i edge according to its alignment status. As mentioned earlier, every placement changes the size and toggles the alignment status of the used free space (line 13). This action can also affect the other free space sizes (line 14) and adds a new free space in the SL (line 15) in addition to the new scheduled task in the TL (line 16).

The main difference between our algorithm and previously proposed algorithms is the additional alignment status of the free space segments and its handling. This status guides our algorithm to make the correct decision on task placement position in order to maximize the free space area and allow earlier placing of further tasks. In addition, our algorithm does not need to compute SUR, therefore it runs faster than the Classified Stuffing.

5   Evaluation

We implemented four different algorithms (the Stuffing [7] [8] (STF), the Classified Stuffing [9] (CTF) and our algorithm using *speed* mode (ISS) and *quality* mode (ISQ)) in ANSI-C and run them on a Pentium-IV 3.4 GHz PC using the same task sets. The simulated device consists of 96 columns to model Xilinx XCV1000 (96x64 reconfigurable units). The task widths and execution times are uniformly distributed in [1,96] columns of reconfigurable units and [1,1000] time units. We generate randomly 20 tasks for each task set and run all algorithms using 100,000 task sets. The evaluation is based on four performance parameters: total wasted area (TWA), total schedule time (TST), total response time (TRT), and total algorithm execution time (TAT) (μs).

Table 1. Experimentation results using 100,000 task sets

Performance parameters	STF	CTF	ISS	ISQ
TWA	1035449499	783069435	367934139	106709691
TST	651128773	648499814	644175488	641454400
TRT	335229077	317655028	276949454	230250447
TAT(μs)	2076694	2184614	2074848	2168651

Table 1 shows that even in *speed* mode our algorithm utilizes the FPGA better (decreasing the wasted area compared to the Stuffing by 64.5 %) with only 0.1 % algorithm time overhead used for saving the alignment status bit. In addition, it makes the overall application execution 1.1 % faster and has 17.4 % shorter waiting time. The *speed* mode is not only faster than the Classified Stuffing (5 % shorter algorithm execution time) but also utilizes the FPGA more effective by decreasing the wasted area by 53 %. Furthermore the application execution is reduced by 0.7 % with 12.8 % shorter total waiting time.

In *quality* mode the wasted area is decreased by 89.7 % compared to the Stuffing with only 4.2 % algorithm execution time overhead (saving the alignment status bit and finding alternative placements). Moreover it makes the application running 1.5 % faster with 31.3 % shorter total waiting time. In respect to the Classified Stuffing the *quality* mode is not only faster by 0.7 % in terms of algorithm execution time but also decreases the FPGA wasted area by 86.4 %. Additionally, the overall application execution time is reduced by 1.1 % with 27.5 % better total waiting time.

6   Conclusions

In this paper we proposed a new algorithm for online task scheduling and show how it outperforms previous art in terms of reduced total wasted area, schedule time and response time. We also evaluated two different modes of our algorithm: the *quality* mode for better placement and scheduling quality and the *speed* mode the algorithm execution time is considered more important.

Acknowledgment

This work is sponsored by the hArtes project (IST-035143) supported by the Sixth Framework Programme of the European Community under the thematic area "Embedded Systems".

References

1. Lysaght, P., Dunlop, J.: Dynamic Reconfiguration of FPGAs. In: More FPGAs, pp. 82–94, EE&CS Books, Abingdon (1993)
2. Eldredge, J.G., Hutchings, B.L.: Density Enhancement of a Neural Network Using FPGAs and Run-Time Reconfiguration. In: Proceeding of IEEE workshop on FPGAs for custom computing machines, pp. 180–188 (1994)
3. Villasenor, J., Jones, C., Schoner, B.: Video Communications Using Rapidly Reconfigurable Hardware. IEEE Transactions on circuits and systems for video technology 5(6), 565–567 (1995)
4. Vuillemin, J., Bertin, P., Roncin, D., Shand, M., Touati, H., Boucard, P.: Programmable Active Memories: Reconfigurable Systems Come of Age. IEEE Transactions on VLSI Systems 4(1), 56–69 (1996)
5. Eggers, H., Lysaght, P., Dick, H., McGregor, G.: Fast Reconfigurable Crossbar Switching in FPGAs. In: Field-Programmable Logic: Smart Applications, New Paradigms and Compilers, pp. 297–306 (1996)
6. Wirthlin, M.J., Hutchings, B.L.: Sequencing Run-Time Reconfigured Hardware with Software. In: ACM/SIGDA International Symposium on Field Programmable Gate Arrays, pp. 122–128 (1996)
7. Steiger, C., Walder, H., Platzner, M.: Heuristics for Online Scheduling Real-Time Tasks to Partially Reconfigurable Devices. In: Cheung, P.Y.K., Constantinides, G.A., de Sousa, J.T. (eds.) FPL 2003. LNCS, vol. 2778, pp. 575–584. Springer, Heidelberg (2003)
8. Steiger, C., Walder, H., Platzner, M.: Operating Systems for Reconfigurable Embedded Platforms: Online Scheduling of Real-Time Tasks. IEEE transaction on Computers 53(11), 1393–1407 (2004)
9. Chen, Y., Hsiung, P.: Hardware Task Scheduling and Placement in Operating Systems for Dynamically Reconfigurable SoC. In: Yang, L.T., Amamiya, M., Liu, Z., Guo, M., Rammig, F.J. (eds.) EUC 2005. LNCS, vol. 3824, pp. 489–498. Springer, Heidelberg (2005)

Data Reallocation by Exploiting FPGA Configuration Mechanisms

Oliver Sander, Lars Braun, Michael Hübner, and Jürgen Becker

ITIV - Universitaet Karlsruhe (TH)
{sander,braun,huebner,becker}@itiv.uni-karlsruhe.de

Abstract. Xilinx Virtex and Spartan FPGAs offer the possibility of dynamic and partial reconfiguration. This feature can be used in self-adaptive systems for providing the possibility to meet application requirements by exchanging parts of the hardware while other parts stay operative. The designer has to pay special attention to the communication wires connecting and crossing the reconfigurable areas. Module interfacing is still relatively complex, resource consuming and inflexible especially when regarding 2-dimensional reconfiguration approaches. In this paper a method is exploitet that overcomes these limitations achieved by using the reconfiguration interface not only for device configuration but also for data transfer between modules. In this paper we describe the approach in detail and present first implementation results.

1 Introduction

Today, field programmable gate-arrays (FPGAs) are used for a wide range of applications. Particularly the possibility of run-time reconfiguration which is supported by some present FPGA architectures allows introducing new ideas for self-adaptive systems [MH06],[JB06] . SRAM or FLASH based FPGAs can be reconfigured many times for different applications. Modern state-of-the-art FPGA devices like Xilinx Virtex family FPGAs additionally support a partial dynamic run-time reconfiguration which reveals new aspects for the designer in order to develop future applications demanding adaptive and flexible hardware. The idea here is to provide the required hardware function for an application only when data has to be processed. Run-time adaptive systems use the flexibility of an FPGA by partially reprogramming the configuration. A function can be substituted by another on demand while used parts stay operative as described in [ea05]. The designer of a dynamic and partial reconfigurable system on an FPGA has to ensure that no signal lines of a module cross the border to another reconfigurable functional block. During reconfiguration such a signal line might cause a malfunction or a short-circuit which destroys the FPGA. Therefore it is necessary to implement interfaces that are used as fixed routing resources. These interfaces, usually called bus macros, are placed in the same position for each functional block. Connecting the modules with signal lines on the same position grants the option to substitute a module by another. Although it sounds very

R. Woods et al. (Eds.): ARC 2008, LNCS 4943, pp. 312–317, 2008.

straightforward this task has a big impact on the overall design flow as any module slot (1- as well as 2-dimensional) has to offer all necessary connections for all possible configuration combinations. Often more than one reconfigurable slot is used, which means each slot introduces a pair of incoming and outgoing macros. Although bus macros are key components of partial and dynamic reconfiguration for data in- and output they introduce a lot of complexity into the overall design process. The possibility of realizing partial dynamical reconfigurable systems without bus macros can improve flexibility and decrease the resource utilization. One approach, namely the usage of the reconfiguration interface for inter module communication, is presented in this paper. The following paragraphs are organized as follows: Related work is summarized in chapter 2. Chapter 3 explains the basic idea, while chapter 4 presents the system that demonstrates the feasibility. Implications are being discussed and the final conclusions are drawn in chapter 5.

2 Related Work

Getting more functionality out of the configuration plane was discussed by Lysaght and Dunlop in [PL93] highlighting the necessity for dynamically reconfigurable FPGAs. Furthermore they mention a close coupling between configuration and the logic circuitry that allows self reconfiguration. The FastMap processor interface introduced in the Xilinx XC6200 device family allowed direct and arbitrary access to the configurable array. This means data can be transported via configuration plane and no extra wiring for logic coupling is necessary. The ideas presented by Brebner in [Bre96] define two different models for coupling of accelerators. The parallel harness model is based on wiring between the different mapped functions defined as swappable logic unit (SLU). In the sea of accelerators model only the configuration plane is used for SLU communication. Further refinement of both models has been done in [Bre97]. The Self Modifying Circuitry approach presented by Donlin [Don98] added the self configuration to the given context. Again the FastMap interface is used for data transfers. Both, communication between the SLUs as well as the configuration of SLUs are managed by the Ultimate RISC core. The impacts of this approach have been discussed by Brebner and Donlin [GB98], analysing several concepts of SLU communication. The conclusions made in this paper are not based but related to the FastMap configuration features only available within the XC6200 architecture. An API giving access to the configuration memory of the Virtex II devices was presented by Blodget et al. [ea03] including several methods for configuration plane modification. While data streams via this API are possible in principle they have not been discussed within this approach. The Virtual File System presented by Donlin et al. [ea04] is another API that gives access to the configuration plane by a file structure added to embedded Linux systems. Data transport using the Virtual File System is feasible but isn't mentioned as application.

3   Exploiting the ICAP Core for Data Reallocation - Overview

3.1   ICAP

The HWICAP core is an IP core to control the Internal Configuration Access Port (ICAP). This core is part of the Xilinx EDK and it is available at the IP catalogue. It supports FPGAs from the Virtex-II Pro and Virtex-II FPGA families. The core allows the user to read and write the FPGA configuration memory through the ICAP at run time and thereby change its configuration including the content of a specific BRAM. Further details can be found in [Xil05b], [BML03] and [Xil05a].

3.2   Methodology

The internal configuration interface is only used for reconfiguration of the FPGA area in state of the art approaches. This means there is no dataflow associated with bitstream configuration. The result is a strong partitioning between the functional units that are configured via the ICAP interface and the data exchanged between the functional units via bus macros. The main idea in our approach is to overcome this traditional system view in FPGA design and use the configuration interface not only for configuration but also for data transfers. This brings both streams for configuration and data together. Being able to feed functional units with data this way leads to much more flexibility because there is no bus macro needed for module communication. A similar approach was also used in [BHB+07] where the content of a LUT was modified by also using the configuration mechanism for controlling switches. We use the BRAMs to store the data that is used by the configurable modules. Therefore each module has to be located next to at least one BRAM block. Besides this fact all modules in this approach can be placed almost freely on the FPGA since no communication infrastructure is needed. The transfer of the utilizable data is managed over the ICAP. A small example and test system will illustrate this approach in chapter 6. In figure 1 left the structure of a typical reconfigurable FPGA-system is shown. In the picture different reconfigurable Blocks are placed nearby at least one BRAM. The modules can be put on any place of the FPGA. The results can be stored into the same or another BRAM. This allows reading back the data via ICAP. It is also conceivable that results that have been processed by a module could also resist within the BRAM and only the processing module is being reconfigured. This can decrease configuration and processing time because no data has to be loaded.

4   System Implementation - Structural Overview

Figure 1 right presents a systematic overview of the system that demonstrates the feasibility. Basically we display an image on a screen. On the left side a VGA controller that loads the image data out of a BRAM memory which works as frame buffer can be seen. On the right hand side one can see a simple PowerPC system that has been designed and implemented on a Virtex2Pro device. This system can read different bitstreams containing just the image data from the attached DDR memory. On the PowerPC there is a simple software running that manages to configure the different bitstreams onto the FPGA. As the data contained in the bitstreams is just image data only the content of the BRAM blocks that build the VGA frame buffer is reconfigured and the new image is displayed. This is done without a logical connection between the two parts of the system. The VGA Core is designed to display a resolution of 640x480 pixels by 3 bit colour depth with a refresh rate of 60Hz. The data displayed on the screen are collected by the VGA core from an enclosed BRAM. The position of this BRAM on the FPGA is known by the controlling PowerPC and thereby the PowerPC can manipulate the content of this BRAM. The PowerPC system includes the

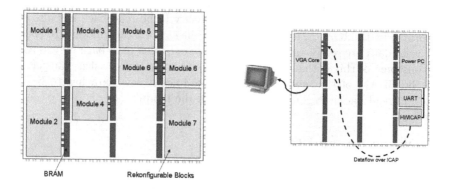

Fig. 1. System Implementation-Overview

HWICAP which is provided by Xilinx as IP Core to use by an embedded processor for internal reconfiguration. Furthermore the RS232 IP Core to communicate with the user and a DDR-RAM controller is implemented to store the different bitstreams which hold the BRAM content for the frame buffer. At startup the system is completely configured on the FPGA including the initial BRAM data. After uploading different bitstreams into the DDR Ram via UART the system is able to perform a partial write operation into the corresponding BRAMs to change the display. The system functions correctly as intended. However, the performance is a big issue. Compared to some other systems that were designed it was observed that the ICAP is running at 5 MB/s. This differs drastically from the theoretical rate of 66MB/s. As this delay mainly depends on the HW-ICAP implementation and not on the silicon there is still potential for increasing the performance of the system. Tests with the ICAP have shown that the data throughput can be increased at least by the factor of 10. Furthermore the ICAP of the newer Xilinx Virtex 4 series has the benefit to provide a 32 bit wide ICAP, that means that it is possible to perform a data transfer which is four times faster than the transfer of the ICAP used in Virtex 2. This shows that the ICAP has a large performance potential which will be utilized in the future and makes this approach much more usable and also feasible for more communication intensive applications. In the test application we presented here we want to show the possibility to use the ICAP as data transfer for systems with lower and non time critical data throughput as the presented frame buffer. To display a complete picture on the screen 640 x 480 pixels with a width of 3 bit has to be transferred. This means 115.2 Kbyte have to be transferred to display a complete picture on the screen. To show a nonstop video sequence at least 25 frames per second have to be displayed. According to our example a data transfer rate of 2.88 MB/s has to be performed. Therefore the data throughput of the conventional HWICAP as it is provided by Xilinx is fast enough. However, for more data intensive applications the transfer rate of the ICAP has to be improved, especially if there is more than one module which has to be allocated by data. Another point to be stressed here is the possibility of the bidirectional communication. Because of the absence of a conventional communication structure, the readback and the monitoring if new data in the modules are ready to be read back has also been performed by the ICAP. Therefore the ICAP has to poll each module to check if new valid data are ready and have to be prepared to be read back by the ICAP. The outcome of this is that the ICAP has to manage three tasks: transfer data into the BRAM of the modules, poll the modules if new data has to be read back and read back the computed data from the modules.

5   Discussion and Conclusions

We believe macro less partial reconfiguration has its advantages for selected applications. However, there are some drawbacks in this approach one has to be aware of. A communication is triggered, planned and executed by the configuration interface in both read and write directions. That means this is primarily a single master multiple slave concept, with the master which is the static slot and the slaves build by several reconfigurable slots or modules. It must be considered that using this approach means to use one interface (ICAP) for all communications and the configurations. Compared to what has been learned from the von Neumann concept we can be sure that this is the overall bottleneck. Similar impacts have been described in [GB98]. Here a placing of the corresponding modules next to each other and establishing a local communication structure can help. Another interesting aspect is temporal parallelism. While in traditional approaches data has to flow to the functional unit we consider functional units to come to the data. As already mentioned one could imagine the data being processed and stored in the same buffer. The functional unit is reconfigured next to the data and works on the data stored in the buffer. One also has to take into account that disregarding macros can make the tool flow much easier. Introducing neighborhood or local communication does not change this fact because there is no module crossing. And additionally there is no overhead for the macros that can stretch over en entire slot. Regardless of the mentioned drawbacks we think it is very important to investigate the potentials given by the reconfiguration interface in the FPGA fabric.

In the approach presented in this paper we demonstrated the feasibility of bringing the reconfiguration stream and the data stream together within the reconfiguration interface of modern dynamically reconfigurable devices. A demonstrator was presented and described in detail. The upcoming bottleneck was identified and methods for solution proposed. For this a faster controller would be necessary. First results gained by using a modified HWICAP implementation achieve a throughput sufficient for a broad field of applications. Further research will focus on detailed performance measurements and evaluation of the overall concept.

References

[BHB+07] Braun, L., Huebner, M., Becker, J., Perschke, T., Schatz, V., Bach, S.: Circuit switched run-time adaptive network-on-chip for image processing applications. In: Hubner, M. (ed.) Proc. International Conference on Field Programmable Logic and Applications FPL 2007, pp. 688–691 (2007)

[BML03] Blodget, B., McMillan, S., Lysaght, P.: A lightweight approach for embedded reconfiguration of fpgas. In: Proc. Design, Automation and Test in Europe Conference and Exhibition, pp. 399–400 (2003)

[Bre96] Brebner, G.: A virtual hardware operating system for the xilinx xc6200. In: Glesner, M., Hartenstein, R.W. (eds.) FPL 1996. LNCS, vol. 1142. Springer, Heidelberg (1996)

[Bre97] Brebner, G.: The swappable logic unit: a paradigm for virtual hardware. In Proc. 5th Annual IEEE Symposium on FPGAs for Custom Computing Machines 16–18, pp. 77–86 (April 1997)

[Don98] Donlin, A.: Self modifying circuitry - a platform for tractable virtual circuitry. In: Hartenstein, R.W., Keevallik, A. (eds.) FPL 1998. LNCS, vol. 1482, pp. 199–208. Springer, Heidelberg (1998)

[ea03] Blodget, B., et al.: A self-reconfiguring platform. In: Y. K. Cheung, P., Constantinides, G.A. (eds.) FPL 2003. LNCS, vol. 2778. Springer, Heidelberg (2003)

[ea04] Donlin, A., et al.: A virtual file system for dynamically reconfigurable fpgas. In: Becker, J., Platzner, M., Vernalde, S. (eds.) FPL 2004. LNCS, vol. 3203. Springer, Heidelberg (2004)

[ea05] Becker, J., et al.: Automotive control unit optimisation perspectives: Body functions on-demand by dynamic reconfiguration. In: Date 2005. Munich, Germany (2005)

[GB98] Donlin, A., Brebner, G.: Runtime reconfigurable computing. In: IPPS/SPDP (1998)

[JB06] Huebner, M., Becker, J.: Run-time reconfigurabilility and other future trends. In: SBCCI 2006. Brazil (2006)

[MH06] Becker, J., Huebner, M.: Exploiting dynamic and partial reconfiguration for fpgas - toolflow, architecture and system integration. In: SBCCI2006. Brazil (2006)

[PL93] Dunlop, J., Lysaght, P.: Dynamic reconfiguration of field programmable gate arrays. In: Grünbacher, H., Hartenstein, R.W. (eds.) FPL 1993. LNCS, vol. 704. Springer, Heidelberg (1993)

[Xil05a] Xilinx. Virtex-ii platform fpga user guide, ug002 (v2.0) (March 23, 2005)

[Xil05b] Xilinx. Virtex-ii pro and virtex-ii pro x fpga user guide, ug012 (v4.0) (March 2005)

A Networked, Lightweight and Partially Reconfigurable Platform

Pierre Bomel, Guy Gogniat, and Jean-Philippe Diguet

LESTER, Université de Bretagne Sud, CNRS FRE 2734, Lorient, France
{pierre.bomel,guy.gogniat,jean-philippe.diguet}@univ-ubs.fr

Abstract. In this paper we present a networked lightweight and partially reconfigurable platform assisted by a remote bitstreams server. We propose a software and hardware architecture as well as a new data-link level network protocol implementation dedicated to dynamic and partial reconfiguration of FPGAs. It requires a network controller and much less external memories to store reconfiguration software, bitstreams and buffer pools used by standard communication protocols. Our measures, based on a real implementation, show that our system can download remote bistreams with a reconfiguration speed ten times faster than known solutions.

Keywords: partial reconfiguration, FPGA, link layer, bitstream server.

1 Introduction

FPGAs provide reconfigurable SoCs with a way to build systems on demand. In particular, Xilinx's Virtex FPGA reconfiguration can be exploited in different ways, partially or globally, externally (exo-reconfiguration) or internally (endo-reconfiguration). Virtex's dynamic and partial reconfiguration (DPR) requires additional resources to store the numerous partial configurations bitstreams. Today, researchers exploit in vast majority local FLASH and RAM memories as repositories. In the best case Huebner et al. [1] reduce up to 50% of the bitstream memory footprint with the help of a small hardware decompressor. Then, we face the migration of silicon square millimeters from FPGAs to memories. Although their low cost, when compared to FPGAs, is in favor of this migration, there are some drawbacks: 1) low reuse rate, 2) increase of number of components and PCB size, 3) reduction of MTBF and 4) impossibility to store all the possible bistreams (FPGA models, bitstream locations, areas shapes) for a single IP.

In the following we review in Sect. 2 the previous DPR related works via a standard LAN. In Sect. 3 we present our contribution in terms of embedded hardware and software and propose a LAN-level protocol adapted to DPR constraints and objectives. In Sect. 4 we describe our experiments and measures about the partial reconfiguration speeds and memory footprints. Finally, in Sect. 5, we conclude.

R. Woods et al. (Eds.): ARC 2008, LNCS 4943, pp. 318–323, 2008.

2   Related Works

Partial reconfiguration of Xilinx's FPGAs goes through the control of a configuration port called ICAP [2] (Internal Configuration Access Port). Virtex2 PRO, Virtex4 VFX and now Virtex5 contain this port. The reconfiguration peak rate announced is exactly of one byte per clock cycle: be 100 MB/s (100 MegaBytes) for 100 MHz systems. Because systems work at different frequencies, we'll express measures in bits transmitted per seconds and per MHz. The reference ICAP bandwidth of 100 MB/s becomes 8 Mb/s.MHz (8 Megabits).

Claus et al. [3] consider that, for automotive real-time video applications, the average bitstreams size is about 300 KB. Claus accepts to loose one eighth of the processing time to reconfigure. For 25 images/s, the processing time is 40 ms, and a maximum of 5 ms is devoted to endo-reconfiguration. The speed constraint is 60 MB/s. The experimental platform is a Virtex2 inside which a PPC405 executes the software managing the DPR. Claus's paper lets us think that no functional system was ready at publication time.

The XAPP433 [4] application note, describes a system built around a 100 MHz Virtex4 FX12. It contains a synthesized Microblaze processor executing the code of an HTTP server. The HTTP server downloads files via a 100 Mb/s Ethernet LAN. The protocol stack is Dunkel's lwIP [5] and the operating system is Xilinx' XMK. A 64 MB external memory is necessary to store lwIP buffers. The announced downloading rate is 500 KB/s, be 40 Kb/s.MHz. This rate is 200 times lesser than ICAP's one.

Lagger et al. [6] propose the ROPES system, dedicated to the acceleration of cryptographic functions. It is build with a 27 MHz Virtex2 1000. The processor is a Microblaze executing νClinux's code. It downloads bitstreams via Ethernet with HTTP and FTP protocols on top of a TCP/IP/Ethernet stack. For 70 KB bitstreams, DPR latencies are about 2380 ms with HTTP, and about 1200 ms with FTP. The max reconfiguration speed is about 60 KB/s, be 17 Kb/s.MHz.

Finally, Williams and Bergmann [7] propose νClinux as a RDP platform. They have developed a device driver on top of the ICAP. Junction between a remote file system and the ICAP is done at the user level by a shell command or a user program. When a remote file system is mounted via NFS/UDP/IP/Ethernet the bitstreams located there can be downloaded into the ICAP. The system is built with a Virtex2 and the processor executing νClinux is a Microblaze. No measures are provided. To have an estimation of such performances we made some measures in a similar context and got transfer speeds ranging from 200 KB/s to 400 KB/s, representing a maximum of about 32 Kb/s.MHz.

3   Contribution

In this section we present our contribution in terms of hardware architecture, software architecture and data-link level protocol for DPR. We present in details the essential points improving the speed and reducing the memory footprint.

The hardware architecture we propose (Fig. 1) relies on a 100 MHz Virtex2 PRO 30. A PPC405 core executes the DPR software. We consider that IPs

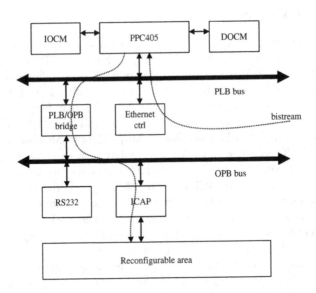

Fig. 1. Bistreams path from Ethernet to ICAP through PLB and OPB buses

communicate with the FPGA environment directly via some pads. Communication with the PPC405 and inter-IPs communication are out of the scope of this article but can be implemented with Xilinx's and Huebner's bus macros [8] and OPB/PLB wrappers as well as with an external crossbar like in the Erlangen Slot Machine of Bobda et al. [9]. We have specified with EDK, XPS and Planahead tools a system which contains a PPC405 surrounded by its minimal devices set for DPR. We have added two memories. These are respectively the IOCM (Instruction On Chip Memory) and the DOCM (Data On Chip memory). The PPC405 communicates with its devices through two buses connected through a bridge. These are the PLB bus for the faster devices and the OPB bus for the slower devices. The Ethernet PHY controller is connected to the PLB. The UART serial line, for instrumentation and trace purpose, is connected to the OPB. Finally the ICAP, connected to the OPB, manages the access and the downloading of bitstreams into the reconfigurable areas. The exo-reconfiguration is done through the JTAG port while the endo-reconfiguration is done through the ICAP.

The software architecture is a two layers one. Bottom (level 1) layer is based on the ICAP and Ethernet drivers. Top (level 2) layer handles the DPR protocol processing. They establishe a data pipeline between the remote bitstreams server and the reconfigurable areas in the FPGA. To uncouple ICAP and Ethernet we have designed a producer-consumer paradigm. The producer is the Ethernet controller and the consumer is the ICAP port. A circular buffer is asynchronously fed with packets by interrupt handlers. Packet reception occurs by bursts and the burst length is less than or equal to the half capacity of a reception packets buffer. Each packet has a maximum size of 1518 bytes and has a maximum payload of

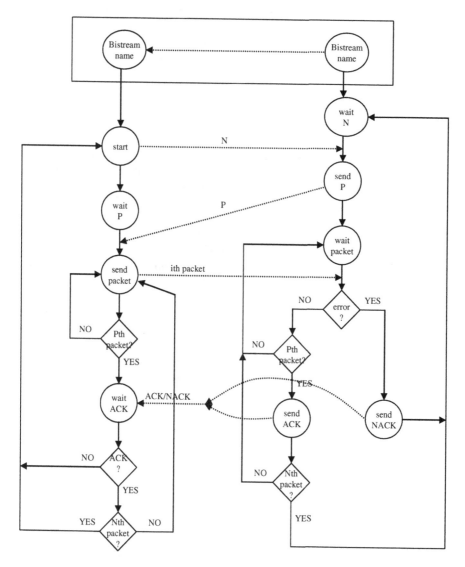

Fig. 2. RDP Protocol state machines for server (left) and target (right)

1500 bytes of bitstream data. The DPR protocol is executed concurrently with the interrupt handlers. It analyzes the packet content and transfers the bitstream data to the ICAP port. The bigger the burst is, the faster the protocol is.

Our protocol (Fig. 2) implements a data link with error detection and flow control. It is qualified as "adaptive" because it is able to adapt itself to the memory resources available in the lightweight system at endo-reconfiguration time. Would an error be detected, the DPR is instantaneously stopped after signalization of the error to the remote bitstreams server and the reconfiguration restarted from the beginning. The Virtex tendancy (Virtex4 and Virtex5) being to systematically reduce bitstreams sizes for partial reconfiguration, we think a bitstream level restart strategy is better than a packet level restart one. This choice is, of course, only valid for small amount of data transmitted over a very low error rate LAN, which is our context. So the Ethernet controller detects all transmission errors and the sequential numbering of packets allows detection of missing, duplicated and moved packets in the packets flow. To implement the necessary data flow regulation, we have chosen a positive acknowledge scheme every P packets. P is determined by the DPR module from the available memory space at the reconfiguration time. The DPR protocol can be used in two different modes. In "optional master" mode (top of Fig. 2) the lightweight system specifies the identity (a file name relative to the bitstream directory managed by the server) of the bitstream to send. In "slave" mode it receives the bitstream without knowledge of its function and location in the FPGA. When a transmission starts, the server sends the total number of packets, N, that will be transmitted for the full bitstream. The target answers with the number P which specifies the burst size. Immediately after this parameters negotiation, and after every positive acknowledge, the server sends a burst of P packets and waits for the next acknowledge. The finite state machine on the left describes the server's behavior and the one on the right the target's behavior. The downloading is constituted by $\lceil N/P \rceil$ bursts of maximum P packets, until the Nth packet ends the session. In case of hardware reset, both state machines come back to their waiting state. Timers on both sides help in the detection of unexpected death of an extremity of the pipeline and restart state machines if necessary.

4   Results

Our measures are based on the repetitive endo-reconfiguration of cryptography IPs like DES and triple DES producing bitstreams file sizes about 60 KB and 200 KB. Results obtained depend, as we could expect, on the producer-consumer

Table 1. Comparative endo-reconfiguration speeds and memory footprints

	Lagger [6]	Williams [7]	Xilinx [4]	RDP [authors]
Speed (Mb/s@MHz)	17	32	40	375-400
Memory (bytes)	$> 1M$	$> 1M$	$> 1M$	$< 100K$

packets buffer size allocated to the DPR protocol. So the speed depends on P. Measures establish that in both cases (60 KB and 200 KB bistreams), when the packets burst has a size greater or equal to three packets (P = 3), a maximum speed ranging from 375 to 400 Mb/s.MHz is reached and is stabilized. The size of the circular buffer being $2P + 1$, it needs room for exactely seven packets, be 10.5 KB (7 ∗ 1.5KB) only. Compared to usual buffer pools of hundredths of KB for standard protocol stacks, this is a very small amount of memory to provide a continuous DPR service. In this context our DPR protocol exhibits a sustained reconfiguration speed about 40 Mb/s. Finally, our DPR software fits into 32 KB of data memory and 40 KB of executable code memory. This memory footprint and the reconfiguration speed enable us to qualify this system as being a "lightweight DPR system". Table 1 sums up the respective speeds expressed in Mb/s.MHz and memory footprints in bytes.

5 Conclusion and Future Extensions

Our DPR platform shows there is still opportunities to improve LAN-level, and probably IP-level, protocols in order to provide an efficient and remote reconfiguration service (or communication service as well) over a standard network. Our implementation exhibits an order of magnitude gain in speed when compared to related works.

References

1. Hubner, M., Ullmann, M., Weissel, F., Becker, J.: Real-time Configuration Code Decompression for Dynamic FPGA Self-Reconfiguration. In: Proceedings of the 18th International Parallel and Distributed Processing Symposium (IPDPS 2004) (2004)
2. Blodget, B., McMillan, S., Lysaght, P.: A lightweight approach for embedded reconfiguration of fpgas. In: Proceedings of Design, Automation and Test in Europe (DATE 2003) (2003)
3. Claus, C., Zeppenfeld, J., Muller, F., Stechele, W.: Using Partial-Run-Time Reconfigurable Hardware to accelerate Video Processing in Driver Assistance System. DATE 2007
4. Web Server design using MicroBlaze Soft Processor, Xilinx, XAPP433 (October 2006)
5. Dunkels, A.: lwIP, Computer and Networks Architectures (CNA), Swedish Institute of Computer Science, http://www.sics.se/~adam/lwip/
6. Lagger, A., Upegui, A., Sanchez, E.: Self-Reconfigurable Pervasive Platform For Cryptographic Application. In: Proceedings of International Conference on Field Programmable Logic and Applications (FPL 2006) (2006)
7. Williams, J., Bergmann, N.: Embedded Linux as a platform for dynamically self-reconfiguring systems-on-chip. In: Proceedings of the 2004 International Conference on Engineering of Reconfigurable Systems and Algorithms (ERSA 2004) (2004) ISBN 1-932415-42-4
8. Huebner, M., Becker, T., Becker, J.: Real-Time LUT-based Network Topologies for Dynamic and Partial FPGA Self-Reconfiguration. In: 17th Symposium on Integrated Circuits and Systems Design (SBCCI 2004) (September 2004)
9. Bobda, C., Majer, M., Ahmadinia, A., Haller, T., Linarth, A., Teich, J.: The Erlangen Slot Machine: Increasing Flexibility in FPGA-Based Reconfigurable Platforms. Journal of VLSI Signal Processing Systems 47(1), 15–31 (2007)

Neuromolecularware – A Bio-inspired Evolvable Hardware and Its Application to Medical Diagnosis

Yo-Hsien Lin and Jong-Chen Chen

Department of Information Management,
National YunLin University of Science and Technology, Taiwan, R.O.C.
g9220805@yuntech.edu.tw, jcchen@mis.yuntech.edu.tw

Abstract. Computer systems have powerful computational capability. However, it is brittle in that a slight program modification can inadvertently change the system functions. Biological systems demonstrate better adaptability than computer systems. An evolvable neuromolecular hardware motivated from some biological evidence is proposed. The hardware was further applied to medical diagnosis with a clinical database of premature babies who are given total parental nutrition (TPN). Experimental results show that the neuromolecular hardware was capable of learning to differentiate data in an autonomous manner.

Keywords: Adaptability, Artificial Brain, Evolvable Hardware, Evolutionary Learning, Medical Diagnosis.

1 Introduction

Computer systems provide effective programmability that allows us to explore various problem domains. It has powerful computational capability in performing repetitive jobs. Intelligent models represent the effort to assist clinicians in making a medical diagnosis. However, most models developed so far are software simulation systems. It is very time-consuming to simulate a population of networks, in particular an ensemble of evolutionary neural networks. Furthermore, computer structures are brittle in that a slight program modification can inadvertently change the system functions [1].

Biological systems demonstrate better adaptability than computer systems. The ability to evolve, self-organizing dynamics, and a close structure-function relation provide organisms with great malleability (gradual transformation) in coping with environmental changes. Malleability characteristics play significant roles in facilitating adaptive learning [2].

Evolvable hardware (EHW) is a new approach that attempts to apply evolutionary learning techniques to a reconfigurable hardware [3,4]. The idea is to combine the merits of biological systems and computer systems together and, hopefully create hardware with better adaptability. EHW might have the following benefits: speed up various evolutionary operations, low hardware design

R. Woods et al. (Eds.): ARC 2008, LNCS 4943, pp. 324–329, 2008.

costs, automatic design, innovative design, better adaptability in dealing with environmental changes, and good fault tolerant capability [3,5].

The artificial neuromolecular (ANM) model [6] was motivated from the molecular mechanisms inside real neurons. The model consists of two types of neurons: cytoskeletal neurons and reference neurons [2]. However, it is still a software simulation system that runs on top of a serial digital computer. The implementation of this model on hardware would allow it to perform on a real-time basis, speedup performance, parallel processing, and to provide an architectural paradigm for emerging molecular or neuromolecular electronic technologies. In this paper, evolvable neuromolecular hardware is proposed. The hardware is further applied to medical diagnosis for premature babies who are given daily TPN treatment.

2   Architecture of Neuromolecularware

In this section, we descript the mechanisms of cytoskeletal and reference neurons and present how to implement the cytoskeletal neuron on digital hardware.

2.1   Cytoskeletal Neurons

The cytoskeletal neurons have significant intra-neuronal dynamics that serves to transduce specific combinations of input signals in space and time to an output signal. The transduction mechanism of the cytoskeletal neurons is motivated by some physiological evidence that the intra-neuronal dynamics of a neuron controls its firing behavior [7]. The cytoskeletal neuron is simulated with a two-dimensional cellular automaton.

The cytoskeleton has three major fibers: microtubules, microfilaments, and intermediate filaments (denoted by C1, C2, and C3 component-type in this model), each of which is responsible for transmitting a specific type of cytoskeletal signal. When an external signal impinges on the membrane of a cytoskeletal neuron, it will activate a readin enzyme at the site of the input. The activation of a readin enzyme will thus trigger a unidirectional signal flow along a chain of neighboring components of the same type. For example, in Fig. 1, the activation of the readin enzyme at site (1,5) will trigger a cytoskeletal signal flow along the C3 components, starting from site (1,5) and running to site (5,5). An activated component will enter a refractory state for a certain amount of time.

These fibers might interact with each other through the proteins (microtubule associated proteins, MAPs) that connect them together [8]. For example, as shown in Fig. 1, a signal will interact the components at sites (5,4) and (6,5) via the MAP connecting them together when it arrives at site (5,5). The strength of the interactions depends on the types of fibers involved. When the spatiotemporal combination of cytoskeletal signals arriving at the site of a readout enzyme is suitable, the readout will be activated and the neuron will fire. Specific combinations of these signal interactions may in turn fire a neuron. Another important feature is that different types of components transmit signals at different speeds.

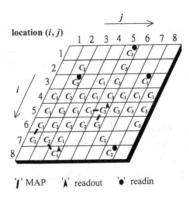

'/' MAP   'A' readout   '•' readin

Fig. 1. Cytoskeletal neuron

2.2   Hardware Architecture of Cytoskeletal Neuron

The cytoskeleton is implemented with a 2-D grid of basic units, molecular units (MUs). Figure 2 shows the digital architecture of a molecular unit, consisting of four evolutionary control parameters (Readin, MAP, C-Type, and Readout) and three signal processing components (Connector, Processor, and Transmitter).

The evolutionary control parameters provide the interface that decides an MU type and its state. There are four MU types: C1, C2, C3, and none. Two bits are used to each MU type (parameter C-Type). Readin serves as receptor to process an external stimulus. One bit is required to determine whether it is on or off (parameter readin). Readout parameter plays the role of determining whether a fire is about to fire (parameter readout). Similarly, one bit is used. As to the connections to the neighbors of an MU, four bits are used to decide their connections with neighboring MUs (parameter MAP). The output of each MU has four channels: S, I, W, and Firing. Channel S, I, and W indicate a signal from a highly activated C1, C2, and C3 component, respectively. For example, channel S will be turned on whenever a C1-type MU is about to send its outputs. The Connector processes all the signals from the channels S, I, and W of each neighboring MU and external signals. The Processor is the major component of MU for integrating each signal from its neighbor. The Processor serves as a recorder, keeping the present state of an MU. Whenever the Processor receives a signal from the Connector, an MU enters a new state. For an MU in the most highly activated state, a neuron will fire if there is a readout enzyme sitting at the same site. If a neuron is not firing, an MU in the highly active state will continue to transmit signals to Transmitter. At the same time, the signal in Processor will decrease over time. The Transmitter is responsible for two tasks. One is to control the transmitting speed of signals. The ratio of signal speed of C1, C2, and C3 is 3:2:1. The other task is to turn off Connector for a specific period of time, indicating an MU is in the refractory state.

All of the digital circuit modules were designed with Verilog using Quartus II software. The final design of circuits was implemented with an FPGA device.

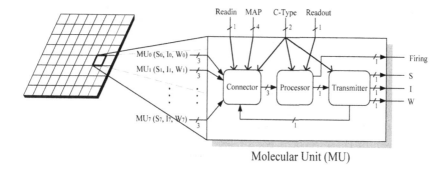

Molecular Unit (MU)

Fig. 2. Digital architecture of molecular unit

2.3 Reference Neurons

Reference neurons play the role of selecting appropriate combinations of cytoskeletal neurons to complete specific tasks (Fig.3). Low-level reference neurons select comparable cytoskeletal neurons in each subnet. High-level reference neurons select different combinations of the low-level reference neurons. The activation of a high-level reference neuron will fire all of the low-level reference neurons that it controls, which in turn fires a specific combination of cytoskeletal neurons. We note only those cytoskeletal neurons indirectly activated by the reference neurons are allowed to perform input-output processing tasks.

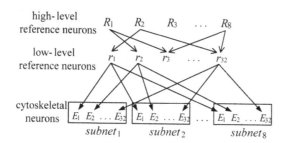

Fig. 3. Connections between reference and cytoskeletal neurons layers

3   Evolutionary Learning and Problem Domain

There are eight comparable subnets, each consisting of 32 cytoskeletal neurons. Comparable subnets are similar in terms of their inter-neuronal connections and intra-neuronal structures. This ensures that comparable cytoskeletal neurons in different subnets will receive the same external stimuli. Five parameters of evolutionary learning are allowed in this system. They are C-Type, MAP, readin enzyme, readout enzyme, and reference neurons (grouping cytoskeletal neurons). Evolutionary learning has three steps:

1. Each subnet is activated in turn for evaluating its performance.
2. The pattern of readout enzymes, readin enzymes, MAPs, connectivities, and other components of best-performing subnets is copied to lesser-performing subnets, depending on which level of evolution is operative.
3. The pattern of readout enzymes, readin enzymes, MAPs, connectivities, and other components of lesser-performing subnets is slightly varied.

In this study, the neuromolecular hardware was employed to differentiate a clinical TPN database of premature babies. The TPN database consists of 274 records. Each of these records comprised 30 parameters: 7 observatory parameters, 12 laboratory parameters, and 11 TPN diet parameters. Based on the degrees of weight changes, these 274 records were further divided into three groups: weight-gain, weight-loss, and weight-sameness group.

Cytoskeletal neurons were equally divided into three classes, corresponding to three groups of records. For each record, we defined that the hardware made a correct response when the class of the first firing neuron was in accordance with the group shown in the database. The greater the number of correct responses made by the neuromolecular hardware, the higher its fitness was.

4   Experimental Results

Two experiments were performed. The first was to test the differentiation capability of the neuromolecular hardware. In the second experiment, we investigated the contributions made by parameter changes during evolutionary learning. These 274 records were divided into two sets: training and testing. The training set consisted of 174 records. The testing set consisted of 100 records. The neuromolecular hardware was first trained with the training set for over 20000 cycles. The experimental result showed that the number of records recognized by the neuromolecular hardware increased continuously during the course of learning (Fig. 4a). Correct classification rate improved significantly in the early stage of learning, but slowed down in the later stage. The classification rates for the training and testing sets were 87.9% and 62.0%, respectively. This result implied that the system possessed a certain degree of differentiation capability.

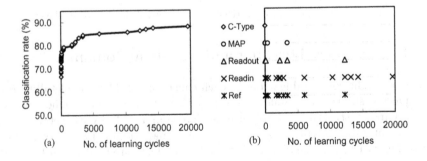

Fig. 4. (a) Learning performance. (b) Learning progress made by parameter changes.

Closer examination of the data showed that learning proceeded in an alternate manner. That is, each parameter more or less contributed to learning progress (Fig. 4b). This suggested synergies occurred among different parameters of evolution, implying that learning at one parameter opened up opportunities for another. We noted that in the early stage of learning contributions were made by several parameters of evolution. This was because the initial repertoire of neurons was sufficient to differentiate the majority of patterns.

5 Conclusion

Computer systems are suited for performing high computing tasks. However, its structure is rigid, lacking flexibility. Relatively, biological systems exhibit high adaptability but with limited computational capability. The neuromolecular hardware presented in this paper is a system lying between these two extremes. The neuromolecular hardware is a model that combines the merits of biological information processing and evolutionary learning techniques into a system. The implementation of the system with digital circuits allows us to create hardware with better adaptability.

TPN is our present application domain. We have demonstrated that the system is capable of learning to differentiate TPN data in a continued manner. That is, it does not stagnate during the learning process. Learning in a continuous manner is an important feature for perpetual evolutionary learning.

Acknowledgments. This research was supported in part by the Taiwan National Science Council (Grant NSC 95-3113-P-224-003).

References

1. Conrad, M.: Bootstrapping on the adaptive landscape. BioSyst 11, 167–182 (1979)
2. Conrad, M.: Evolutionary Learning Circuits. J. Theoret. Biol. 46, 167–188 (1974)
3. Yao, X.: Following the path of evolvable hardware. Comm. ACM 42(4), 47–49 (1999)
4. Sipper, M., Ronald, E.M.A.: A new species of hardware. IEEE Spectrum 37(3), 59–64 (2000)
5. Gordon, T.W., Bentley, P.J.: Towards Development in Evolvable Hardware. In: Proc of the 2002 NASA/DoD Conference on Evolvable Hardware (2002)
6. Chen, J.-C., Conrad, M.: Learning synergy in a multilevel neuronal architecture. BioSystems 32, 111–142 (1994)
7. Hameroff, S.R.: Ultimate Computing. North-Holland, Amsterdam (1987)
8. GriPth, L.M., Pollard, T.D.: The interaction of actin filaments with microtubules and microtubule-associated proteins. J. Biol. Chem. 257, 9143–9151 (1982)

An FPGA Configuration Scheme for Bitstream Protection

Masaki Nakanishi

Graduate School of Information Science, Nara Institute of Science and Technology
Takayama, Ikoma, Nara 630-0101, Japan
m-naka@is.naist.jp

Abstract. FPGAs are widely used recently, and security on configuration bitstreams is of concern to both users and suppliers of configuration bitstreams (e.g., intellectual property vendors). In order to protect configuration bitstreams against the threats such as FPGA viruses, piracy and reverse engineering, configuration bitstreams need to be encrypted and authenticated before loaded into FPGAs. In this paper, we propose a new FPGA configuration scheme that can authenticate and/or decrypt a bitstream. The proposed scheme has flexibility in choosing authentication and/or decryption algorithms and causes only a small area overhead since it utilizes programmable logic blocks to implement authentication and/or decryption circuits.

Keywords: FPGA configuration, bitstream protection, bitstream encryption, bitstream authentication.

1 Introduction

FPGAs are widely used recently, and security on configuration bitstreams is of concern to both users and suppliers of configuration bitstreams (e.g., intellectual property vendors). Configuration bitstreams are exposed to the threats of piracy, reverse engineering and code theft. Moreover, a tampered configuration bitstream can be an FPGA virus [4], which is a hardware analogue of a computer virus. In order to defend against such threats, we need encryption/decryption and authentication of bitstreams at configuration. Some commercial FPGAs have a cryptographic circuit in it [1,8]. Also various methods that protect bitstream security have been proposed [2,3,5,6,7]. Most of them equip dedicated decryption and/or authentication circuits in an FPGA. This causes a hardware overhead. Note that circuits for asymmetric cryptography need large area. Because of the overhead, dedicated decryption and/or authentication circuits equipped in an FPGA are limited to symmetric key cryptography. On the other hand, a method that utilizes reconfigurable logic blocks to implement a decryption circuit was proposed [2]. This might solve the area overhead problem. However, the whole circuit cannot be encrypted because at the end of a configuration, the decryption circuit is replaced with a part of the target circuit whose bitstream is a plain text. This limits the size of the decryption circuit to be implemented

R. Woods et al. (Eds.): ARC 2008, LNCS 4943, pp. 330–335, 2008.

since a large part of the target circuit cannot be encrypted if we implement a large decryption circuit. In addition, it needs a dedicated authentication circuit in order to authenticate the bitstreams of the decryption circuit, causing an area overhead.

In this paper, we propose a new configuration scheme such that the whole circuit can be encrypted while the proposed scheme causes only a small area overhead. In our scheme, a decryption circuit is implemented using reconfigurable logic blocks, and a bitstream of (a part of) the target circuit is decrypted using the decryption circuit. At the end of a configuration, the decryption circuit is replaced with the remaining part of the target circuit whose bitstream is one-time padded. Thus, the whole circuit can be securely downloaded into an FPGA. To do this, we use a part of the target circuit as a one-time pad for the bitstream to be loaded in the last phase of the configuration.

Since the proposed scheme can use a large reconfigurable area to implement a decryption circuit, it can handle computationally demanding cryptography such as public key cryptography.

This paper is organized as follows. In Sect. 2, we describe the proposed scheme. In Sect. 3, we discuss the security of the proposed scheme. In Sect. 4, we show how to enhance security and flexibility of the proposed scheme. In Sect. 5, we describe architecture requirements for realization of the proposed scheme. And Section 6 concludes the paper.

2 The Proposed Scheme

Our concern is to protect designs from piracy, reverse engineering and code theft. So we focus on encryption/decryption of bitstreams in this section, although our enhanced scheme can be used to authenticate bitstreams as we will describe later. That is, a bitstream supplier encrypts the bitstream of a circuit, then send it to a user. The user's FPGA (not the user!) decrypts the bitstream and the decrypted bitstream is stored in the configuration memory. The important point is decryption is completed within an FPGA, i.e., a user cannot access to the decrypted bitstream. To do this securely, only an authenticated (or built-in) decryption circuit should be implemented in an FPGA. We describe the proposed scheme in the following.

We divide Configurable Logic Blocks (CLBs) into two sets; One is the set that consists of CLBs chosen regularly skipping several blocks, and the other consists of the remaining CLBs. (See Fig. 1.) We also divide a bitstream into three bitstreams. The first one is a bitstream for configuring CLBs in set A, the second one is for CLBs in set B, and the third one is for the routing information.

Our main idea is as follows. We first implement a decryption circuit using CLBs in set A, decrypt a bitstream for set B and configure CLBs in set B by loading the decrypted bitstream. Then the decryption circuit is replaced with the remaining part of the target circuit by reconfiguring CLBs in set A. The bitstream used in the reconfiguration of CLBs in set A is one-time padded, and the decrypted bitstream for set B is used as the one-time pad. So we need

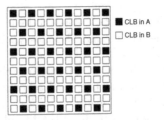

Fig. 1. Grouping CLBs

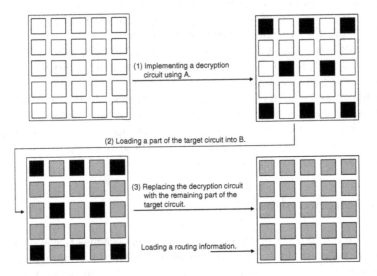

Fig. 2. Configuration flow

no decryption circuit for reconfiguration of CLBs in set A; just XORing the encrypted bitstream and the one-time pad is enough to decrypt it. After finishing configuration of CLBs, routing information is loaded. The configuration flow is illustrated in Fig. 2.

In the following, we describe the configuration scheme in detail.

Phase 1: Implementation of a decryption circuit - Configuration of A
The configuration memory of each CLB in set A has initial values, which are fixed during manufacturing. It is initialized by the initial values at start-up of a configuration. This initial configuration implements the decryption circuit. Similarly, the routing configuration memory has initial values, and is also configured by initializing them.

Phase 2: Decryption of a bitstream for B - Configuration of B
An encrypted bitstream is passed to the decryption circuit. And then, the decrypted bitstream is loaded into CLBs in B, which implements (a part of) the target circuit.

Phase 3: Implementation of the remaining part of the circuit - Reconfiguration of A and reconfiguration of routing information

A configuration bitstream, which is encrypted by one-time pad, is loaded into CLBs in set A. Each CLB loads the configuration data by XORing them with the configuration data of the neighboring CLB, i.e., using the values stored in the configuration memory of the neighboring CLB as a one-time pad. And then, routing information, which is a plain text, is loaded.

Note that we can use large reconfigurable area in an FPGA to implement a decryption circuit, so that we can implement a large circuit such as public key cryptography.

3   Security of the Proposed Scheme

In this section, we discuss the security of the proposed scheme.

Confidentiality of the target circuit

The confidentiality of part B of the target circuit is guaranteed since its bitstream is encrypted. As for the confidentiality of part A of the target circuit, the one-time pad might be weak since it is not a random bit string but the configuration data of the neighboring CLBs. However, we can enhance the randomness of the one-time pad as we will describe later. The routing information is not encrypted in the above scheme. This is because for an evil user, obtaining the routing information alone makes no sense. However, for higher security, it can be encrypted as we will describe later.

Security of the embedded secret key

Our FPGA architecture has an embedded secret key, which is used by the decryption circuit in Phase 2. Only the decryption circuit in Phase 2 can access to the embedded secret key; After Phase 2, the connection port to the secret key is disabled. Note that the decryption circuit is fixed during manufacturing. Thus, the embedded secret key is securely managed.

4   Enhancing Security and Flexibility

In this section, we describe how the security of the bitstream for part A and the routing information can be enhanced. We also describe an enhanced configuration scheme that can implement an arbitrary decryption and/or authentication circuit instead of the built-in decryption circuit.

4.1   Encryption of the Bitstream for A and the Routing Information

As we described in Sect. 2, the secret key (the one-time pad) for the encryption of the bitstream for A is not a random bit string but a configuration bitstream stored in a neighboring CLB. However, we can enhance the randomness of the key by generating a key by bitwise XORing the bit strings stored in the neighboring four CLBs instead of using a single bit string in a neighboring CLB as a key.

Routing information can also be encrypted similarly by using configuration data stored in CLBs that are placed around the routing configuration memory in order to create a one-time pad.

4.2   Enhancing Flexibility of Decryption Algorithms

In the configuration scheme described in Sect. 2, we can use only the built-in decryption circuit in Phase 2. However, we can enhance the configuration scheme so that the authorized suppliers of configuration bitstreams (e.g., the authorized intellectual property vendors) can distribute arbitrary decryption circuits for the use of the decryption in Phase 2. Moreover, a circuit to be implemented in Phase 2 is not limited to a decryption circuit. We can implement an arbitrary cryptographic circuit such as an authentication circuit. We describe the enhanced configuration scheme below.

We divide CLBs into two sets, A and B, as in Sect. 2. We also divide set B into two sets, A' and B', similarly. Then, we replace Phase 1 with Phase 1' below.

Phase 1': Implementation of an *authenticated* decryption circuit

First, we implement an authentication circuit using CLBs in A'. Similarly to the case of the decryption circuit described in Sect. 2, the authentication circuit is built-in, and is configured just by initializing the configuration memory. The authentication keys that are generated by the authorized suppliers of configuration bitstreams are also embedded, i.e., they are fixed during manufacturing. Then it loads an arbitrary decryption and/or authentication circuit into A while verifying the MAC for the bitstream of it. Thus only the decryption and/or authentication circuits authorized by the suppliers of configuration bitstreams can be implemented.

The remaining phases are the same as in the configuration scheme described in Sect. 2. The configuration flow is illustrated in Fig. 3.

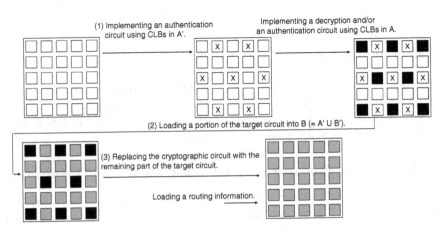

Fig. 3. Enhanced configuration scheme

5   Architecture Requirements

In this section, we describe architecture requirements for realization of the proposed configuration scheme. In order to configure A, A', B and routing information, four configuration systems (chains of configuration memories) are needed. Each configuration memory of a CLB in A' has its initial value, and can be initialized at the start-up of a configuration. A memory controller for dealing with this initialization is needed. As for the management of the embedded secret keys, a connection port to the embedded secret keys can be disabled after finishing Phase 2.

All the above features together with a controller that manages the whole configuration procedure realizes the proposed configuration scheme. All the above features are easy to implement, and the area overhead is very small.

6   Conclusion

We proposed a configuration scheme that can securely download a bitstream into an FPGA. By using the proposed scheme, we can encrypt the whole circuit with only a small area overhead. Also the proposed scheme has flexibility; An arbitrary cryptographic circuit can be implemented.

References

1. Altera Corp., http://www.altera.com/
2. Bossuet, L., Gogniat, G., Burleson, W.: Dynamically configurable security for SRAM FPGA bitstreams. International Journal of Embedded Systems 2(1/2), 73–85 (2006)
3. Drimer, S.: Authentication of FPGA Bitstreams: why and how. In: Diniz, P.C., Marques, E., Bertels, K., Fernandes, M.M., Cardoso, J.M.P. (eds.) ARCS 2007. LNCS, vol. 4419, pp. 73–84. Springer, Heidelberg (2007)
4. Hadžić, I., Udani, S., Smith, J.M.: FPGA viruses. In: Lysaght, P., Irvine, J., Hartenstein, R.W. (eds.) FPL 1999. LNCS, vol. 1673, pp. 291–300. Springer, Heidelberg (1999)
5. Kean, T.: Secure configuration of field programmable gate arrays. In: Proc. of 9th IEEE Symposium on Field Programmable Custom Computing Machines (FCCM2001), pp. 259–260 (2001)
6. Kean, T.: Secure configuration of field programmable gate arrays. In: Brebner, G., Woods, R. (eds.) FPL 2001. LNCS, vol. 2147, Springer, Heidelberg (2001)
7. Parelkar, M.M., Gaj, K.: Implementation of EAX mode of operation for FPGA bitstream encryption and authentication. In: Proc. of IEEE International Conference on Field-Programmable Technology, pp. 335–336 (2005)
8. Xilinx Inc., http://www.xilinx.com/

Lossless Compression for Space Imagery in a Dynamically Reconfigurable Architecture

Xiaolin Chen[1,*], C. Nishan Canagarajah[1], Raffaele Vitulli[2],
and Jose L. Nunez-Yanez[1]

[1] Department of Electrical and Electronic Engineering, University of Bristol, UK
{Xiaolin.Chen,Nishan.Canagarajah,J.L.Nunez-Yanez}@bristol.ac.uk
[2] European Space Agency (ESA), On-Board Payload Data Processing Section,
The Netherlands
Raffaele.Vitulli@esa.int

Abstract. This paper presents a novel dynamically reconfigurable hardware architecture for lossless compression and its optimization for space imagery. The proposed system makes use of reconfiguration to support optimal modeling strategies adaptively for data with different dimensions. The advantage of the proposed system is the efficient combination of different compression functions. For image data, we propose a new multi-mode image model which can detect the local features of the image and use different modes to encode regions with different features. Experimental results show that our system improves compression ratios of space image while maintaining low complexity and high throughput.

1 Introduction

Advances in remote sensing facilities generate massive amounts of data. For instance, SAR (Synthetic Aperture Radar) and the LANDSAT can produce hundreds of gigabytes of data per day, not to mention the 224 bands hyperspectral image from AVIRIS (Airborne Visible/Infrared Imaging Spectrometer). These data are transmitted to the Earth for further processing. However, the data volume is often several times larger than the transmission capacity of the downlink circuit, which limits the scientific data return from the spaceborne instruments. This is known as the "Bandwidth vs. Data Volume" challenge for modern spacecraft [1]. An effective solution to this problem is compression. As space data is costly and subject to processing, all the information in the data should be preserved. Therefore, lossless compression is necessary in space applications.

There are various kinds of data that need to be sent from spacecraft to the Earth, such as 1-D general data, 2-D image data, 3-D multispectral image data or video, etc. These data are likely to be transmitted along the same physical channel. Therefore, a system that can compress different types of data with real-time adaptation is of interest to space applications. The Consultative Committee for Space Data Systems (CCSDS) recommended an ASIC device PRDC (Payload

* Thanks to the support from EPSRC under grant EP/D011639/1.

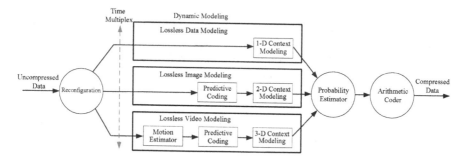

Fig. 1. Architecture of the Lossless Compression System

Rice Data Compressor) [2] for 1-D data, and NASA proposed a FPGA device [3] based on the LOCO algorithm [4] for 2-D image compression. However, in terms of compression ratios, there is still a gap between the performance of hardware and software-based algorithms. Examples of the latter include the context-based PPMZ [5] for 1-D data, and CALIC [6] for 2-D data.

To bridge the performance gap between software and hardware algorithms, and to meet the challenge of data transmission, we propose a reconfigurable architecture targeting to FPGA devices for lossless compression of various types of data from space imagery. Fig. 1 shows the architecture of the system, which consists of four modules: reconfiguration, dynamic modeling, probability estimator and arithmetic coder. The novelty of our proposed system is to effectively combine the statistical models for different data types with the reconfiguration technique. We design three hardware amenable models dedicated to each type of data in the dynamic modeling module. These models share a similar structure, which utilizes contexts, a common probability estimator and arithmetic coder. The reconfiguration technique takes advantage of this feature and efficiently reallocates the hardware resources to execute only the required functionality, in order to minimize the silicon requirements and power consumption. The switching between different models is done adaptively according to the incoming data type. Experimental results show that we achieve superior compression ratios to other state-of-the-art schemes while still keep the system complexity low.

The rest of the paper is organized as follows. In Section 2 we introduce the reconfiguration module. In Section 3 we explain the details of the dynamic modeling, followed by the probability estimator and arithmetic coder in Section 4. We show the performance comparison result with other current hardware amenable algorithms in Section 5 and conclude our work in Section 6.

2   Reconfiguration

Our proposed system is a real-time processing system that encodes and decodes data on the fly. As illustrated in Fig. 1, the reconfiguration module works as the brain of the system, controlling the activities of the dynamic modeling and probability estimator. It detects the data type of the incoming data by examining their file extensions or headers, and activates the corresponding hardware resources in other modules during the coding process. To be more specific, we use a Leon3 processor as a reconfiguration controller, which is connected with the dynamic modeling module, probability estimator, and an external memory. Once a function is requested, the controller loads the configuration data from the memory to the dynamic modeling module and probability estimator. This technique integrates all the modules into a system and reuses the hardware resources, resulting in a reduced amount of resources usage and power consumption.

3   Dynamic Modeling

The dynamic modeling module carries out the major algorithmic tasks. The three models in this module are all context based. *Context*, here means the previously seen symbols in 1-D data, or the surrounding symbols of the current symbol in 2-D or 3-D data.

3.1   Lossless 1-D Data Modeling

Lossless data modeling deals with 1-D data. It is based on the PPMH algorithm implemented in the high-speed hardware compressor Byacom [7]. According to the variable-order Markov modeling mechanism, the variable-order contexts are formed and searched in a context tree, which is built dynamically as more data is seen. The context of the current symbol is stored in a FIFO, whose length is configurable and depends on the maximal model order. The main part of the model is implemented as a context tree, which enables fast search operations with low complexity. A single-cycle reset and rescale of the tree are also implemented to speed up the operation of the model. Once a context is matched, the context area address and the context symbols are sent to the probability estimator.

3.2   Lossless Image Modeling

Lossless image modeling handles image or any data which has two-dimensional correlations. We propose a segmentation-based lossless image model. Segmentation, here means partitioning of an image into multiple regions according to its features. We use this idea to group pixels with similar features and use different modes to compress them. A new ternary-mode is proposed to detect and encode the edges, while the run-length coding [4] is adopted to encode the homogeneous regions. The rest of the image, mostly the texture regions, is compressed with a regular-mode, which is based on the Gradient-Adjusted Prediction (GAP) from CALIC [6] but is simplified. As the mode selection is made by adaptive online checking of neighboring symbols, no side information is transmitted.

We identify certain conditions for entering each mode. If the four nearest symbols of the current symbol are the same, a homogeneous region is assumed and the run-mode is triggered. If the current symbol is identical to its previous symbol, the symbol occurrence, called *run*, increases by one; otherwise "run"

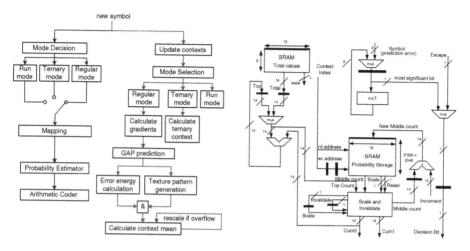

Fig. 2. 2-D data modeling architecture

Fig. 3. Architecture of the probability estimator

stops and the current *run length* is encoded. In regions where edges are present, we examine if there are no more than three distinct symbol values in a small neighborhood of the current symbol and the ternary-mode is triggered. Thus only four symbols are needed to encode this group of symbols and lower entropy can be obtained. When the entry conditions for run-mode or ternary-mode cannot be met, or when coding in other modes fails, the regular mode is used.

Fig. 2 illustrates the dataflow of the image model. The implementation is achieved with two pipelines running in parallel. Line 1, indicated by the flow on the left, operates on the current symbol and yields the prediction error with the selected mode for the probability estimator; Line 2, indicated by the flow on the right, calculates the prediction value and context index for the next symbol under the selected mode. Since complicated calculation on coefficients are not needed, and simple division is done by small lookup table, this model is hardware amenable. Note that this model is the base of the video model and can be extended to handle multispectral images. The details of the image compression algorithm is reported elsewhere.

3.3 Lossless Video Modeling

Lossless video modeling compresses data which contains three-dimensional correlations, typically videos or multispectral images. Based on the 2-D model, the video model incorporates the decorrelation in spectral domain and temporal domain. An inter-band prediction is used to exploit the correlation in spectral domain and a switching strategy is designed to switch between intra-band and inter-band prediction, according to which correlation is stronger in the local area. For temporal domain, we intend to use a zero-side-information (no motion vectors) motion estimator to remove redundancy between frames. Implementation details of this model are currently under investigation.

Table 1. Lossless Image Compression Bit Rates (bpp) Comparison

image	CCSDS	PRDC	JPEG-LS	JPEG2000	SPIHT	ICER	proposed
coastal_b1	3.36	3.56	3.09	3.13	3.09	3.07	3.00
coastal_b2	3.22	3.32	2.90	2.97	2.94	2.92	2.84
coastal_b3	3.48	3.68	3.22	3.23	3.21	3.20	3.14
coastal_b4	2.81	2.91	2.41	2.53	2.57	2.55	2.37
coastal_b5	3.16	3.30	2.81	2.94	2.91	2.89	2.79
coastal_b6h	3.02	2.75	2.50	2.60	2.71	2.54	2.52
coastal_b6l	2.35	2.03	1.76	1.96	2.02	1.87	1.84
coastal_b7	3.45	3.66	3.17	3.22	3.17	3.15	3.10
coastal_b8	3.66	3.93	3.42	3.40	3.35	3.31	3.28
europa3	6.61	7.48	6.64	6.52	6.46	6.30	6.42
marstest	4.78	5.39	4.69	4.74	4.64	4.63	4.60
lunar	4.58	5.23	4.35	4.49	4.43	4.40	4.20
spot-la_b3	4.80	5.20	4.53	4.69	4.70	4.56	4.43
spot-la_panchr	4.27	4.87	4.00	4.13	4.11	4.03	3.90
average	3.82	4.09	3.54	3.61	3.59	3.53	3.46

4   Probability Estimator and Arithmetic Coder

The probability estimator is shared by all the models in the dynamic modeling module. Fig. 3 shows a simplified diagram of the probability estimator. It is a SRAM memory where the probability of symbols in each coding context is stored. *Coding context* is defined by the local feature of the data and is used to group symbols in the way that a lower conditional entropy can be achieved. Each coding context is represented by a balanced binary tree with n (n is the alphabet size of the data) nodes associated with each symbol. The values of the tree nodes reflect the symbol occurrence adaptively and are used to calculate the symbol probability. This module maps the probability data into a set of binary decisions (left or right, represented by 0 or 1) from the root to the leaves through each context tree. The binary arithmetic coder is driven by these decision bits and the probability data. It is multiplication-free, resulting in an improved clock ratio of the system. One decision bit is processed per clock cycle, and hence 8 cycles are needed for encoding one byte. More details can be found in [7].

5   Performance Comparison

The experimental result of image compression ratios is presented in this section. We use the 8-bit CCSDS reference image set as test images. As the proposed system is intended for high-speed spaceborne application, test results relevant for this purpose are presented. We compare the proposed scheme with some state-of-the-art low complexity schemes. CCSDS is the current Recommendation for space image compression; PRDC is the CCSDS Rice coder; JPEG-LS is the lossless image compression standard; JPEG2000 [8] is the current standard for lossy to lossless compression; SPIHT [9] is a low-complexity progressive image compressor; ICER [10] is another progressive wavelet-based image compressor. When strip-based and frame-based options are available for these algorithms, the better ones are chosen in this comparison. Table. 1 shows that the proposed system outperforms the others in terms of bit rates. The proposed system processes 1 bit per clock cycle, which is translated into a throughput of 100Mbits/sec on a Xilinx Virtex-4 SX35 FPGA. Results on general data can be found in [7].

6   Conclusions and Future Works

A novel dynamically reconfigurable FPGA architecture for lossless compression of space imagery is presented. The proposed hardware amenable algorithms produce superior image compression ratios and the reconfiguration technique efficiently combines models for different data types with online adaptation. These features make our system suitable for space application. The complete hardware implementation of the system and its extensions is part of our future works.

References

1. Katz, D.S., Some, R.R.: NASA Advances Robotic Space Exploration. Computer 36, 52–61 (2003)
2. Vitulli, R.: PRDC: An ASIC Device for Lossless Data Compression Implementing the Rice Algorithm. In: Proceedings of IEEE International Geoscience and Remote Sensing Symposium, IGARSS, pp. 317–320 (2004)
3. Klimesh, M., Stanton, V., Watola, D.: Hardware Implementation of a Lossless Image Compression Algorithm Using a Field Programmable Gate Array. TMO Progress Report 42–144, Jet Propulsion Laboratory, California, US (2001)
4. Weinberger, M.J., Seroussi, G., Sapiro, G.: LOCO-I: A Low Complexity, Context-based, Lossless Image Compression Algorithm. In: Proceedings of Data Compression Conference, pp. 140–149 (1996)
5. Bloom, C.: Solving the Problems of Context Modeling (1998), http://www.cbloom.com/papers/index.html
6. Wu, X., Memon, N.: Context-based, Adaptive, Lossless Image Coding. IEEE Trans. Comm. 45, 437–444 (1997)
7. Nunez-Yanez, J.L., Chouliaras, V.A.: A Configurable Statistical Lossless Compression Core Based on Variable Order Markov Modeling and Arithmetic Coding. IEEE Trans. Comp. 54, 1345–1359 (2005)
8. Taubman, D.S., Marcellin, M.W.: JPEG2000 Image Compression Fundamentals, Standards and Practice. Kluwer, Dordrecht (2002)
9. Said, A., Pearlman, W.A.: A New Fast and Efficient Image Codec Based on Set Partitioning in Hierarchical Trees. IEEE Trans. Circuits Syst. Video Technol. 6, 243–250 (1996)
10. Kiely, A., Klimesh, M.: The ICER Progressive Wavelet Image Compressor. IPN Progress Report 42-155, 1-46 (2003)

Author Index

Lecture Notes in Computer Science

Sublibrary 1: Theoretical Computer Science and General Issues

For information about Vols. 1– 4661
please contact your bookseller or Springer

Vol. 4835: T. Tokuyama (Ed.), Algorithms and Computation. XVII, 929 pages. 2007.

Vol. 4818: I. Lirkov, S. Margenov, J. Waśniewski (Eds.), Large-Scale Scientific Computing. XIV, 755 pages. 2008.

Vol. 4800: A. Avron, N. Dershowitz, A. Rabinovich (Eds.), Pillars of Computer Science. XXI, 683 pages. 2008.

Vol. 4783: J. Holub, J. Žďárek (Eds.), Implementation and Application of Automata. XIII, 324 pages. 2007.

Vol. 4782: R. Perrott, B.M. Chapman, J. Subhlok, R.F. de Mello, L.T. Yang (Eds.), High Performance Computing and Communications. XIX, 823 pages. 2007.

Vol. 4771: T. Bartz-Beielstein, M.J. Blesa Aguilera, C. Blum, B. Naujoks, A. Roli, G. Rudolph, M. Sampels (Eds.), Hybrid Metaheuristics. X, 202 pages. 2007.

Vol. 4770: V.G. Ganzha, E.W. Mayr, E.V. Vorozhtsov (Eds.), Computer Algebra in Scientific Computing. XIII, 460 pages. 2007.

Vol. 4769: A. Brandstädt, D. Kratsch, H. Müller (Eds.), Graph-Theoretic Concepts in Computer Science. XIII, 341 pages. 2007.

Vol. 4763: J.-F. Raskin, P.S. Thiagarajan (Eds.), Formal Modeling and Analysis of Timed Systems. X, 369 pages. 2007.

Vol. 4759: J. Labarta, K. Joe, T. Sato (Eds.), High-Performance Computing. XV, 524 pages. 2008.

Vol. 4746: A. Bondavalli, F. Brasileiro, S. Rajsbaum (Eds.), Dependable Computing. XV, 239 pages. 2007.

Vol. 4743: P. Thulasiraman, X. He, T.L. Xu, M.K. Denko, R.K. Thulasiram, L.T. Yang (Eds.), Frontiers of High Performance Computing and Networking ISPA 2007 Workshops. XXIX, 536 pages. 2007.

Vol. 4742: I. Stojmenovic, R.K. Thulasiram, L.T. Yang, W. Jia, M. Guo, R.F. de Mello (Eds.), Parallel and Distributed Processing and Applications. XX, 995 pages. 2007.

Vol. 4739: R. Moreno Díaz, F. Pichler, A. Quesada Arencibia (Eds.), Computer Aided Systems Theory – EUROCAST 2007. XIX, 1233 pages. 2007.

Vol. 4736: S. Winter, M. Duckham, L. Kulik, B. Kuipers (Eds.), Spatial Information Theory. XV, 455 pages. 2007.

Vol. 4732: K. Schneider, J. Brandt (Eds.), Theorem Proving in Higher Order Logics. IX, 401 pages. 2007.

Vol. 4731: A. Pelc (Ed.), Distributed Computing. XVI, 510 pages. 2007.

Vol. 4728: S. Bozapalidis, G. Rahonis (Eds.), Algebraic Informatics. VIII, 291 pages. 2007.

Vol. 4726: N. Ziviani, R. Baeza-Yates (Eds.), String Processing and Information Retrieval. XII, 311 pages. 2007.

Vol. 4719: R. Backhouse, J. Gibbons, R. Hinze, J. Jeuring (Eds.), Datatype-Generic Programming. XI, 369 pages. 2007.

Vol. 4711: C.B. Jones, Z. Liu, J. Woodcock (Eds.), Theoretical Aspects of Computing – ICTAC 2007. XI, 483 pages. 2007.

Vol. 4710: C.W. George, Z. Liu, J. Woodcock (Eds.), Domain Modeling and the Duration Calculus. XI, 237 pages. 2007.

Vol. 4708: L. Kučera, A. Kučera (Eds.), Mathematical Foundations of Computer Science 2007. XVIII, 764 pages. 2007.

Vol. 4707: O. Gervasi, M.L. Gavrilova (Eds.), Computational Science and Its Applications – ICCSA 2007, Part III. XXIV, 1205 pages. 2007.

Vol. 4706: O. Gervasi, M.L. Gavrilova (Eds.), Computational Science and Its Applications – ICCSA 2007, Part II. XXIII, 1129 pages. 2007.

Vol. 4705: O. Gervasi, M.L. Gavrilova (Eds.), Computational Science and Its Applications – ICCSA 2007, Part I. XLIV, 1169 pages. 2007.

Vol. 4703: L. Caires, V.T. Vasconcelos (Eds.), CONCUR 2007 – Concurrency Theory. XIII, 507 pages. 2007.

Vol. 4700: C.B. Jones, Z. Liu, J. Woodcock (Eds.), Formal Methods and Hybrid Real-Time Systems. XVI, 539 pages. 2007.

Vol. 4699: B. Kågström, E. Elmroth, J. Dongarra, J. Waśniewski (Eds.), Applied Parallel Computing. XXIX, 1192 pages. 2007.

Vol. 4698: L. Arge, M. Hoffmann, E. Welzl (Eds.), Algorithms – ESA 2007. XV, 769 pages. 2007.

Vol. 4697: L. Choi, Y. Paek, S. Cho (Eds.), Advances in Computer Systems Architecture. XIII, 400 pages. 2007.

Vol. 4688: K. Li, M. Fei, G.W. Irwin, S. Ma (Eds.), Bio-Inspired Computational Intelligence and Applications. XIX, 805 pages. 2007.

Vol. 4684: L. Kang, Y. Liu, S. Zeng (Eds.), Evolvable Systems: From Biology to Hardware. XIV, 446 pages. 2007.

Vol. 4683: L. Kang, Y. Liu, S. Zeng (Eds.), Advances in Computation and Intelligence. XVII, 663 pages. 2007.

Vol. 4681: D.-S. Huang, L. Heutte, M. Loog (Eds.), Advanced Intelligent Computing Theories and Applications. XXVI, 1379 pages. 2007.

Vol. 4672: K. Li, C. Jesshope, H. Jin, J.-L. Gaudiot (Eds.), Network and Parallel Computing. XVIII, 558 pages. 2007.

Vol. 4671: V.E. Malyshkin (Ed.), Parallel Computing Technologies. XIV, 635 pages. 2007.

Vol. 4669: J.M. de Sá, L.A. Alexandre, W. Duch, D.P. Mandic (Eds.), Artificial Neural Networks – ICANN 2007, Part II. XXXI, 990 pages. 2007.

Vol. 4668: J.M. de Sá, L.A. Alexandre, W. Duch, D.P. Mandic (Eds.), Artificial Neural Networks – ICANN 2007, Part I. XXXI, 978 pages. 2007.

Vol. 4666: M.E. Davies, C.J. James, S.A. Abdallah, M.D. Plumbley (Eds.), Independent Component Analysis and Signal Separation. XIX, 847 pages. 2007.

Vol. 4665: J. Hromkovič, R. Královič, M. Nunkesser, P. Widmayer (Eds.), Stochastic Algorithms: Foundations and Applications. X, 167 pages. 2007.

Vol. 4664: J. Durand-Lose, M. Margenstern (Eds.), Machines, Computations, and Universality. X, 325 pages. 2007.